Date	Name	Address
10.9.83	R. G. Mugabe	Prime Minister / Prime Minister's
19.6.'84	Conor Cruise O'Brien	Very friendly please...
	Máire Cruise O'Brien	As above!
14 July '84	+ Tomás Cardinal Ó Fiaich	Thanks for the historic day on which Fr Niall O'Brien came home.
25 July	Édouard d'Estaing	FRANCE
20/10/84	Felipe González	Prime Minister of Spain
	Dennis Taylor	1985 World Snooker Champion
21.6.85	Chaim Herzog, President of Israel	[Hebrew text]
	Pat Kenny	RTE – there are no clouds for this silver lining!
	明仁	Crown Prince / Crown Princess of Japan

Signatures from the distinguished visitors' book, Dublin airport

CHARLES J. HAUGHEY,
Taoiseach, 1982
RAY MacSHARRY,
Tanaiste & Minister for Finance, 1982
BRIAN LENIHAN,
Minister for Agriculture, 1982
SANJIVA REDDY,
President of India, 1982
JACK LYNCH,
former Taoiseach, 1982
DESMOND O'MALLEY,
Minister for Trade, Commerce & Tourism, 1982
MOTHER TERESA OF CALCUTTA,
1982
DR PATRICK HILLERY,
President of Ireland, 1982
LEONARD FIGG,
British Ambassador, 1982
PETER BARRY,
Minister for Foreign Affairs, 1983
MR & MRS ROY DISNEY,
California, 1983
JAVIER PEREZ DE CUELLAR,
Secretary-General, United Nations, 1983
HENRY KISSINGER,
United States, 1983
GEORGE BUSH,
U.S. Vice-President, 1983

ROBERT MUGABE,
Prime Minister, Zimbabwe, 1983
DR CONOR CRUISE O'BRIEN,
1983
MÁIRE CRUISE O'BRIEN,
1983
TOMÁS CARDINAL Ó FIAICH,
Primate of All Ireland, 1984
VALÉRY GISCARD D'ESTAING,
President of France, 1984
FELIPE GONZALEZ,
Prime Minister of Spain, 1984
DENNIS TAYLOR,
World Snooker Champion, 1985
CHAIM HERTZOG,
President of Israel, 1985
PAT KENNY,
RTÉ, 1985
CROWN PRINCE & PRINCESS AKIHITO OF JAPAN,
1985

DUBLIN AIRPORT: THE HISTORY

DUBLIN AIRPORT:
The History

HUGH ORAM

AerRianta

First published 1990 by
Aer Rianta, Dublin Airport.

Copyright © Hugh Oram, 1990. All rights reserved.

British Library Cataloguing in Publication Data
Oram, Hugh, 1943–
   Dublin Airport: The History
   I. Dublin. Airports. Dublin Airport, history.
   I. Title
   387.7360941
   ISBN 0-9516193-0-6

PRODUCED IN IRELAND BY MSA LTD., 13 UPPER LAD LANE, DUBLIN 2
DESIGNED BY JARLATH HAYES
COLOUR SEPARATIONS BY PENTACOLOUR INTERNATIONAL LTD., DUBLIN 2
TYPESETTING BY REE-PRO LTD., DUBLIN 6
PRINTED BY CRITERION PRESS LTD., DUBLIN 11

for Bernadette

Contents

CHAPTER I
The early years   1

CHAPTER II
Sheep graze in the Emergency   41

CHAPTER III
Concrete at Collinstown   61

CHAPTER IV
The end of a monopoly   97

CHAPTER V
The real birth of Aer Rianta   127

CHAPTER VI
Preparing for the Pope   163

CHAPTER VII
Up to the present   207

POSTSCRIPT   286

A CHRONOLOGY OF EVENTS   288

SOURCES   290

AER RIANTA CHAIRMEN AND DIRECTORS,
DUBLIN AIRPORT STATISTICS   291

INDICES OF ILLUSTRATIONS AND TEXT   293

The Aer Rianta View

AER RIANTA itself can claim a little more history than the fifty year span of Dublin airport. The company was originally formed in 1937, managed Dublin airport since its opening and took on responsibility for Shannon and Cork in 1969. Airport history in Ireland really starts, however, with Dublin and the airport remains of crucial importance to the whole basis of civil aviation in Ireland. I am, therefore, very pleased to see the entire history of the airport, from its very earliest days right up to the events of this summer, recorded in so much detail in this book.

The successful onward development and progress of Dublin airport has been a vital part of the success of Aer Rianta as a company and the enormous strides made at the airport over the years by its highly dedicated Aer Rianta team (which now numbers nearly one thousand people) has contributed in no small measure to the health and vitality of our company. The commercial strengths developed at Dublin airport have given Aer Rianta the capacity and will to operate as an entrepreneurial organisation and have helped us to market Irish airport management skills in many other countries. We are constantly exploring and developing new opportunities within Aer Rianta, opportunities that will strengthen the company still further. But Dublin airport remains in the key pivotal position in our company's operation and I am pleased to see so many aspects of the airport's development over the years recorded here for posterity.

While the technical and statistical progress of the airport remains highly impressive, Dublin airport depends in a fundamental way on the skills and resources of our staff. Aer Rianta has always been blessed in this respect. The professionalism, the commitment and especially the warmth and humanity of our Dublin airport staff give the airport a special flavour.

Dublin airport's team have the entirely laudable ambition of wanting to make it the best airport of its size in the world. I am glad to see so many of their efforts put on record, so that we have here a permanant tribute to the people who have worked at the airport over the years.

DEREK KEOGH,
Chief Executive, Aer Rianta.

Dublin Airport: The History

THIS year is the fiftieth anniversary of Dublin airport and many events are taking place to mark the momentous occasion on January 19, 1940, when the first scheduled flight took off from the airport. Much of the previous history of the airport and its immediate area has only been preserved by word of mouth and we were very keen to ensure that the airport's history was fully documented and preserved as a fitting part of the celebrations that are taking place this year.

The Collinstown area is of great historic interest, and since World War I, has had a close link with aviation. Much of this early history was in great danger of being lost, but we have now preserved it within the covers of this book. The airport itself has been developed from small origins and again this book documents progress, not just on the technical side, but on the human side too. Over the years, many people have contributed greatly to the development of the airport, and their efforts are recorded also in the book. The very early years of aviation on the Collinstown site, chosen with such great perspicacity in 1917, are well covered. I am particularly fascinated by the photographs in Chapter I showing Collinstown as it was in 1925 and exactly the same area today, the heart of the modern airport. Building the airport in the late 1930s, its official opening exactly fifty years ago and the lean years of the Emergency, all are meticulously set down for posterity. Even more exciting is the development of the airport over the past forty-five years, to its present crescendo of activities and services. We have travelled such an immense distance and the innumerable facets that merge to form the airport of 1990 are recorded in depth and detail. With its extensive collection of photographs, the book is truly a history of Dublin airport in its many parts, over very many years, a fascinating panoply of events and personalities. They all intermingle to make a history of our times, for Dublin airport, since it was opened in 1940, has played a crucial role in the history of our country.

TOM CULLEN,
General Manager, Dublin airport.

A word of thanks

Many people have helped in putting together the history of Dublin airport. Firstly and most importantly, I should like to thank my wife, Bernadette, for her endless patience and wise counsels; without her help, it would have been impossible to have completed the book to such a demanding schedule. I should also like to thank Tom Cullen and Owen Clarke of Aer Rianta for their support and encouragement for the book; Owen Clarke has been an invaluable help with the research for the book. All the Aer Rianta staff have been immensely helpful and always good humoured; it has been a most agreeable and rewarding experience working with the company. Martin Swords, marketing consultant to Aer Rianta, and his staff, Gráinne Murray and Gerry McGovern, have been unfailingly efficient in providing back-up services. Gráinne Murray of MSA is deserving of especial thanks for her always cheerful efficiency. Robert Ballagh is thanked for his cover design and Jarlath Hayes for his work on the design and layout of the book, laced with unbounded enthusiasm and fine humour. I must not forget Murphy his constant studio companion. On the photographic front, I have had invaluable assistance from Robert Allen Photography, Neil MacDougald, Michael and Grace Duncan and Frank Fennell Photography. Fennell's staff were extremely efficient in organising duplicates of numerous historic photographs. The Duncans' photographic collection has yielded many rare gems for the book and the Duncans went to immense trouble in providing these prints of great historic value. Thanks are due to *The Irish Times* library and photographic departments, for their efficient and patient help. Philip Doherty supplied fascinating line drawings. Jonathan Williams checked the entire text as did Cecil Prentice of Matheson Ormsby Prentice; their help is duly acknowledged. Helen Litton prepared the indices, a task of great intricacy. Louis McConkey of Ree-Pro, who did the typesetting, and Noel Masterson of Criterion Press, the printers, brought a much appreciated dedication and enthusiasm to the production of the book. The undernamed are thanked for their contributions in various forms to the book; many provided photographs and other visual material.

Elaine Adams (Aer Rianta)
Aer Lingus *(John Allen, Eithne Pettit)*
Aéroports de Paris
Air France *(Marcel Henri Lamarque, Eoin Scott)*
Robert Allen (Robert Allen Photography)
An Post *(Mary Kelly)*
An Post museum *(Barra O'Muirthile)*
Jack Bannon (head of airport security)
William Beck, Kendal, Cumbria
Dr Thekla Beere
Padraig Beirne (group photographic editor, Independent Newspapers, Dublin)
late Billy Bizzell
Frank Boland (former chairman, Aer Rianta)
Freddie Bond, Palmerstown, Dublin
Bord Fáilte communications' department *(John Brown, Gillian McDermott)*
Mona Bouchier-Hayes
Patrick ("Pakie") Bourke, Malahide, County Dublin
British Embassy, Dublin
Budget Travel, Dublin
Brian Byrne (deputy general manager, Dublin airport)

Nicky Byrne (technical supervisor–boilerhouse)
Jim Campbell
Noel Carroll (Aer Rianta public relations)
Catholic Press & Information office, Blackrock, County Dublin
Brendan Clancy (assistant chief executive–technical services, Aer Rianta)
Seán Clancy (head waiter and assistant manager, Silver Lining restaurant, Dublin airport)
Owen Clarke (head of administration, Aer Rianta, Dublin airport)
Flan Clune (press and public relations manager, Aer Rianta)
CM Kent Consultants *(Patrick Crane)*
Colman Corcoran (Aer Rianta)
Paddy Corrigan
Charlie Craddock
Tommy Cranitch
Claire Cronin (Dr Garret FitzGerald's office)
Tom Cullen (general manager, Dublin airport)
Terry Cummins (airport police/fire service)
Christy Darcy
Fintan Deere (Department of Tourism and Transport, Dublin)
Peter Delamer
Frank Delaney, Julianstown, County Meath
Delta Airlines
Dr J. F. Dempsey (former chief executive, Aer Lingus)
Department of Defence *(Tom Aherne, David Ash, Regina Murphy)*
Department of Foreign Affairs, Dublin
Dermot Desmond (chairman, Aer Rianta)
Philip Doherty (Dublin airport technical supervisor–plumbing — line drawings)
Helen Donovan (Aer Rianta)
Jack Doyle (former Dublin airport manager)
Noel Drumgoole (manager, Silver Lining restaurant, Dublin airport)
Neil Duffy, Boston, US
Martin Dully (executive chairman, Bord Fáilte, former chief executive, Aer Rianta)
Michael and Grace Duncan (G. A. Duncan Photography, Dublin)
Caroline Dunlop, Stepaside, County Dublin
EC Commission Office, Dublin *(Rosemary McCarthy)*
Embassy of the United States of America
Gerard Fanning
Frank Fennell Photography
Jack Flahive, Shankill, County Dublin
Liam Flood (assistant to company secretary, Aer Rianta)
Fergus Flynn, Howth
Dr Garret FitzGerald, TD
John Gallagher (former Aer Rianta press officer, now Department of Justice)
General Valuation Office, Ely Place, Dublin
Gerard Giltrap, (Trinity College, Dublin)
John Gunning (retired field supervisor), Garristown, County Dublin
Jack Hanley, Portmarnock, County Dublin
Bernard Hanratty, Howth Lodge Hotel, Dublin
Gerard Harvey (former marketing director, Aer Rianta)
Hertz Rent-a-car, Leeson Street Bridge, Dublin
Iarnród Éireann press office *(Cyril Ferris, Mary Linehan)*
Ned Keating
Derek Keogh (chief executive, Aer Rianta)
Johnny King (retired head of personnel, Aer Rianta)

Jim Lambert (Air Navigation Services, Department of Tourism and Transport)
Lensmen photographic agency, Dublin
David Lord (retired manager, Silver Lining restaurant)
Lufthansa *(Joe Moore)*
Brian McCabe (editor, *Runway* magazine)
J. C. B. McCarthy (former secretary, Department of Transport and Power)
Helen McDonnell, (Aer Rianta)
Jim McDonald (former head of security, Dublin airport), Santry
Neil MacDougald
Edward F. MacSweeney, (RTÉ)
Caroline Martin (Park Public Relations/Manx Airlines)
Christopher Martin (retired accountant, Aer Rianta)
Joe McGuinne (general manager–technical, Aer Rianta)
Myra Moore (Aer Rianta)
Gráinne Murray (MSA)
Lt. Col. Frank Neill (retired), Santry
Paddy and Rita O'Daly, Trim, County Meath
Carol O'Donohue (airport police/fire service)
Tom O'Loughlin (senior air traffic controller, Dublin airport)
Office of Public Works *(Chris Flynn)*
Johnny Oppermann, Blainroe, County Wicklow
Ordnance Survey, Phoenix Park, Dublin
P. P. O'Reilly, Naas, County Kildare
Joe O'Rourke (retired head of airport fire service), Swords, County Dublin
James O'Sullivan (former chief executive, Aer Rianta)
R. W. O'Sullivan, Killiney, County Dublin
Phoenix Maps, Dublin
Public Relations of Ireland/British Airways *(Áine MacGillicuddy)*
Kathleen Riordan, Ballybough, Dublin
Sabena *(Catherine Grennell-Whyte)*
Sean Rothery (School of Architecture, College of Technology, Bolton Street, Dublin)
Royal Netherlands Embassy, Dublin
RTE illustrations library *(Leni McCullagh)*
Ryanair *(Captain George White, Louise Heneghan)*
Jack Scully
SIPTU, Dublin
Squadron Leader Peter Singleton (retired), London
Billy Stenson
Imogen Stuart
Martin Swords (MSA)
Jean Taylor (advertising and promotions officer, Aer Rianta)
The bike boys and girls
The Cahill family (Iona National Airways)
The FitzGerald family
The Irish Times *(Rachel Burrowes, John Gibson, Tony Lennon, Gordon Standing)*
The Times, London
Michael Thompson (air traffic control instructor, Dublin airport)
Benny Traynor (Dublin airport hairdresser)
Margot Wall (John Sisk & Son)
Leo Ward, Abbey Films, Dublin
Peter White (Fine Gael press office)
Jonathan Williams, Sandycove, County Dublin
Joe Whoriskey

A pilot's eye view coming in to land at Dublin airport.
Photograph: Neil MacDougald

The country landscape surrounding Dublin airport, 1990.
Photograph: Neil MacDougald

Near Dublin airport, 1990.
Photograph: Neil MacDougald

Aerial view of the apron at Dublin airport.
Photograph: Neil MacDougald

CHAPTER I

The early years

FRIDAY, January 19, 1940 was a bitterly cold day in Dublin; snow was piled high in the streets and even the canals were frozen. People were going to the zoo in the Phoenix Park not to see the polar bears, but to skate on the frozen ponds. Up at Collinstown, on the heights to the north of the city, blasts of pure icy wind swept in, unhindered, from the sea; they had come from eastern Europe, tempests of deep, bone gnawing cold, for the whole continent, gripped in war, was also blasted by sub-zero weather conditions. On the night of Wednesday, January 17, the temperature recorded in Dublin fell to the astounding figure of 21 degrees Fahrenheit below freezing.

Despite the weather, the inaugural flight took off from the new airport at Collinstown, on schedule, at 9 am. The critics were wrong; the airport was destined to succeed over the next fifty years in a manner far beyond the elaborate imaginings of the project's most fervent proponents. The night before the first flight took off, a talk was given to members of the Irish Junior Aviation Club, at the now defunct Moira Hotel in Trinity Street, off Dame Street, by a Mr C. Bruton, who said of the construction of the new airport terminal, then well under way: "it is sometimes suggested that the number of planes visiting a Dublin airport would not warrant the enormous cost of building one but until an airport is built, it is impossible to say what the traffic would be". The day after Mr Bruton's little homily, there was one departure from the new airport. It came exactly 155 years after the first aeronautical ascent in Ireland on January 19, 1785, when Richard Crosbie took off in his balloon from Ranelagh Gardens in Dublin, landing across the bay in Clontarf.

On January 19, 1990, the fiftieth anniversary of the departure of that very first flight, there were 302 aircraft movements, scheduled, charter, cargo, newspaper and mail services. A total of 10,796 passengers arrived at or departed from Dublin airport.

The evening before the great day in January, 1940 two Aer Lingus Lockheed 14 aircraft had flown in from Baldonnel aerodrome, arriving at 3.20 pm. At 6 am next day, Patrick "Pakie" Bourke was first to arrive at the airport, putting heaters in the aircraft. One of those aircraft made the inaugural flight from Dublin to Liverpool on the Friday morning and was seen off by a delegation of dignitaries, including Major G. T. Carroll, general manager, Aer Lingus Teo, T. J. O'Driscoll, from the aviation section of the Department of Industry and Commerce, J. F. Dempsey, secretary of Aer Lingus and S. M. O'Connell, the fledgling airline's press officer. The plane flew twenty feet above the roof of the Boot Inn, causing the then owner, Matt Weldon, to jump out of bed in alarm. On the front page of the following day's *Irish Press*, two photographs showed the aircraft on the grass taxi-ing apron. In the background could be clearly seen the new airport terminal building, designed by Desmond FitzGerald to resemble the graceful curving lines of the bridge of an ocean liner; it was still under construction. The finished outline of the building could be distinctly made out, since building work was at an advanced stage in January, 1940, but the wooden scaffolding was still in place. However, the new radio station at Collinstown was operational that very first day, broadcasting its call signs "EIJ" and "Dublin" on 348 kcs/862 metres and providing radio communication and direction finding for aircraft.

Elsewhere on those front pages of long ago, the aerial news was of a martial nature, for on January 19, 1940 Europe was in the 142nd day of a world war, between Germany and the Allied forces, led by Britain. The *Irish Press*, on January 20, 1940, beside its two photographs from the Collinstown inauguration, had a small news paragraph headlined "One a side air battle off Scotland". An RAF plane on patrol off Aberdeen had encountered a Luftwaffe Heinkel. Another report, this time in the Dublin *Evening Mail* of January 19, said that orders to American plane-makers could triple, since the Allies were said to want another 8,000 machines.

War had been declared on September 3, 1939 and, for the rest of that year, there had been a "phoney" war, when there still seemed some hope that the global holocaust could be avoided. In January, 1940, the *Evening Mail* stated, with unbridled optimism, that according to a primitive opinion poll in Germany, ninety-five per cent of the German people did not want war. Yet all the signs were there of the dogs of war being unleashed; the most active war zone was in Finland, where Finnish and Soviet troops were engaged in a huge battle near Salla. The *Irish Independent* ran a photograph of Finnish troops discussing their exploits by lamplight, huddled in their tents in temperatures twice as cold as those being experienced in Dublin. Denmark declared its neutrality, although that declaration did not save it from a later German invasion, and in the Netherlands, the ice was described as forming a Maginot line.

German soldiers were pictured on the Siegfried line, in arctic conditions. David Lloyd George, the Welsh political wizard, celebrated his seventy-seventh birthday. He was British prime minister and First Lord of the Treasury from 1916 to 1922, saw the end of World War I and signed the treaty with Ireland in late 1921 that saw the end of the War of Independence. A religious exhortation in 1940 gave every sign of the coming ferocity on the war front: Dr Temple, the Archbishop of York, said that the war was one for Christian civilisation and a righteous war. Goebbels, the German propaganda minister, declared that the German aim was to "destroy the English". One war was recently over, however, the civil war in Spain, which had ended in 1939 with General Franco victorious over the Republican cause. The *Irish Independent*, in January, 1940, ran a series of articles in praise of the new Spain.

While the world war was sucking most of the European nations into its net, the events of that war were extensively reported in the Dublin newspapers, *The Irish Times*, *Irish Independent* and *Irish Press*, as well as the *Evening Herald* and the now defunct Dublin *Evening Mail*. But in a sense, it was very much a "phoney" war for Dublin readers, since none of the events described on the various war fronts impinged directly on their lives. Jottings by Man about Town and the Mandrake cartoon were main features in the *Evening Mail*, while the *Irish Independent* gave one detailed paragraph to a court case in which a man was fined £2 for stealing a bicycle at Lucan.

The official opening of air services from the new airport at Collinstown merited a reasonable amount of coverage — the two photographs in the *Irish Press* were the greatest amount of space given to the event — while a proposal under discussion in Dublin Corporation also merited an amount of editorial space. Some councillors were keen on the idea of a new bridge across the Liffey, to the east of Butt Bridge.

An early 19th century map, showing the general Collinstown area, still very rural, six miles into the country from the city centre.
Phoenix Maps, Dublin

This idea had to wait rather longer for fruition than the notion of a great airport operating successfully at Collinstown. But some newspapers, like the Dublin *Evening Mail,* made no mention of that first Dublin–Liverpool flight.

Two local news stories attracted far more interest for the sub-editors than either the new airport or international events in the war zones of Europe. In Church Street, Dundalk, a tragic house fire early on the Thursday morning killed a total of eight people from two families, the Colemans and the Morans, and the newspapers devoted many photographs to the tragic scene; water from the firemens' hoses had frozen into great icicles. A court hearing also attracted much interest; Thomas MacCurtain was further remanded in custody, charged with the murder of Det. Officer John Roche in Patrick Street, Cork, on the night of January 3, 1940. Murder was so rare in Ireland in those times that if one occurred, it caused enormous public excitement, reflected in substantial newspaper coverage. Another sad event was the cause of much musing in print, the funeral of Elizabeth Corbet Yeats, sister of W. B. Yeats, the poet; he had died in the South of France in 1939.

There was little sign of the forthcoming food rationing that was destined to become such a feature of Dublin life from 1941 for the duration of the Emergency, and the fashion shops of Dublin promoted their wares with vigour. Pims, the great store that once stood in South Great George's Street, advertised extensively on the front pages of the main newspapers — those front pages were all advertisements, mostly classified — while at Griffith's shoe shop in Talbot Street, ladies shoes were priced at 5s 11d (30p). Readers were also advised to protect their kidneys with Doans pills. A tube of Rowntrees fruit gums was selling for 2d; they are still going strong today. Pony racing at Dolphin's Barn racecourse was advertised in the Dublin *Evening Mail* on January 20 — it again failed to mention the inaugural flight from Collinstown — while there was widespread concern that the Red Cross 'chase at Leopardstown would have to be postponed because of the bad weather.

There was concern too at the mounting level of unemployment, which in this month of January, 1940, stood at 113,455, or half the present-day total. The building trade was badly hit by a fall in business and it was reported that week that 260 bricklayers were signing on in Dublin, a record number. One of the few large-scale construction projects under way at the time was the terminal building at the airport, although it was moving towards completion.

The band played on; the entire staff of Hely's, the Dame Street stationers, attended the company's staff dance in the Metropole in O'Connell Street. The gentlemen were attired in formal suits, many complete with the old-fashioned wing collars, while the ladies invariably wore the voluminous crinoline-style dresses popular then. An excellent night was had by all, dancing away the bewitching hours to music by Phil Murtagh and his band. There were many other entertainments, too. At the Olympia, Cinderella, the Christmas pantomime, was just finishing its run, while Jimmy O'Dea, that great Dublin comedian, was putting the finishing touches to the Theatre Royal concert he was about to give in aid of the Capuchin foreign missions. In the city centre cinemas, there was an excellent choice of films, such as Boris Karloff in *Mr Wong in Chinatown* at the Carlton and Edward G. Robinson in *Blackmail* at the Savoy. Interspersed with the feature films made in Hollywood, California, and Ealing, England, were the Movietone News newsreel films, depicting the war in a light favourable to the Allies and unfavourable to the Germans, just as in the cowboy films of that era, the good man won over the bad, and the sheriff ran the "baddies" out of town. Cinema- and theatre-going was immensely popular; the notion of home entertainment was barely catching on, since the Radio Éireann service was only fourteen years in existence. It went on the air at 5.30 pm daily and closed down at 11 pm. Some typical programmes on January 19, 1940 included *Town Hall Tonight*, a rendition of *Arrah na Pogue,* and *Ireland is Singing* with Donagh MacDonagh. Very often, the batteries would start to run down at the crucial moment and would need recharging.

An air of near normality pervaded the newspapers; *The Irish Times* for January 19, 1940, devoted much feature space to covering the latest Paris fashions. With the fall of Paris six months in the future, haute couture had a little more time to run. A minister in the French Defence Department was quoted in that same issue as warning the people of France of the dangers of mass air attacks on the country by the Nazis. Foreshadowing the National Lottery, such a popular feature of life in Ireland in 1990, *The Irish Times* carried an advertisement in one of its other publications, the *Weekly Irish Times:* "The names of the 3,860 prizewinners in this week's Sweepstake draw will be published".

The contrast between the newspapers of January, 1940 and those of January, 1990 could not be more striking. News of war was less muted, since the only open conflict was in the Soviet republic of Azerbaijan, where Soviet forces were moving in to quell a near-insurrection and the threat of a civil war between the Islamic Azerbaijanis and the neighbouring Christian Armenians. The Dublin newspapers were full of photographs of Soviet troops being sent to the front. Elsewhere, the international news coverage was of the unscrambling of Communist rule in eastern Europe. At

Corballis House, Dublin airport. The house dates back to the 17th century and is now used by the Aer Lingus technical ground school.
Illustration: Philip Doherty

home, controversy reigned over the remarks of Dr Desmond Connell, the Catholic Archbishop of Dublin, on the nature of homosexuality, a topic that was totally taboo for any kind of discussion fifty years ago. There was a big change in the weather, too. At the meteorological station at Dublin Airport, the maximum temperature reading for January 19, 1990 was seven degrees Centigrade or forty-five degrees Fahrenheit, and weather conditions were sunny. It was all a vast improvement on the snow conditions in 1940, when the new Dublin airport was described as having a cold and frosty start. The events of that momentous day in January, 1940 were commemorated exactly fifty years later, when a plaque was unveiled on the airport complex by the Minister for Tourism and Transport, Seamus Brennan.

The area on which the airport was built at Collinstown is one of ancient historic interest and two of the buildings on the present airport site, both now in the care of Aer Rianta, are of considerable vintage. The earliest reference to the Cloghran area is found in 1169, when annals record that Owen Gwyneth, Prince of North Wales, had a "sonne called Ryryd, Lord of Clochran". The name Cloghran derives from the Irish for "stone of song", a reference to the limestone hillock on which the church is built; in ancient times, several hundred years ago, harpists and bards assembed here once a year to compete for prizes. Collinstown, on the other hand, has no such derivation from Irish; the name comes from the family that once owned this townland. Corballis, too, is intimately connected with the present-day airport and was the townland nearest to the modern centre of the airport. The earliest written record of Corballis was in 1536 when King Henry VIII, he of the many wives, granted to one Gerald Nugent "general livery of seisin and pardon of intrusion" in different lands, including Corbally.

Just over a century later, in 1641, the area of Corballis was described as extending to some 100 acres and having a stone-built house of modest dimensions, with an orchard and garden. There were less substantial dwellings, probably cabins made from mud and thatch, and described as being valued by a jury at £20. Eighteen years later, the townland of Corballis was documented as having ten residents, four English and six Irish. Collinstown was similary sparsely populated; in 1659, it had a population of three English and six Irish. In the latter part of the 17th century, the lands of Collinstown were owned by one Patrick Birmingham of Corballis, but on January 20, 1669 King Charles II granted Collinstown to James, Duke of York. In these early times, the southern part of what was later to become the townland of Collinstown was called Donas or Dowanstown and when the grant of land was made by the English king, it included Collinstown and Dowanstown. At the start of the next century, there was a further transition of ownership, when a Dr Thomas Molyneux of Dublin bought the lands of Collinstown and Dowanstown, a total of 236 acres, for the grand sum of £1,184, which for the time was the equivalent of Ballsbridge property prices in 1990. Even at that early stage, in the early 18th century, there were references to the limestone quarries that stood at Collinstown; the quarries filled with water and made a substantial lake that remained until modern times, only being filled in when the airport was being extended in the 1970s.

Some of the hamlets — villages would be too elaborate a description — in the vicinity of the present airport no longer exist; their disappearance is due to factors other than the enormous expansion of the Collinstown airport site over the last forty years. On the track from Cloghran to Artane, itself a country area until after World War I, when it was built up to house veterans returning home from service in the British Army in the trenches of Flanders and north-eastern France, there was a tiny settlement called the Baskin. During the potato famine of the late 1840s, this village faded out of sight, as its inhabitants died off and the houses were abandoned, to fall into roofless ruin. Another settlement very near the present airport site has also vanished into the mists of history, but there were fewer local regrets about its oblivion.

Toberbunny drew its name from the Irish for the well that was once noted there; the water in the well had a white quality, due to its alkaline salt. In Irish, it was tobar bainne, the "well of milk". The one-time inhabitants of Toberbunny seemed to have had less than the milk of human kindness flowing in their veins; a report dated 1838 said that the little village of scattered houses, called after the townland, was better known as "Robbers' Town", because of its lawless inhabitants. Just over ten years later, there was a certain local satisfaction in the fact that the famine caused Toberbunny to be wiped off the face of the map. There was another tragedy, too, in the village, in the year of 1798, the time of the bloodily suppressed insurrection.

Tubberbonney House in the village was built in the late 16th century; at the end of the 18th century, when the house was a venerable mansion, two centuries old, and occupied by one William Sneyd, tragedy struck. Sneyd, described as a loyalist, a supporter of the Crown, was out at the Ascension Day fair at Kilsallaghan on May 17, 1798 when he was shot dead by an unknown assailant. After his death, the house fell into ruin and about 1829 it was totally demolished by a man called John Morgan, who had the tenancy rights. Of the house and the little hamlet itself, described as far back as 1641 as having one stone-built house and three cottages, not a trace has existed for well over 100 years. It has disappeared as completely as the Augustinian priory that once stood on the site of the present airport and which had to be abandoned in the 16th century at the time of the dissolution of the monasteries. In time, the priory fell into dust and so too did the adjoining graveyard, living on only in the memory of some local residents until the earlier years of this century.

Some of the old buildings still remain, however, giving a certain aspect of Collinstown in the old times. Corballis House, which is beside the main road leading to the present airport terminal, has antecedents going back to the early 17th century. It was built on the site of a previous house, owned, until its demolition, by the De La Noyde family. The history of the site can be traced back even further than this family, to the 14th century, when it was in the possession of the Taillour family.

Castlemoate House as seen from the old graveyard at Cloghran. The church here was dedicated to St Doulogh; by 1630, it had forty-eight parishioners, but, by 1831, that number had jumped to 541. The church was rebuilt in 1712 and was demolished in 1950.
Illustration: Philip Doherty

They were the first to own this parcel of land, which, in the early 15th century, passed to the Hollywood family. The present house, originally called Tamora House, was built using stones from the ancient castle that was believed to have stood on what is now the site of the Ryanair hangar. In the 18th century, the house was occupied by the Wilkinson family; Thomas Wilkinson was Lord Mayor of Dublin in 1719/20. Carolan, the 18th century harpist, was said to have given his last public performance here. In 1795, when the great house was occupied by his grandson, Sir Henry Wilkinson, Recorder of Kilkenny, it was raided one night by men looking for arms, for robbery or insurrectionary purposes. The Wilkinson family had quite a collection of muskets and other weapons — presumably not all for self-defence — but the entire collection was taken during that raid in the middle of the night, an eerie precursor of the IRA raid on Collinstown in 1919 when it was a British military base. The two-storey Corballis House, in the custody of Aer Rianta, and leased to Aer Lingus for use as its technical ground school, has been well preserved and refurbished, retaining its original outlines and slate roof. Much of the facade of the building is draped in an ancient vine, which turns red at the approach of autumn. Corballis House, whose name derives from the Irish Cor-bhaile, meaning "odd town", passed from the ownership of the Wilkinson family in the early 19th century. By the 1880s, it was owned and occupied by a venerable old lady of the manor, a Miss Wall. Nowadays, this piece of north county Dublin's architectural heritage is safely in the hands of Aer Rianta. Only one element of the house no longer remains, a tower.

This circular tower, standing twenty feet high, with a castellated parapet, was immediately adjacent to Corballis House. Two storeys each had a room, twelve feet in diameter, each lighted by two small windows facing north, but the roof fell in — literally — in the early 19th century and the remains of this tower had to be demolished about 1844.

Otherwise, Corballis House, with the fine tiling in the entrance hall, is much as it was, both inside and outside, although there is no trace today of the hand-made nails that were found when a major refurbishment of the house took place about ten years ago. These nails dated back to the original construction of the house and were

This aerial photograph by the Air Corps taken from a height of about 400 feet, shows the old RAF aerodrome at Collinstown, as it looked in 1925, with the hangars and accommodation still intact. In the forefront of the photograph is Corballis House.
Photograph: Stationery Office

probably made by one of the local blacksmith's forges that once hammered out horseshoes and other ironwork in the vicinity, until the early years of this century.

The other old house at the airport, also in the care of Aer Rianta, is Castlemoate House, which stands just off the main Dublin to Belfast road, opposite the Coachman's Inn. The house was built in the early 19th century, using stones from the same ruined castle that was the source of building materials for Corballis House. Castlemoate House derives its name from this old castle, and its moat. Local people used to believe that ancient treasure was buried in the grounds of the house, but when the owner ploughed up the adjacent rath in 1822, only a few copper and silver coins were found, together with a number of pikes, abandoned after the 1798 rebellion.

In the old days, the house was known as "Castle Moat"; in 1877, it was bought by Christopher Dodd, who promptly enlarged the building, adding a new front in the Italian stucco style, which was popular then. He also laid out new gardens. In the immediate vicinity was the hamlet of Cloghran, consisting of eleven thatched cottages, a pub, the Coachman's Inn, itself dating back two centuries, a post office, a forge and the local national school. From the early 1960s, the house began to fall into disrepair, but in 1975 Aer Rianta took it over and began a substantial restoration programme, which included restoring the broad entrance foyer to its original splendour. Now, the house and its gardens are in excellent condition; the building is used as the Aer Rianta training and conference centre.

Other buildings in the area of the airport are living proof of the great antiquity of human habitation in the Collinstown district. There are some ancient buildings still standing as living testimonies to the old settlements of Collinstown and surrounding

This photograph was taken in 1990 from a similar position, showing the same section of the airport site.
Photograph: Neil MacDougald

townlands, long before anyone dreamed of the possibility of flying and the need to build a great airport, by far the largest in Ireland. Just down from the airport, on the old main road into Dublin, is Collinstown Cross, which is a Y-shaped junction; once, it had thatched cottages on either side of the road. One of those cottages still remains; it is said to date from 1661, and was built in the traditional single-storey style. Since the 1920s, it has been known locally as the "dairy cottage of the O'Donohues".

The road to the left of this junction led to Forrest; this name and the name of the present-day golf course, Forrest Little, are reminders of the great forest, of oaks and other traditional Irish trees, that once covered much of the land to the immediate west of the modern airport.

The ancient highway from Dublin to Derry also ran to the west of the airport. A little settlement clustered around the Boot Inn, which was built in the 16th century and is said to be the oldest pub in County Dublin, so called because it was in the boot shaped townland of Pickardstown. There may have been a previous pub on this site going back even further in history. Outside the front door of the Boot Inn is a stone mount, once used for riders when mounting their horses, and staples for tethering the beasts. Of another venerable inn here, the Forrest Tavern, nothing remains except a section of stone wall. Several of the single-storey cottages here are quite old, around two hundred years, but the little shop that was in the Maxwell family for generations is now closed up.

Also on the western side of the airport, not far from the end of the new runway, opened in June 1989, is the well-preserved Dunsoghly Castle at St Margaret's. A

The Coachman's Inn, on the main Swords road, near Dublin airport. Over two centuries ago, the pub used to be known as the Blandford Arms.
Illustration: Philip Doherty

castle stood near the present ruin, as far back as the end of the 13th century; it was then owned by the Finglas family, who took their name from the ancient village of that name.

A member of the powerful and pervasive Plunkett clan built the present castle in the 15th century; the tablet over the door to the small chapel beside the main tower reveals the provenance of the castle: "built by John Plunkett of Dunsoghly and his wife Genet Sarsfield in the year 1573". After four centuries, the castle remains in comparatively good condition, standing over seventy feet high and consisting of a tower with four rectangular turrets at each corner. The main walls are over four feet thick and there is a substantial principal room.

This whole area of north County Dublin remained as it was until the middle of World War I. It was good farming country, with isolated farmhouses and a scattering of small communities, like Cloghran and Collinstown Cross, thatched cottages still much in evidence. Over in the direction of the Naul, to the west of the present airport site, there were still extensive woods, a substantial reminder of that ancient Irish forest that once girded hundreds of acres. The bustle and liveliness of Sackville Street, now renamed O'Connell Street, and central Dublin, with its trams gliding hither and thither, early open motor cars and horse-drawn vehicles, was six miles away and far distant.

One woman who was resident in this immediate area some sixty years ago remembers the quiet, undisturbed countryside. Kathleen Riordan, who used to live in the thatched cottage that once stood on the site of the present airport church, recalls that the whole area was very rural.

Collinstown was as out of the way as the most remote part of County Galway, she remembers, and people living in the area rarely went to Dublin, which was regarded as a distant metropolis, beyond their immediate concern. Even though the British guns that shelled Sackville Street and the GPO as Easter Week, 1916 drew to a violent close, could be heard quite clearly at Collinstown and the flames and smoke of destruction could be seen rising into the sky, it all seemed somehow irrelevant. For many of these years, the Bewley family had their farm here, keeping their prize herd of Jersey cows at Knocksedan, near the present airport; for the family, it was a quiet country location, far removed from the city centre cafés that drew their milk and cream from the family farm in this district. World War I, or the Great War, as it was known at the time, the war to end all wars, also seemed far away to the inhabitants of the Collinstown and Cloghran areas, even though many households saw their sons go off, many never to return, to fight for what they thought was the freedom of small nations.

Yet this very same war brought aviation to Collinstown. The Royal Flying Corps had been set up on April 13, 1912, on the recommendation of the Committee of Imperial Defence. Just over a year later, the first military aircraft arrived in Ireland, in September, 1913. The seeds were sown for the new military aerodrome at Collinstown, from which site grew the present civil airport.

In September, 1913, large-scale military manoeuvres were held throughout these islands and it was decided to deploy aircraft from No 2 Squadron, based in Montrose, Scotland, to Limerick. Six aircraft in total made the journey; one of the BE2A machines flew over Dublin, where it was seen by many people in the Phoenix Park. The next major development was in November, 1915, when a Royal Flying Corps training school was set up at the Curragh. From 1916 onwards, the British Government decided that Ireland, relatively calm after the Easter Rising of that year, and far removed from the fighting in Belgium and France, would make an ideal place for training. More aerodromes were needed and the man selected to choose the sites not only had a family connection with Ireland, but forty years later, sat on the board of Aer Lingus as the British European Airways representative.

Sholto Douglas, who was later to become Lord Douglas of Kirtleside and Marshal of the Royal Air Force, was a pilot in 1917 with 43 Squadron, RFC, based at Treizennes in France. Taking off one day, he failed to notice a horse in the field; the undercarriage of the plane hit the animal. The Sopwith aeroplane overturned and Douglas was sufficiently injured to warrant his removal to hospital in London. His father was the director of the National Gallery of Ireland, in Merrion Square, Dublin, and the young aviator spent some time in Dublin recuperating, until he was eventually passed fit for light flying duties. He was unable to return to his squadron in France, but was given an unusual assignment in Ireland.

Sholto Douglas, the man who recommended in 1917 that Collinstown should be developed as a military aerodrome. Later, he became a Marshal of the Royal Air Force and chairman of British European Airways.
Photograph: John W. R. Taylor

Earlier that year, it had been decided that the Royal Flying Corps should be expanded to 106 service squadrons and 97 reserve squadrons which needed a parallel increase in training programmes, so when Douglas had recovered, he was sent on a tour of Ireland to find eight sites that could be used as training aerodromes by the RFC. There were no aerodromes in Ireland at that stage, and the Lands Officer at Irish Command had picked out some likely sites; it was up to Sholto Douglas to inspect them and make recommendations. Irish Command was going to provide him with a car and driver, but he decided that flying would save a lot of time, so he flew a BE2C from Scotland, over the North Channel, by way of Stranraer and Larne. He landed his aircraft in the Phoenix Park, near the Vice-Regal Lodge, which is now the official residence of the President of Ireland. Douglas warned the two sentries on duty to guard the plane with their lives: this was less than a year after the 1916 Rising and Douglas was concerned about any threat of sabotage. During that summer of 1917, Sholto Douglas selected eight aerodrome sites throughout Ireland, including Baldonnel, Gormanston and the Curragh. He also chose the sites at Collinstown and Aldergrove, which were to become the two largest civil airports in Ireland, in terms of annual passenger throughput.

Once he had selected a site from the air, he went by car to make detailed ground inspections. Despite the fact that the sight of a British Army uniform was becoming increasingly unpopular in Ireland, Douglas received a fairly warm welcome.

He recalls in his autobiography, *Years of Combat,* that when he travelled by car, corner boys lounging at the street corners in the villages almost invariably threw scowls at him; some were audacious enough to throw stones. But any time he landed in a field near a village, the young men of the area would come running onto the field, cheering and shouting, throwing their caps in the air, because few of them had seen an aeroplane before. When his selection task was completed, Douglas flew back to London and reported to his superiors on the sites he had recommended, including Collinstown. The other sites chosen by Douglas included Fermoy, County Cork, and Cookstown, Tallaght, near the site of the present Cookstown industrial estate. The specifications were simple: the grass fields had to give good take-off runs of five to six hundred yards in any direction. Despite its original choice on these most simplistic grounds, Collinstown proved to be the ideal site in the greater Dublin area for a large civil airport requiring runways nearly five times longer than those needed in the closing stages of World War I.

Once work started on the chosen sites, construction was fairly straightforward. The grass had to be treated and any potholes or bumps removed — paved runways at Collinstown were thirty years in the future — and buildings, such as hangars, were constructed. As work was starting on the Collinstown base, an interesting exhibition was held at the Earlsfort Garage in Hatch Street, Dublin, in December, 1917.

The Air Services Exhibition, organised by the Countess of Drogheda, was designed to tell the complete story of aeronautics, using models, paintings, photographs and actual aircraft, with the aim of raising funds to build hospitals for wounded airmen. Throughout 1917, the exhibition had toured Britain, where it was seen by over a million people. When it came to Dublin, it created equal excitement, with the aircraft on display including an RFC Sopwith Camel and a captured German Albatross DI, both of these fighter planes used in France. There were many relics of German Zeppelins, the airships that caused some havoc and terror in eastern England during the war. During the exhibition, music for the visitors was played by the band of the Royal Berkshire Regiment. In his opening speech, the Lord Lieutenant of Ireland, the Rt. Hon. Ivor Churchill-Guest, 2nd Baron of Wimborne, said there would soon be a great development in aerodromes and airship stations. He even forecast the use of Ireland as the best European base for trans-Atlantic flights to the United States. One young teenager was greatly impressed by the sights of the exhibition, R. W. (Dick) O'Sullivan, who in the mid-1930s played such a key role in the Government choice of Collinstown as the site for Dublin's new civil airport.

On April 1, 1918, the Royal Flying Corps and the Royal Naval Air Service were amalgamated to form the Royal Air Force. On this date, Collinstown aerodrome was

View of Castlemoate House from the old graveyard at Cloghran.
Illustration: Philip Doherty

The gate lodge to Forrest West, demolished in 1988.
Illustration: Philip Doherty

reported as being twenty-two per cent built and scheduled for completion in June. In the event, work was not finished until well into 1919.

Four of the new aerodromes in Ireland were designated as training depot stations; a reorganisation of the training programme had taken place, with an emphasis on economies in the use of personnel and transport, and also in the use of farming land, so the Collinstown base was built on a smaller scale than originally intended. Each one of the four Irish training depot stations, Baldonnel, Collinstown, Gormanston and Tallaght, were built to exactly the same specifications, with the intention of having a complement of seventy-two aircraft at each base. Out of the four bases, the one at Collinstown was marginally larger than the others and covered in total 234 acres. The layout of the four stations was the same; at Collinstown, there were six aeroplane hangars, or sheds, as they were known at the time, each measuring 170 feet by 100 feet and built in three pairs. There was one repair section shed of similar size, standing on its own. Other technical buildings included a salvage shed, motor transport shed, workshops for wood and metal working, oil and petrol stores, technical stores, instruction huts, where subjects like gunnery, photography and radio could be taught, offices, a power house, a guard house, a compass platform, a machine gun range and an explosives' store. Regimental buildings included the officers' mess, officers' baths and latrines, and similar but separate facilities for sergeants and enlisted personnel. There was a woman's hostel for women serving at the station. At Collinstown, a total of 142 officers were stationed, and 626 other ranks.

Quite a number of women worked at the Collinstown RAF base, seven forewomen and 154 rank and file, as well as fifty-four women with what were described as household duties. In July, 1918, the scheme for the new Irish training depot stations was finalised and the Collinstown base became fully operational during September and October, 1918. Besides the RAF personnel based at Collinstown, some American personnel manned an aeroplane repair section. They belonged to the United States Air Service, which only became active in the war in Europe in April, 1918, a year after the US entered the war. In addition to its use as a training centre, there is also some evidence that, in the last year of the war, the base at Collinstown was used to hold German internees. Kathleen Riordan, a long-time resident of the immediate area, has quite vivid memories of these troops being held at the base.

But the base at Collinstown was no sooner running at peak efficiency than the war ended, far quicker than the military planners had envisaged. With the signing of the Armistice on November 11, 1918, the military authorities began the run-down of the vast training section within the RAF. Armistice Day was celebrated with enthusiasm. In Dublin, reported *The Irish Times*, "aloft were to be seen aeroplanes, gracefully

The Boot Inn, on the old coach road from Dublin to Drogheda, at the western edge of the airport. The pub dates from the 16th century.
Illustration: Philip Doherty

gambolling in a cloudless sky, their wings flashing in the sunlight".

The first withdrawal of flying units from Collinstown began on November 12, the day after the Armistice, when a flight of 156 Squadron was moved to Cambridgeshire in the east of England.

The next withdrawal came on December 9, when a flight of 163 Squadron was moved out, also to a base in Cambridgeshire. Collinstown, in common with the other three training bases in Ireland, only enjoyed a very brief period at full training capacity, from August to December, 1918, although there was reduced flying training until the early summer of 1919. The extensive facilities built at Collinstown quickly became under-utilised, as did Collinstown House itself, a three-storey brick-built house with slate roof dating back to the mid-19th century, and which was used as the 3rd training wing headquarters.

In addition to the four main training bases, the RAF had a large administrative presence in Dublin; its recruiting headquarters was in the Maples Hotel in central Dublin, while the Standard Hotel in Harcourt Street was used as a reception depot. The medical headquarters for the RAF in Ireland was at 65 Fitzwilliam Square, while the medical board was based at 23 St Stephen's Green. At the Collinstown base itself, there were four hospital beds for officers and seven for non-commissioned ranks, all carefully segregated. Yet less than a year after the Armistice, the run-down of the RAF in Ireland was almost completed. Collinstown, Gormanston and Tallaght bases were all evacuated and the RAF concentrated all its flying activities on Baldonnel aerodrome.

Perhaps the greatest excitement during the existence of the RAF base at Collinstown was the IRA raid in March, 1919. A large party of about 50 men entered the base and seized a quantity of arms and ammunition. The raid took place at about 2.30 am on March 20, a clear moonlit night. The twenty or so sentries were disarmed and tied up, while another party from the raiding expedition collected the arms and ammunition. The haul amounted to seventy-five rifles and bayonets and 5,000 rounds of ammunition. As a final "shot", the raiders immobilised the twenty or so military cars garaged at the base.

In reporting the raid, *The Irish Times* said that when its reporter visited the aerodrome, Major Woods, the officer in charge, declined to make any comment. Enquiries to the Dublin headquarters of the RAF also failed to elicit any reponse. But continued the newspaper: "the aerodrome was not enclosed with a fence, so that the raiders could have made off in any direction and the roads around the airfield were so rutted" — country roads were not tarred in those days — "that no indication could be gleaned of which direction they went in".

After the high excitement of the raid, life returned to comparative quiet at the aerodrome, which even then was coming to the end of its short life as a military base. In 1922, there were some relatively minor incidents at Collinstown.

In July, 1922, a Bristol fighter was damaged while landing on the grass at Collinstown, while in August that year, another Bristol fighter was damaged on take-off, when the engine failed. The observer in the plane, Private McCafferty, was injured. No aircraft taking off from Collinstown suffered the ignominious fate of one machine taking off from Fermoy aerodrome in north County Cork, in November, 1920: it struck a cow.

There were some incidents involving military mail planes en route to Collinstown, like the flight from Aldergrove in October, 1922, when a Bristol fighter missed its flight plan because of heavy mist and ended up in Lough Neagh, although neither the pilot nor his commanding officer were injured. After the War of Independence and the Treaty, the main function of the base at Collinstown was facilitating the military mails aircraft. In June, 1922, this service was started between Collinstown and Aldergrove, operating three times a week. The most complicated instructions were given to the pilots to avoid detection by the IRA and in the event of a forced landing, the pilots had to burn the mail. In July of that year, the flight frequency was increased to one a day, with a second aircraft being used as needed. The truce in the War of Independence came into force on Monday, July 11, 1921, and three months later, the London conference began, that led to the signing of the Treaty in December, 1921. At 4.15 am on the morning of Wednesday, June 22, 1922, the government artillery started firing on the Republicans who had taken over the Four Courts the previous April. The civil war had started.

During the April of that year, it had been decided that Baldonnel aerodrome would have to be evacuated, since it could not be adequately guarded. Collinstown

Christopher McGuinness, who owned Rock House, Collinstown, and who died in 1933, is pictured at his front door. Later, the cottage was occupied by the Riordan family.

Copies of the *Daily Mail* leave Collinstown airfield, June, 1920, bound for Galway, on what is believed to have been the first commercial flight from Collinstown.

was selected as the base for the Irish Flight, the RAF section that was to remain in southern Ireland until the final British withdrawal, planned for December, 1922. On May 1, 1922, the Irish Flight was transferred from Baldonnel to Collinstown, immediately after services such as the meteorological office had moved over. The aerodrome at Baldonnel was handed over to the Provisional Government on May 4; one of the first people to join the embryonic Irish air corps was Colonel W. P. Delamer, the manager of Dublin airport between 1946 and 1966, when he retired. He often attributed his survival in the Great War to the fact that his training instructor crashed when Delamer had just reached the mandatory level of twenty hours' dual instruction. Instead of being sent off to fly solo missions, Delamer took over his instructor's duties and by the time he was flying solo missions, he had eighty hours' flying experience. Delamer served at the front line in north-eastern France and had two lucky escapes; on one occasion, the future airport manager was brought down when German bullets hit the petrol tank of his plane. He was wounded twice, on one occasion seriously enough to be evacuated to hospital in London. He never served in the RFC in Ireland. In 1922, when the Irish Air Corps was being set up, he transferred immediately from the RAF and went on to spend twenty-four years in the service.

Although Collinstown had not been used as a training base since May, 1919, it continued to be occupied as a barracks by soldiers in the British army. As from May 1, 1922, following the closure of Baldonnel as a British military aerodrome, Collinstown became once again an RAF station, while the RAF headquarters in Ireland was moved from Baldonnel first to General HQ at Parkgate, near the Phoenix Park, then to the army barracks at Islandbridge.

During that month of May, the newly redesignated RAF base at Collinstown was busy enough, with nearly twenty-eight hours of operational flying. Four troop trains from the Curragh and Newbridge to Dublin were given aerial escorts and there was a reconnaisance mission flown in search of cars stolen by Republicans. But by the end of May, 1922, with the civil war becoming more likely by the day, there was a considerable reinforcement of the RAF's presence in the South of Ireland. No. 2 Squadron, which had withdrawn from Fermoy, County Cork, to England, was ordered back to Aldergrove, by way of Collinstown. A total of twelve machines made the journey over a two-day period; their landings at Collinstown were an impressive enough sight. Heavy reinforcements were sent to the aerodrome; by July, Bristol fighters were arriving, fitted with 112 lbs bomb bays, so that they could carry out bombing missions where required. The military mail service between Collinstown and Aldergrove was also in full flight, the first instance of mails being carried by aircraft in Ireland. On July 5, one of the Bristol planes was handed over to the new Air Corps, and made the short flight from Collinstown to Baldonnel.

The civil war started on June 28, 1922, and ironically, it led to the development of civil oriented flying activities at the Collinstown aerodrome, for the first time in its history. The tragic events in Ireland were of considerable interest to the British newspapers and their readers, not least because there were still substantial numbers of British troops stationed here, even though the Treaty had been signed the previous December. Civil aircraft were hired from the De Havilland Aeroplane Hire Service in England to bring news copy and photographs from Dublin to London. This company had been formed in March, 1921, at Edgware in Middlesex, not far from the present Heathrow airport, by Alan Cobham, who was its chief pilot. The new company's first aircraft were DH9s, unused military airframes converted for civil use. The firm charged £8 an hour, or two shillings a mile, for the hire of its aircraft.

The involvement of Cobham's company with Collinstown in the summer of 1922 was a precursor of his great level of activity in Ireland in subsequent years, not least for the Cobham flying circus. Garret FitzGerald, later to become an employee of Aer

The ball alley that once stood beside the Boot Inn; it was demolished in 1937 when the airport site was being developed.
Photograph: Irish Press

Lingus at Dublin Airport, and later still, a Taoiseach, who gave his older brother Desmond some friendly advice on the design of the first terminal at Dublin airport, remembers it. He was first introduced to the thrills of flying when he saw one of the flying circuses, run by Cobham, by now Sir Alan Cobham, over Dungarvan, County Waterford, in 1935.

The origins of Cobham's involvement with Collinstown are fascinating in themselves. On June 28, 1922, he had just returned from a trip to Bucharest in Romania when word came in that a London newspaper wanted a plane to go to Dublin immediately to pick up editorial copy and photographs. He detailed one of his pilots, C. D. Barnard, for this flight in a DC9C. Within a few minutes, a call came through for another plane, so he sent Hubert Broad in an identical aircraft. Both Barnard and Broad were to become well-known for their aerial antics in the Cobham flying circus. Then came a call for a third aircraft and there was only one pilot available at this stage, Cobham himself. He flew to Collinstown, into a fierce westerly gale, and waited at the aerodrome for several hours while his precious cargo for the London newspaper was made ready. He later reported for the newspaper, the august London *Times,* how the Irish Sea lay sparkling for thirty miles ahead of him. Then the thin band of darkness, the Irish coastline, came up and, before long, he could see the outline of Dublin with a long tail of smoke from the fires that were burning in the city moving out to sea on a north-westerly wind.

A few moments later, he was over the city. He saw that the Four Courts were barricaded with sandbags, but otherwise, he could make out nothing of the fighting. "I still have the impression of emptiness under that strange curling drift of smoke, as though tragedy veiled the face of the city".

He had to wait for two hours for permission to take off from the Irish Free State authorities; he left at 8.30 pm, as the sun was setting. Dublin was still burning and the plume of smoke was drifting ten to fifteen miles out to sea.

Throughout the summer of 1922, the military mail flights continued from Collinstown to Aldergrove and, in August, there was great commotion with the assassination of Michael Collins at Beal na Blath in west County Cork. The funeral service of the great Irish political leader was held in the Pro-Cathedral, Dublin, with due pomp and circumstance, as befitted a national hero. The circumstances of his death created much interest for the readers of the London newspapers, so once again, Cobham's air service was in action, flying into Collinstown to collect press photographs. The

Top left: The thatched cottage once occupied by the Riordan family; it stood near the site of the present airport church. In the lane beside the cottage, Eamon de Valera and his wife, Sinead, often came for Sunday afternoon walks in the early 1930s.

Top right: members of the Riordan family with greyhounds at the door of their Collinstown cottage, early 1930s.

Bottom left: on the old aerodrome site.

Bottom right: the quarry at Collinstown, early 1930s.
Photographs: Kathleen Riordan

Irish Flight at Collinstown ceased flying on October 14, 1922; the day before, a convoy of lorries travelled down from Aldergrove to collect stores in preparation for the disbandment. The Fifteen Acres of the Phoenix Park in Dublin, where Sholto Douglas had landed on his first reconnaissance mission to Ireland back in the summer of 1917, was turned into an emergency landing ground as Collinstown base was being closed down. The wireless station at Collinstown was dismantled and eventually shipped to Aldergrove, while the last of the stores went back to England, along with the remaining personnel from the base. The Irish Flight was disbanded as from November 1, 1922. Some British army troops remained at Collinstown, men of the First Battalion of the Cameronians.

When they evacuated the Collinstown aerodrome, it was handed over to the Irish Free State government. The last RAF presence in southern Ireland was that of seven men at the Phoenix Park temporary base, which closed down at 4 pm on December 14. Three days later came the final withdrawal, when three thousand men from four British army regiments marched from their barracks in different parts of Dublin to the North Wall, where they set sail on six cross-channel steamers, which were escorted by *HMS Venomous*. The officer commanding British forces in Ireland, General Sir Neville MacReady, left Kingstown harbour aboard *HMS Dragon*, which was equipped with an aircraft hangar.

The War of Independence, the truce and the Treaty had all come and gone; the following year, 1923, the civil war was brought to an end. In future, military aviation in Ireland would be in the hands of the Air Corps, who made Baldonnel, rather than Collinstown, their headquarters. Collinstown was never again used for substantial military aviation activities, although it was a further fifteen years before it was decided to turn the aerodrome into the Dublin civil airport. Although the land and buildings at Collinstown passed into Irish Government ownership at the end of 1922, the former military aerodrome had no immediate role in aviation in the new Irish Free State and was left to the fate of the elements. The grass started to grow on the runways.

One of the features of the old RAF base was the eight acres of land designated for sports; on this patch of land, there were two squash courts. Of all the buildings left behind at Collinstown when the RAF left at the end of 1922, these courts, turned into handball alleys, were the best appreciated by local people. Jack Hanley, who worked at the airport for thirty-four years from 1950, mainly on the maintenance side, remembers the alleys, "under the one roof, a back wall and all, and a gallery, lovely". He recollects that there was a great tradition of handball in the area and claims that the handball alleys at Collinstown were the best in the country. "There wasn't a dead bit in any of the walls, you would get the same response off different parts of the wall". He remembers that championship matches were sometimes held here.

Hanley's family lived in the Collinstown area for many years — he and his family now live just outside Portmarnock — and when his father and mother married, after the Great War, they lived in one of the two red brick cottages that stood opposite the old quarry, the site of the entrance to the present boiler house.

When Jack Hanley was growing up here, the area was so rural that the main interest lay in the numbers of animals; the fields were overrun with rabbits. The Board of Works rented out the old aerodrome fields, some of them to a man called Mick Cuddy. Jack Hanley well remembers helping his uncle to gather sheep on these fields. Times were hard; his father worked in the city for fifty years. In his younger days, Hanley's father worked in Crumlin, sticking cabbages, and walked to work from Collinstown every day. He also remembers his mother: if she was lucky she might get a lift in a horse and cart. Life was very hard in those days, but his family, in common with most of the other families in the district, grew their own vegetables, succulent cabbages and floury potatoes. "Times were tough, but if you had enough to eat, you were all right".

Collinstown in the late 1920s, with the buildings on the aerodrome starting to fall

Dunsoghly Castle at St Margaret's on the western edge of the airport. The present castle was built by a member of the Plunkett family in the 15th century.
Illustration: Philip Doherty

Kathleen Riordan: vivid memories of Collinstown before the development of the airport, when the area was totally rural.
Photograph: Neil MacDougald

into disrepair, had little to recommend itself to the children of the time. Kathleen Riordan, who was reared in the area, recollects that the main attraction for the children was picking blackberries, or maybe resting awhile from their play, on the old-fashioned hayricks that used to dot the fields in summer. The only bit of excitement came in the evenings; she and other children in the area often claimed to see ghosts in the area near the Boot Inn. There were long memories of the late 18th century robber, called Collier, who held up the Drogheda coach with great regularity. Recollections of him years later often used to frighten the children, especially after dark.

There was also the ghost of a headless captain, reckoned to be a relic of the military occupation of the district during the Great War; he was taken seriously enough by local people, so much so says Kathleen Riordan, that no-one would come over to their house, making the evenings very quiet. There was a real and palpable fear of meeting the ghostly rider moving silently up one of the little lanes that criss-crossed the district. But there used to be real people with real guns, hunting parties for, years ago, the Domville estate, better known as the Santry Demesne, had shooting rights over much of the land at Collinstown, extending as far as the forest that once stood at Forrest Little, at the back of the present airport.

Her family took over the rights to the thatched cottage near the quarry, from Christopher McGuinness, in 1931. The cottage had been built in 1800 and had few amenities, although Kathleen's father had the two-roomed cottage re-thatched, put in proper windows and also a range. She has a receipt from the solicitors who handled the transaction over the cottage; the rights to it cost her father £30. The solicitors were Grimes, in Cavendish Row, at Parnell Square; a curiosity about the receipt is the telephone numbers for the solicitors, who would have been one of the early users of telephones. Their numbers were Dublin 2053 and Ballsbridge 592.

Kathleen Riordan remembers well the early buses that used to do the run from Dublin to Swords and Skerries. Way back in the late 1920s, most of the vehicles used in the locality were horse-drawn; cars were a real novelty. Then came the buses; there was a great proliferation of private bus services. Kathleen remembers the bus service that started at Railway Street, near what was then Amiens Street station, and ran as far as Skerries. Then came the Blue Line, then the Red Line, before all the private bus services were taken over by CIE. But even in those very early days of bus transport, sixty years ago, Kathleen remembers double decker buses on the Swords route. The buses had the advantage of relative speed and frequency and were not too expensive — Dublin to Swords in the 1930s cost eight old pennies. The buses also gave the young people of Collinstown a chance to have a lift at least one way into Swords on a Saturday night to the parish ceili nights. After the dance was over, it was a question of walking home, at two o'clock in the morning, although sometimes there would be a lift from one of the dairymen. Even so, Kathleen was afraid to come up to her cottage in the middle of the night unless she was in a group of five or six people together: "we were afraid of the horse running round with a captain with no head".

One day, a real life visitor attracted the attention of Kathleen Riordan, her sister and a young playmate called George Kavanagh.

In the words of Kathleen Riordan: "the three of us were lying there and the sun was beaming on us". A tall man came by, arm in arm with his wife, a woman of much smaller height. In the hedgerows in the lane that led past the Riordan family cottage, there was an abundance of wild flowers and the tall man stooped to pick some of them. Kathleen continues: "George ran after him and said something to him, but when he came back, I said to him, 'do you know who that is?' 'No, I don't'. 'Well, I said, that's de Valera and his wife (Sinead)'". When the young boy heard who it was, he ran back to de Valera to apologise. The Taoiseach, elected to office in 1932, was a frequent visitor to what is now the airport area, and Kathleen Riordan remembers him coming out on many a Sunday afternoon, with the customary detectives walking behind him and his wife. The purpose may have been to have a quiet Sunday afternoon stroll in what was then real country, six miles from the city centre, but untouched by any modern development. Sixty years ago, the nearest building development to Collinstown was away on the Drumcondra Road in Dublin. But de Valera may have had another purpose in mind: interest in civil aviation was quickening and with that gathering interest came the inevitable need for a civil airport; de Valera may have been coming out to do his own reconnoitre of the Collinstown site.

Civil aviation had already started, but not at Collinstown. Hugh Cahill began Ireland's first aircraft operating company, Iona National Airways, in 1930. He used Kildonan airfield at Finglas.

The land at Collinstown was being used for grazing sheep and training horses, but there is evidence that in 1932, just ten years after the RAF abandoned the aerodrome as part of the British withdrawal from the southern part of Ireland, there was some flying activity here. Some sources even suggest that a commercial flight from Collinstown took off in June, 1929, with a cargo of newspapers for Galway. A Waterford-based company, called Irish Air Lines, had started up operations, using three aircraft, two Avro 504Ks and a Blackburn Bluebird. For a short time in 1932, the firm had a rental arrangement with the Government to use the old runways at Collinstown and in fact the company based one of its aircraft at the old aerodrome. However, its aeronautical ambitions were short-lived, a matter of months, and it then withdrew from Collinstown.

Nineteen thirty two, the year of the great Eucharistic Congress, which brought tens of thousands of visitors to Dublin, by sea, also saw some interesting aviation developments, but using the facilities of the Irish Air Corps base at Baldonnel. The Dutch airline KLM, founded in 1919 and one of the earliest national airlines in Europe, started a passenger and mail service from Dublin to Berlin, using a Fokker F.XII aircraft. Early in the morning of October 24, 1932, a Fox Moth, EI-AAP, took off

A NEW DUBLIN AIRPORT
100 Acres Acquired near Collinstown

By Our Air Correspondent

The Free State Government has been responsible for the acquisition of 100 acres of land at Cloghran, County Dublin, to form part of the new Dublin civil airport. The land was the property of Mr. Michael Monks.

The new site adjoins the disused military aerodrome at Collinstown, just off the main road from Dublin to Belfast, between Santry and Swords. It is within fifteen minutes' journey from the centre of the city.

A considerable amount of levelling and draining requires to be done before the airport will be ready for use, and this work will create employment for a large body of unskilled labour. The hangars, some of which have collapsed, will be reconstructed to house aircraft operating from the airport.

The Irish Times,
January 19th, 1937.

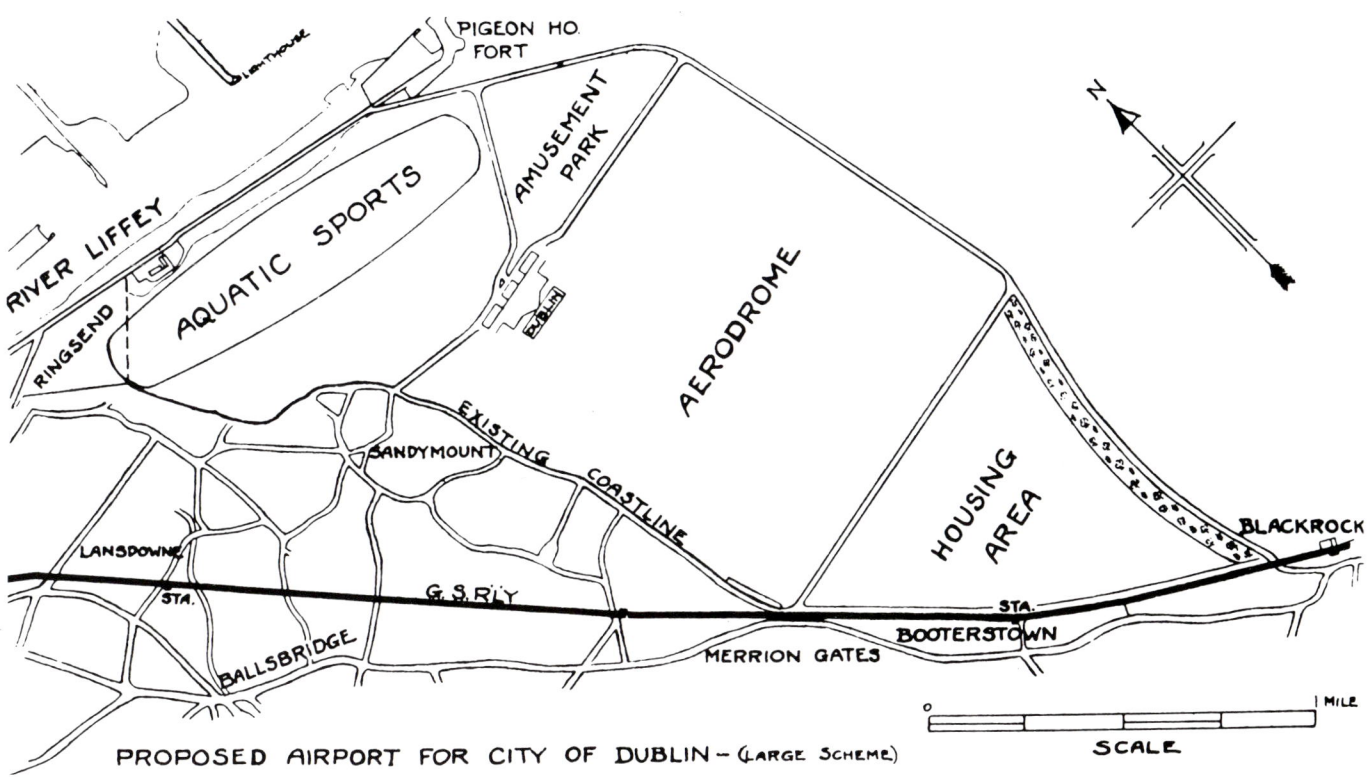

One of the proposed sites for Dublin airport: a plan for Sandymount strand drawn in 1935.
Studies *magazine*

PROPOSED AIRPORT FOR CITY OF DUBLIN – (LARGE SCHEME)

Derelict RAF hangars on the old Collinstown military aerodrome site. This photograph was taken in January, 1937, prior to their demolition for the new airport development.
Photograph: The Irish Times

from Galway and landed at Baldonnel at 7.30 am with a cargo of mail, which was transferred to the waiting Fokker. This latter aircraft departed shortly afterwards, with the mail bags and a passenger complement of thirteen. It was routed Croydon–Rotterdam–Berlin and the flight took eight hours; there were no further flights on the route.

This flight from Baldonnel to Berlin was the first out of Ireland by a foreign commercial carrier, a portent of times to come, fifty-eight years in the future, when some fifteen foreign carriers would be operating regular, scheduled services out of Dublin airport. The year after that KLM flight, Baldonnel, although still the Air Corps headquarters, was designated as the civil airport for Dublin. For the following three years, until the infant Aer Lingus started scheduled services, Baldonnel was used, for commercial flying purposes, by private and charter flights. In one famous incident, in July, 1933, the surgeon and writer turned senator, Oliver St John Gogarty, renowned for his cutting wit, brought his plane in to land at Baldonnel and ran into a flock of sheep on the runway. He remarked on the country's principal aerodrome being let as a sheep ranch.

Events were moving fast, if jaggedly. In Cork, Richard O'Connor, the county surveyor, presented a scheme in 1933 for creating an international airport at Belvelly, on the northern side of Great Island in Cork Harbour. His plan called for the development of an airport that could service both land- and sea-based aircraft. One of O'Connor's two partners in the Cork scheme was Colonel Delamer, later to become manager of Dublin airport, but his involvement in the Belvelly project was short-lived. The Department of Defence refused him permission to serve on the board of a private company. In Dublin, a much more viable airline scheme was put forward by Colonel Charles Russell, another pioneering aviator.

He wanted to set up a company called Irish Air Transport. In 1934, Seán Ó hUadhaigh, a Dublin solicitor and personal friend of the Taoiseach, Eamon de Valera, brought together the two groups, Colonel Russell's and Richard O'Connor's, to merge their interests in the formation of a national airline. O'Connor never saw his Cork airport project take off, but to him goes the credit for devising the name of the national airline, Aer Lingus. There had been a proposal to run cross-channel air services in conjunction with Sir Alan Cobham's London-based company, but these fell through. Cobham was well-known in Ireland, from 1933 onwards, for his flying circus. In the first of his 1933 tours, he was based at the small Kildonan airfield in Finglas, run by Hugh Cahill. The show attracted huge numbers of people to the airfield, about 14,000, and anticipated by over fifty years the air spectaculars that have been sponsored by Aer Rianta in recent years. The Kildonan show was opened by Alfie

MR. H. CAHILL, PROPRIETOR IONA NATIONAL AIRWAYS, WITH SIR ALAN COBHAM (LEFT) AT KILDONAN.

The first commercial aircraft registered in Ireland, August, 1930. The plane was operated by Iona Airways air taxi service and flying school.

When Cobham's flying circus came to Dublin in 1933, Sir Alan Cobham (left) was pictured with Hugh Cahill, a north Dublin garage owner who founded Iona National Airways.

The Iona Airways' fleet at Kildonan aerodrome, early 1930s, with (inset) a coterie of flying club enthusiasts.

In July, 1933, Cobham's flying circus arrived at Kildonan airfield, Finglas, at the start of an Irish tour that went to Waterford, Clonmel, Cork, Limerick, Galway's Oranmore aerodrome, Bundoran, Derry, Belfast and Dundalk. In this photograph, aircraft from the flying circus are seen over Dublin, with the Liffey estuary and Ringsend below.

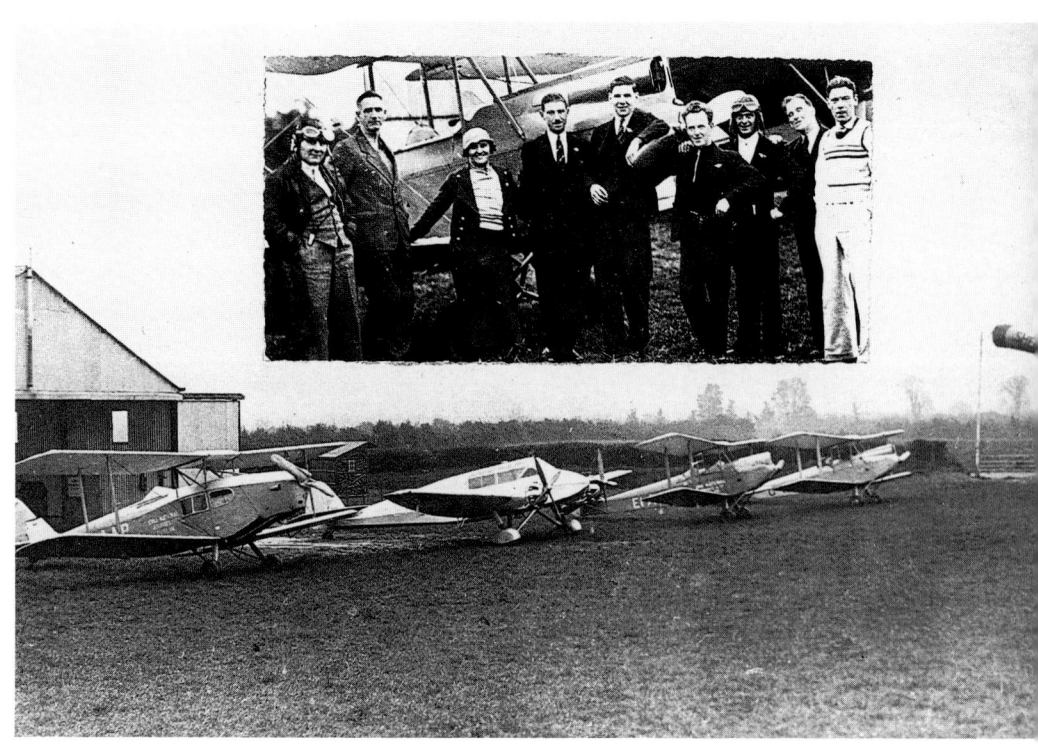

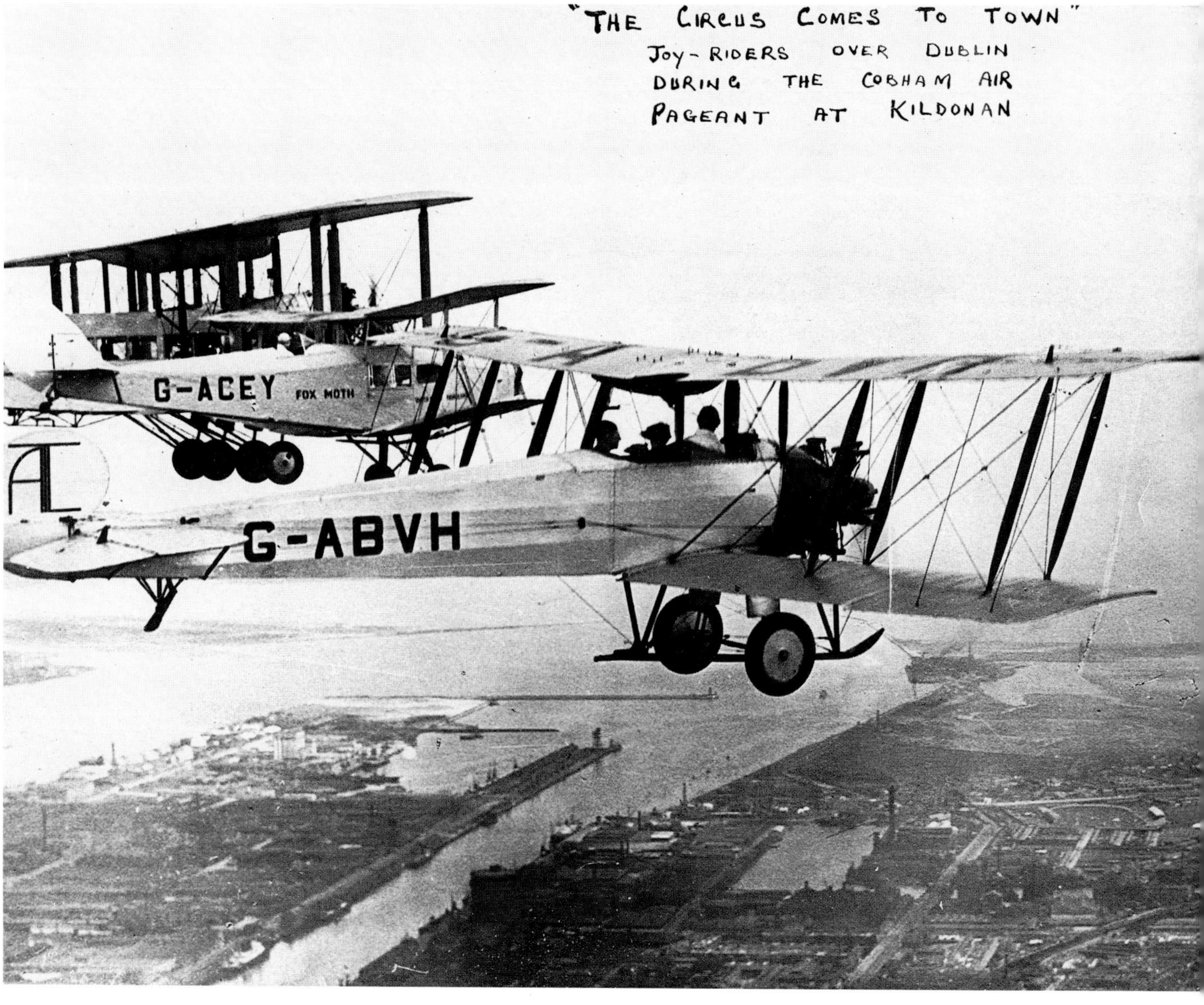
"THE CIRCUS COMES TO TOWN"
JOY-RIDERS OVER DUBLIN
DURING THE COBHAM AIR
PAGEANT AT KILDONAN
G-ACEY
FOX MOTH
G-ABVH

Byrne, who was Lord Mayor of Dublin for practically the entire decade of the 1930s. Byrne was a keen and far-sighted advocate of civil aviation and one of the first proponents of a properly established civil airport for Dublin. In pressing the advocacy of his cause, he welcomed Cobham's flying circus as a means of giving as many people as possible the chance to see these marvellous flying machines in action. On the Saturday, the day before the show, ten circus planes flew in formation over Dublin to publicise the event. The promotion had a dramatic effect: the city was mesmerised, as all eyes turned skywards.

Such was the popular enthusiasm for flying that the Dublin *Evening Mail* even ran a cartoon series called Pat and Pete the "aero twins". They undertook all sorts of fantastic flying adventures, like going to Everest and back for tea, pure fantasy then, nearly fact now. With the passing of the Air Navigation and Transport Bill of 1936, the setting up of Aer Lingus came ever closer; the airline was to be set up with a nominal share capital of £100,000 and it was to operate services between Ireland and Britain in conjunction with Blackpool and West Coast Air Services. Events were finally moving at a fast pace.

While Aer Lingus was being set up, the airfield at Baldonnel was being made ready for civil flights. Ireland was alone among the countries of Europe in allowing its military aerodromes to be used without restrictions by civil aircraft. In March, 1936, Captain Ned Stapleton of the Air Corps, and his assistant, Captain Michael

Construction work under way at the southwest end of the main runway, 1937

Above: seventeen horses were used on the construction of the runways at the new Dublin civil airport, which began in 1937. Among their duties was towing wagonloads of earth from the foundations, as seen in this photograph.
Robert Allen Photography

Sods of turf are laid for the first runways at Collinstown, 1937.
Robert Allen Photography

An elaborate network of tracks was set up on the airfield in 1937, for the horse drawn wagons, which were used to remove soil from the runway foundations.
Photograph: Irish Press

Cumiskey, described how they had taken part in a course in Britain on civil air traffic control, an art new to Ireland. Charlie McConnell, the founder of McConnell's advertising agency, who had a very keen interest in aviation and was a close friend of Colonel Russell, had his agency prepare some extravagant copy for the launch of Aer Lingus: "Eire has always had her place among the nations in Art, Drama and Literature — now she is in the Air.

"Her scattered sons look homewards, proudly conscious of the Motherland's achievements in many spheres — not least her position in international transportation. Now are the 'Wild Geese' linked more closely with Eire, not only in spirit, but in fact". The Aer Lingus terminal at Baldonnel, telephone Clondalkin 39, consisted of a wireless hut with a passengers' hut, which also had rooms for crew members. A bus service was organised from Aston Quay by the Dublin United Tramway Company. Air services began in May, 1936, using a five-seater De Havilland Dragon to Bristol. The first ticket ever issued by the airline was held by the wife of Seán Ó hUadhaigh and the only freight on that first flight was a parcel of *The Irish Times*, bound for London. But even at this embryonic stage in the development of the national airline, there was a clear perception that Baldonnel was unsuitable for long-term development as Dublin's civil airport.

In June, 1935, nearly a year before Aer Lingus started flying from Baldonnel, Alfie Byrne asked Sean Lemass, then Minister for Industry and Commerce, to consider the construction of an airport for Dublin as an urgently needed relief scheme; Ireland was in the grip of the Economic War with Britain and there was widespread unemployment. Byrne suggested the Collinstown site. Somewhat ironically, Lemass,

Workmen with wheelbarrows and shovels helping to lay the main runway, 1937.
Photograph: Robert Allen Photography

The bicycle brigade: workers going home from the first runway construction at Collinstown, 1937.

who later became a staunch advocate of aviation and airport development, did not seem to be consumed by the urgency of the situation and told Alfie Byrne that the provision of an aerodrome was a matter for Dublin Corporation.

A number of sites came up for discussion; the most fanciful was one proposed by Desmond McAteer, who prepared an elaborate article, with accompanying plans, which were published in *Studies* magazine in 1935. McAteer proposed reclaiming much of the land at Sandymount Strand in order to create an aerodrome with hard runways. The site he outlined would have been over a mile square, with provision for both housing and recreation. He further proposed that construction work would be phased over five years, because of the huge cost involved; he reckoned the project would cost £1½ million, an enormous sum of money before World War II. One advantage of the plan was that the new airport would have easy access to the Great Southern Railway line at Booterstown. The main disadvantage of the scheme, as perceived at the time, was that the whole strand, from Blackrock to Ringsend, would be built over, even though McAteer planned such delights as an amusement park and an aquatic sports area. The site would have been feasible for the type of aircraft in use in the mid-1930s, but highly unsuitable for modern jet aircraft. Another rather far-fetched possibility was the Phoenix Park, which would have had the advantage of easy access to the city centre. However, although the park had been used for air displays in the early 1930s, and for military aviation purposes in the Great War, it was not a serious contender in the battle to site the new Dublin airport. But the rumours were so strong that in late 1936, James Dillon, that master of parliamentary oratory, was prompted to take action.

By means of a Dail question, he asked the Government for an assurance that the Phoenix Park would not be used as the site for the proposed new municipal airport. He was told that such a move would be "most unlikely". Officially, remembers R. W. O'Sullivan, who was closely involved in the preparatory work for Collinstown, the

Wheelbarrows and shovels were primary equipment in the construction of the airport.
Robert Allen Photography

Excavations at Dublin airport, 1937.
Robert Allen Photography

Phoenix Park was disregarded because of its vulnerability to river fogs, as well as its proximity to built-up areas in the west of the city.

It was decided by all relevant interests, Government technical services, the Air Corps and the new Aer Lingus, that Baldonnel would become an exclusively military aerodrome. There was an alternative possibility with another former RAF base, the disused military aerodrome at Cookstown, Tallaght, but R. W. O'Sullivan says that this site was ruled out on two grounds. First of all, the airfield was too close to the Dublin mountains, which created much turbulence in the vicinity of the airfield, and secondly, because it was so close to Baldonnel, there would have been serious air traffic control problems separating flight paths by military and civilian aircraft. One other civilian site came up for consideration, Kildonan at Finglas. In the mid-1930s, Finglas was a small rural village, with one main street and a cluster of houses, two miles from the nearest built-up part of Dublin, the suburb of Glasnevin, which was even then in the process of extension. About a mile north of Finglas village, just off the main road to Ashbourne, was the Kildonan airfield.

The airfield, which was run by Hugh Cahill, was on land owned by a family called Fitzpatrick. There was a hangar, a clubhouse, a windsock and a petrol pump, yet despite the extent of its use for private flying in the early 1930s, the Kildonan site was never seriously considered as suitable for the development of a large civilian airport. That left just one site in the choice being made by Major Gerry Carroll of Air Corps and R. W. O'Sullivan, then assistant aeronautical engineer with the Air Corps. They were instructed to make a recommendation to the Minister, Sean Lemass, which they did, in favour of the development of Collinstown. Situated 200 feet above sea level, with clear approaches from every direction, unhindered by mountains, and not prone to foggy conditions, it turned out in retrospect to have been the best possible choice for an airport in the Dublin region.

The official Government announcement about Collinstown was made on December 9, 1936, just eight months after the start of the Aer Lingus scheduled services from Baldonnel. It was planned to develop a total of 717 acres, of which some 258 were already owned by the Office of Public Works. The cost of the work was estimated at £150,000, including £30,000 for land acquisition from over six farms, to be divided between the Government, Dublin Corporation and Dublin County Council; the State paid half and Dublin Corporation £58,000. Costs soon soared; shortly afterwards, the total estimate went up to £162,000. By June, 1937 it was up to

£360,000. Apart from the terminal, works were to include a workshop hangar with a 250 feet span and 150 feet deep, the largest in western Europe.

At least one daily newspaper, the *Irish Independent,* published a daily column showing arrivals and departures of prominent people by air and sea. True, the volume of people arriving by sea was much greater; long lists were recorded for the Royal Mail steamers arriving at Rosslare Harbour and for other cross-channel ships arriving at the North Wall, Dublin, and Dun Laoghaire, renamed in 1930 from Kingstown. A typical entry, for October 30, 1936, shows that the principal arrival at Baldonnel airport was Mr Kingsley Martin, the English socialist writer. At this stage of aviation, travel was usually confined to the rich upper classes and the aristocracy;

This photograph, taken near Corballis House in 1939, shows thirty-eight men in a work gang on the construction of the initial stages of Dublin airport. Only a handful are still alive, Peter Gannon, who lives in Swords and who worked in Savage's supermarket in Swords in recent years; Jim Markey, who lives in the St Margaret's area; Tommy Markey, who lives in Swords; the third Markey brother, Mick; and Kit Nulty, who lives in Baskin cottages, Swords. Out of the gang, only seven men were wearing ties and thirty-three were wearing headgear.

Front row, left to right: unidentified, J. O'Rourke, John Monaghan, Billy Rickards, Jim Dennis, Henry Savage, Jack Crosby, Josie Maguire.

Second row, left to right: Tom Hand, Ned Butler, Nick Valentine, Jack Brown, Kit Nulty, Tom McGuirk, Mick Markey, Tommy Markey, Jack Manning, J. Kavanagh, Mick Savage.

Third row, left to right: Jack Brown, — Dardis, Johnny O'Rourke, Jim Galvin, unidentified, Mick Hughes, Kit Nulty, Billy Keogh, Jack Hanley, "Stacks" Henry.

Back row, left to right: Bill Ryan, Joey Ryan, Micky Ferris, Peter Gannon, Jes McKettrick, Jim Markey, Mick Donnelly, Peter Tierney, Bill Nagle and Mick Cronin.

Billy Ryan worked later as the airport's vermin exterminator, while Jim Galvin was the first security man at the airport.

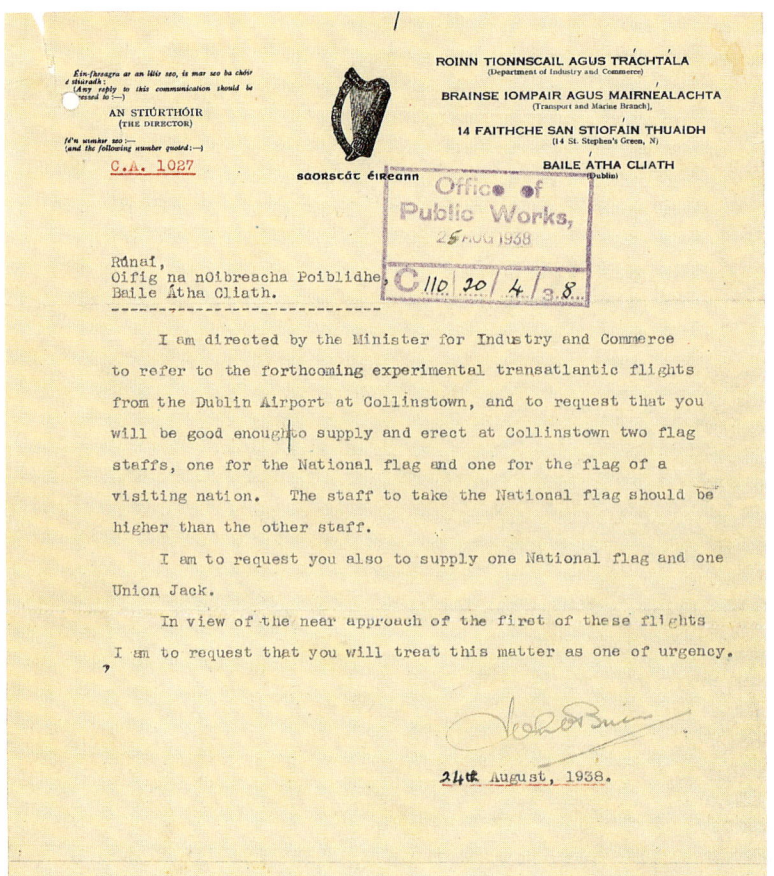

Strict instructions from the Department of Industry and Commerce.

that same passenger detail shows that among those departing Baldonnel that day was the Marquess of Sligo. Two years later, the new general manager of Aer Lingus, Robert Logan, who took over from Major Carroll, the man who had worked on the airport survey site, had some pointed remarks to make about the unsuitability of Baldonnel for civil use. He said that the terminal building was inadequate, conditions at departures were chaotic and there were fire hazards. Just to add to the general air of gloom, Logan noted that passengers on the airport bus from Aston Quay were obliged "to ride in company with labourers in a cloud of smoke".

Within four months of the Government announcement being made about the Collinstown site, work started on its preparation. In early 1937, the Government acquired one hundred acres of land from Michael Monks; it was adjacent to the site it already owned. Other acquisitions included the grounds of St Margaret's coursing club. The famous ball alley at the Boot Inn was bought and demolished. A degree of urgency had been injected into the proceedings because of an inter-governmental agreement between the Irish Free State, Canada, the United Kingdom and the United States of America for the provision of facilities for trans-Atlantic air services. There was much discussion at the time about the relative merits of land and sea planes; in 1936, Rineanna, on the County Clare side of the Shannon estuary, had been designated as the land airport, while Foynes, on the opposite side of the estuary, in County Limerick, was designated as the seaplane base. The two operating companies on the trans-Atlantic service, Imperial Airways and Pan American Airways, both said that experimental flights across the Atlantic by land-based aircraft were likely to come into operational use far sooner than had been expected. Shannon was still being prepared, so it was decided to provide alternative, temporary facilities for trans-Atlantic flights at Collinstown. The inter-departmental airports construction committee believed that a suitable area could be provided at Collinstown by August, 1937. It would be suitable for use by the De Havilland Albatross aircraft which were

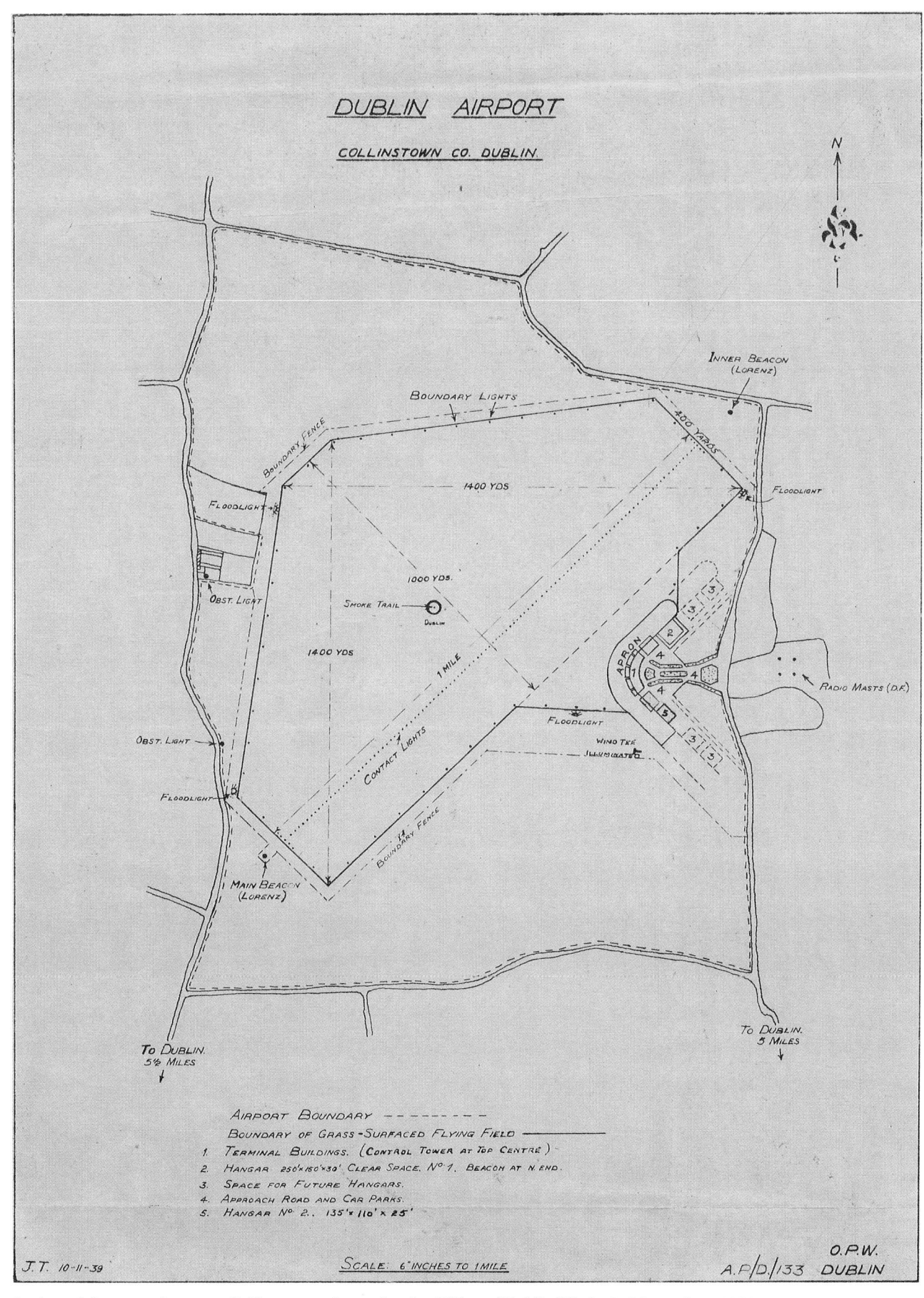

A plan of the new airport at Collinstown, drawn by the Office of Public Works in November, 1939.
Illustration: Office of Public Works

Desmond FitzGerald, architect of the first terminal building at Dublin airport. His father, also Desmond, was the first Minister for External Affairs and following the assassination of Kevin O'Higgins in 1927, was appointed Minister for Defence. After the 1932 general election, he remained a T.D. until 1937. When Desmond FitzGerald was designing the airport terminal, his younger brother, Garret, later a Taoiseach, gave him plenty of youthful advice.
Photograph: Lafayette

intended to be used for land plane services to Newfoundland.

The site at Collinstown lent itself to ready expansion, remembers R. W. O'Sullivan. By April 1, work was well in hand preparing the main runway, one mile long.

A great deal of grading, levelling and resurfacing work was done on the site and miles of drains were laid, despite the bad weather in early 1937. A system of powerful floodlights was installed by Chance Brothers, the lighthouse specialists, and arrangements were made for putting in a Lorenz ultra shortwave landing aid and an up-to-date Adcock medium wave direction finding installation. While the first work was on the preparation of the site, giving much-needed relief work to unskilled labourers, the preparation of other facilities only came later. However, just after the work had started, there was a forceful complaint from Matthew Caul, secretary of the Swords branch of the Irish Labour Party, that a big number of married men were being laid off from the site. At its height, just over 1,000 men were employed by the Board of Works on the airport construction, although by July, 1937 there were just 215 men on site.

On April 1, 1937, work began on clearing hedges and fences; equipment in use included a steam navvy and a dragline. All went well until the unskilled men went on strike on April 29. They complained, with great vehemence, that the rate being paid for the levelling and drainage construction work both at Collinstown and at Rineanna was well below trade union rates. The unskilled workers were earning twenty-nine shillings a week. However, the strike did not deter planning work for the new airport and tenders were invited for the demolition of the disused RAF hangars and adjacent buildings.

The month the strike started, April, 1937, also happened to be the month that Aer Rianta was established. It was set up as the national company with the responsibility of investing shares in the joint operating company responsible for running the trans-Atlantic service. Aer Rianta was also charged with aviation development generally. It was stated to be in control of Aer Lingus. The first directors of Aer Rianta were Col Charles F. Russell, Seán Ó hUadhaigh, W. H. Morton, J. J. O'Leary and J. Flynn, assistant secretary, Department of Industry and Commerce.

The strike of the unskilled labourers lasted until early June, when it collapsed. During the course of the dispute, there were many bitter allegations and, at one stage, Dublin County Council was urged to withhold its funding for the airport until the contractors on site ceased what was described as their "unChristian behaviour" in under-cutting trade union rates. Yet the wages were just over £2 a week. Local

The main hall and booking office of Le Bourget airport, Paris, which was opened on November 12, 1937, with a design not dissimilar to that of the FitzGerald designed terminal at Collinstown.
Photograph: The Times, London

farmers were paying a mere £1 10s a week. When the strike collapsed, the men gained nothing from the withholding of their labour over a six week period; work resumed on the runways. By July, plans were in progress for the building of a hangar, measuring 200 feet by 150 feet. Also by July, work on the runways was going so much to schedule that it was confidently forecast that the main runway would be ready for use by October 1. Temporary accommodation had been secured for the meteorological staff, pending the completion of permanent buildings. The house of Sean Kavanagh, the former caretaker on the airport site and now a labourer there, burned down. An amazingly complicated bureaucratic wrangle went on for three months before the man was finally housed in a new cottage at the Baskin. The fact that he was a member of Casement's brigade in the War of Independence was used to promote his case.

There were two unauthorised landings. On November 14, 1937, a plane belonging to a Mr Rogers of the Curragh and piloted by Denis Greene from Foxrock, a member of the Irish Aero Club, tried out the airfield, while an unidentified landing by a light plane was made on October 22, 1938.

When Alfie Byrne was Lord Mayor of Dublin for most of the 1930s, he was one of the earliest advocates of an airport for Dublin.
Photograph: The Irish Times

By the beginning of September, 1937, site clearance on the main runway area was ninety per cent completed, while most of the demolition work had also been finished. Demolition of the small cluster of houses to the north-east of the main runway was being put in hand. In October, as predicted, the work on the main runway was finished, but the arrangement for the installation of the blind landing equipment was suspended because of delays in the delivery to Imperial Airways of the Albatross aircraft, caused by major design modifications. On October 6, two Air Corps planes landed on the new runway.

However, by November, 1937, the medium wave direction finding equipment was put into place. At the end of that year, which had seen employment on the site reach its peak of over 1,000 men, work on the secondary runways was well progressed and work was going ahead on the construction of approaches to the building sites, where the terminal building was to be built. At the start of the new year, plans for the terminal building were completed and tenders invited.

The architect of the terminal building was Desmond FitzGerald, an elder brother of Dr Garret FitzGerald. Desmond was an architect on the staff of the Department of Industry and Commerce and there were some complaints at the time, from the architectural profession, that the design was not put out to competition. In the event, Desmond FitzGerald designed a graceful, curving building that echoed the lines of the bridge of a great ocean-going liner. He had great difficulty at the outset trying to persuade the Department to be more ambitious in its thinking: Dr Garret FitzGerald says that his recollection is that his brother had great difficulty in persuading the Department to build more than a couple of rooms. In 1936, the year before Desmond started design work on the new terminal building, the traffic records showed that total Aer Lingus passengers were only in the hundreds and for the authorities there was little expectation that there would ever be sufficient traffic to warrant such an ambitious terminal.

In fact, the building was designed in such a way that its system of open buttresses formed the framework for a further level of offices. The terminal building was designed to be flexible in use; later, during the Emergency, when he was working for the Office of Public Works, FitzGerald designed the hotel at Foynes in County Limerick for the crews and passengers of the flying boats. But as far as Dublin airport was concerned, Desmond FitzGerald eventually had his plans accepted, although another piece of forward planning had to wait years to be implemented. In the original design, he allowed for the provision of covered walkways from the terminal building to aircraft, at four points, but this design feature was not put into practice for a further twenty years.

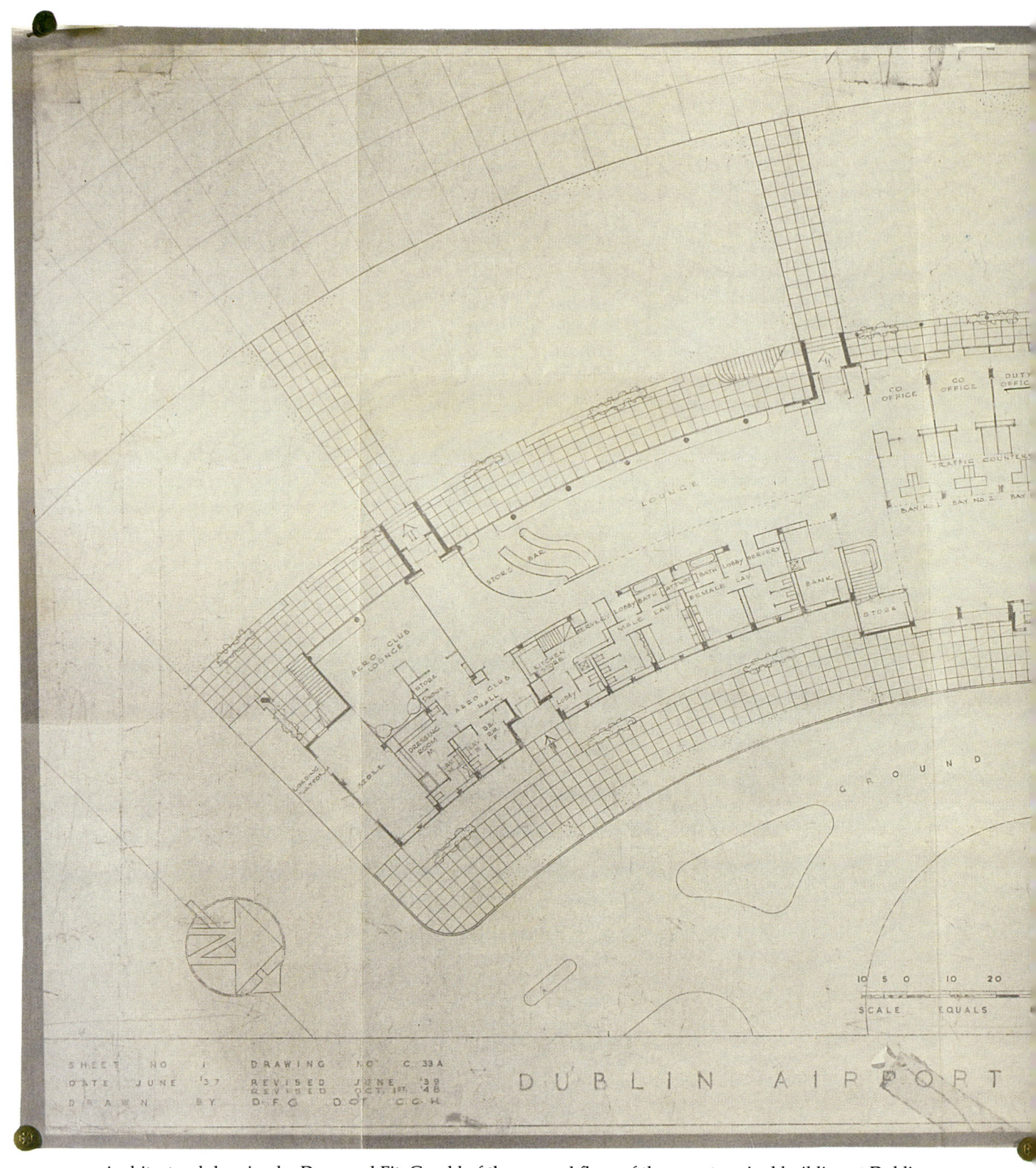

Architectural drawing by Desmond FitzGerald of the ground floor of the new terminal building at Dublin airport.
Illustration: Office of Public Works

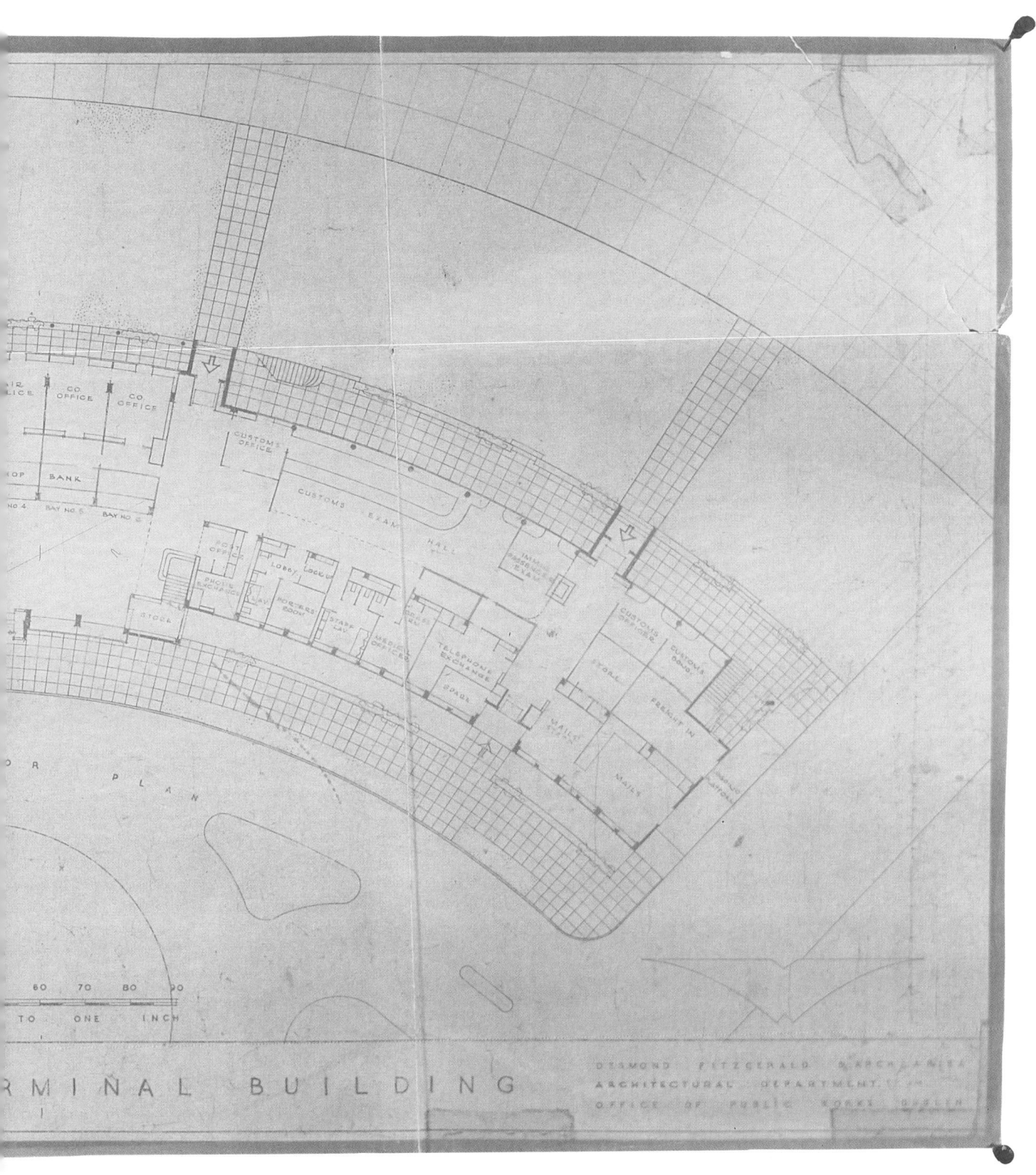

The terminal building at Collinstown, under construction, 1939.
Robert Allen Photography

In 1940, there was considerable official discussion about the use of Irish at the new Dublin airport. This drawing of the proposed airport identification sign was prepared by the Office of Public Works; the letters were to be made in concrete, so as to be visible to incoming pilots. The final version, which read simply "Áth Cliath", had to be approved by Eamon de Valera, the Taoiseach, before its construction that year.

Tenders for the building of the terminal had to be in by March 9, 1938. The method of heating for the terminal building was under much consideration. By June, it was hoped to place the contracts for the erection of the terminal building and the hangar very shortly and work was under way on bringing the electricity supply to the airport. Also in March, a house at the south-west end of the runway was demolished, even though it had been built only a year previously. The following month, July, the main runway was ready for experimental use and was tested by the Air Corps. In August, the contract for the terminal building was placed and work began almost immediately on excavating the foundations. In February, there had been a dispute over holiday pay for the men looking after the seventeen horses being used on the site. Eventually, the workmen were given six days' annual paid leave. In November, 1938, it was recorded that work on the new terminal building was very slow, due to another strike, this time by six carpenters. This dispute lasted from the first to the twenty-eighth of the month.

After the resumption of work, the contractors had nearly three weeks of satisfactory progress, until the severe frost of December 17, 1938, when a halt was called to all concreting work. By the time 1939 had arrived, there were regular site reports that work on the new terminal building was "proceeding". August, 1939 saw the virtual completion of all field work and the new airport runways were declared fit for use by aircraft. Despite the great progress in the building of the airport, the hesitancy over the introduction of trans-Atlantic services from Collinstown continued.

The military, from 5th battalion, Eastern Command, arrived at the airport on September 1, first occupying the offices of Murphy's, the main contractors for the terminal. September, 1939 was a momentous month in more ways than one. At international level, it saw the declaration of war by Britain on Germany, following the German invasion of Poland. Neville Chamberlain's speech on the Sunday morning, September 3, 1939, sounded eerily on the wireless. Many people throughout Ireland were filled with foreboding by that declaration of war, even though it was clear at that stage, that de Valera was determined to keep the southern part of the country out of the war, which also meant an end to all the grandiose civil aviation schemes that were being proposed in the late 1930s. But up at Collinstown, despite the general gloom at the announcement of war in Europe, work continued unabated

Drawing by Frank Delaney of aircraft types at Dublin airport, 1940. Delaney was the flight engineer on the first Aer Lingus flight to leave the new Dublin airport, January 19, 1940.

on the new airport. With the terminal building, structural work was almost completed; plastering and finishing were delayed because of the late arrival of heating equipment and window frames.

But work on the two hangars was nearly completed and the temporary apron for aircraft parking was virtually finished. On September 13, the meteorological office opened at the airport with a small staff, providing daily synoptic observations. Progress reports on the airport were suspended because of the war and were not resumed until January, 1940. The weather was appalling; heavy frosts were followed by a spell of wet weather. Yet everything was made ready and the emergency equipment, including one ambulance, was handed over to the Department of Industry and Commerce.

The management of the new airport was entrusted to Aer Rianta; the time for the transfer of Aer Lingus flights from Baldonnel to Collinstown was drawing near. Thanks to fog, Aer Lingus anticipated the event. On Wednesday afternoon, December 8, 1939, an Aer Lingus aircraft returning from Liverpool was unable to land at Baldonnel because of the fog. Instead, it made a safe and uneventful landing at the new Collinstown airport. Next day *The Irish Times* described the event in these words: "this was, therefore, the first time an airliner carrying passengers used the new airport. In the very near future, Irish Civil Aviation will have its new headquarters at Collinstown. The airport is noted for being remarkably free of fog".

Work on the aerodrome and buildings was described as continuing slowly because of difficulties in obtaining essential supplies caused by war-time shortages and strikes. The most damaging strike was in the cement factories in Ireland.

When the time came for the transfer of Aer Lingus services to Collinstown, the terminal building was still unfinished. The buildings were ready for completion in the early part of that year; within a few months of the terminal building being made ready, Desmond FitzGerald won the triennial gold medal of the Royal Institute of the Architects of Ireland.

But the very first Aer Lingus flight from the new airport at Collinstown took off at an early hour, 9 am, on Thursday, January 19, 1940. The new airport was born, but because of the war-time conditions, the official ceremonies were low key and Collinstown's new civil airport was inaugurated in bitterly cold weather, with only a handful of officials from the Department of Industry and Commerce and the airline to see the Lockheed 14 aircraft take off for the hour-long flight to Liverpool. Dublin airport immediately settled in for six years of quiet, almost non-existence, as World War II raged around Europe, close enough to Ireland for the aircraft searchlights at Holyhead in north Wales to be seen by people out for a night-time walk on the east pier at Dun Laoghaire.

NEW DUBLIN AIRPORT
FIRST PASSENGER LANDING

As a result of fog, which at times enveloped the Dublin area on Wednesday afternoon, the second Aer Lingus airliner returning from Liverpool found conditions at Baldonnel rather difficult for landing, and advantage was taken of the somewhat better conditions prevailing at the new Dublin airport at Collinstown, where a successful landing was subsequently effected.

This was, therefore, the first time an airliner carrying passengers used the new airport. In the very near future Irish Civil Aviation will have its new headquarters at Collinstown. The airport is noted for being remarkably free from fog.

The Irish Times,
December 8th, 1939

The Irish Times, January 19, 1940, the day that the new Dublin airport at Collinstown was officially opened for commercial traffic.

CHAPTER II

Sheep graze in the Emergency

AFTER the first commercial flight took off from the brand new airport at Collinstown on January 19, 1940, the airport promptly went into a trance-like hibernation for the duration of the Emergency. Not until 1944 were the first steps taken to develop the airport further, when it became clear that World War II was coming to an end. But in January, 1940, the aviation world was increasingly restricted by the war and because Aer Lingus had nowhere to fly apart from Liverpool, the new airport was put into mothballs.

The Irish Free State declared itself neutral in late 1939; one of the first steps taken by the Government of Eamon de Valera to put the country on a "war" footing was to ban all private flying. Each aircraft was disabled by the official removal of a vital part and all private airfields and landing strips that were not occupied by the defence forces were staked with railway sleepers to ensure that aircraft could not use them. From early 1940, the war soon tightened its grip; by June of that year, Paris had fallen to the Germans and the newspapers were full of the hasty flight from the city by hundreds of thousands of people, who fled to the west of France as best they could. Cars loaded with luggage, pony traps even, all joined the vast and slow-moving cavalcade out of Paris. Nineteen forty was one of the darkest years of the war; in the Battle of Britain, fought over the skies of south-eastern England that year, the Luftwaffe came close to winning a decisive victory over the RAF, in the biggest aerial battle ever fought. There was animated discussion at the airport that summer over the use of Irish. The new airport identification sign, Áth Cliath, made in concrete letters, had to be approved by Eamon de Valera, the Taoiseach, before work could start.

This Emergency concrete bunker was built to the west of Castlemoate House, while another is located on the Forrest Little Golf Club. At Cloghran graveyard, a gun emplacement overlooks Swords.
Illustration: Philip Doherty

Above: Aer Lingus Lockheed 14 aircraft at Dublin airport on the morning the airport was officially opened to commercial traffic, January, 19, 1940.

Pictured beside a Lockheed 14 at Dublin airport in 1940, from left: Gerry J. Carroll, general manager, Seán Ó hUadhaigh, chairman and Gerry Dempsey, accountant, all Aer Lingus.

Dublin airport drawing office, 1943.

The Aer Lingus plans for a grandiose extension of its routes looked impressive while the world war was still in its "phoney" stage, but by the time the first flight of the airline left Collinstown, these plans were utterly unrealistic. A joint meeting of the Aer Lingus and Aer Rianta boards had taken place at the end of November, 1938, which laid ground rules for these expansion plans, designed for a five-year period. The first year of the plan, which extended to April, 1940, called for the extension of the Dublin-London route to Paris or Amsterdam. In the event, the Paris route was not opened by Aer Lingus until June 17, 1946, while the Dublin to Amsterdam route, via Manchester, did not open until July, 1947. Year Two of the grand scheme, 1940/41, envisaged a Cork to Paris route operated in pool with Air France. In the outturn, Cork airport did not open for a further twenty years. Year Three, 1941/42, was marked down for direct services between Dublin and either Paris or Amsterdam. Even when the grand plan was being drawn up, world events were sufficiently menacing for Aer Lingus and Aer Rianta to inject a note of cautious realism into their thinking: "it is difficult to see developments as far ahead as years four and five, when there are so many incalculable variants".

Just after Aer Lingus moved into the new airport at Collinstown, so too did the army; for the second time in its history, the airfield at Collinstown was under military occupation, although the one that began in 1940 and lasted until 1945 had one crucial difference compared to the earlier military occupation that began in 1917. Then, the site was occupied by the Royal Flying Corps and from 1918 onwards, the RAF. The military occupation that ran for the period of the Emergency, as the years of World War II were known euphemistically in Ireland, was by the Irish army. It stationed a garrison at Collinstown for the duration of the war, because for most of the war period Ireland faced a very strong invasion threat from both the main belligerents in the conflict.

The Irish army immediately set about building pillboxes around the perimeter of the airfield (some were there until recent years) and also installed anti-aircraft guns. The twelve pounder guns were considered effective against all enemy aircraft, but in the event, they were never used during the Emergency to bring down a hostile aircraft, although there was at least one close call with an intruding American bomber in 1943. However, despite the stringent precautions, designed to put off any outside invasion force from thinking of using Collinstown as the entry point to a neutral Irish Free State, the army managed to bring its usual style to the occupation.

Turf being loaded onto a Grand Canal barge. Behind the barge is the bridge carrying the Harcourt Street railway line towards Bray.
Photograph: G. A. Duncan

Collecting turf in the Dublin mountains.
Photograph: G. A. Duncan

Another load of turf in the Dublin mountains.
Photograph: G. A. Duncan

The officers' mess, located in one of the temporary huts on the site, was warm and comfortable, a refuge of bonhomie with the odd tincture of whiskey. Otherwise, the main difference the war made to the new airport was on the perimeter. Rationing did not start in earnest until 1941. Severe restrictions were placed on the consumption of most items of food; tea was rationed to half an ounce per person per week and sugar was down to half a pound per person per week. There were many restrictions on the use of gas and electricity and the "glimmerman", who toured houses looking for people using the remnants of the gas supply when they were not supposed to, became a familiar symbol of the Emergency. Everyone used bicycles to get about and by 1944, when the trams had to be taken off the streets of Dublin altogether, fleets of bicycles could be seen at rush hour, rather as they are in present-day China. Even the army, which had nearly 20,000 men during the Emergency, had its cycling squadrons, known in informal parlance as the "piddling panzers".

But by 1942, the squeeze on imports became so severe that bread rationing was introduced. Flour from Canada and other countries could no longer be imported and the resultant bread made in Ireland was a dark unpalatable-looking colour. The year before bread was officially rationed, postmarks on letters had borne the slogan "grow more wheat", aimed at farmers, and "eat less bread", aimed at families. The Collinstown airport came to play its part in the native wheat-growing campaign.

All the land on the edges of the runways was sown with wheat, some 257 acres in all, which made Collinstown one of the largest wheat farms in the country. Grazing for about 500 sheep was also provided. When an aircraft was coming in to land, a red flag was run up a flagpole in the middle of the airfield to let the shepherd know to bring in his flock of sheep. There were other amusing instances, too, brought about by the war-time rationing. John Leydon, who was chairman of Aer Lingus and Aer Rianta from December 1941 until March 1949, was secretary of the new Department of Supplies, set up shortly after the start of the Emergency. Dr J. F. Dempsey, who was general manager of Aer Lingus and Aer Rianta for thirty years, from 1937 until 1967, remembers how Leydon once asked him how the hay was being mown at the airport. Dr Dempsey explained that petrol-driven machines were being used. "Ordinary people are going to jail for doing exactly the same thing", thundered Leydon. A solution was quickly found: horses were brought in and added to the war-time list of sundries and the hay-making at the airport was carried out for the rest of the period of the Emergency by horse-drawn machines.

Despite the privations of war, Aer Lingus maintained its one daily flight to Liverpool as best it could. The airline used its two Lockheed aircraft until April, 1940, when they were sold to Guinea Airways.

That same month, people like Dr Dempsey and Frank Delaney, the flight engineer on the first Aer Lingus flight out of Collinstown on January 19, 1940, were involved in hair-raising adventures in Belgium. The first DC3 for Aer Lingus arrived in Belgium from the US, but in part form. The parts had to be assembled by Fokkers into a whole aircraft, which was then flown to Dublin by way of Britain; the flight back with the party was quite a close call, because the German army was advancing into the Netherlands and was not more than fifty miles away from the new Aer Lingus plane. The new aircraft was brought into service on the Liverpool route on May 7, 1940, but in June it was replaced by a DH86 because of the fall-off in traffic. The DC3 did not return to the route until early 1941. P. P. O'Reilly, for forty years a broadcaster with RTE, who retired in 1989, and who has always had a keen interest in aviation, remembers flying to Liverpool on the DC3. All the windows were blacked out, so that the passengers could not see any of the aerial defences constructed round Liverpool's Speke airport. Among those using the service from Britain was a regular group of cattle dealers, who came over to Dublin to buy beasts at the old markets on the North Circular Road. On the night they concluded their

The new terminal building at Dublin airport, shortly after its completion.
Photograph: G. A. Duncan

deals, they managed to imbibe considerable quantities in local hostelries and, on the way back to Liverpool the next day, engage in continuous poker games. There was blackout too at the airport; in March, 1941, Clery's were asked to supply 2,200 yards of English-made blackout curtains for the terminal. The cost was about £90. In December, 1940, an underground air raid shelter had been completed at the airport, at a cost of £724 0s. 9d.

For part of the Emergency, from 1941 onwards, the Aer Lingus flights to Liverpool were reduced to two a week. The balance of services was maintained by West Coast Airlines, which used a DH86. The route was operated until April, 1944, when it was suspended at the request of the British authorities because preparations were being made for the D-Day landings in Normandy on June 6 that year. The Liverpool service was not resumed until September, 1944. One other route was serviced, albeit temporarily, during the war. A Dublin-Shannon route was opened in September, 1942, using an Aer Lingus DH86; the new service operated one round trip a day; flying time was one hour and the return fare was £5 10s. The service was designed to feed passengers into the trans-Atlantic flying boat services whose Irish terminal was at Foynes, County Limerick, but it did not attract sufficient traffic and was suspended at the end of October that year. There was one other service operated, briefly, during 1941 and 1942, when BOAC operated a Dublin-Bristol route between July 4, 1941 and February 21, 1942. Plans were made during 1942 for other regional flights from Dublin to Cork, Galway and Waterford, even though there was no airport at any of these locations. With the severe war-time shortages, those plans did not materialise. Apart from those two brief exceptions, Dublin-Liverpool remained the only service operating out of Collinstown on a regular basis for virtually the entire war period. Since there was one flight a day in each direction, the new airport had a ghostly appearance and the staff were decidedly underworked. There were some staff problems, too: in 1943, the airport superintendent was found guilty of larceny of petrol and oil and falsification of records.

Such cases were not isolated; many people were convicted during the period of most severe rationing, from 1941 until 1945, under the very strict Department of Supplies' rationing regulations, so the case involving the airport superintendent was one among thousands.

The air of boredom at the airport, because there was so little to do, was broken from time to time by unauthorised landings by foreign aircraft, all British, with the exception of one American plane. No Luftwaffe planes landed at Collinstown during the war. A series of lookout posts was established all over the country, so there was plenty of advance warning of enemy aircraft coming in. The first such incident to affect Collinstown took place on January 28, 1942, when an RAF Hawker Hurricane landed in the late afternoon at 3.52 pm, when the sun was starting to set. The pilot turned out to be American, a Sergeant Salvatore Walcott from New York, who told the intelligence officer investigating the landing that he had been training with the RAF for the previous three months. He had taken off from a base in Cumberland at 2.15 pm but had lost his way. Down to his last twelve gallons of fuel and "perished with the cold", he decided to make an unauthorised landing. The pilot was revived with traditional Irish hospitality and the next morning, at 10.20 am, he

Members of the 26th battalion ready to board a train at Kingsbridge railway station for training exercises. For most of the war period, the 7th battalion of Eastern Command guarded the airport.
Photograph: G. A. Duncan

Above: O'Connell Street, Dublin, at the height of the Emergency. On the right-hand side of the photograph is the old Metropole.
Photograph: G. A. Duncan

A jaunting car carries passengers along O'Connell Street, Dublin.
Photograph: G. A. Duncan

took off. A report of the time says that the skies around Collinstown reverberated to the sound of the plane's Merlin engine, as the first ever foreign military visitor to the new airport took to the skies.

The workers at Collinstown had to wait over a year for the next touch-down by a foreign military aircraft, this time American. It was the only war-time visit to Collinstown by a United States air force plane, a Boeing B-17F flying fortress. There was plenty of advance warning: lookout posts all over Ireland had sighted the aircraft as it wandered aimlessly, while the crew tried to decide where they were. At 11.55 am that day, the plane was seen approaching Dublin from a westerly direction; it passed over the village of Clondalkin and continued towards the city. It then made a left-hand turn at Baldonnel, but suddenly made a further turn towards Collinstown. The anti-aircraft guns at Collinstown fired three shells, which exploded harmlessly near the aircraft, but the pilot managed to get his undercarriage down. The army officer commanding the garrison at Collinstown ordered all the guns to be manned. A party of men was placed at the southern edge of the airfield and another party was placed at the northern end of the terminal building. These parties were ordered to converge on the aircraft as it landed while at the same time covering the advance of the rest of the company, which was organised into a striking force, aboard two lorries. When the B-17F touched down, it was immediately surrounded as it taxied in. The officer in charge went on board and was assured that none of the crew were carrying firearms. There were ten people on board, four lieutenants and six sergeants; it turned out that they had been delivering the plane from the US to Europe, via North Africa.

The crew had lost their bearings, which explained why they had been flying continuously since 8 pm the previous evening. They had had to land at Collinstown because the plane was so low on fuel. There was no love lost between the pilot and

An army gun emplacement during the Emergency; similar installations were in place around the perimeter of the airport at Collinstown from 1939 until 1945.
Photograph: G. A. Duncan

A queue for the trams in O'Connell Street, Dublin.
Photograph: G. A. Duncan

the navigator, as the former blamed the latter for his incompetence in losing their direction. When they landed, the crew asked for a drink, which the commanding officer at Collinstown promptly produced, two bottles of whiskey out of his jacket pocket. After rest and relaxation, the plane took off, bound for Britain.

Just over two months later, the airport had another unexpected visitor, this time from the RAF. Like the B-17F, the Anson was another mass production plane; 12,731 B-17s and over 11,000 Ansons were constructed. Three RAF Ansons landed at Collinstown during the war, although many more came to the airport after the war, in civilian guise. This particular Anson took off from an RAF base in Wales on June 29, 1943, but its crew soon lost their directions. They were seen flying over County Waterford, into County Kilkenny, then back to County Wexford, before flying up the east coast to Dalkey, then across Dublin Bay to Collinstown. It arrived there at 2.25 pm and was allowed to leave for Wales at 5.10 pm.

Some months later, on October 12, 1943, another RAF Anson got hopelessly lost and landed at Collinstown. The plane had taken off from Bishopscourt airfield in Co. Down, following a towed target on a gunnery practice run. The aircraft became separated, and the navigator, trying to set a course back to Bishopscourt, went completely off his route. The weather was very bad, with poor visibility, and the pilot flew around in circles for some considerable time, trying to get a fix on the landscape below. Soon, the fuel tank was down to twenty gallons and the pilot was about to ditch the plane in the sea off north County Dublin when he spotted Collinstown and made a routine landing. The Air Corps provided eighty-one gallons of precious aviation fuel, and an equally useful route forecast, and the plane left again later that day, at 5.40 pm.

Not until March 12, 1944, did the next incident occur with a straying foreign aircraft. Five crew, four Canadians and an American, were aboard an RAF Armstrong Whitworth Whitley twin-engined bomber, a type that had been used extensively by the RAF for bombing missions in the earlier years of the war. This plane had taken off from a base in England, but had drifted off course because of the cloud cover and high winds. After seven hours in the air, the crew thought they were over the south of England; the pilot received a considerable shock when he saw the name "Eire" painted on the ground at the Air Corps airfield at Baldonnel. He turned with the intention of ditching at sea, then changed his mind and made for Collinstown, putting out a distress signal as he did so. It was a Sunday and the airport was closed. Captain Murray, who was then commanding the 7th Battalion at Collinstown, recognised the distress signal.

He had the sheep cleared from the main runway and ordered a soldier to stand out in the open with a sheet, to show the wind direction. The pilot was cleared to land with a Verey light and he touched down at 5.54 pm. The crew decided to stay

Three management people from Aer Rianta photographed during the Emergency. Shown in this photograph taken at Mass parade from the 43rd battalion of the Local Defence Force in Portobello Barracks, Dublin, in 1942, were James O'Sullivan (No. 1, later a chief executive, Aer Rianta), Leo Phillips (No. 2, later ground services, Dublin airport) and Joe Madigan (No. 3, later airport development manager).

A cart load of cabbage is tipped out in Moore Street, Dublin.
Photograph: G. A. Duncan

overnight; the plane was put in the hangar and the crew slept on board. They were given food, cigarettes and blankets and were very appreciative of the army's generosity. The following morning the plane was refuelled and it took off for a base in Northern Ireland at 11.15 am.

Since there were no commercial flights in or out of Collinstown between Friday evening and Monday morning at this stage during the Emergency, there were suggestions that the control tower should be manned seven days a week, in case there were any more unauthorised landings by foreign military aircraft. The suggestion was not followed up and the airfield remained closed every weekend, although of course it was always heavily guarded by the 7th Battalion.

The last incursion of the war came just a month before Germany surrendered in May, 1945. An RAF Anson took off from the Air Navigation School at Bishopscourt base in County Down, on April 5, 1945, for a training flight routed over Blackpool and the Kish lightship in Dublin Bay; over the Kish, there were problems with the port engine and the crew decided to make for Collinstown, landing at 2 pm. Aer Lingus technical staff repaired the burst oil pipe that was causing the difficulties and it was recorded that the Collinstown coffers had been enriched by the sum of £1 7s. 7d. This was for six whiskies, two rums, four minerals and some cigarettes. The visitors took off at 5.35 pm that evening, heading for Bishopscourt. With the departure of that RAF Anson into the evening sky, the wartime intrusions at Collinstown came to an end. For the airport, it had been a remarkably uneventful war, contrary to the expectations of 1940, when a British invasion was expected from the North and there was an equal threat of a German invasion from the south coast.

During the course of the war, there were a few minor alterations and extensions to the airport buildings. In 1943, ownership of a hayshed on the airport lands was

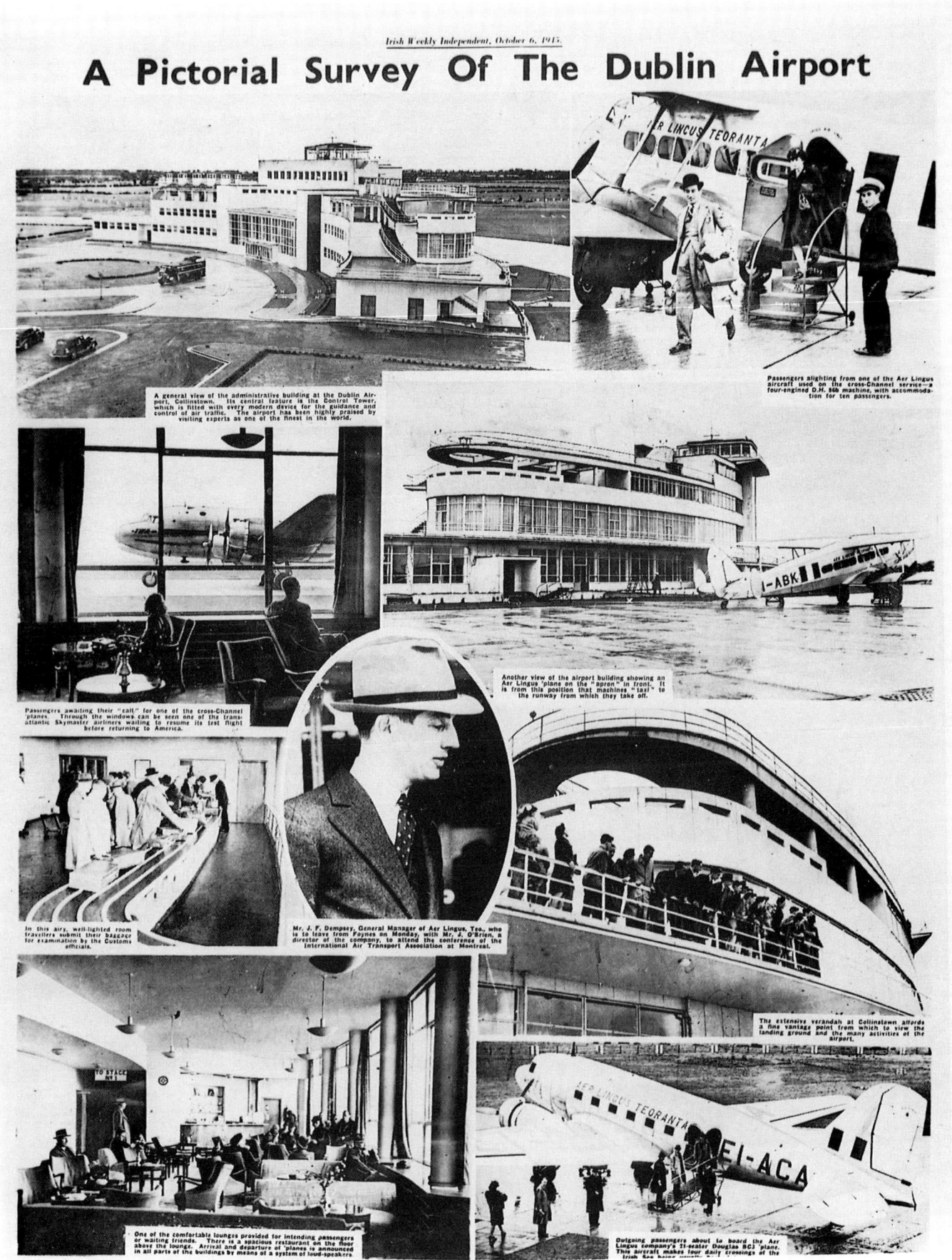

On October 6, 1945, the *Irish Weekly Independent* ran a full-page photographic feature on the new Dublin airport.

J. F. Dempsey, appointed general manager of Aer Lingus and Aer Rianta in 1943.

transferred to Aer Rianta. The main No. 1 hangar, which bore the legend "Eire" on its roof, was built concurrently with the terminal building and was ready for the first Aer Lingus operations out of the airport in 1940. That year also saw the completion of a small, second hangar, on a temporary basis, which was used for overhaul work. All the field work on the airport was completed during the early summer of 1940. The internal roads and car parks were completed and handed over to Aer Rianta in January, 1942; the main four-storey terminal building was finally completed a short while later. The first floor contained the restaurant and the second, the meteorological staff and banks of teleprinters. Facilities at the airport remained extremely limited, especially with the electricity rationing. The airport closed at 5.30 pm every day, after the one and only inward flight of the day had arrived from Liverpool and the airline and airport staff went home either on a bus that was laid on for the disembarking passengers, or by bicycle.

With many of the people who worked at the airport living in either Santry or Swords, getting home by bicycle was a pleasant enough experience, since there was virtually no motor traffic at all on the main Dublin to Belfast road. Severe petrol rationing meant that only people like doctors, performing a vital community service, had fairly ready access to petrol supplies. For the rest of the population, petrol coupons were almost as rare as hen's teeth. Supplies could be swiftly withdrawn for breaches of the regulations; Mrs M. A. Fanning, the maternity nurse at Garristown, a village in north County Dublin not far from the airport, had her permit removed because her motor car was allegedly being used by a member of her family to carry workmen and farm machinery components. A few car drivers with an engineering turn of mind had gas cylinders fitted to the roofs of their motor cars so that they could run on gas, but, in general, a car or even a bus on the main airport road during most of the Emergency became something of a novelty. Nevertheless, there was one expansion of note at the airport; in 1943, it was decided to open a small café in the terminal building. As Dr J. F. Dempsey remembers, it was extremely small and served little more than tea and sometimes coffee, with an odd biscuit if supplies were reasonable. When the job of manageress was advertised, for the princely sum of £3 a week, there was an enormous rush of applicants, 159 in all.

Despite over 100,000 people actively engaged in the Local Defence Force and ancillary services, like the civil defence, unemployment was a huge problem, with around 70,000 people officially registered as unemployed during the Emergency. With the new café, the airport was able to offer meagre refreshments to passengers, complementing this service later in 1943 with the opening of the first airport lounge bar. Patrons, if they waited long enough, could see an aircraft arrive or depart; the alternative was a contemplation of the sheep grazing peacefully on the main grass runway.

There was a little movement too on the managerial side of the airline and the airport, which although allegedly under the control of two separate companies, with Aer Rianta in law being the company that controlled airline services, in practice the running of the airport came very much under the wing of Aer Lingus. Seán Ó hUadhaigh, a Dublin solicitor who had been prominent in the setting up of the national airline, was chairman of Aer Lingus from May, 1936 until November, 1941, when he was succeeded by John Leydon. Ó hUadhaigh remained a director until 1944, and again was appointed a director from 1957 until 1959. The British authorities were not keen on him as chairman, given his political background and friendship with German internees. But in Ireland, he was regarded as a man of very great integrity, who did much for the development of civil aviation. Although he was chairman of Aer Lingus, followed by John Leydon, in practice this meant being chairman also of Aer Rianta; the two companies were becoming one and the same in working practice. In 1943, Dr J. F. Dempsey, who was also secretary of Irish Shipping during the Emergency, was appointed manager of both companies, Aer Lingus and Aer Rianta, and continued to act as secretary for both.

Aer Rianta had so little to do during the war years that Dr Dempsey inaugurated a scheme in conjunction with the Department of Education to encourage young people to take an interest in aviation matters. The appetite of many young people had been whetted by the spectacular shots of aerial battles, depicted on the Movietone News, then a popular feature at the cinemas, between the "short" and the main feature film, as often as not a cowboy film. But Dr Dempsey well foresaw that, when the war was over, there would be an unprecedented development of aviation for civilian purposes. Rare excitement came to the airport workers in 1942, when the All-Ireland ploughing championships were held at Cloghran, an interesting diversion for a few days.

Even at this early stage, halfway through the war, many people working at the airport were keenly anticipating the day when restrictions on flying development would be lifted and an Irish trans-Atlantic service could be started. Apart from the input into the educational system, children were also encouraged to come to Dublin airport and see what it was like for themselves. Many of those children, twenty or thirty years on, were among the devotees of the original airport restaurant in its heyday, run by Johnny Oppermann, when it was one of the most popular social venues in the Dublin area.

Behind the scenes, the work continued at the airport. Charlie Craddock, now retired from Aer Rianta, joined Aer Lingus in October, 1941, and was transferred to the Aer Rianta payroll the following year. He was the first tradesman employed by Aer Rianta, and he had charge of runway maintenance and also the original terminal building, which at that stage was not completed. The ground floor area, scheduled for check-in purposes, still was not finished. As did practically everyone else

A horse-drawn Post Office wagon passes the Goodwill restaurant in Pearse Street, Dublin. A chain of these wartime restaurants provided low-cost meals.
Photograph: G. A. Duncan

Saving the hay at Dublin airport, just after the end of the Emergency. Fieldmen at work, from left to right: J. Lawlor, C. Finn, P. Hanley, J. Browne, unidentified, T. Stafford, unidentified, P. Caul, D. Kelly, J. Collins, T. McGuirk and J. Carroll.

working at the airport, Craddock had to use a bicycle to get to and from work. He was living in Swords at the time and remembers vividly that there was no regular bus service to the airport; one had to walk down to the main road to catch one of the infrequent buses en route to Swords.

Train services were badly hampered by the lack of coal; only low-grade coal and slack was available to fire the steam locomotives. On the Great Southern Railway's most prestigious line, from Kingsbridge to Cork, there were sometimes only two trains a week and the 165-mile journey often took twenty hours. On one memorable occasion in 1942, a train from Killarney to Dublin took twenty-three hours for a journey that normally occupied less than five hours. In these conditions, Charlie Craddock made an endlessly tedious journey to Sligo in search of a saw; in the event, he found his saw but he never went on a train again.

The Boot Inn was one of the adjacent "watering holes" for people working on the airfield, sometimes providing meals for airport staff and flight crews. Jim McDonald, who was in charge of airport security for many years, also has memories of the airfield in the early days of the Emergency. He remembers the field foreman of the

Dublin airport passenger lounge, 1945.

time, the late John Cronin, and says that things were so quiet then, with only one flight a day, that very often a gang of workers would walk across the fields to the Boot Inn, to savour a bit of crack.

There were two wardens based at the terminal building, Jim Galvin and Paddy Hughes, and if there was ever any hint of trouble, all they had to do was call in the army battalion.

The two men had an "easy job", remembers McDonald, although one army man who joined the warden's staff at the airport took his duties seriously. Any time anyone approached the gate, whether or not they were on the airport staff, he took a great delight in challenging them. Jim McDonald says that this man treated the airport exactly like the military garrison it was, although other people guarding the place were more easy-going in their approach, but not more lax in their efficiency. McDonald saw the whole security system at the airport from the inside, because he served in the army during the war; he was on the medical services' side. He remembers well the airport garrison, with its infantry company and an anti-aircraft unit with its three gun emplacements. The 7th Battalion headquarters was in Santry Court, about two miles distant from the airport, and after the 7th handed over to the 22nd Battalion, there was a disastrous fire at the house, which was reduced to a shell. McDonald spent some time at Santry Court before being transferred to Gormanston air base, another former RFC/RAF base converted after World War I to Air Corps use. He joined the army medical services there and was eventually transferred back to Collinstown as its medical orderly. He was based there from 1942 to 1943, a strange introduction to the place where he later worked for so many years, until his retirement at the end of 1983.

Paddy O'Daly well remembers the primitive state of the airfield during the war, when the runways were grass. To him, the airport was a "desperate" place, because there was so little activity, just one service a day. When life was hectic, there were two services a day. The operation of those services during the winter was especially difficult, because when the aircraft landed on made ground, the wheels would cut huge furrows in the turf. There were several fieldmen working at the airport then, whose job it was to go out and patch those furrows. O'Daly was living in a bungalow at the side of the airfield and he walked across to the terminal every morning to work, so he got a good knowledge of the condition of the grass. When he saw which way a pilot wanted to take off — the original runways were designed so that planes could take off in any direction, depending on the wind — he would go out and find hard patches on the ground and then get tracks put down on them so that the pilot could get a purchase on the ground when he was taking off. But O'Daly remembers that during the war there were only forty civilians working at the airport, between Aer Lingus and Aer Rianta. The work of Aer Rianta was modest, consisting of maintaining the airfield and the terminal building; a team of about a dozen people, including carpenters, an electrician and painters, worked under O'Daly keeping the place in order.

One of Paddy O'Daly's jobs was maintaining the "stake system", which was designed to prevent unauthorised aircraft landing.

This grid system was also designed so that the airfield could be turned into a detention camp for prisoners, but the airfield was never used for this purpose during the Emergency. The stakes, which were actually old railway sleepers, were sunk into the ground in a 1234 pattern, with a gap between each corner. When an aircraft was expected, a gang of men would go out to pull up the stakes. A small permanent gap was left in the middle of the staked area to facilitate landings by Aer Lingus, and at night, when there were no aircraft movements, the army placed carts across this area. For much of the Emergency, there was a strong fear that Collinstown would be used by an invading force.

Aer Lingus, Aer Rianta and the army shared a relatively easy occupancy of the airfield. Aer Lingus had the ground floor of the new terminal building — their head office, which also contained the two secretarial staff of Aer Rianta — was in O'Connell Street — and also in one of the hangars. The other hangar was occupied by the army. In the terminal building itself, beyond the concourse with its check-in desk, was the customs hall and also a small cargo room. The scale of the entire operation can be judged by the Aer Lingus turnover figures for the war years; between 1939/40 and 1944/45, a total of 34,112 passengers flew Aer Lingus, or about 120 every working week. In the last year of the war, 1944/45, Aer Lingus had an operating revenue of £21,079.

There was one slight problem for Paddy O'Daly and that was keeping the airport in good trim; the sheep did their grazing job so efficiently that, when the winter came, the grass was cropped so short that a lot of work had to be done cutting and repatching the turf. As the war progressed, the wheat grown on the one-hundred foot wide stretch of land running all round the perimeter of the airfield became progressively weaker. But one man and his dog came well out of the war, the Aer Rianta shepherd, a man called Ferris, and the Aer Rianta sheepdog, called Terry, looking after the 500 sheep. The latter had a permanent food "ration" all his own, sanctioned by Gerry Dempsey in his role as chief executive of Aer Rianta. The dog did well, paid five shillings a week (no deductions!), enough to give him about twenty pounds of meat a week and a bottle of milk a day. There were never any twin lambs delivered at Collinstown; only later was it discovered that someone was helping himself to the other lamb.

Yet despite all the hardships of the war, there was a realisation in 1944 that Ireland had a vital part to play in the development of aviation in the post-war world. Sean Lemass, who had been the Minister presiding over the birth of Aer Lingus in 1936, spoke encouragingly in 1944 of the role Ireland could play in trans-Atlantic services, but centred on Shannon. Nevertheless, there was keen determination not only within Aer Lingus and Aer Rianta, but also within the Department of Industry and Commerce to develop Dublin airport. In January, 1944, a proposal was considered for an alternative scheme for three hard-surfaced runways, a big improvement on the grass, following up the initial considerations of the subject, made in 1943.

Another piece of important forward planning came in the winter of 1944, when the American Government called an international civil aviation conference in Chicago. Included in the delegation were Robert Brennan, the Irish Minister to the US, John Leydon, secretary of the Department of Industry and Commerce and Denis Devlin of the Department of External Affairs, also a noted poet. The conference quickly began dealing with technical matters, so a select group of experts was sent for, including R. W. O'Sullivan, chief aeronautical officer in the Department, and T. J. Monaghan, engineer in chief of the Department of Posts and Telegraphs. The head of the Meteorological Service, A. H. Nagle, was unable to travel. A total of fifty-one states attended the conference; the resulting convention came into force in 1947, giving a broad base for the development of international civil aviation in the post-war world.

The war in Europe ended in May, 1945, although it dragged on in the Far East for another year. However, it was some months before Collinstown was taken off a war footing and civil aviation was able to start getting back to normal. The Emergency petered out, even though the end of the war saw vociferous displays of delight and joy in many countries of Europe, as well as in North America. In Dublin, there were celebrations, some by people with nationalist inclinations, others by people of a unionist persuasion, but even though the war officially ended, some rationing lasted until the early 1950s.

But even though the army garrison at the airport began withdrawing its anti-aircraft guns and moving out of its accommodation on the airfield, a certain military tendency was to remain at Collinstown for the next ten years, since many of the people who were about to come to the airport in a civilian capacity, like Colonel Delamer, who was made first airport manager in 1946, came from military backgrounds. Dublin airport provided a useful new role for military personnel who had been serving in the defence forces during the Emergency and this sense of the military was heightened by Aer Lingus recruiting numbers of ex-RAF personnel, not necessarily Irish, to fly the airline's post-war expanded fleet. For the airport at Collinstown, just five years in existence, the lull of its initial years which lasted well into 1945, was the prelude to the rapid development of the airport as civil aviation literally took off after the war, out of the preserve of a wealthy and socially exclusive elite. The real history of the airport at Collinstown, as it exists today, did not begin until peace came to a weary and ruined Europe.

An aerial photograph of Collinstown taken in 1945, just after the end of the Emergency, showing the Éire identification still painted on the main hangar.

CHAPTER III

Concrete at Collinstown

THE drums of war stopped beating, and the memories of the worst shortages began to fade from the public mind in the early summer of 1945. Dublin airport started to equip itself for the peace, when all the experts predicted, correctly, that there would be an enormous upsurge in civil aviation.

Dublin airport was fortunate because solid foundations had been laid well in the late 1930s and the early years of the war, in the shape of the new terminal building and the two hangars. All the first-class facilities were there, a product of the perceptive long-term planning that has always characterised Irish aviation development. The first major appointment at the airport after the war ended was Colonel Bill Delamer who was officer commanding the Air Corps from 1940 until 1946. The colonel was brought up in a wealthy household not far from Mullingar in the midlands; Dr Thekla Beere, who, as secretary of the Department of Transport and Power in the 1960s, played a crucial role in the further development of civil aviation in Ireland, remembers well the Delamer home from her childhood. Delamer had served in the Royal Flying Corps, which subsequently became the RAF, during the Great War of 1914-18.

His son, Peter, who is managing director or Technico Communications in Dublin, still has his father's World War I log book. When the Air Corps was being set up in 1922, Colonel Delamer transferred to it and was to spend the next twenty-four years of his life based at Baldonnel. John Leydon, who was secretary of the Department of Industry and Commerce and was also on the board of Aer Lingus and Aer Rianta, asked Delamer to take over the airport job in 1946, which he did, arriving at Collinstown in a civilian capacity at the age of forty-seven. It was not a substantial transition for him, because he was able to set his own pace at the airport. By the nature of things, the discipline he brought to the airport job was militaristic; many other former military personnel went to work at Collinstown, like Colonel Eamonn Rooney, who went to Aer Lingus to head its publicity department. Sometimes, Delamer was considered to have taken the military approach too far; one story, often related in airport circles, tells how he went out on an inspection of the lawns at the airport one day, and finding some evidence that the grass had not been cut as scheduled, picked a few clumps, put them in an envelope and sent them to the appropriate overseer.

Colonel Delamer was always amused to see the sign over the shop in the airport: "Colonel W. P. Delamer, licensed to sell tobacco". His staff at the airport would have been intrigued to see their boss in such a state, since he had a rather austere and aloof reputation. In the first years of his tenure at the airport — he retired in 1966 — he did not have an overwhelming workload.

In the airport boilerhouse, 1946, Paddy Byrne (left), boilerman and Charlie Craddock, foreman.

Below: John Gunning, former field supervisor, with two of the paraffin flares used on the grass runways.
Photograph: Robert Allen Photography

At work in the Aer Rianta carpenters' shop, a converted Nissen hut, in 1949, were Paddy Noonan, John Monaghan, Hugh O'Hagan, Kit Johnson, Joe Noonan, Frank Shortall and Larry Shields.

His assistant was another military man, Colonel Michael Tuohy, a native of Feakle, County Clare, and the two of them struck up a close friendship, working together in harmony, although Tuohy was a more flamboyant character, who had been active in the struggle for independence. At one stage, Tuohy was sentenced to death by the British authorities for his involvement in IRA activities, was reprieved, then sentenced again, before winning a permanent reprieve. It must have been an unnerving experience, but Tuohy made light of it in any occasional references he made to the subject. There were other echoes of the harrowing days of the War of Independence and civil war, which had ended only just over twenty years previously. With the immediate post-war expansion of the airport, many people were recruited into the police and fire service at the airport. Their backgrounds were markedly different; some had strong Republican sympathies from civil war days, while others had served in the Free State army. Sources say that the presence of two such disparate groups in such a sensitive area as policing could have had potentially controversial results, and while these could surface in a pub late at night, when these men were on duty, professionalism prevailed, an equity of mind attributed to their service in the Irish army during the Emergency.

One of the early realities that Colonel Delamer had to deal with was the newly unionised workforce. The fieldmen had complained vociferously about their conditions, just as the labourers and skilled men constructing the airfield in the late 1930s had done.

This time there was no strike, but the men got a powerful ally on their side, "Big" Jim Larkin, the man who lifted the unskilled workers of Dublin off their feet during the 1913 lockout and who became the first general secretary of the Irish Transport and General Workers' Union. Shortly before he died in 1947, he gave the airport fieldmen precious advice on organising themselves under the umbrella of a trade union. Such matters were quite foreign to Delamer, since trade union activity had never been permitted in the Defence Forces, but despite the intervention of Larkin,

The Aer Rianta accounts department, 1946. From left: Jack Hudson, Leo Mooney, Tom Hallinan and Mike Murphy.

The Aer Rianta maintenance department held its first annual Christmas dinner at the Central Hotel, Exchequer Street, Dublin, in 1946. Included in the photograph are Colonel Delamer (airport manager), fourth from left, sitting, Paddy O'Daly (superintendent of maintenance), sixth from left, sitting and Bill Beck (airport engineer), seventh from left, sitting. On the immediate right of Beck is Charlie Craddock, general foreman.

the fieldmens' grievances were settled with reasonable speed and harmony. Delamer was able to report to his boss, Gerry Dempsey, that the airport was continuing to work well under partial union membership. Delamer would have enjoyed that sense of continuity.

Apart from "Big" Jim Larkin, the other person who arrived at the airport shortly after the end of the war and had an equally important influence on the progress of the airport, but in an entirely different direction, was Johnny Oppermann, brought in by Colonel Delamer to build up the catering facilities.

Dublin Airport also went public for the first time; the new airport was revealed when the July 28, 1945 issue of the *Irish Builder* was published. The editor of the magazine stated: "war-time censorship alone must take the blame for the lateness of this description of Dublin airport and its buildings". This very censorship is often blamed for the lack of recognition that its architect, Desmond FitzGerald, deserved for the very fine modern four-storey building he had designed in 1937. FitzGerald had been very perceptive; the *Irish Builder* pointed out it was the first airport designed to supply a long periphery to accommodate planes. The magazine said that the principle was the same as used in the design of many other international airports, notably Washington in the US. But even in small matters, FitzGerald was ahead of his time; in the restaurant, he included a rostrum for the orchestra and a space for dancing, measuring twenty-three feet in diameter. The restaurant had a superb setting, looking out on the entire airfield with a totally clear line of vision, yet because of the many cramping but necessary restrictions of war-time, it was never used as a restaurant until peace resumed. Johnny Oppermann came in and breathed energetic life into the airport catering, making the restaurant a legend in its own lunchtime, a legend that is fondly remembered by countless Dubliners of a certain age.

Oppermann had worked in the North and in Dublin. First of all, he had opened a hotel in the Glens of Antrim, then he came to Bray in County Wicklow, where he managed the International Hotel. In 1944, he moved on again, to the Moira Hotel (since demolished) in Trinity Street, off Dame Street in the heart of Dublin. The Moira was a favourite with Dublin businessmen (there were precious few businesswomen in those days) and thanks to Johnny Oppermann's expertise, the Moira became as popular as the Dolphin, Jammets, the Red Bank and the Russell, all now very sadly defunct. Oppermann remembers that when Aer Lingus started its flights to Paris in July, 1947, he had to get the inflight refreshments and food prepared; the cylindrical flasks were prepared in the airport kitchen, which he says was "absolutely primitive". The inflight food consisted mostly of sandwiches and there were tales told, darkly, of workers coming in late at night and watching mice and other rodents scurrying out of the way. Very often, remembers Oppermann, he would get a call from the airport at 4.30 in the morning to say that weather had caused trans-Atlantic planes to be diverted from Shannon to Dublin. The minute and rather grubby kitchen was called upon to muster up three or four hundred breakfasts. As always, the airport staff rose to the occasion, magnificently.

Johnny Oppermann brought a Swiss precision and an Irish flamboyance to catering; all along the way, there were innovations, since this was a time for building and creating, often without the necessary financial resources.

He recalls the very first "fast food" equipment that was installed at the airport not long after the end of the war; it was a unique Swiss-made device that tenderised steak as it was being grilled, and when Johnny Oppermann and Colonel Delamer came to see the device in action, they were like two little schoolboys with the latest gadget.

There were other kinds of excitement, too. The Cuckoo Stream, which runs along the southern boundary of the airport, but which has long since been covered, burst

Preparing the sub-grade for the new runways, 1947.

Pouring joints on the new runways, July, 1947.

A beam vibrator at work on the construction of the new concrete runways, 1947.

Construction work on the new runways at Dublin airport during the winter of 1947/48 became seriously bogged down by bad weather.
Photograph: H. W. Harrington

its banks and caused quite substantial flooding. For a while that February, the airport had to be closed. The ground became much too soft and the new Aer Lingus DC3s were unsuitable for operation from Baldonnel. August, 1946, saw an amazing escape for a planeload of passengers, when a French Navy Junkers, on its descent to Collinstown, crash landed on the top of Djouce mountain, in County Wicklow, thirty miles out from the airport. Most of the crew and the passengers, twenty-five French girl guides, walked out of the wreckage. Some of the passengers had major injuries.

In the summer of 1945, there had been some "unlicensed" intrusions into Irish air space by US war planes. During one incident, a twin-engined aircraft flew in low from the Sandymount direction, nearly hit a factory chimney, and skimmed over the Bank of Ireland in College Green. It banked so steeply as it flew over the city centre that its wings were nearly vertical. In the atmosphere of joviality and hilarity that followed the ending of the war in Europe, the public was not too censorious, but one newspaper leader said that Aer Lingus should not be allowed to continue its recently introduced practice of flying over the city of Dublin.

Although the public was now allowed to go to the airport merely for sightseeing purposes, a pastime that grew to be very popular in the late 1940s and early 1950s, immediately after the war public comments were made, in the newspapers, that the "authorities" wanted to chase away members of the public as trespassers, if they came too close to the airport. The first major aircraft movement into Dublin after the war was by TWA, which had been set up in America in 1930 as a domestic carrier. In 1944, it decided to expand its routes internationally, and sent a Douglas DC4 to sound out the two Irish airports, flying first to Shannon, then going on to Dublin.

Quidnunc in *The Irish Times* gave an eloquent description of the first trans-Atlantic flight to land at Collinstown: "Twice the Skymaster circled over Dublin, and then back she came again, lower now with the engines throttled down. She made a circuit of the airfield, flying quite slowly, disappeared for a moment behind the terminal building and suddenly appeared beyond the hangar on the right, her outsize pair of double wheels almost touching the grass. She touched down and seemed to sink a little into the ground. The Skymaster weighs more than thirty tons and as yet, there are no concrete runways at Collinstown. She turned almost in her own length and

The first Constellation arrives at Dublin airport, 1947, in Aerlínte colours. In the front row of the welcoming party, from left, are John Leydon, Seán Lemass and Gerry Dempsey.
Photograph: G. A. Duncan

came riding back across the grass with her four engines roaring. The moment Collinstown had been waiting for was over. For the first time in history, a transAtlantic commercial plane had landed within a few miles of the heart of Dublin City".

Captain W. G. Golien, the pilot, was equally enthusiastic: "Dublin airport is magnificent and given concrete runways would make an ideal alternative to Rineanna". Two days later, on September 27, 1945, another Skymaster arrived, this time belonging to American Overseas Airlines, overflew Dublin airport, but did not land. Twenty years later, this plane did land at Dublin, when it was working on charter flights for meat companies. However, on December 10, 1945, an American Overseas Skymaster landed at Collinstown, carrying the airline's vice-president, who had discussions with officials of the Department of Industry and Commerce.

While these American arrivals had caused great excitement among airport staff, Aer Lingus was gearing itself up to an increasingly busy flight schedule. On November 9, 1945, it reopened its Dublin to Croydon direct service, which had been suspended since the outbreak of war. Before the war, this service had included a stop at Bristol, but when it resumed in late 1945, it was a direct flight. The return leg of the flight, which took 2½ hours, was undertaken by West Coast Airways; the single fare cost £6 10s. Christmas, 1945, the first peacetime Christmas since 1938, was subdued because of the continuing shortages of food, although Dubliners going down the country reported no difficulties with butter and other provisions.

The early days of the New Year, 1946 saw the introduction of a revolutionary new service at Collinstown. On Tuesday, January 15, the aerial mail service between Ireland and Britain began. On that day, a Railway Air Services DH.86 Express flew from Liverpool to Collinstown with four thousand letters and packages and returned with 1,500 letters. From that day to this, air transport has been a vital part of Ireland's interconnection with the international postal network. But the conditions for planes landing and taking off at Collinstown remained relatively spartan. The runways were still grass, and although there were quite sophisticated systems like the Lorenz blind landing system, some of the technology was decidedly primitive. In the years immediately after the war, the paraffin flares, which played such an important part in

Crowds gather at the airport to watch the arrival of one of the Aerlínte Constellations, 1947; it was destined for the proposed new transAtlantic service, which was scrapped as soon as the Inter-Party government came to power in 1948.
Photograph: G. A. Duncan

guiding planes down in poor weather, were still in use. The containers were circular in shape, so that whatever direction they rolled in, they returned to the upright position; the wicks drew paraffin from the container and burned brightly enough to give, in tandem, a satisfactory flare path for the pilots. The only such flare still in existence has been lovingly restored by John Gunning, a former airfield supervisor, who lives in retirement at Garristown in north County Dublin, not very far from the airport perimeter.

A new sight was to be seen at Dublin airport, apart from the DH.86 Express running the new mails' service. From the end of January, 1947, several Royal Canadian Air Force C–47 aircraft landed at Collinstown, bringing members of the Canadian forces still stationed in Britain into Ireland for what is called in military parlance, R & R. The title had nothing to do with the Rathmines and Rathgar Musical Society; it referred to "Rest and Recreation". If Canadian accents were heard around town, then the extraordinary aircraft sighted at Collinstown created a great deal of interest, enough to match that of the young, unattached maidens of the city. Even more exciting times lay ahead; as Aer Lingus augmented its post-war fleet, the first deliveries came through from California, two brand new Douglas DC3 aircraft, which arrived on Sunday, February 24, 1946, after their delivery flight from the west coast of the US. They were shining silver, painted in the Aer Lingus colours, in sharp contrast to the former American Air Force planes purchased recently by Aer Lingus.

There were still more arrivals at Collinstown; Joseph P. MacHale, who worked at University College, Dublin, mainly as secretary and bursar, for nearly forty-eight years, came to the airport in 1946. He joined Aer Rianta in 1946 as assistant secretary and two years later, just before his departure to UCD, he was made accountant.

He notes, pertinently, that at that time, the administration of Aer Lingus and its holding company, Aer Rianta, was shared between the two companies. As assistant secretary of both Aer Lingus and Aer Rianta, he was closely involved with the planning of new routes and new developments at the airport. Work was being done in Dublin to lay the foundations of trans-Atlantic air traffic; the North Atlantic route conference was held in Dublin over a three-week period from March 4, 1946. A total of 200 delegates and observers from eighteen countries attended the proceedings. Although it was nearly a year since the war in Europe had ended, the delegates were given their ration cards for butter, sugar and tea. As a result of those lengthy deliberations in Dublin Castle, many aspects of trans-Atlantic air travel were sorted

Grass cut at the airport was harvested to make cattle feed. This photograph, taken in the late 1940s, shows grass-cutting operations in progress.
Photograph: G. A. Duncan

Air Corps photograph taken on April 7, 1947, showing the plan of the airfield and its runways.
Photograph: Stationery Office

Pandit Nehru, Indian prime minister, arrives at Dublin airport, 1948, not long after India won her independence.
Photograph: G. A. Duncan

out, such matters as air sea rescue, meteorology and air traffic control. The weekend before the conference started was the busiest ever experienced at Collinstown until then, for at one stage there were as many as thirteen aircraft on the ramp, with more incoming planes in the "hold" position, awaiting clearance to land. It was a foretaste of things to come, as civil aviation developed at a fast pace.

From the following month, West Coast doubled the frequency of its Croydon to Dublin flights, but the airline's days in Dublin were numbered, for the bilateral agreement between Ireland and Britain, covering air transport between the two countries, was signed on April 5, 1946.

Under the terms of the agreement, Aer Lingus was given the sole right to operate scheduled services between Ireland and Britain, a right that existed for the next ten years, although during that period, many independent UK companies operated charter flights into Dublin. The agreement also meant a financial restructuring of Aer Lingus; forty per cent of the airline's share capital was to be held by British Overseas Airways Corporation and British European Airways.

The remaining sixty per cent of the shares were held by Aer Rianta, as the national air transport holding company. Out of that forty per cent UK holding in Aer Lingus, ten per cent was controlled by BOAC and thirty per cent by BEA. One of the other terms of the agreement was that all parties to the agreement were to ensure that no other airline should operate any scheduled services in competition, meaning that for the next ten years Aer Lingus had a total monopoly on all cross-channel routes. The nominal capital of Aer Lingus was increased from £100,000 to £1 million, of which Aer Rianta held that sixty per cent stake. The UK side was to nominate three out of the seven directors of Aer Lingus; with fitting irony, a UK director from 1949 until 1964 was the same Sholto Douglas, who later became Lord Douglas of Kirtleside. Thirty years previously, it was he who had selected the Collinstown site as being particularly suitable for aviation purposes.

At the same time that the Aer Lingus share capital was increased, so too was that of Aer Rianta, whose capital was doubled from £1 million to £2 million. Deputies in their Dáil questions reflected the confusion in the public mind as to the difference between Aer Lingus and Aer Rianta, and who did what. Deputy Liam Cosgrave, later to become Taoiseach, asked the Minister about the necessity for maintaining both companies. It was explained that Aer Rianta was the senior company, that it was completely owned by the Irish State. Its role was to manage Dublin airport, contribute

Edwina Lady Mountbatten flies in, 1948. Her husband, Lord Louis Mountbatten, killed in County Sligo in 1979, had just overseen India's transition to independence.
Photograph: G. A. Duncan

Billy Morton, the man behind Santry stadium and a legendary figure in Irish athletics, prepares to leave Dublin airport with a team, late 1940s.
Photograph: G. A. Duncan

capital to Aer Lingus and to operate trans-Atlantic services. Aerlínte had not yet been formed to operate the trans-Atlantic service and Shannon airport, the only other airport in the State, was controlled by the Department of Industry and Commerce. West Coast disappeared from the aviation scene, having been absorbed into BEA, while Railway Air Services, which operated the mail service, was also taken over by BEA.

Some aspects of the flying business were very different then. Jack Doyle, subsequently an airport manager, remembers that when he started working at the airport in 1948, there was a complete lack of ground transport. The traffic department of Aer Lingus, in which he first worked at Collinstown, employed about eighty people between clerical officers and more senior grades of management, yet those eighty people could muster only two motor cars between them. Some of the others had bicycles, but most people had to rely on the very sporadic bus service.

Members of staff were heavily dependent on the buses and Doyle recollects that if someone missed the bus into town, it was a substantial disaster, since there was a two hour wait until the next bus. For the lucky few who could afford the real luxury of air travel in those days, the airport had a delightfully quiet and civilised atmosphere. Passengers would alight from their cars, or more often than not, their chauffeur driven limousines, and be greeted by the airport staff almost as long lost friends, out for the day. Joe Whoriskey, who worked for many years with Aer Lingus, says that in those far-off days just after the war, "every passenger had to be almost packed in cotton wool and loaded onto the aircraft. You could nearly name all the people one week who were going to travel the next week, and those people were all rich". Some people arrived at Dublin airport in their own aircraft, like the Aly Khan, who exuded an air of extreme, and very elusive wealth. But there were so few passengers on the Aer Lingus flights to Britain, France or the Netherlands, that within a week or two, ground staff at the airport would get to know regular travellers extremely well. As Joe Whoriskey remarks, the passengers would be greeted on arrival at the airport by name. In 1945/46, Aer Lingus carried a total of 21,235 passengers. Sometimes, the passengers even arrived accompanied by their horses, destined for a cross-channel race meeting. It was also quite usual for these wealthy passengers to travel with mountains of luggage, which would block the terminal concourse.

In 1948, Aer Rianta set up a short-lived charter and air taxi division with four aircraft. One of the aircraft, a three-seater Miles Gemini, is seen on the apron. A Gemini from the fleet crashed in Kent, England, in 1954, while one of the Consul aircraft crashed in Leopoldville, in the Belgian Congo, now Kinshasa, Zaire, in June, 1957.

Seán Lemass pictured at the controls of one of the Aer Rianta aircraft, 1948.
Photograph: G. A. Duncan

Crew beside a Consul aircraft in the Aer Rianta colours, 1948.
Photograph: G. A. Duncan

As Joe Whoriskey recollects, quite often passengers would bring thirty or forty kilos of luggage with them, enormous cases, even if they were going away only for three days. Going by air in those far-off days, forty years ago, had the rarified atmosphere of an exclusive gentleman's club, to which ladies were permitted access in certain favourable circumstances. But while the lords and ladies of the aristocracy and the racing fraternity enjoyed the convivial pre-take-off chatter among their friends, out at Collinstown work was beginning on the new runways, which would have the effect of broadening the scope of civil aviation and making it more accessible to far greater numbers of people. The grass runways had proved useful, but the time had come for them to be updated. The grass also provided a useful by-product; it was cut three times a year between May and November, dehydrated into pellets in a small plant beside the airfield and then sold for use as cattle feed.

But all over Europe and North America, civil aviation gathered momentum, swiftly, once the war was over. Heath Row, as it was then called, was the UK's main international airport was under construction since 1944. The longest runway under construction was 9,000 feet long and the estimated cost of the new London airport project was £10 million. In 1946, Le Bourget, the airport for Paris, was being reconstructed after war damage; that year, it welcomed 300,000 passengers.

When Le Bourget airfield was handed over to the French civil authorities in 1945, at the end of the war, it was a total ruin, with the terminal and control tower destroyed by bombing. But just as Collinstown graduated from being a military airfield to a civil airport, so too did the French authorities decide, in 1946, to start turning the heavily damaged military airfield of Orly into a second airport for Paris. At Zurich, in Switzerland, a public vote was taken to start construction work on the airport, which is the only one in the world where all major building projects have to be submitted to public vote. What was happening at Collinstown, Heathrow and Zurich was being mirrored in other airport developments in much of Western Europe and North America. It was not all peaceful; in 1948, Colonel Delamer went to see for himself the breaking of the Berlin blockade by vast fleets of allied aircraft; the Berlin situation had threatened to rekindle the war.

Work was about to get under way in earnest on the new runways at Dublin airport; the peak construction period was between August and October, 1947. The construction of the runways was carried out by the Department of Industry and Commerce, under the superintendence of T. L. Hogan. Captain D. Campbell was the resident

The first departure bar, Dublin airport, 1948.

engineer and the contractors were T. J. Moran & Co. of Dublin, a continuance of their pre-war work on the site.

Neil Duffy, who has lived in Boston, US, since 1948, remembers well his two-year spell working on the construction of the new concrete runways. Many of the workers came from County Donegal; he does not believe that there were many more than about 100, since the work was far more automated than the previous work on the runways, in the late 1930s. Five trucks full of freshly prepared concrete ran a continuous "shuttle" to the runway site and two vibrators were used in the laying of the concrete. Some of the foremen still come to mind, like Michael Joyce, Michael Noone and John Logue. When Duffy was working Saturdays on the new runways, he was bringing home nearly £7 a week, a large sum of money in those days.

The Aly Khan, whose lavish hospitality at his County Kildare stud farm brought many famous screen personalities like Rita Hayworth to Dublin airport.
Photograph: G. A. Duncan

The construction of the three concrete runways, to replace the four grass ones in use until then, was a substantial task for the contractors. This type of pavement construction was more at the mercy of the elements than any other type of construction work and the very wet weather during the autumn of 1946 and snow during the winter of 1946/47 hindered progress. There were also the immediate post-war shortages, of both cement to make the concrete, and the equipment for laying it, but the contractors managed, with a degree of improvisation, to overcome these problems and the difficulties caused by the weather, and keep the project on schedule. In the late 1930s, aircraft seldom weighed more than 30,000 lbs gross, yet by the time the runways were being put down, aircraft with a gross weight of 100,000 lbs were commonplace and far larger and heavier aircraft were on the drawing boards of the manufacturers, especially in the United States. The new runways at Dublin airport were designed to take a 50,000 lbs single-wheel load, equivalent to the weight imposed by an aircraft weighing up to 150,000 lbs gross. The designer of the runways had to avoid making them stronger than necessary, because of the substantial extra cost this would entail.

The soil on the airport site was a silty clay, with about fifteen per cent of gravel and stones. Most of the concrete runways were placed in position with vibratory finishing machines, which gave a very good finish, far better than if the concrete had been laid by hand.

Forming the joints posed another headache for the construction teams; it was a problem that was never satisfactorily solved. Making sure that the subgrade, or the foundation upon which the concrete was laid, was in good condition proved tedious, since the almost continuous rain during construction caused a significant deterioration. Some 16,000 tons of stone and hardcore were used to form durable foundations for the concrete, but what often happened was that a perfect section of subgrade was prepared, then a night's heavy rain would do substantial damage. Next day, before concrete laying could progress, stone, gravel or hardcore had to be put in place, a time-consuming and costly exercise. On several occasions, material could be moved only by bulldozer, because other machines had broken down. The runway had to be laid in short sections of about 600 feet; most of the stone, gravel and hardcore used during this airport construction project went on the foundations for the east-west runway.

Neither was all the plant delivered on time; some of the machines arrived six months late, hampering work. A central mixing plant was set up, the first ever used in Ireland, which batched all materials mechanically, rather than manually. It worked practically without a hitch, giving the contractors many advantages in the production of the concrete for the runways. Overall, says Neil Duffy, the workload was well organised and bad weather was not too disruptive.

By the beginning of 1948, the new runways were completed. The main runway, which was designated 06/24 (it later became 05/23), was 5,300 feet long. The two

The RAF Meteor jet at Dublin airport in 1948, the first jet aircraft ever to land at Collinstown.

Another view of the RAF Gloster Meteor jet on the apron at Collinstown, May 27, 1948.

secondary runways, 17/35 and 12/30, were each 4,500 feet long. The concrete runways were to serve the airport well; the first extension to runway 17/35 did not come for a further twelve years, when Aer Lingus took delivery of its first commercial jet.

The new runways were much appreciated by aircraft pilots and the ground staff at the airport; they represented an enormous improvement on the former grass runways. Ironically, the first Aer Lingus service to use Collinstown, the route to Liverpool which was opened from the new airport in January, 1940, gave the airline's pilots a chance to see for themselves the benefits of a hard runway; since before World War II, Speke airport in Liverpool had had a tarmacadam covering on its runway. The Emergency, euphemism for many shortages, including financial investment, meant that the concreting of Dublin's runways did not happen until the airport had been eight years in use. There was a palpable air of excitement at the airport when the enormous task of concreting was completed; one young man got totally carried away. Some of the workers in the hangar were motor cycling enthusiasts and looked forward every year to the big Skerries races. One worker, overcome by his enthusiasm, tried out his motor cycle on the new runways, the ideal location to really open up the throttle. For his trouble, he got sacked.

Colonel Bertie McCormick, publisher of the *Chicago Tribune*, pictured after his arrival at Dublin airport in 1948 aboard his own Constellation.
Photograph: G. A. Duncan

The winter of 1946/47 was one of the worst for years, with heavy falls of snow that remained on the ground for weeks. Aircraft operation was made very difficult and it was equally difficult for people getting to work in the airport, since most of the airport workers still depended on bicycles or on the spasmodic bus service from Santry or Swords. The snowfalls were so heavy that the Swords Road was virtually blocked by snow; the airport was almost cut off from the city it served. There were other matters of general interest that were subjects of great conversational interest, like the sudden death of "Big" Jim Larkin, the trade union leader, who had played his part in organising some of the airport workers. His funeral to Glasnevin at the beginning of February, 1947, when the Dublin streets were still laden with snow, was an impressive event, watched by tens of thousands of people.

The snow did bring some cash benefits to airport workers, however. Jack Scully, who started work at the airport in 1946, as an electrician on £2 10s a week, remembers that during the bad weather of 1947, he was working literally day and night on snow clearance (the airport did not have a proper snowplough in those days) and, one week, he was paid the staggering sum of £60 because he had worked so much overtime.

Another person who joined the airport staff in those early post-war years was Bill Beck, the airport engineer, one of the great personalities at Dublin airport for over thirty years. He was born and brought up in Phibsboro', and served his time as a fitter in the Dublin dockyards. Then eventually, he went to Trinity College, Dublin, from where he graduated with an engineering degree in 1936. After working for three years with Metropolitan Vickers in Manchester, he returned home to become works engineer with Gouldings, the fertiliser manufacturers. In 1944, he went to work for a phosphate mine in County Clare and, while there, was given the tip-off about the airport job. He remembers that the official title of the job was airport engineer, but in practice, he was "dogsbody" to Colonel Delamer. Bill Beck also remembers how insistent Delamer was on the spelling of his name: "if any one put an 'e' at the end of it, they were for the high jump!" Delamer's assistant, Colonel Tuohy, was much more easygoing than his boss, who brought a strong tradition of military discipline to the running of the airport. On one occasion, Delamer and Beck fell out over the design of a high pressure hot water heating system for the airport. The new system had an unfortunate tendency to "backfire" with an embarrassing sound. This sound, called cavitation, erupted all over the terminal building, and on one particularly awkward occasion, remembers Bill Beck, it happened when the

Prince Bernhard of the Netherlands, pictured at the Dublin Horse Show in 1947. He visited the event on several occasions, piloting a DC3 of the Dutch royal flight into Dublin airport.
Photograph: G. A. Duncan

An Aer Lingus DC3 being refuelled by Shell and BP at the airport, late 1940s.

airport priest was saying Mass for the workers in the hangar. "A lot of the fellows were more devout than they let on and when the priest nearly fell off the altar, they were deeply shocked", he remembers. After a blazing row over how the problem would be solved, Delamer, never a popular man with the airport staff at the best of times, fired Beck, who nevertheless quickly returned to the payroll when tempers had cooled. He was able to resume where he had left off, including attendance at Delamer's regular weekly meetings, when the strict colonel insisted on drawing up detailed schedules for the week ahead. Despite Delamer's approach to managing the airport, Bill Beck feels that the colonel did much to put the airport management on a sound footing, a contribution that has not always been recognised.

But the airport was still operating on a small scale; Jack Scully remembers that there was no system of radio communication between the tower and airport vans on the field. When a van or truck driver wanted to cross the runway, he had to flash his lights at the tower, which would respond with a green or a red lamp. From the end of 1947, when the appropriate runway lighting systems were installed, the airport could remain open for night flying, a little-used novelty.

The airport also acquired its first fire engine, a Merryweather machine, which Joe

O'Rourke, who headed the team of seven firemen then stationed at the airport, remembers as being very cumbersome. The fire risk was greater in those days, because high octane petrol was being used as aviation fuel, not the special grade aviation fuel that is used today, and Joe O'Rourke recollects that if a plane had come down in the middle of the field, the Merryweather would not have been able to reach it unless the ground was dry. The early aircraft were made of very inflammable materials, like wood and canvas, but by this immediate post-war stage, metal was the standard material for aircraft body construction. Yet despite the start of rapid development at the airport, there was still plenty of room for the "characters" and the "crack". Myles Magee, a security man, was known as a great wit around the airport; on one occasion, a passenger, seeing him in his uniform, thought he was a pilot and asked if they had just come in over Howth. "I couldn't tell you, I was sitting behind you", came Myles' reply. A fieldman called Laurence Hoey also fell into the same category.

Most of the people on the airport payroll were local, from Swords or elsewhere in north County Dublin. Nicky Byrne, the man in charge of the present-day boilerhouse, who has worked in the airport since 1946, remembers them well, and also the hardships of those far-off days. There were no cooking facilities in the boilerhouse, where the boiler was fired by turf; there was a hook for hanging a kettle and the shovel was used for fry-ups. If hot water was wanted for washing, it was drawn straight from the boiler. In those early days, just after the war, Nicky Byrne remembers John Monahan, who eventually became a plumber on the airport staff, and Charlie O'Reilly, the foreman electrician. Over everyone was Paddy O'Daly, who became superintendent of maintenance. Just inside the main hangar, there was a primitive cookhouse, run by a man called Kavanagh. Nicky Byrne remembers: "He had a huge big pan and when we got his back turned, we used to toddle across and, with our forks, fry up our bread".

The Hanleys, from the immediate airport area, were very involved with the airport, mostly on the labouring side, John, who was known as "Plant", Paddy, who was called "Butsey", Peter, who was "Guy" and the other Paddy Hanley, who was nicknamed the "Gaffer". They all had their nicknames, like the other workers at the airport. But all the time, recalls Nicky Byrne, the Aer Rianta personnel were living very much in the shadow of "Big Brother", Aer Lingus.

From the Aer Lingus side, Nicky Byrne has fond memories of general manager,

Timmy Ryan (left) and John Hanley, stoking the domestic hot water boiler at the airport, late 1940s. This boiler system was in use from 1939 until 1950.

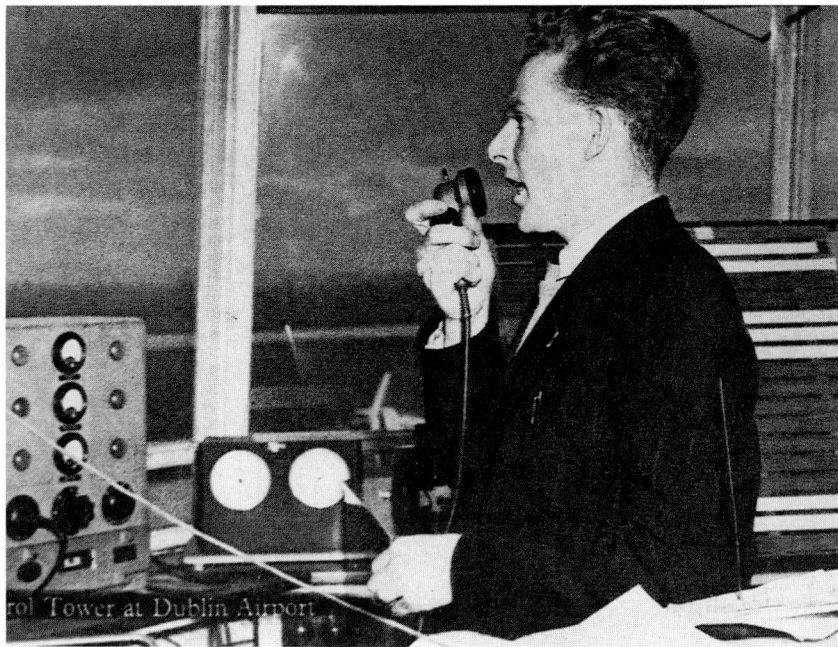

Control officer Noel Brabazon is seen in the Dublin airport control tower, 1948.

Gerry Dempsey: "A fantastic man, he knew everyone by their first name. I suppose he made Aer Lingus, no-one else would have done what he did, a beautiful man". Then there was Dr Bouchier-Hayes, the airport doctor, who was also well-known to everyone on the airport staff, along with Nurse Egan. But the equipment in use by the airport tradespeople remained primitive: Joe O'Rourke remembers that in the hangars, there were just hand saws. "When they got a circular saw, they were nearly throwing a party".

Bicycles were very much in vogue and if anyone wanted a quick repair job done on their machine, they came to the boilerhouse. Just like the famous biscuit tin that held the first set of spares for Aer Lingus when it started in 1936, the boilerhouse staff kept a large tin for bicycle spares. A veritable mound of spare parts was built up and if anyone had trouble with their bicycle, they would leave it into the boilerhouse on their way to work in the morning. In the evening, when everyone was going home, it was like the Charge of the Light Brigade, in Nicky Byrne's colourful estimation.

As a little light relief from the hardships of the post-war years, there were always little "gags", although the airport staff have always taken their work very seriously, and kept all the practical jokes at a minor level, that did not interfere in any way with the workings of the airport. Bill Beck, the engineer, used to work in a hut with a galvanised iron roof. One of the carpenters used to clamber on the roof when he knew that Beck was inside trying to work; the carpenter would run up and down the roof, making the most terrible racket. When Beck rushed outside, all he saw was one of the other carpenters, standing quite innocently, with a hammer and a saw under his arm; his colleague would be lying low on the roof. On other occasions, the tradespeople would be gathered for their tea break in a hut with an old stove for heating; one of the workers would stuff an old satchel down the chimney to smoke out his colleagues. A favourite spare-time occupation with some of the fieldmen was catching hares, for the local greyhound tracks. On one occasion, a purchaser came for his hare, which was put into a sack. Unknown to him, someone had cut a hole in the sack and the hare escaped. There was general consternation at seeing £3 running up the road, after all the trouble that had been taken to catch the animal in the first place.

Once, a lifesize photographic cut-out of a girl model caused equal consternation

Top left: American film star, Judy Garland, arrives at the airport, late 1940s. A temperamental star, her arrival was anticipated with some trepidation by airport staff.
Photograph: G. A. Duncan

George Formby, the north of England comedian famous for his banjo ukulele, arrives at Dublin airport in 1948 with his wife Beryl.
Photograph: G. A. Duncan

American film star and comedian, Danny Kaye, arrives at the airport, late 1940s.
Photograph: G. A. Duncan

Greyhounds ready to board an Aer Rianta charter plane, 1948.
Photograph: G. A. Duncan

John A. Costello, Taoiseach of the Inter-Party government that scrapped the proposed trans-Atlantic air service in 1948. The following year, 1949, *The Irish Times* said that "he ran away to Canada to declare the Republic".
Photograph: The Irish Times

in the boilerhouse. Nicky Byrne remembers that it showed a girl in a polka dot dress, using a Kodak camera. He put an overcoat round the cut-out and propped it up in a shady corner of the boilerhouse; one of the other airport workers was convinced, until the day he died, that it was for real and he always used to say to Nicky Byrne: "I seen what I seen".

There was a great Dublin phrase, much in vogue at the time, which summed up well the public perception of the airport. If someone was asked what they were going to do for the weekend, they would often as not reply: "I'm going out to Aer Lingus". They meant going out to what had already become known in the pubs of the area as the "White Elephant", the original FitzGerald terminal building. But the confusion extended all the way to the top; Jimmy O'Sullivan, who was recruited in 1947 and who later became chief executive of Aer Rianta, remembers that the letter calling him to the job interview came on an Aer Rianta letterhead, while the subsequent letter of appointment came on Aer Lingus paper. Even in those early days, remembers O'Sullivan, when Aer Lingus was beginning its dramatic post-war growth, the terminal building was starting to show its limitations, not only in a lack of space, but in its lack of functional practicality. Even by July, 1947, the terminal building, still only five years completed, was becoming congested with the extra passengers generated by the new Aer Lingus flights and also by the new KLM and Sabena flights.

May, 1947, saw a most significant step forward at Dublin airport: on May 20, KLM arrived at Collinstown at 5.25 pm with a DC3, to begin the first ever service from the airport by a continental European carrier. KLM was starting the Dublin–Manchester–Amsterdam service that it was to run for a further twenty years. The new month saw the first of the Vickers Viking aircraft arrive in Aer Lingus livery; all of them were delivered by the September of that year.

The lifespan of these Vikings with Aer Lingus was short; the fleet was disposed of within a year. Of equally short duration was Aer Rianta's role as a charter aircraft operator. Although Aer Rianta was charged with managing Dublin airport and also acted as a holding company for Aer Lingus, it was decided in 1946 that Aer Rianta would go into the charter business. During the summer of 1947, aircraft became available and the first plane in Aer Rianta livery, a Miles Gemini, arrived at Collinstown on June 9, 1947. Later than year, another Miles Gemini was brought in, along with two Airspeed Consuls.

Aer Rianta was ahead of its time: one of the aims of its new charter division was to operate feeder services from around the country, linking passengers into the main scheduled services. Personnel from the company did a 'Sholto Douglas', travelling round the country looking out for suitable landing sites for the light Gemini aircraft. In the event, it was not until the mid-1980s that the concept of regional airports feeding traffic into the scheduled services from the main airports became a working reality. The other intention of the new division was to operate air taxi and light charter services, but not even Aer Rianta's service to the public in using one of the aircraft to provide sightseeing trips over Dublin could save the concept of the charter service from a fairly swift descent into oblivion. For a time, the four aircraft were used for training purposes by Aer Lingus, before all four were sold off.

On Tuesday, May 25, 1948, a further arrival at Dublin airport gave another glimpse into the future, although, again, much time had to pass, twelve years in fact, before jets came into commercial use with Aer Lingus. The principle of the jet engine had been established during World War II by Sir Frank Whittle, who proved

Mass being celebrated in the main hangar for Dublin airport workers, late 1940s.
Photograph: G. A. Duncan

French film and stage star, Maurice Chevalier, at the airport, late 1940s.
Photograph: G. A. Duncan

that the revolutionary transition from propeller-driven aircraft to jet propulsion did work, and work very effectively. The RAF Gloster Meteor was flown into Dublin on a sales mission by the British Government, which wanted to sell this type of fast combat aircraft to the Air Corps. The jet flew from the RAF base at Horsham St Faith near Norwich in East Anglia (that base is now the civil airport for Norwich) to Dublin in just fifty minutes. The Meteor was followed by a RAF Dakota, with an engineering and maintenance support team.

The sight of the Meteor sitting on the apron at Collinstown proved slightly perplexing for some of the journalists covering the event; clearly, they were a little baffled by the new technology. They commented on the "swallow like" appearance of the new aircraft and said that in flight, it had a peculiar high-pitched whine or whistle, while at close quarters a heat haze could be seen streaming from the jet engines. The newspapers reported that the demonstrations of the new aircraft would take place as far away as possible from the terminal building, because of the intense heat generated by the engines.

The following day, the Meteor was put through its paces on the demonstration flight for the Air Corps. It was a spectacular affair, with the jet roaring across the airfield at 600 mph, vapour trails flaming from the engines. The plane rolled in the sky and dived directly down towards the airfield, from heights of up to 15,000 feet. It made its final run at full speed, just thirty feet above the ground. Flight Lieutenant Scannell, the pilot, looped and rolled, flew upside down, shot straight into the air, rolled over in clouds and flashed down in steep dives with breathtaking speeds, according to one contemporary account. The jet age had arrived at Collinstown in a truly exciting style, yet remembrance of that outstanding event in the history of the airport is curiously muted in the minds of most people who were present at Collinstown that May. More technically knowledgeable people at the airport were quick to realise that jet propulsion was the way of the future for commercial aircraft as well as for defensive purposes. The pilot of the Meteor flew off into the glowering skies, to give final, brief demonstrations at Gormanston and the Curragh, before turning east and heading home.

A much more down-to-earth topic caused as much discussion among the airport workers that May of long ago. Dublin's bakers went on strike; these days, it is very hard to imagine that such an event would cause the slightest ripple in the public consciousness, but in those days it was a matter of grave concern. The dispute went on for three weeks. The bakers eventually settled for an extra eleven shillings a week, a lot of money then; the average craftsman's wage in the airport was about £3 10s a week. But the bakers' strike caused such consternation in the Dublin area that the few bakery shops that were able to provide their own supplies attracted huge queues of people. There was much hardship at the airport, too, at this time, when deflationary measures were taken as a corrective to the over-optimism of the immediate post-war years.

In 1947, a sister company of Aer Lingus was formed, Aerlínte Éireann, to operate a trans-Atlantic service. Five Lockheed Constellations were ordered; one of them, the *Saint Brigid,* was the first to fly into Dublin airport, on Saturday, September 27, 1947. Its arrival created an enormous amount of public excitement and interest and, despite the fact that, not for the first time, there was a CIE bus strike, some 12,000 people flocked to Collinstown on the Sunday to see the newly arrived "Connie". They came by car and bicycle, and even walked up the airport road from Santry, such was their enthusiasm. But no sooner had Aerlínte Éireann taken delivery of the new "Connies" than the incoming Inter-Party government decided, on economy grounds, to scrap the proposed trans-Atlantic service before it had even begun. The five Constellations were put into service on Aer Lingus' European routes, but they were too big; by the summer of 1948, all the "Connies", symbol of a brave new

Clement Attlee, the British prime minister, arrives at Dublin airport during the term of the Inter-Party government, 1948-51. His escorts include from left, Seán MacBride, Minister for External Affairs, William Norton, Tánaiste and Lord Rugby, British Ambassador. Attlee was a taciturn man; of him, it was said that he never used one word where none would do.
Photograph: G. A. Duncan

aviation venture that did not work out, had been sold to BOAC.

Jimmy O'Sullivan, who was the Aer Lingus personnel manager at the time, was given the unpleasant task of giving the many people recruited for this new service their cards, as well as a small "sweetener" in the form of a bonus. As a result, O'Sullivan was given the nickname of "Sack 'em O'Sullivan", which is remembered even to this day by older stalwarts who were in the airport in the late 1940s. The political decision of February, 1948 to abandon the trans-Atlantic plans was not the only harsh measure being taken at Aer Lingus. In the first six months of 1948, 259 Aer Lingus workers were laid off; it was a time of great economic hardship and jobs of any kind were virtually non-existent. Grown men, used to the ways of the world, were seen leaving the airport for the last time, as airline employees, in tears. Some of the routes which had been opened up to then were closed down, like Dublin–Belfast and Dublin–Rome. Sabena withdrew its new Dublin–Brussels service. As a further economy measure, the concession of free travel on the airport bus, which ran from Cathal Brugha Street in the centre of Dublin, near the Gresham Hotel, was withdrawn and passengers now had to pay a one shilling fare.

Despite the economies, there was growth in the use of the airport. In 1946, passengers using Collinstown totalled 70,082 and the following year, that figure doubled to 140,404, while aircraft movements were a healthy 18,525. Nevertheless, at this period, Aer Rianta was not making a profit; in its financial year to March, 1947, it turned in a deficit of £19,220.

A young economist who had just joined Aer Lingus, Garret FitzGerald, came up with the idea of reduced fares for midweek flights. Nineteen forty-nine saw the introduction of the highly successful Dawnflights and Starflights to London — they were less successful to Paris — which enabled passengers to travel off-peak at reduced fares. This innovation began to swell the numbers of passengers using the airport. Although all the economy measures taken in 1948 had affected very largely Aer Lingus staff, and had little impact on the fifty or so people who worked at the airport under the Aer Rianta banner, the increases in the numbers of people using Aer Lingus services only boded well for the future. There was even a start made to the business of pilgrimage flights; in those early years of aviation, Aer Lingus did not have the capacity to cope with the numbers of Irish pilgrims who wanted to go to

Maureen O'Hara, the Irish film actress who made her name in Hollywood, arrives home at Dublin airport, late 1940s.
Photograph: G. A. Duncan

Margot Fonteyn, the English dancer, signs the airport restaurant visitors' book for Johnny Oppermann, the restaurant manager, 1949. That year, she won her first international acclaim, for her performances in the US in *Sleeping Beauty*.

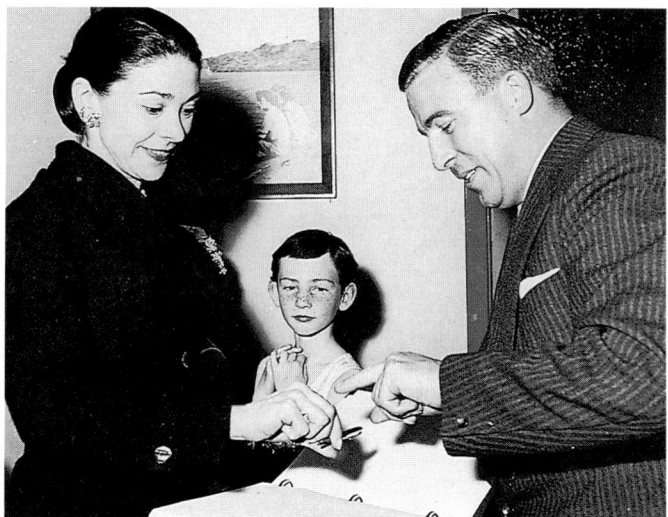

Lourdes, so all this traffic was handled by charter companies. The first major charter pilgrim flight was organised by Sabena, and flew from Dublin direct to Lourdes on August 16, 1948; it was a tedious flight in a DC3, taking some five hours.

In October that year, a sad event took place, when two United States Air Force C-47 aircraft flew into Dublin with the bodies of Irishmen who had been killed in Europe fighting in the American forces during World War II. Seven bodies were returned home and there was a moving religious service on the airfield (the church had yet to be built), before the coffins went to their various home towns for burial.

In October, 1948, Collinstown nearly received its first diversion from Shannon, a Trans Ocean Airways DC4, with a party of Italian emigrants flying to Venezuela. Shannon was closed because of fog, so the pilot diverted to Dublin, but he was unable to make contact with the control tower, since there was not have a common frequency. The multi-channel VHF radios now used had not been developed then, and aircraft were restricted to a limited number of frequencies. The pilot of this aircraft made a 180° turn and flew back to Shannon, where the weather had lifted sufficiently to enable the plane to land. It was not until the summer of 1950 that Dublin airport received its first diversion from Shannon.

Fog indirectly caused the crash of a charter flight out of Dublin airport on November 11, 1948. A Rapide of Mannin Airways, based at Ronaldsway, Isle of Man, was chartered to bring a party of holidaymakers back to the island from Dublin. It collected its passengers at Collinstown and took off without refuelling. Fog over the island prevented the plane landing at Ronaldsway, so it diverted to Liverpool. The dramatic Mayday message came through from the pilot as the plane was flying up the Mersey: "out of petrol, going down". The plane crashed into the river and only one of the nine people on board survived, by swimming ashore.

Interesting aircraft came to Dublin during 1948, as Aer Lingus sought the successor to the DC3, which was a pre-war design, even though it was consolidating its fleet with DC3s at the time.

The first of the "hopefuls" to arrive was a Saab Scandia, which flew from Sweden on August 16, 1948, to be demonstrated to Aer Lingus and government officials. In the event, the Scandias were not bought and the Vikings being used by Aer Lingus were quickly sold off in favour of its DC3 fleet consolidation. It was some years before the airline started using Viscounts and Fokker Friendships. Some extensions took place at the airport, with the construction of freight and cabin service depots for Aer Lingus and a garage for the maintenance of airport vehicles. A staff restaurant was provided in temporary accommodation. Work started on additional taxi strips, on an extension to No. 2 hangar and on the construction of a third hangar.

Nineteen forty-nine proved to be a buoyant year for the airport, with a total of 204,737 passengers, of whom 193,000 were carried by Aer Lingus. The remaining 11,737 passengers were carried by KLM to Amsterdam and by charter companies, mostly operating pilgrimages. During the year, both Sabena and KLM operated pilgrimage flights to Lourdes out of Dublin. Dublin airport had some distinguished visitors, too. Prince Bernhard of the Netherlands piloted the DC3 of the Royal Dutch Flight, on August 1, 1949. He was met at the airport by the President, Seán T. O'Kelly; the prince was en route to the Horse Show. Over the years, this plane, sometimes with the prince at the controls, was a frequent visitor to Collinstown, well into the late 1960s. Subsequently, the plane was preserved at the Aviodome museum at Schiphol airport, Amsterdam.

Another aircraft visitor in royal livery that year was a C–47 of the Royal Flight of King Farouk of Egypt. The plane was on an unofficial visit to Dublin; the crew had been to the Paris air show and then received Sikorsky helicopter training in Britain. Group Captain Hassan Akef, ADC to the king, had been to Dublin in March, 1946, for the North Atlantic route conference and in June, 1949, had decided to fly over from London to renew acquaintance with the city.

The previous month, May, there had been a visit by a thirty-six strong delegation

The airport football team, 1949/50.

Aer Rianta carpenters and painters at work May, 1946. In the photograph are from left to right: Jimmy Ellis and Johnny Butler (both painters), John Monaghan (labourer), Charlie Craddock (foreman) and Kit Johnson (carpenter).

from Iceland, including that country's president and eight members of the Althing (the Icelandic parliament), who were on a tour of Scandinavian airports and decided to take in Dublin on the way home. After lunch in the airport, organised with his customary aplomb by Johnny Oppermann, the party went on a sightseeing tour of the city before departing for Reykjavik. Before they left, the Icelandic consensus was that the Dublin airport terminal was one of the most magnificent in the world.

A distinguished visitor from a new independent state came to Dublin as well, Pandit Nehru, the Indian prime minster. India had only gained its independence from Britain in 1947, so the party created considerable interest at Collinstown. The aircraft was a Beechcraft Expeditor, the military version of the Beech 18, and it flew in from Northolt, near London, on April 29, so that Nehru could visit the President and see the Dáil in session. At the airport, he ended up checking the correct time with P. P. O'Reilly, who had recently begun his long commentating career with Radio Éireann, now RTE. The Taoiseach, John A. Costello, was not amused by this leap over protocol boundaries.

In the August of that year, there was another distinguished visitor from abroad, Lt General Beyers, chief of the general staff of the South African armed forces. He had been on official business in London and decided to fly over to Dublin in a South African air force C–47, in order to pay a brief courtesy visit. He was greeted at Collinstown by the Chief of Staff of the Irish army. Politicians were very much in the news that year, because it was in 1949 that the declaration of the Republic was made. John A. Costello, as head of the Inter-Party government, was attending a conference in Canada, when Hector Legge, then editor of the *Sunday Independent,* ran a feature suggesting that Costello was about to declare the Republic. The day after that feature appeared in print, Costello was goaded into making the declaration; *The Irish Times* said that he had run away to Canada to declare the Republic.

A new newspaper hit the streets in September that year, the *Sunday Press.* Sean Lemass, who in government had done so much to promote the progress of Irish aviation in the mid- and late 1930s, was at this stage out of political office, but was managing director of the *Irish Press* and as such was responsible for the launch of the *Sunday Press.* Eamon de Valera, also out of political office, was present at the launch to sign copies. But the year saw the end of a long era in public transport in Dublin; the last tram ran from Nelson's Pillar, by the GPO, to Dalkey, during the summer of 1949, amid scenes of nostalgic excitement. Huge crowds turned out, not only to take a last trip on the tram, but to see the end of one of Dublin's landmark institutions.

As the tram service was being wound down, KLM upgraded its service from Dublin through Manchester to Schiphol. The airline replaced its DC3s on the route with Convair 240 aircraft, which reduced the flying time from Dublin to Manchester to one hour. Ironically, when Aer Lingus pilots went on strike, just for the day, during that same month, to protest against the company's failure to provide them with a superannuation scheme, a charter plane arrived at Collinstown carrying Lord Douglas of Kirtleside, chairman of BEA and another titled gentleman, Lord Amhurst, a BEA director, who both flew in to attend an Aer Lingus board meeting. Another unusual visitor to Dublin airport was a horse, due to take part in the Champion Stakes at the Curragh. It had been planned to ship the horse to Ireland, but bad weather at Holyhead for several days meant that in order to ensure that the horse arrived on time, a Silver City Airways Bristol freighter flew the animal in at the last minute.

A trial consignment of ox tongue and liver, packed in barrels, was flown out from Collinstown on board an SAS DC4, bound for Gothenburg, but it was not until the mid-1960s that the airport built up a substantial charter traffic in frozen meat exports. More pilgrims flew out to Lourdes, the traffic handled by Sabena and KLM.

A US government delegation had discussions with the Irish government to try and secure landing rights at Dublin for American carriers, but the Irish side stuck fast to its established position that Shannon was the designated trans-Atlantic airport. A new type of aircraft was seen at Collinstown for the first time in 1949, the prototype Viscount that made the 285-mile flight from Northolt, near London, in 70 minutes. Its arrival coincided with an IATA technical conference being held in Dublin under the auspices of Aer Lingus. The plane came to Collinstown in early December; reporters who went for a flight in the plane noted that the weather at ground level was dreary, with a cold, biting wind and much rain. At 15,000 feet, the sun shone warmly and a rainbow appeared through the clouds. The flight was smooth and the cabin comfortable; the Viscount went on to become a mainstay of the Aer Lingus fleet for many years and became a very familiar sight on the apron at Dublin airport.

Despite the increase in aircraft movements, the number of people directly employed by Aer Rianta remained static, at around the fifty mark. Landing fees by Aer Lingus and other airlines had to be paid to Aer Rianta, but James O'Sullivan, later to become Aer Rianta chief executive, remembers that everything was done to avoid paying Aer Rianta too much. Systems were primitive, as Paddy O'Daly recollects. Initially, export cargo was handled from two temporary huts put up at the back of the boilerhouse, later moving to more spacious accommodation in one of the hangars. But all the sheets containing information relating to the cargoes were literally pigeon-holed and staff had to look up individual sheets if they wanted any details of a cargo, a far cry from today's computerised methods.

A vivid instance of the rivalry between Aer Lingus and Aer Rianta at that time is given by Paddy O'Daly. Michael Dargan, who later became chairman of Aer Lingus, was personnel manager and O'Daly remembers him coming into his office one day, announcing that he (Dargan) was setting up the staff and services department. He took all the personnel files.

In 1949, there was another appointment at the airport, Canon Kelly, parish priest of Swords, who succeeded Fr Toher. Shortly afterwards, negotiations began for the provision of a site at Collinstown for the building of an airport church, although this was a protracted process, not completed until 1964, when it became the first modern church in the Dublin diocese. Aer Rianta maintenance men had already devised a temporary solution to the problem of offering Mass: they built a wooden altar, and this served, like the ancient Ark of Israel, being carried around from place to place in the airport. Mass was originally offered in the then customs hall at the north end of the original terminal building by Fr Toher, who on occasion had a "deputy", a priest from a religious order in Raheny. From its first location, Mass was offered in a variety of locations, including the staff canteen, No. 1 and No. 2 hangars and back to the terminal building, until such time as the church was finished.

Bill Beck, the airport engineer, had a number of exceptionally able and interesting "characters" working under him, like Paddy O'Daly, superintendent of maintenance, who was Beck's chief assistant, and Charlie Craddock, who was general foreman. Jim Gormley was cleaning supervisor. Charlie O'Reilly was the airport electrician. Jack Bannon, the present head of the airport police, has a long family connection with the airport, going back almost until its opening; his father, Jim, was a foreman at Collinstown.

Bill Beck remembers the cleaning ladies: the elite. Mary McDonald introduced herself to him as the senior charwoman (there was a strict hierarchical structure at all levels of airport staff), while another name of note on the cleaning staff was Mrs Salmon, whose territory was the staircase in the terminal building. Beck also remembers a typical story about Gerry Dempsey. One night in the late 1940s, when Johnny Oppermann was starting to build up the original airport restaurant, Bill Beck was standing in the concourse when Dempsey came along, checking early, as was his fashion, that all the small points of detail were in proper order. He asked Beck

The first fast food equipment at the airport, 1949. Jimmy Kilbride (left) demonstrates the new Swiss device that not only tenderised steak but grilled it too, before the intrigued gaze of Johnny Oppermann (centre) and Stan Clifford, then the head chef.

Paddy O'Daly, superintendent of maintenance when the airfield was being developed after the Emergency. His son, Colin, trained in the airport restaurant and now runs the Park restaurant at Blackrock, County Dublin.
Photograph: Neil MacDougald

the name of the woman scrubbing the stairs. "Mrs Salmon", was the reply. "How do you spell it?" "Just like the fish". "Should I know her?" "Well", replied Beck, "she was here when the terminal was being built". Dempsey did not know her, but he went over to her. Mrs Salmon curtsied. Dempsey said: "Good evening, Mrs Salmon, are you keeping well? You know, you're a long time with us". Beck recalls that the cleaning lady was delighted with the recognition and recollects that Dempsey had this same "hands on" approach to everyone working at the airport.

Dr Bouchier-Hayes had an emergency case one day at Collinstown. Colonel Tuohy, the assistant airport manager, collapsed at the airport, bleeding heavily. An ambulance was summoned by Dr Bouchier-Hayes; Tuohy was taken to Mercer's Hospital for an emergency operation. A few days later, when Tuohy came round, Beck went to see him in hospital and he confided in Beck: "The doctor came round here this morning with the usual matron and nurses, but he told them to get lost, as he wanted to talk to me privately. He sat on the end of the bed and said: 'Michael, I operated on you a week ago and it was a near thing. You've had your last drink and that's a fact'". Until the day he died, five years later, he never touched another drop. Arthur Walls, who is now chairman of Ryanair, who started working for Aer Lingus in 1947, remembers that Aer Lingus was frequently criticised at the time for employing people who were either lazy, incompetent or had drink problems. The number of bad managers then was high; his explanation was simple. With civil aviation expanding so fast, the only people with experience and in any way suitable for recruitment all had experience in the armed forces. The talents required there were very different from those needed to manage a budget or handle union problems, he recollects. This syndrome of recruiting from the military extended also to Aer Rianta, although as Bill Beck recalls, not all recruitment channels were quite so orthodox. According to Beck, Charlie O'Reilly, the electrician, had been in jail in Crumlin Road, Belfast, in the early 1920s. A then colleague of his, also in for political activities, was Seán Ó hUadhaigh, the first chairman of Aer Lingus.

O'Reilly had been working as an electrician at the ESB and wrote to Ó hUadhaigh asking him for a job, reminding him of the jail episode. The airport job soon followed. Others came by more conventional routes: James Moran, the chief accountant, came from Stokes Kennedy Crowley, and had an insistence on tried and trusted traditional ways of presenting the accounts. Up to thirty versions of the annual accounts could be produced, although the final version did not differ greatly from the first. Christopher Martin, now retired, who joined the accounting staff of Aer Rianta in 1949, remembers that it was one of the very few areas where the company had a degree of autonomy at this time. He remembers well James Moran and his rather austere approach; Moran was responsible for the accounting functions in both Aer Lingus and Aer Rianta, although both organisations presented separate sets of accounts. There were some fine people on the accounting staff then, recollects Martin, including Alf Donohoe, who was Liverpool Irish and who always prided himself on his trade union connections. At this stage, the Aer Rianta and Aer Lingus head offices were in Upper O'Connell Street and Martin remembers that the Aer Rianta accounts office had a variety of central locations, including one in Beresford Place. It was physically separate from the rest of Aer Rianta functions, which only extended to Dublin airport (Shannon was the responsibility of the Department of Industry and Commerce and Cork airport was still at the gestation stage).

Since it was so physically separate from the airport operations, the small number of staff, no more than two or three, in the Aer Rianta accounts office, enjoyed a certain autonomy that was the envy of their colleagues at the airport. More often than not, the main contact between the accounts office and the airport was in the form of phone calls to Pearl Kirwan (a member of the Fairview family of undertakers), who was secretary to Colonel Delamer. As Paddy O'Daly remarks: "Aer Rianta was born and died before being born again". This period during the late 1940s was a deadly time at the airport, as Aer Lingus ran the operations side of the airport very much as a subsidiary to its own aviation operation. The shades remained

A view of a staircase inside the original terminal building at Dublin airport.
Photograph: Neil MacDougald

The original Dublin airport terminal building.
Photograph: Neil MacDougald

down on Aer Rianta for nearly another twenty years. But the 1940s came to an end with a certain feeling of optimism, both nationally, because of the declaration of the Republic, and at the airport, because of the clear signs that aviation was the way of the future in the world of transport. There were transports of delight, too, at the New Year's eve dinner dance organised by Johnny Oppermann in the airport restaurant, to see out the '40s and toast in the '50s with his customary exuberant style. In aviation terms, the 1950s could only be better than the 1940s.

Front page, *The Irish Times*, January 19, 1950 — ten years after Collinstown was officially opened.

CHAPTER IV

The end of a monopoly

THE new year, 1950, was seen in with the customary dinner dance in the airport restaurant, organised with his usual panache by Johnny Oppermann. There was much banter and chatter over the dinner; even the formal Colonel Delamer, the airport manager, was seen to enjoy the proceedings, while his deputy, Colonel Tuohy, was able to let his hair down and really enjoy the evening. After the dinner came the dancing, which went on until the small hours. There was still no late-night flying into or out of the airport, so it was a special concession for the airport restaurant to stay open so late. The rostrum area for the band, and the special floor area for dancing, so carefully designed by Desmond FitzGerald when he was designing the terminal building fifteen years previously, were being put to good use. Nineteen fifty was Holy Year and the immediate intentions of many of the people enjoying the New Year's dinner dance that night was to take part in the celebrations, in Rome, if at all possible. Later the Pope imparted his pastoral apostolic benediction to the staffs of Aer Rianta and Aer Lingus; they had presented him with a set of vestments during Holy Year.

Colonel Bill Delamer, Dublin airport manager, 1946–66.
Photograph: G. A. Duncan

But the start of the decade was signalled by much more than a rapid development of the pilgrim traffic out of the airport. Many of the people who were to play a key role in the future development of Dublin airport, like Martin Dully, later to become a chief executive of Aer Rianta, were beginning their careers at Collinstown in the early 1950s. For the decade as a whole, one of the most important events was the start of London–Dublin services in 1957 by British European Airways, which was the first breach in the near monopoly of services held until then by Aer Lingus.

The other event of lasting significance, as far as the airport was concerned, was the recommencement of the Aer Lingus trans-Atlantic service in 1958, followed by the introduction of commercial jets on the route in 1960, just twelve years after the first jet had put in an appearance at Collinstown.

But in January and February, 1950, detailed planning started for the great number of charter flights that were scheduled to go to Rome for the Holy Year. The traffic began in April and one British charter company, Hunting Air Travel, did particularly well out of the interest in travel to Rome. It advertised in the *Catholic Herald* for charter flights from Dublin to Rome; the special fare was £27, compared to the normal return air fare then, of over £50. The company's Viking aircraft could carry 27 passengers and, with each party, a priest was carried free of charge. Hunting Air Travel ran the charters on behalf of Aer Lingus and various religious organisations. On April 28, Dr D'Alton, Archbishop of Armagh and later Primate of all-Ireland, went to Rome on one of Hunting Air Travel's Vikings. These flights continued throughout the Holy Year and, while the traffic between Dublin and Rome was very

Airport viewing balcony, 1950.

heavy, so too was the pilgrimage traffic to Lourdes in south-west France building up. In September, 1950, Hunting Air Travel flew seven flights to Lourdes, carrying 189 invalids from the Dublin diocese, accompanied by medical attendants and nurses.

Throughout the 1950s, the traffic to Lourdes became steadily more concentrated, so much so that in 1958 Aer Rianta erected a large wooden shed. This was quickly dubbed the "Lourdes terminal" and had special facilities for coping with the wheelchairs of many of the invalid travellers. The terminal was in use for this pilgrimage traffic until the end of the 1960s. On August 19, 1950, the airport sports day saw some notable wins for Aer Rianta staff, including John Hanley. He won the Garland Cup and the Aer Lingus Social & Athletics Association Cup and was presented with his prizes by Mrs May Dempsey. Gerry Giltrap, then of Aer Lingus, won in the 16 lb shot class.

Some tragic crashes occurred during the decade. In March, 1950, an Avro Tudor, a new type of aircraft for the airport, arrived with a party of Welsh rugby supporters, en route to an international match in Belfast. The Avro Tudor stayed at Dublin airport for two days, until 2 pm on the Sunday, March 12, when it took off for its return flight to Llandow airport, Cardiff. Attempting to land at Llandow, the aircraft overshot the runway and eighty out of the eighty-three people on board were killed. It was the heaviest death toll in a civilian air crash until then. At the beginning of 1952, the first crash of an Aer Lingus plane caused a deep sense of sorrow at the airport. Ironically, at the end of 1950, Aer Lingus had been awarded the Cumberbatch Trophy by the Guild of Airline Pilots and Navigators for safety and reliability in operations. The *St Kevin,* a DC3, returning to Dublin from London on the night of January 10, 1952, came down in Snowdonia, Wales, with the loss of all twenty passengers and three crew.

The cause of the crash was never discovered and neither was the wreckage of the DC3 recovered: it became a permanent tomb for the unfortunate souls on board.

The early 1950s were a quiet time at the airport; the heady days of expansion in the late 1940s were over and the main ambition of Aer Lingus was to consolidate its cross-channel routes. It was rather a dull, uneventful time at the airport, which matched in many ways the mood of the country. True, there was high political drama in 1951, when the Archbishop of Dublin, Dr John Charles McQuaid, and other bishops, objected to the "Mother and Child" scheme, which was intended to give free medical care to mothers and their children up to sixteen years of age. Dr Noel Browne, the Minister for Health, resigned, precipitating the collapse of the Inter-Party government. In the general election of that year, Fianna Fáil returned to power, with Eamon de Valera as Taoiseach once again. There had been other kinds of drama, too, like the two month-long bank strike, while the old Abbey Theatre burned down in a spectacular fire.

A golf dinner in the airport restaurant, 1950. From left: Colonel Bill Delamer, airport manager, Mrs May Dempsey, Mrs Helen Delamer, Johnny Oppermann and J. F. Dempsey, general manager, Aer Lingus and Aer Rianta.

This new inward passenger lounge was opened at Dublin airport in 1950.

A scene in the departures bar, Dublin airport, 1950. From left: Angela Cogan (deceased), June Greene, Tony Gavin, Carmel Duff and Jack Doyle, then with Aer Lingus, later to be a manager of Dublin airport.

But in the country at large, life was quiet and humdrum, a reaction perhaps to the years of austerity during the Emergency. The last of the wartime rationing and shortages were being phased out, but as yet, there were no great signs of prosperity on the horizon and the biggest queues remained those for the mail boat at Dun Laoghaire, packed with suitcase-laden emigrants, heading for a new life in Britain. At the airport, the most striking event of that year was on Sunday, June 11.

An open air terrace café was opened, located near the tarmac and adjacent to the terminal building, where on fine sunny days, intending passengers and visitors to the airport could sit and nonchalantly enjoy a drink or two, watching the DC3s taxiing. In July that year, there was a real touch of show business at the airport, when a United States Air Force band arrived aboard four Fairchild C–82 Packets. These capacious aircraft carried the band and all their equipment, on their European tour; they parked in a line on the south ramp near No. 1 hangar. When the band arrived at the airport, Aer Rianta organised some stylish hospitality in the form of a cocktail party in the airport restaurant. Colonel Delamer, Colonel Tuohy and all the other military men then connected with the airport were in their element, surrounded by the American air force musicians. The USAF band gave a foot-stomping performance in the Theatre Royal that night (in the early 1950s, as now, Dublin often hosted concerts and performances by leading international celebrities) and flew out the next morning, in their Packets, to their next engagement, at Frederickshaven in Germany.

Statistics released in August of that year, 1950, showed that in the financial year 1949/50, Dublin airport had enjoyed its busiest ever time, with a record total of 212,661 passengers. In addition, there were 2,358 tons of freight and mail carried, almost double the previous year's total. Interestingly, Aer Rianta had reversed its earlier policy of discouraging visitors other than intending passengers from going to the airport.

Visitors had to pay for this new-found privilege, however, and in the 1949–50 period, 82,113 visitors paid a total of £2,865 to see the airport. Further improvements were being carried out at the airport at that time, including the building and commissioning of runway 23 ILS and the installation of radio direction finding equipment. Alterations were made to several huts, to improve facilities for flight crews and for cargo handling. But in the Aer Rianta fiscal year of 1950/51, there was still a fairly substantial deficit — £10,953 — in running the airport, and landing fees, which were the main source of airport revenue, were increased by 12½ per cent.

Ned Keating, who had joined Aer Rianta in 1949 as a cleaner and who transferred to the police and fire service eight years later, has very clear recollections of the type of passengers using the airport. Despite the big rise in passenger numbers, air travel was still very much the prerogative of the wealthy and the upper class (not necessarily synonymous). In those days, he recollects, most of the people travelling seemed to belong to the Ascendency class, lords and ladies up from the country, retired colonels; very seldom would a working man take to the skies, unless in a family emergency, like a bereavement. One lord of the realm whom Ned Keating recalls well was Lord Powerscourt, who used to come to the airport in a big, gas-guzzling American car. Later, he exchanged it for a more down to earth and practical Morris Minor. Keating has memories of his lordship getting into a tantrum over car parking.

Another man well-known at the airport in those far-off days was a businessman nicknamed the "sweet man", because he owned a sweet factory in Dublin. He had the lavish habit of tipping airport staff with £1 notes, equal to a third of a week's wages in those days, and staff almost queued up to carry his bags. Then there were the really wealthy people who used Dublin airport, like the Aly Khan, who had a stud farm in County Kildare. He did not use scheduled flights, as he had his own aircraft. Film stars like Rita Hayworth would come to Ireland to stay at the Aly Khan's stud farm and the limousine came up to the airport to collect them. Then there were the other film stars of the 1950s who came to Dublin to promote a new film, or perhaps take part in a charity event, people of world renown like Bob Hope and Bing Crosby. The Artane Boys Band stood on the apron, playing out Crosby in style. "I remember Bing Crosby walking towards them, with a dour look; then as he approached, it all changed and he went into his 'Bells of St Mary's' routine. He picked up like a real actor, conducting the band, saying farewell to all the boys in the band". Danny Kaye was another regular passenger through Dublin airport in the 1950s. Apart from film stars and the religious groups, headed by Cardinal D'Alton, going to or from Rome, there were no State visits. But there was a regular procession of politicians.

Ned Keating recollects one rather forlorn occasion at the airport, involving Eamon de Valera and Frank Aiken, who had a distinguished career as Minister for External Affairs. During the Coalition Government of the mid-1950s, when de Valera and Aiken were out of office, they were at the airport. Keating recalls them standing in the concourse, talking to a third party, waiting for nearly an hour for a car to pick them up. Protocol at the airport is always a matter of exquisitely timed niceties and in the 1950s, the approach to protocol was even more formal than it is today. Keating says that not one person on the airport staff on that occasion would approach de Valera and Aiken, to offer even a cup of coffee, for fear of breaking the rigorous protocol arrangements.

Protocol was well observed in November, 1950, when Colonel Oswald W. Lunde, air attaché at the US embassy in Dublin, decided to ask some friends for the weekend. They arrived in two Boeing B–50D aircraft of Strategic Air Command which were by far the largest aircraft ever to have touched down at Collinstown. Although Colonel Lunde insisted that the thirty airmen had come to Dublin simply to enjoy the weekend, the event was marked by a splendid party on the Sunday afternoon at the airport. The Taoiseach, John A. Costello, attended, and so too did members of the government, the judiciary, the army, the air corps and the diplomatic corps, who were also shown over the vast aircraft. The public appetite for unusual aircraft was whetted by the arrival of these enormous American bomber aircraft. *The Irish Times* reported: "Between 3 and 4 pm on the Sunday afternoon, the approaches to the airport were jammed with cars, cyclists and people on foot and eventually, the assistance of the civic guards had to be obtained to clear the traffic. The crowd, believed to be the biggest ever assembled at the airport, far exceeded the airport authorities' expectations". For a mere weekend party, it was some event! When the two planes left at noon on the Monday, the roar of their engines drowned out all conversation in and around the airport. There was no wind at Collinstown that day and when the B–50Ds took off from runway 23, they took the entire length of the concrete to get airborne. In time-honoured military tradition, the two planes came back round for a low level circuit of the field, dipped their wings in salute and finally headed for home, having given Collinstown and Dublin a weekend to remember.

January 19, 1951, was the eleventh anniversary of the opening of Dublin airport. It was close to handling its millionth passenger. By the end of the previous year, Dublin airport had recorded 920,000 passengers and was the third busiest airport in these islands, only exceeded by the two London airports of Heathrow and Northolt. Nineteen fifty had seen a total of 233,576 passengers using Dublin airport, and a grand total of 19,510 aircraft arrivals and departures.

At the beginning of January, 1951, there was a rare visit to Dublin by a BEA aircraft; that airline's scheduled services between Dublin and Heathrow did not start for another six years. The charter DC3 came to Dublin with delegates of the Committee of Purchasers of Aviation Materials, which was meeting in Dublin; the

This Merryweather foam carrier, the first to be stationed at the Dublin airport fire station, is seen rolling out in 1950.

Air traffic control, Dublin airport, 1952.

New Year's Eve gala dinner dance at the Dublin airport restaurant, 1951. Included in the photograph are Colonel Delamer, airport manager (third from right), Johnny Oppermann (second from left), Jimmy Flahive, head chef (second from right) and Liam Lynch, airport restaurant manager (third from left). Note the size of the cigar boxes, and also the soda water syphon.

purpose of the flight was to show what could be done by a British instrumentation company, Smiths, to assist a European company to avoid dollar expenditure. The same plane returned to Dublin in the late 1950s, when it was operating on BEA scheduled routes. Another charter early that year, in March, was by KLM and brought the German soccer team to Ireland for a match. All commercial aviation was banned in Germany by the four powers occupying the country, a ban that was not lifted until 1955, when Lufthansa became operational. For its financial year to March 31, 1951, Aer Rianta turned in a profit of £3,884. When Gerry Dempsey announced the news to the staff, there was an "almighty roar of applause", according to *Aer Scéala*, the Aer Lingus staff magazine.

There were some unusual visitors to Dublin airport on the pilgrimage charters during the summer of 1951: three Savoia Marchetti SM.82s, in the colours of the Order of St John of God of Jerusalem (the Order of Malta). These planes were bombers belonging to the Italian air force, temporarily converted, but they flew thirty-four flights between Dublin and Lourdes that year, with one of the hangars being used as a clearing station. At the end of the year, bad weather caused the temporary closure of Shannon, since the runways there were flooded, and many flights were diverted to Collinstown. These diversions were not too popular with the airport catering staff. They had to prepare breakfast for the passengers and crew of the first TWA Constellation to arrive. Such was the public excitement with all the diversions from Shannon during those storm-bound days at the end of December, 1951, that unusually large crowds of sightseers came to Collinstown to see the "Connies" arriving and departing, including one TWA flight from New York en route to Bombay. A total of 275,994 passengers used the airport in 1951.

Nineteen fifty-two was a quiet year at Dublin airport, although from May 1, it opened for twenty-four hours a day. Previously, it had closed at midnight. The other necessary development at the airport was the provision of a new staff cycle park,

An unusual view of the terminal building, early 1950s, from a car interior.

A dusk view of the terminal building at Dublin airport, 1952.
Photograph: Aer Lingus

beside No. 2 hangar. A new boiler plant was installed under the supervision of Bill Beck, the airport engineer. 5,000 square yards of apron was relaid and grass areas between the terminal building and the apron were concreted. An extra storey was added to the terminal building. Colonel Michael Tuohy was promoted to assistant airport manager. One of the last aviation links with World War II, a converted Halifax bomber, paid its last visit to Dublin during 1952. The Lancashire Aircraft Corporation was using one of these aircraft types to bring in newspapers as late as June, 1952, and the last visit to Collinstown by a Halifax took place in September that year. Also at the end of that year, an attempt was made to restart the trans-Atlantic service. Agreement was reached with an American airline, Seaboard & Western, for Aer Linte to lease DC4s, and, with a Fianna Fáil government back in power, official

An aerial view of the airport complex at Collinstown, in the early 1950s.

approval was given for the project. But unacceptable limitations by the US Civil Aeronautics Board meant that the service had to be postponed until 1958. In March, 1952, the joint committee of Aer Rianta and Aer Lingus workers, set up the previous year to raise funds for the proposed airport church, began work in earnest. Fundraising events included a dance in Clery's Ballroom. Admission was five shillings. It took until 1959 to raise £9,000.

One development, however, did get under way in 1952; Bord Fáilte was set up to promote Ireland's attractions as a tourist destination. It was destined to play a major role in developing Ireland's tourist traffic and hence the numbers of passengers using Dublin airport. However, the following year, 1953, there was a serious slump in the tourist trade. Hotel bookings by English visitors to Ireland were a quarter lower in 1953 than in 1952. Since almost a third of Aer Lingus passengers at this stage were British tourists coming to Ireland, the revenue implications for Dublin airport were serious. Passengers travelling by air accounted for just under twenty per cent of people travelling cross-channel from Dublin: the rest went by sea.

By a strange coincidence, the year that Bord Fáilte was started, Martin Dully, its current executive chairman, began his aviation career with Aer Lingus. Jack Bannon, who is the head of the police and fire service at Dublin airport, and whose father had worked as a foreman at the airport, remembers vividly that Dully began as clerk in cargo. "He was a great worker and it sticks in my mind that a man could come in at the very bottom and work his way up to become chief executive of Aer Rianta".

Two events in 1953 remain in the public consciousness. One had little direct connection with the airport, except for the increase in passenger numbers. An Tostal was designed as a community festival on a nationwide scale. Today, it only survives in one place, Drumshanbo in County Leitrim, but nearly forty years ago, it generated immense excitement in a country dulled by years of shortages and rationing. Yet despite all the excitement of that festival, one incident remains in the public mind. The large flower bowl on O'Connell Bridge, which was hurled into the River Liffey

The main bar, just outside the restaurant in the terminal building, 1952.

The first walk round shop was opened at Dublin airport in the early 1950s. Since air sickness tablets and other medicaments were sold, a qualified pharmacist had to be employed. That pharmacist was Maura Edwards, who was later killed in a tragic car crash near Swords, along with her two children. Also in this photograph are Johnny Oppermann (left) and Frank Hanratty.

Dublin airport restaurant, 1952.
Photograph: Jack Coady

by a group of students, was promptly christened the "Tomb of the Unknown Gurrier". The other big event of 1953 caused even more controversy: the opening of Busáras, the central bus station, at Store Street. It was designed by the late Michael Scott and owed something of its design genesis to the *avant garde* work of Desmond FitzGerald on the original airport terminal. Busáras was Dublin's first modern office block and was instantly derided for its modernity: it became known as the "glass house", but that term of abuse did not last. Over the years, it has become familiar to countless thousands of air passengers as the city terminal of the airport bus service.

Despite the best efforts of the promoters of An Tostal, who even flew in twelve city officials from Philadelphia and a number of American newsmen, 1953 was again a disappointing year at Collinstown. Financial results for Aer Lingus and Aerlínte, the trans-Atlantic company, combined, for 1952/53 show a deficit of £83,718, while in the following financial year, 1953/54, the deficit was only slightly reduced, to £62,663.

Seán Lemass was once again Minister for Industry and Commerce. His department announced, at the beginning of 1954, that it was not prepared to take action for the provision in the estimates for public service of the amount required to meet the Aer Rianta share of the Aer Lingus losses in the year 1953/54. The Minister wanted, at an early date, a statement from the board of Aer Lingus setting out its views on the actions that needed to be taken.

Ronnie Delaney, victorious in the 1956 Melbourne Olympics. On his return home, he received a rapturous welcome at Dublin airport.
Photograph: G. A. Duncan

A telling vignette of the workings of Aer Lingus and Aer Rianta is provided in the August, 1953, edition of *Aer Scéala*. Much of that issue was given over to the workings of the Aer Lingus accounts department, which was divided into about a dozen sections. The Aer Rianta accounts branch was described as being separate from these sections. The magazine notes that "Christy Martin in Aer Rianta has a miniature realm all to himself, assisted by M. L. Slater and nearly a dozen others, divided between Dublin airport and the city". It was noted that their records were quite distinct from those of Aer Lingus. "They keep accounts of landing fees and rents and of the catering business and other activities that provide the revenue for the management of the airport. They prepare their own estimates and costs, look after the Aer Rianta stores' records, produce weekly and monthly financial returns and half yearly and yearly accounts".

In 1953, there was a very visible symbol of progress at the airport, with the completion of the new control tower and beacon atop the central terminal building. The control tower is still in place today, facing the new tower built in conjunction with the new runway which was opened in 1989. But even seventeen years after the airport was opened, there were many signs in 1953 that the terminal building was less than adequate for the increasing volume of traffic. This was the year that J. C. B. McCarthy, later to become secretary of the Department of Industry and Commerce, was first given responsibility within the department for aviation matters. His duties included chairmanship of the airport construction committee, which dealt with such problems as architecture, engineering and air traffic control.

Dublin airport was still run by Aer Lingus, with Aer Rianta playing a relatively subdued role, responsible for areas like maintenance. McCarthy remembers clearly Colonel Delamer, the airport manager; at this stage, the Department controlled Shannon directly. McCarthy says of Dublin at this point in its existence: "one had to be conscious of the fact that there was something slightly odd about an airport operated by one airline, but used by many other carriers. There was always a danger of allegations of discrimination, but fortunately, there was a very good airport manager in Colonel Delamer who understood all these things". Even so, J. C. B. McCarthy soon found a certain air of conservatism at the airport.

"When I first got responsibility for the airport, I found that the terminal building was being treated as an architectural gem, something that had to be preserved at all costs. But aviation technology seemed to be changing every five minutes and if we

Johnny Oppermann points to the scene of his culinary triumphs in the old terminal building at Dublin airport.
Photograph: Robert Allen Photography

were going to be bound by the architectural beauty of the building, it created headaches". Assistant secretary to J. C. B. McCarthy was Dr Thekla Beere, who later as secretary of the Department of Transport and Power, became the first female secretary of a Government department. The daughter of a Protestant clergyman, her family came from the Mullingar area, where they knew the Delamers well. The Delamers were a family of wealthy farmers. When Dr Beere graduated from Trinity College, Dublin, in the late 1920s, she had the great difficulty, shared by all graduates then, of finding employment at home. Eventually, she got a Grade 3 temporary clerical post in the civil service, on £2 a week, and worked her way up the civil service hierarchy from there. She well remembers John Leydon, the secretary of the Department of Industry and Commerce in the 1940s, who played such a pivotal role in the development of aviation in Ireland. She remembers him as having a very agile mind and, in ways, he introduced her to the ways of aviation, of which he was a very keen advocate. Gradually, Thekla Beere became acclimatised to the technicalities of aviation and as the airport developed in the 1950s and 1960s, became increasingly involved in the allocation of monies for its development.

While administrative movements were taking place in the Department of Industry and Commerce in 1953, with J. C. B. McCarthy beginning his long involvement in aviation and airport matters (he retired in 1972), Collinstown had some unusual aircraft movements. At the end of February, 1953, four Republic F–84 Thunderjets flew into Dublin airport from their base in West Germany. Such military arrivals at Dublin airport were treated with an air of relaxed nonchalance that would not be possible today: they were as commonplace then as they would be impossible now. The American aircraft stayed rather longer than their pilots had anticipated, because a thick covering of fog descended on Collinstown. Fog of this nature is very rare at Collinstown, yet on this occasion the last of the Thunderjets had to wait nearly a fortnight before it could get away. The pilots had been scheduled to make an overnight stay in Dublin!

When the last two Thunderjets left, they did so in a truly flamboyant style, noisy and low level, that brought office workers in the city centre to their windows. Passers-by in the street stopped to look upwards in awe, for advanced military jets of this type were still a big novelty.

On April 1, 1953, there was a sad footnote to a small chapter in Irish aviation. A Miles Gemini, that had once belonged to the short-lived Aer Rianta fleet in the late

1940s, crashed into the Irish Sea. The pilot and his passenger were killed, but of them and the plane, no trace was ever found. The passenger, Walter Bradley, was an employee of BEA, who had been trying unsuccessfully all day to get a seat to Belfast.

In June that year, there were more Thunderjets back at Dublin. Four USAF planes flew in from the Chaumont air base, 250 miles south of Paris. Interestingly, France was then in NATO, and had American air bases but that was before the accession to power of General de Gaulle in the late 1950s. The jets from Chaumont made the 660 mile journey to Dublin at a cruising speed of 560 mph, making a flying time of just ninety minutes. Officials and airport technicians rushed onto the tarmac as the planes came in. The *Irish Press* described the scene in its next day's issue: "with vapour trails streaming like banners behind them, the planes gave the traditional salute as they made their landing approaches. One by one, they banked suddenly until they seemed to stand upright on their wing tips, then just as suddenly, they rolled away at right angles and they were flying in line again".

The four Thunderjets parked on the grass in front of the fire station. No doubt, the pilots noticed the other improvements that were taking place on the field that year, including the relaying of 5,000 square yards of apron and the concreting of the grass areas between the terminal building and the apron. On the cargo side, No. 1 hangar was pressed into service as a temporary cargo depot. There were improvements, too, inside the terminal building, for the benefit of passengers, with the installation of new check-in desks.

However, the pilgrims that year did not benefit too much: thanks to the chaos caused by a nationwide transport strike in Paris, the Dublin Diocesan Pilgrimage to Lourdes ran into heavy weather, metaphorically speaking. Only the affluent and the terminally ill went on airborne pilgrimages then; most people could afford to travel only by sea and train. But the French strike meant that the pilgrims travelling surface only got as far as Paris and had to return, while the Order of Malta aircraft went to

President Seán T. O'Kelly is presented with a model of a Viscount aircraft after he had been for a flight round Ireland on the aircraft in 1954; it was then a new type for Aer Lingus. Also in the photograph, second left to right, are Mrs Phyllis O'Kelly, wife of the president, Seán Lemass, Seán Ó hUaidhaigh and J. J. O'Leary.
Photograph: G. A. Duncan

Going home by bicycle: maintenance staff leave the airport, early 1950s.

In 1956, the terminal building at Dublin airport was extended. The Aer Lingus staff magazine, *Aer Scéala*, "doctored" this photograph to announce the building work being carried out by the Aer Rianta "wall busters".

Lourdes to retrieve their pilgrims when the 1953 pilgrimage was cancelled. Towards the end of the year, KLM introduced the Convair 340 on its scheduled route from Amsterdam to Dublin. On the inaugural run, the plane was piloted by an Irishman, Captain W. H. Gardiner, later to become well-known in the Irish aviation business as the director of operations at Aer Turas, the Irish-owned air freight company.

Also at the end of that year, there was a spectacular arrival at Collinstown of twelve USAF aircraft. The planes brought teams and a band, all destined for Croke Park to play a benefit baseball match in aid of the Irish Red Cross. American Air Force planes were quite frequent visitors to Collinstown during the middle and late 1950s, but have not been seen at the airport now for many years, except when arriving for the annual Aer Rianta-sponsored air spectacular.

In February, 1954, the airport had its first visit from a BEA Viscount, which had been diverted from Nutt's Corner, then the airport for Belfast. Aldergrove was still an RAF base. The next month, on March 7, Aer Lingus took delivery of the first two Viscounts in its fleet. A large crowd gathered at the airport to see the two planes come in; they performed a number of low level fly bys before they landed, an impressive sight in the sun, with their unpainted metal finish. The Aer Rianta surplus for the year to March 31, 1954, was £24,201, mainly landing fees and rents paid by Aer Lingus. September of that year saw an impressive event in the civilian world outside the airport: the *Evening Press* was launched on an unsuspecting public in Dublin, with the help of the ITGWU band, two elephants borrowed from the zoo and a vast medley of bit players, who brought the city centre to a standstill. Three months after its launch, the *Evening Press* secured a sensational scoop, when it revealed the Berrigan baby kidnap, a case that enthralled the nation.

On the political front that year, there was a change of Government, when John A. Costello again became Taoiseach of a Coalition Government.

The River Tolka flooded badly and local residents had to be rescued by rowing boat. There was an interesting diversion from Shannon late that year, not because of bad weather, but because the emergency services went on strike. One diverted aircraft to land at Collinstown was a Seaboard & Western DC4, flying from London to Gander, in Newfoundland, with, of all things, a cargo of monkeys. The major aviation event towards the end of that year was the closure of Northolt as a civil airfield on October 3. Henceforth, all London flights changed to Heathrow, which had been under construction since 1944.

With the dawning of the New Year, on January 1, 1955, Dublin airport prepared for another spectacular "first". Its first ever helicopter was due, a Bristol Sycamore, which was air freighted into Dublin by Aer Lingus and reassembled in one of the hangars at Collinstown. Bad weather curtailed its demonstration flights on January 15 and 16, although it landed at Leopardstown racecourse, Blackrock College and the Royal Dublin Society. It had been due to go to the Baily lighthouse on the tip of the Howth peninsula, to give a demonstration of winching down a relief lighthouse keeper, but this trip had to be cancelled because of the weather. The large crowds that turned up at Howth that day were bitterly disappointed. Nevertheless, over the next few days, the novel machine gave demonstrations to the Air Corps.

The machine also flew to Arás an Uachtaráin, where it landed in the grounds to collect President Seán T. O'Kelly and give him his first ride in a helicopter.

A few days later, there was another unusual "visitor" to the airport, a C–47 aircraft of the French Armée de l'Air, which brought André Moynet, Secretary of State to the French Prime Minister, to Dublin for the international rugby match between Ireland and France. M. Moynet had sixteen in his party, including several French air force officers. Some fifteen years later, this plane was sold to the notorious Emperor Bokassa of the Central African Republic.

While many varied piston-engined aircraft were coming and going at Collinstown,

Dr Thomas Bouchier-Hayes, the airport's first doctor, as drawn by Seán O'Sullivan in April, 1953.

the aviation enthusiasts also saw traces of the future in the skies above them. Overflying jets then did not fly at the altitudes of modern jets, so there were very clear glimpses to be seen of overflights. An interesting overflight was the Swissair DC–4 flight, which operated once a week, beginning in Zurich and ending in New York. It was the first ever all-freight scheduled trans-Atlantic service and, since its route took it from Manchester to Shannon, it passed directly over Dublin. Military jets flying at very high altitudes created contrails or flyovers clearly visible at ground level, and since jets were not yet in use at Dublin airport, these signs of evidence of the jet age to come caused much public interest. Newspapers even reported them on occasion.

There were two particularly unusual events at the airport that year. Dr Paris Panaytou was a Greek doctor who had qualified in Ireland. He flew home to Tanganyika, now Tanzania, where he was taking over his father's medical practice. His parents had given him a nice little present, a Cessna 180, which was shipped in from the US and reassembled by Aer Lingus engineers. On March 4, 1955, he set off from Dublin airport on the first leg of his flight to Africa. At the end of that month, two plane loads of furniture were flown in, aboard Yorks. They contained the entire contents of a castle, for they belonged to Brigadier Jephson-Norreys, who was moving house from Norfolk to Mallow Castle in north County Cork.

In 1955, Aer Lingus was continuing to use DC3s, but some strange aircraft came to Dublin on demonstration flights, like the French HD.32, which had a 150 feet wing span. Other unusual aircraft came to Dublin at the end of May that year, to take part in the air display held at Weston airfield in County Kildare. It attracted a crowd of 50,000 to the first air display held in the Dublin area for nineteen years. There was considerable public agitation over the opening of the new airway, overhead Killiney to Strumble in west Wales. This new airway was used for all London-bound traffic. In the newspapers of the time, it was noted that on busy days, when runway 24 was in use, there seemed to be a regular procession of aircraft following the course of O'Connell Street and passing over Dalkey.

At this period, there were some interesting developments at the airport, with an enlarged cargo depot, an automatic standby electricity generating plant, new approach lighting on runway 24, better apron lighting and a private automatic telephone exchange. In what was really a sign of the times, the first expansion of car parking

Below left: The first newsagent's shop was opened at Dublin airport in 1953. Its manageress, seen here, was May Wyse, who later married and went to live in California.

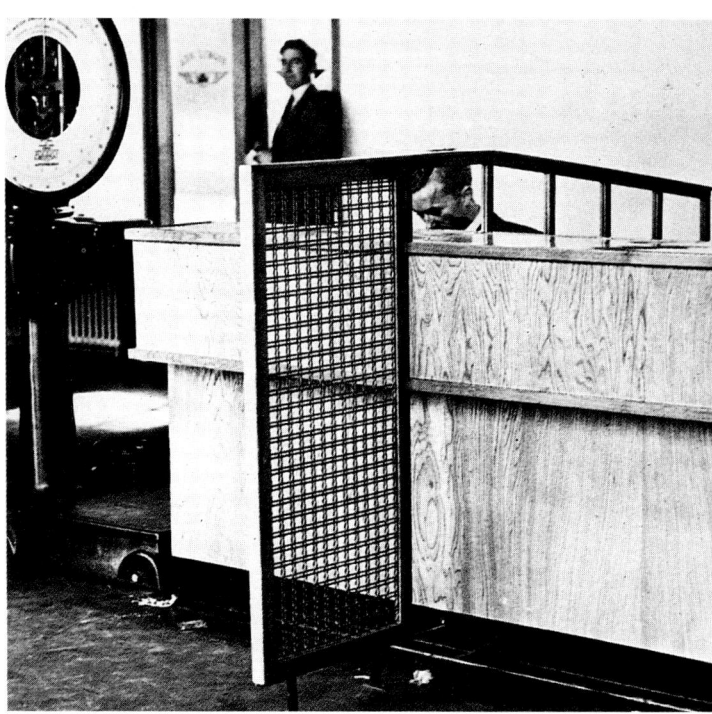

Check-in desk at the airport, 1950s.

This photograph, taken in 1956, at a fancy dress party, shows from left: Captain J. C. Kelly-Rogers, Colm Fitzgerald, Aer Lingus purchasing superintendent, Arthur Walls, Aer Lingus engineering, Frank Delaney, deputy chief engineer, Aer Lingus and Paget McCormick, chief engineer, Aer Lingus.

facilities was made. For the first time, cars were becoming popular means of transport, although they remained very expensive for the ordinary person in the street. A new Hillman Minx cost about £635 and a new Ford truck cost around £1,100. Air fares were expensive for the time, too; a tourist return ticket from Dublin to Manchester cost less than £7, while £30 bought a return ticket from Dublin to Frankfurt. But the average weekly wage for a working person in the mid-1950s was between £3 and £5.

In 1955, there was something of an upturn in the aviation business. Aer Lingus reported that in July of that year nearly 60,000 passengers were carried, an increase of 8,000 on the same month of the previous year. Ironically, the demands on the Aer Lingus fleet at peak periods meant that the airline was unable to service the Red Island holiday camp charters, which it had catered for when they started the previous year, 1954. Red Island was a popular holiday camp on the north County Dublin coast at Skerries, owned and run by Eamon Quinn, father of Feargal, the Superquinn man. The Saturday flights into Dublin airport for holidays at Red Island became quite popular, but in 1955, they were handled by independent operators from Britain.

The most exciting new service that started out of Dublin airport that year was Dublin to Biarritz in the south-west of France. Biarritz has long held a reputation as a fashionable seaside resort of great elegance, but it is also in reasonable proximity to Lourdes, and the rationale behind the Aer Lingus decision to open the service to Biarritz was motivated mainly by the increasing traffic to Lourdes.

Another, rather more prosaic, feature of that year was the mass meeting of members of staff of Aer Lingus and Aer Rianta, called by general manager Gerry Dempsey on July 29. The meeting was in No. 2 hangar and was attended by about 400 workers in total; not more than fifty were on the Aer Rianta payroll. Dempsey had a simple fact to tell the staff: in the 1954/55 financial year, Aer Lingus and Aer Rianta together had made a profit. It was not a handsome amount, even by the standards of the times, around £25,000, but it represented a substantial return to the black at the airport for the first time since the start of the decade, when traffic fell far below expectations and there were substantial losses in the two previous financial years, amounting to about £150,000. Since the end of the Emergency in 1945, total

Cary Grant, the American film actor, arrives at the airport, 1958.
Photograph: G. A. Duncan

Anna Neagle, the British film star, arrives at Dublin airport in 1956, en route to a festival in Cork. She is seen being greeted by Sidney Safir, the British Lion film representative in Ireland.
Photograph: G. A. Duncan

Cardinal John D'Alton, who was cardinal from 1953 to 1963, is seen arriving at Dublin airport aboard a BEA flight in the late 1950s.
Photograph: G. A. Duncan

losses over the decade amounted to nearly £1½ million. So a modest return to profitability at Collinstown merited some celebration and Dempsey insisted on calling together as many of the workers as possible to tell them the good news and raise morale.

There was a more lighthearted gathering at the airport in the summer of 1955, when scenes from a film were shot on the apron. The production was *The March Hare,* starring Terence Morgan and Peggy Cummins, and while most of the interior scenes were shot at Shepperton Studios near London, the producers asked permission to shoot some scenes at Collinstown. A Viscount was used as a "prop", to show Terence Morgan arriving at the airport. The scene of Morgan coming down the steps from the aircraft was filmed half a dozen times before the director was satisfied with the result. Many members of the airport staff played "bit" parts as passengers, and when the scene was completed, producer George More O'Ferrall thanked the Aer Rianta watch office and members of staff at the airport for their services. Further sequences for the film, which showed Collinstown in glowing Cinemascope colour, were shot in Bray, County Wicklow.

By 1956, said contemporary reports, Dublin airport was being taken for granted by the media. Flying was no longer the novelty it had been in the immediate post-war years. For the 1956/57 financial year, the total number of passengers using the airport, both on scheduled and charter flights, was 444,000: flying was moving away from being a preserve of the wealthy and the aristocrats.

Outside the airport, two events caught the public imagination, one sad, the other joyous. The sad occasion was the passing of Alfie Byrne, who had been Lord Mayor of Dublin ten times between 1930 and 1955. He was nine times Lord Mayor in the 1930s, making a final return to the Mansion House in Dawson Street the year before his death. Byrne was a dapper little man and was often seen at functions in the city, his mane of white hair neatly brushed into place. He always wore a three-piece suit, with watch chain, a fashion throwback to a much earlier era of sartorial elegance. In his appearance and his cultured manner, people at the airport sometimes likened him to the late Billy Bizzell. Billy Stenson, who joined the airport staff in 1956 as a carpenter, and who retired in 1987 as building superintendent of maintenance, remembers Bizzell as one of the many wonderful characters who have peopled the airport over the years. But for Billy Bizzell, he had especial words of tribute: "he was very loyal and he knew everything and anything about his trade, a terrific tradesman".

As for Alfie Byrne, he had been one of the very earliest proponents of the airport development scheme in the mid-1930s, when he saw, correctly, that aviation was the transport medium of the future and that, in the immediate future, the construction of the airport would provide desperately needed jobs for the working men of Dublin.

One event in 1956 brought much joy on the national stage, Ronnie Delaney's win in the Melbourne Olympics.

When Delaney won the 1,500 metres race at the Melbourne Olympics that year, the cheers could be heard from one end of the country to the other. True, there had been earlier Olympic wins for Ireland, such as that of Bob Tisdall, also a runner, in the 1932 Games, but somehow, this win by Delaney really caught the public imagination. It was also the first time that such a major sporting event was covered in some depth by the new mass media. The newspapers naturally ran extensive coverage, but so too did Radio Éireann on its news and sports programmes, and cinemagoers were able to see the Movietone or Pathé Pictorial newsreels of the event. In 1956, BBC television was transmitting from Belfast, but Ulster Television did not go on the air until 1959; in the year of Delaney's win, very few homes in the Republic had television sets. By today's standards, the media coverage of the Melbourne Olympics was sketchy, but nevertheless, the populace at large heard about it quickly enough and when Ronnie Delaney returned in triumph, there was a tremendous turnout for him at Dublin airport, with every possible viewing balcony packed to capacity. He was awarded film star treatment.

But the real drama at Dublin airport that year was behind the scenes, couched in precise legal terminology. In September, 1956, the new bilateral air agreement between Ireland and Britain was signed after some considerable negotiations. Under the terms of this agreement, Aer Lingus lost its ten-year monopoly on Ireland–UK air services.

The previous Anglo-Irish air agreement had come into effect in 1946 and its replacement was as significant for the future development of the airport at Collinstown as the decision to grant Ryanair operating licences in competition with Aer Lingus thirty years later. The new agreement allowed British European Airways (now part of British Airways) to operate services between Britain and Ireland, side by side with Aer Lingus. At the same time, independent British carriers were also allowed to service cross-channel routes. The month after the agreement was signed, BEA's holding in Aer Lingus was reduced, by transferring 285,000 shares to Aer Rianta.

Another new service that was started into Dublin in 1956 was the Sabena thrice weekly cargo flight between Brussels and Dublin, for which the airline used a DC3. This new route began in November, and was the prelude to the start of Sabena's

Clergy participate in the official opening of the Lourdes terminal at the airport, 1958.
Photograph: Lensmen

The newly built Lourdes terminal, 1958.
Photograph: Lensmen

passenger operation between Ireland and Belgium, which began the following April.

Dublin airport had some notable aircraft arrivals that year. At the 1956 Weston air display, the star of the show was an RAF Meteor jet aircraft, which demonstrated its new high speed ejector seat. Using the seat, a pilot could be ejected from the aircraft while it was still on the runway and live to tell the tale. The day after its appearance at Weston during the bank holiday that May, the jet made a similar display, flying out of Dublin airport.

Another distinguished visitor to Dublin that year was the Indian prime minister, Pandit Nehru. He had first visited Dublin in 1949, shortly after India had gained her independence. This 1956 visit was of longer duration, five days; Nehru arrived aboard an Indian Air Force Viscount 700.

One piece of construction carried out near the airport and completed in the summer of 1956 intrigued local residents. It was a steel building without windows and topped by a cylindrically shaped "hat"; its presence in the middle of a cornfield at Rolestown, near Swords, four miles from the touchdown point on runway 17, excited much local comment. The curious structure was in fact the Dublin VOR. This VOR equipment had already been fitted in all the Aer Lingus Viscounts and its installation was in progress in the remaining DC3s. GCA radar was on the way, moving *The Irish Times* to comment that the effect of these improvements was to make Dublin one of the most modern airports in the world. Another improvement, this time in the terminal building, was the opening of the new Shamrock lounge and snack bar. For its construction, the Aer Rianta "wall busters" were in action again. Gardener "Pee Jay" Power and his staff kept lawns and flower beds in immaculate condition.

The following year, 1957, saw much larger extensions to the terminal, which was beginning to burst at the seams. In July of that year, work started on the annexe to the north of the terminal, which became the arrivals building when it opened in June, 1959. Other work at the airport included the provision of more offices for State radio and meteorological staff on the third floor of the terminal building and extra public viewing areas on the upper floors of the terminal. The Aer Rianta educational programme continued and included co-operation with the Irish Aviation Club and the Model Aeronautics Council of Ireland.

In addition to the work on the terminal, extra buildings were provide for aircraft victualling and extra aircraft parking space was provided in front of No. 3 hangar.

April, 1957, saw the bilateral agreement between Ireland and Britain take effect. On Sunday, April 14, a BEA Viscount inaugurated the company's London–Dublin service. The following day, BEA's Birmingham–Dublin service began and on the Tuesday, the Manchester–Dublin route was opened. On Wednesday, April 17, the first British independent carrier opened a route into Dublin, when BKS Air Transport inaugurated its service from Newcastle, using a DC3. At the end of May, Aer Lingus celebrated its 21st birthday in some style, with a flypast over the airport and over the city of Dublin. It was led by a Rapide, borrowed from Weston, which represented the company's first aircraft, a Dragon, and also included six DC3s and two Viscounts. A Fokker Friendship 27 was also included; the first Fokker to join the Aer Lingus fleet was still being constructed in the Netherlands.

Later that year, on September 28, there was an emergency at the airport when an Aer Lingus Viscount en route to London lost an engine on take-off from runway 06 and overran the end of the runway. It ploughed through 600 feet of soft ground before coming to a standstill in a ditch beside the perimeter road. Although the aircraft was badly damaged and was out of commission for some months, none of the fifty-four passengers, or the crew, was hurt.

In November, 1958, Aer Lingus introduced its new Fokker Friendships to its fleet.

The opening of the North terminal 1958. From left: Patrick Lynch (chairman, Aer Lingus), Seán Lemass (Minister for Industry and Commerce), who performed the opening, Leo M. Carroll (senior airports' architect, Department of Industry and Commerce), J. C. B. McCarthy (secretary, Department of Industry and Commerce) and Niall Weldon (assistant services manager, Aer Lingus).
Photograph: Aer Lingus

Arthur Walls, who is now chairman of Ryanair and chief executive of Clery's department store in Dublin, was the project engineer. The first of the aircraft to go into service was the *St Fintan*; the forty-seater high wing turboprop planes proved popular with crews and passengers alike. By the beginning of 1960, Aer Lingus had cut back its DC3 fleet to five, used mainly for cargo work and stretcher traffic to Lourdes.

An even more important event for Dublin airport in 1958 was the start up of the trans-Atlantic service. The Inter-Party government had scrapped the first such service in 1948, before it began, but after a ten-year gap, it did start up. Fianna Fáil had returned to power in 1957 and a decision to open up the trans-Atlantic service was made in December, 1957. Arrangements were completed to lease Super Constellations from Seaboard & Western Airlines; the service from Dublin and Shannon to New York began as a thrice weekly service, became daily that summer and in October that year was extended to Boston. The start of the new service on April 28, 1958, was the cause of grand ceremonial at Dublin airport. A full attendance of dignitaries saw Eamon de Valera, the Taoiseach, inaugurate the service, a milestone for Irish aviation and for Dublin airport. The Super Constellations were leased until the end of 1960, when Aer Lingus took delivery of its first jet aircraft.

While the launch of the new trans-Atlantic air service by de Valera marked an important turning point in the fortunes of Dublin airport, a major era in politics was coming to an end. When Eamon de Valera performed that inaugural ceremony at the airport in 1958, he was seventy-five years of age. The following year, he retired as Taoiseach and moved to Áras an Uachtaráin as President. He was succeeded as Taoiseach by Seán Lemass, who, as Minister for Industry and Commerce during several Fianna Fáil governments, had done much to encourage the development of Irish aviation and Dublin airport, after an initial scepticism.

Some important physical developments took place at the airport in 1958. No. 1 hangar had been converted into the cargo terminal and the wooden building known as the Lourdes Terminal was put up to cope with the extra traffic for the Lourdes centenary year. Aer Lingus chartered planes to over two hundred pilgrimage groups and, in 1958, over 12,000 pilgrims were flown to Lourdes. This airlift was the biggest ever undertaken out of the airport and Aer Lingus converted some of its Viscounts so that they could take fourteen stretcher patients along one side of the cabin. Some members of the airport staff performed voluntary duty as helpers for the Lourdes passengers, a charitable service that has been operated to this day. The wooden building was meant to have been of a temporary nature, but fate decreed otherwise. After its use as the Lourdes terminal, it became the Aer Lingus operations department building.

Paddy O'Daly had the legend "due for demolition 1969" painted on the roof; the building is still in place, over twenty years after it was scheduled to be pulled down. It is used for storage and that lettering can still be made out, faintly. Another development in 1958 was on the western side of the field; Iona Airways was set up in 1930 and for some years, operated out of Kildonan airfield in Finglas. But in the late 1930s, Hugh Cahill, the perceptive founder of Iona, bought land near the airport. Iona had closed down in the mid-1930s, only to be revived by Pearse Cahill, son of the founder. In 1958, he was offered the present site by Aer Lingus and started to build up Iona; the first sign of this expansion was the erection of the six aircraft hangar in 1958.

Another arrival at the airport in 1958 was Seán Clancy, the present head waiter in the restaurant. He had worked in the old Metropole in O'Connell Street (now demolished and the site of the British Home Stores). Johnny Oppermann recruited Clancy to the airport, where he has worked for thirty-two years, and from which he is due to retire in the autumn of 1990. In the 1950s, the Metropole had been a popular venue for Dubliners, but during that decade, the airport restaurant had become a new location of almost equal popularity. Sean Clancy remembers that the Saturday evening dinner dances were very popular, attracting capacity crowds of around three hundred. When the Super Constellations began the service to the United States, they departed at around 9 pm and many people would come out to the airport to see friends and relatives off, making dinner at the Collar of Gold restaurant an integral part of the evening.

At the Metropole, Seán Clancy often cooked a very popular veal dish at table; after he came to the airport restaurant, many customers followed him and he ended up cooking the same veal, with mushrooms, sherry and wine, at table, where it was served in a rechristened format. It was now known as "Veal Viscount". Even Gerry (Jeremiah) Dempsey had a dish named in his honour, a Steak Jeremiah. Those were the high days of the airport restaurant, when Johnny Oppermann, catering controller, held sway and Jimmy Flahive, head chef, soon to find fame as the TV chef on RTE, made bounteous concoctions. The real highlight of the year came on New Year's eve, when the gala dinner started at 7 pm and finished at 6 am on New Year's Day. It was a celebrity occasion, when the restaurant would be booked solid; the reservations were made from the previous New Year's "do", such was its popularity. In 1959, the airport restaurant won a UK catering magazine Oscar, which placed it on an equal footing with the Côte d'Azur airport, Nice, and the Golden Door restaurant at Idlewild airport, New York.

In the financial year 1958/59, the number of Aer Lingus passengers finally broke through the half million barrier, to 500,574. Aer Lingus revenue, which included Aer Rianta, was just over £3,750,000. Rather surprisingly, there was a separate account for Aer Rianta. It was described as managing Dublin airport on behalf of the Minister for Industry and Commerce. The airport area embraced 1,000 acres of lands, including all the buildings, runways, taxiways, parking areas and roads. Aer Rianta provided security and also medical services. Aer Lingus, it was noted, was the chief operator at Dublin airport and, between landing fees and rents, contributed about £155,000 a year to Aer Rianta revenue.

The airport catering facilities occupied the entire first floor of the terminal building; catering revenue in 1958/59 amounted to £262,898, yielding a surplus of

Apron scene, Dublin airport, 1958.

£20,005. For the first time, the accounts noted, airport revenue (excluding catering), exceeded £200,000. The year under review had seen strong growth in revenues, with the Lourdes centenary flights and the start of the trans-Atlantic services being particularly responsible for the increase in Aer Rianta income.

Landing fees accounted for seventy-three per cent of Aer Rianta's income, while a further nineteen per cent came from rents. A mere two per cent came from concession fees, while car parking charges yielded a similar amount. Other revenue gave four per cent of income and included the sale of grass. All the grass cut on the grass surrounds to the runways was sent to a factory established on the perimeter of the field, where the cuttings were turned into pellets for cattle feed. Further runway extensions were planned, to the main runway, then 5,288 feet long, at the Ballymun Road end, and to the 4,800 feet long secondary runway, running parallel to the Ballymun Road at the Santry end. In the Aer Rianta section of the accounts, it was stated that looking to higher landing fees as a source of improved revenue would be counter-productive and that activities would have to be concentrated on developing revenue from non-aviation sources.

Airport car park, April, 1958.

Aer Rianta continued to provide material on general aviation matters, primarily for teachers and students all over the country; this service had begun during the Emergency. Nineteen fifty-eight saw the start of the tour train service, which took visitors around the apron. On a lighter note, and with a delightful Freudian slip, it was noted that the Aer Lingus golfing society, of which Johnny Oppermann was captain, held its captain's prize outing to Sherries (Skerries) golf club.

By the end of the decade, Dublin airport had played host to aircraft from twenty countries, from as far afield as Argentina. Some of the news was sad as the decade closed, like the return home in October, 1958, of the coffin of Liam Whelan, the Irish soccer star, who was one of the Manchester United players killed in the Munich air crash. But, generally speaking, by the time the decade had ended, considerable

---

This photograph was taken on the night of the inaugural flight of the night air mail service for the Department of Posts and Telegraphs, between Dublin and Manchester, on March 12, 1951. From left: Leon Ó Broin (secretary, Department of Posts and Telegraphs), William Norton (Tánaiste and Minister for Social Welfare), J. McKeon (Aer Lingus pilot), James Everett (Minister for Posts and Telegraphs), and Eamon McCarron (chairman, Aer Lingus).

The postal flight to Manchester left at 8.25 pm every night. By this date, a certain amount of overseas mail was being sent by air. The first air mail flight between Dublin and Britain had been inaugurated on January 16, 1946, but as early as 1937, Aer Lingus had started an experimental mailflight between Baldonnel and Ronaldsway, Isle of Man. The first series of airmail stamps was launched by the postal service in 1948, with the issuing of a 3d blue and a 6d magenta, showing the Angel Victor carrying the Voice of the Irish (Vox Hiberniae) over the shrines of Lough Derg and Croagh Patrick respectively.
Photograph: An Post museum/Independent Newspapers

The new Aer Lingus cargo terminal and office extension under construction, August, 1958. The building is now used by Aer Rianta, as part of its head office.
Photograph: Lensmen

progress had been made at Dublin airport. Aer Lingus no longer had the monopoly on cross-channel flights and it had begun its trans-Atlantic services. And as the DC3 came to the end of its useful life with Aer Lingus, the jet age was about to begin at Collinstown, a change that would result in dramatic developments at the airport. Seán Lemass, then Tánaiste and Minister for Industry and Commerce, opened the new North terminal for all arriving flights. Behind the scenes, the airport scored a world first with the installation of closed circuit TV to transmit weather forecasts from the airport meteorological office to the operations room for briefing air crew. With fitting irony, in 1959, just as Collinstown was about to enter the era of commercial jets, one of the most loved transport links in the Dublin area was closing down. For just over a century, the railway line from Harcourt Street station to Bray was popular with Dubliners going on seaside excursions or to the races at Leopardstown, but in the interest of saving £40,000 a year, Dr Tod Andrews, the chairman of CIE, decided the axe had to fall.

The Irish Times, January 19, 1960 — twenty years after the airport opened.

CHAPTER V

The real birth of Aer Rianta

THE sixties was when Ireland came alive; for a brief decade, until the start of the Northern troubles, the country was full of energy and optimism, bursting with a new, youthful vigour. Part of the new-found dynamism came from the economic progress set in train as the Lemass government put into practice the aspirations expressed in Dr T. K. Whitaker's blueprint for economic progress. Ireland was moving forward, and this young persons' enthusiasm, not to be repeated, in some measure, until the late 1980s, was reflected in the music of the age. The Beatles, that unlikely group of Liverpool lads, epitomised the new spirit of the "swinging sixties". They too left their mark on Dublin airport, for when they arrived in 1963 for a never-to-be-forgotten concert at the Adelphi cinema, the crowds lined the balconies of the terminal building at Dublin airport and left not an inch of spare space.

There was similar enthusiasm for the various presidents, heads of state and royal families that came to Ireland on the first State visits seen since the time Queen Victoria visited Dublin in 1900. Of all the great visits of the 1960s, none generated so much excitement as that by President John F. Kennedy of the United States in June, 1963. It was a decade of great hope at the airport, beginning with the arrival of the first Aer Lingus jets in 1960 and reaching a crescendo, in 1968, with the separation of Aer Rianta from Aer Lingus into a totally distinct company.

Nineteen sixty, the first year of the bright new decade, had an exciting opening, and some sad events, too. The most joyous occasion was the arrival at Dublin airport on November 19, 1960, of the first jet to go into service with Aer Lingus. Amazingly, it was only twelve years since Collinstown had seen its very first jet, an RAF Meteor, but in the intervening period, jet aviation technology had developed at a tremendous rate. Dublin photographer Michael Duncan, who covered many events at the airport in the late 1940s, through the 1950s, into the 1960s and 1970s, remembers being in Rome in 1953 covering religious ceremonies and managing to get a "lift" back to London on a Comet 1, the world's first commercial jet aircraft. Only four of the type were built and the series ended after a number of mysterious crashes. The technological lead passed to the Boeing company in Seattle, in the north-western United States, and it began developing its series of jets for commercial traffic. The first of these to come into service for the Aer Linte trans-Atlantic service, a Boeing 720 named *St Patrick,* landed at Dublin airport after a record-breaking flight. The New York to Shannon leg of the journey took just four hours and fifty-seven minutes. Nineteen sixty was also the year that saw runway 17/35 at Dublin airport extended to 6,000 feet.

There was an air of expansiveness about the airport that year, when Aer Lingus

began the first step in its diversification programme. The first move was the acquisition of a share in Irish Intercontinental Hotels, in 1960.

The Aer Lingus partners in this venture were Aer Rianta (its first involvement in a hotel investment project), a subsidiary of Pan Am, the Gresham Hotel, Dublin, and other Irish and international interests which had minor stakes. The hotel company, which was designed to improve the infrastructure in the tourist industry and encourage more visitors, particularly American, to come to Ireland, was problematic at the beginning, but it became successful. In time, the ownership of the three hotels, one in Dublin, one in Cork and one at Limerick, passed to the Jury's company, although Aer Lingus continued to hold its twenty-five per cent share. The Aer Rianta stake was later divested. The hotel project ran quite smoothly compared to the Shannon Repair Services saga; this was a private company set up at Shannon to provide engineering and maintenance services for foreign airlines. It was in direct competition with Aer Lingus and Erskine Childers, who had become Minister in charge of the new Department of Transport and Power in 1959, and who was to enjoy a ten-year term of office there, was uneasy with the involvement by Aer

Lingus in an operation that could be handled just as efficiently by the private sector. Dr Thekla Beere, the secretary of the new department, was the conduit for correspondence between the Department and Aer Lingus over the Shannon Repair Services' issue; at times, the argument became quite heated, with the airline accusing the Department of interfering in its day-to-day managerial decisions.

At the time, Gerry Dempsey, then chief executive of Aer Lingus and also Aer Rianta, said: "If you hire a dog, you shouldn't bark yourself". Eventually, the episode was settled to the satisfaction of Aer Lingus; when the Shannon company got into financial difficulties, it was Aer Lingus that bailed it out, making it a wholly owned subsidiary in 1966. But with an energetic Minister, Erskine Childers, heading the new department with control of aviation matters and Seán Lemass, the new broom Taoiseach, with a long-standing interest in aviation and airports, change became inevitable. The acute controversy between Aer Lingus and the Department of Transport and Power over the Shannon company may have set minds thinking about the exact role of Aer Lingus. These new thoughts coalesced in the Air Transport Bill in 1966, which proposed the separation of Aer Lingus and Aer Rianta and the setting up of the latter as a separate company, with specific responsibility for managing Dublin airport, on behalf of all users, including Aer Lingus.

Outwardly at the airport that year, there was little sign of stirrings underneath the surface. Johnny Oppermann's restaurant operation in the central terminal building continued to be highly successful, although in 1962/63, there was a serious fall in catering turnover, for the first time in several years. Many a wedding was celebrated in that restaurant, prior to take-off on honeymoon. For lunches and dinners, the restaurant was often full and always renowned for its great buffet meals.

The table literally creaked with the weight of the sumptuous creations of Johnny Oppermann and his team of chefs. Besides the people working in the kitchen to prepare meals for the public restaurant, there was a vast team of 120 people working away at the airport in 1960 to prepare meals for inflight catering. Little more than ten years previously, inflight catering consisted of flasks of tea and coffee and a selection of sandwiches, but especially with the opening of the Dublin–Shannon–Boston–New York trans-Atlantic services, a far greater sophistication of cuisine was demanded, and provided. Among the publicly well-known people who came to the airport restaurant and enjoyed its fare at this time were celebrities like Tyrone Power, the American film actor, Margot Fonteyn, the English dancer, and Clementine Churchill, wife of Winston Churchill, Britain's great leader in World War II. Princess Grace of Monaco came to Dublin from time to time, before the first official state visit in 1961. She had been the plainly named but strikingly good-looking Grace Kelly, the American film star of Irish ancestry, who married Prince Rainier of Monaco. There were Irish celebrities, too, who were often given the VIP treatment leaving or arriving at Dublin airport, like Frederick Boland, who became president of the United Nations in 1960. This year also saw the first plane loads of Irish soldiers leave from Dublin airport for UN duty in what had been the Belgian Congo; that country had degenerated into a bloody civil war after independence and UN forces tried to keep the peace.

The Irish contingent played a substantial role and, at a later stage, two years after the initial departures from Dublin, ten soldiers were killed in an ambush at Niemba. The murders made national news, at a time when any kind of murder was still a rarity in Ireland, and drove every other topic from the newspapers and radio news, as well as everyday conversation, as the dreadful deeds of the Baluba tribesmen were recounted. The homecoming to Baldonnel of the coffins draped in the flags of Ireland and of the United Nations was poignant and touching.

Shortly afterwards, in September, 1961, there was nearly another tragedy. Wits at the airport attributed the 100 per cent survival rate to the quantity of Lourdes water

Opposite page:
The first Aer Lingus jet arrived at Dublin airport, November 18, 1960. The Boeing 720-048, named *St Patrick*, had set a record flight time for its journey from New York to Shannon of four hours, fifty-seven minutes. Pictured on the apron at Dublin airport were, from left: James Gorman (secretary, Aer Lingus), Seán Lemass (Taoiseach), Patrick Lynch (chairman, Aer Lingus), Erskine Childers (Minister for Transport and Power), Jack Lynch (Minister for Industry and Commerce) and J. F. Dempsey (general manager, Aer Lingus).
Photograph: Aer Lingus

Seán Lemass and his wife Kathleen.
Photograph: The Irish Times

Interior of the terminal building, early 1960s.

Another view of the terminal interior, early 1960s.

Passenger check-in, Dublin airport, 1960.
Photograph: G. A. Duncan

Interior view, main terminal, Dublin airport, 1960.
Photograph: G. A. Duncan

Cardinal Cushing and Mother Mary Martin (Medical Missionaries of Mary, Drogheda) at the airport, 1960. The solemnity of one of the Cardinal's departures from the airport was marred when he turned round at the top of the steps and shouted to an archbishop seeing him off: "See you, Arch!"
Photograph: G. A. Duncan

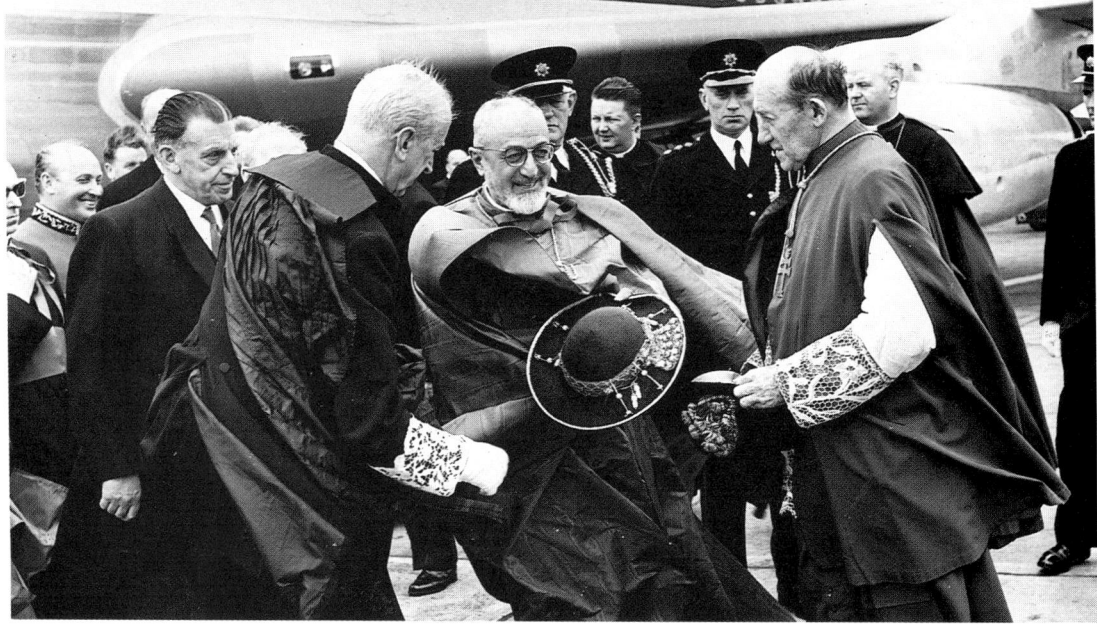

Cardinal Agaginian arrives for the Patrician Congress, 1961. Also in the photograph are Seán Lemass (far left) and Archbishop John Charles McQuaid (right).
Photograph: G. A. Duncan

being carried on the Douglas DC4 which came down on the main Dublin–Belfast road, outside the airport. The plane was being operated by Starways, a British charter company, and was returning from a pilgrimage flight to Lourdes when it started running out of fuel. In taking evasive measures, the pilot put the aircraft down, not on the runway, but across the main road. One wing was embedded in a hedge, as were two of its four engines when the plane came to a halt. There were no serious injuries among passengers or crew. The next morning, crowds of sightseers flocked to the airport to see the crashed plane, but by this stage, it had been towed onto the side of the road. Apart from the crack about the holy water saving the plane, one other story did the rounds of airport workers and is recalled by Joe O'Rourke, now retired.

He was then in charge of the airport fire service and was among the first people on the scene. He remembers that one woman had to be helped from the aircraft, apparently suffering from severe shock. "I was down there and a couple of other fellows and myself were trying to get her onto the bus to take her back up to the terminal. We were almost carrying her; she was a terrible weight. All of a sudden, the woman remembered that her handbag was still on the plane and the lads could not keep up with her running back to the aircraft. Up to a few moments previously, she had been dying!" Joe Kelly remembers that the people working in hangar No. 2 thought they were going to die as well: "as the aircraft made a final approach to runway 24, it lost all starboard power and veered sharply to port. The Aer Lingus staff working in the hangar threw themselves on the ground, as it seemed the plane would come straight through the hangar doors". When the passengers disembarked, many thought they were on the tarmac of the runway. In keeping with tradition, the pilot was the last to leave the aircraft, and asked Joe Kelly and some of his friends to look after what he thought was a half gallon container of vodka in row two. It was not vodka, but Lourdes water.

Lourdes pilgrimage flights were increasing in popularity and so too were scheduled flights. In 1960/61, Aer Lingus carried in total nearly 720,000 passengers; out of that total, some 400,000 were arrivals and departures from Dublin airport. Around

Prince Rainier and Princess Grace of Monaco arrive at Dublin airport for their State visit in 1961. It was the first such State visit to Ireland since Queen Victoria arrived in 1900. The photograph shows the Monagesque royal couple being greeted on the tarmac at the airport.
Photograph: G. A. Duncan

Michael Leo Skentelbery, who was a familiar figure at Dublin airport in his role as chief of protocol at the Department of External Affairs, meeting many foreign dignitaries on their arrival. He held this post from 1957 until 1962, when he was appointed Minister and later Ambassador to the Argentine. The Irish Embassy in Buenos Aires is the only diplomatic representation in South America; he remained there until his retirement in the early 1970s.
Photograph: Lafayette

10,000 tonnes of cargo and mail were carried to and from Dublin.

At Dublin airport in 1961, the main development was the extension of runway 06/24 to 7,000 feet. Aer Lingus opened yet another Continental route, Dublin to Rennes, a year after the start of the new Dublin–Cherbourg service. At £18, the return fare to Rennes was the cheapest to mainland Europe. But in 1961, the aviation focus was elsewhere, on Cork, where the first flight into the new Cork airport at Ballygarvan, on the Kinsale side of the city, touched down on October 12 that year. The official opening, a few days later, was performed by Seán Lemass, the Taoiseach. Discussions about the siting and opening of Cork airport had gone on, seemingly interminably, since the early 1930s; a variety of sites had been proposed, ranging from Great Island to Mitchelstown. When Aer Rianta was set up as a separate company in 1968, it assumed control of Dublin airport; the following year, management of Cork airport passed to it, along with Shannon, which had been managed by the Department of Transport and Power. The first manager of Cork airport, Vincent Fanning, later became manager of Dublin airport.

Apart from the opening of Cork airport, the other main event that year was the opening of Telefís Éireann, the new Irish television service. On the last day of the year, amid a driving snowstorm, the ceremonies were performed in the ballroom of the Gresham Hotel in O'Connell Street, Dublin. For some years, viewers in the Dublin area and northern counties had been able to pick up the BBC service transmitted from Belfast, and also the Ulster television service, begun in 1959.

With the opening of Telefís Éireann, a whole new media era began in Ireland. One of its earliest stars, a young broadcaster named Gay Byrne, already well-known for his sponsored shows on Radio Éireann, soon came to prominence on the new television service. The *Late Late Show* was devised as a summer "filler" in 1962; it is still running, the longest running such TV chat show in the world. But in the early days of his television career, Gay Byrne was spending part of each week working for Granada TV in Manchester and coming home at weekends. One Friday night, he

Interior of the North Terminal, Dublin airport, 1962.
Photograph: Aer Lingus

hitched a lift on an Aer Lingus plane coming back from Manchester; as the plane touched down at Dublin airport, the nosewheel collapsed. The aircraft eventually came to a halt, surrounded by the emergency services; the crew scrambled out down the escape ladder. Jack Doyle, who was later manager of Dublin airport, was on that plane and remembers that a very pale man stepped out between the pilot and the first officer. The decidedly pale passenger was Gay Byrne, who had been travelling incognito in the cockpit. Waiting for him that night, recalls Doyle, was a woman in a trench coat, Kathleen Watkins. The next day, Gay and Kathleen announced their engagement.

Other things collapsed the following year, 1962. The saddest passing was the Dublin *Evening Mail*, which closed down in July. It had been an institution in the city since the early part of the 19th century. "Man about Town", Letters to the Editor and cartoons like Mandrake were part of the folklore in many a Dublin household.

Newsboys used to shout out at street corners: "Herald o Mail", but first the arrival of the *Evening Press* in 1954 and then the start of Telefís Éireann programmes on January 1, 1962, both put nails in the coffin of the *Mail*. Another great Dublin institution bit the dust in 1962, the Theatre Royal in Hawkins Street. It was the last in a number of theatres that had been built on the site; the first was opened in 1821 and burned down in 1880. The second theatre was opened in 1897 and right up to the 1950s, with its vast auditorium, held capacity audiences for all kinds of shows, from variety with the Royalettes' dancers to performances by visiting comedians like Danny Kaye and full-scale symphony orchestras. Its demise, to make way for a large office block called Hawkins House, was greatly regretted by the populace of Dublin, who saw another piece of their heritage being torn down.

But while a place of theatrical pageantry was being torn down in the centre of Dublin, a new kind of ceremonial was being organised at Dublin airport. When Queen Victoria visited Dublin in 1900, the year before she died, it was the last big ceremonial State visit to the city for over sixty years. When Prince Rainier of Monaco and Princess Grace came to Dublin in 1961, they started a whole new wave of official visits. Lt. Col. Frank Neill was the man responsible for army protocol at the airport and remembers vividly when the State visits started. A whole protocol regime was established and the degree of ceremony depended on who was arriving.

The highest ceremony was reserved for Heads of State, who had a 21 gun salute, a guard of honour and an escort of honour. For them, there was the Captain's Guard, with one hundred men. For slightly lesser mortals, like prime ministers, there would

Above left: Tony Murray-Jones, Aer Lingus outdoor catering manager, seen with a special guest at an airport function, 1962.

Above: Alec Guinness, later knighted, the distinguished British actor, arrives at Dublin airport, 1962.
Photograph: G. A. Duncan

A new CIE bus in Aer Lingus colours, supplied for the bus service from Dublin city centre to the airport, early 1960s.

Bing Crosby and his wife Cathy arriving at Dublin airport, October, 1965.
Photograph: Michael O'Reilly

be a Lieutenant's Guard, with half that number of men. The Army No. 1 band, conducted by Jim Doherty, provided the music and Lt. Col. Neill remembers once when Prince Bernhard of the Netherlands, on one of his many visits to the Dublin Horse Show, was marching back to his plane on his departure. The band struck up *Come back to Erin* and he halted in his tracks, thinking that it was the Irish national anthem. There was also close liaison with the Department of External Affairs (it became Foreign Affairs in 1971); on one occasion, the Minister, the late Frank Aiken, wanted to know why the airport ceremonial was not produced in Irish. The document, running to forty foolscap pages, covered every aspect of the ceremonial welcome to be given to an incoming VIP. The document was duly translated into Irish, and it was not until about eight years later, going through his files, that Frank Neill discovered that six pages were missing from the Irish version of the document; no-one had noticed at the time.

He liaised very closely with Colonel Tuohy, the deputy airport manager, in these ceremonial affairs. Colonel Delamer, being more involved in the administration of the airport, had little involvement, Neill recalls.

Lt. Col. Neill says that with aircraft noise in the background, it can be difficult to hear commands, and that if this happens, the whole drill movement is lost. However, Mick Tuohy was very good at ensuring that everything ran smoothly. The Monagesque visit in 1961 was the first big State occasion at the airport and, during the 1960s, there was a whole string of such visits. Religious arrivals were always important, and included such luminaries as Cardinal Agaginian. Frank Neill remembers the airport ceremonies in 1965 when Cardinal Conway returned from Rome with the red hat. But a whole succession of other world dignitaries graced the tarmac at Collinstown during the 1960s, from Maurice Couve de Murville, the gracious French foreign minister, to President Sukarno, the Indonesian head of state. The visit of Prince Rainier and Princess Grace was merely, however, the appetiser for the big visit of 1963, that by President Kennedy.

There were changes in the offing in the running of the airport, as Jack Doyle clearly remembers. In 1957, BEA had broken the Aer Lingus monopoly on scheduled services in and out of Dublin; now, there were stirrings about the actual management of the airport.

Since the bilateral aviation agreement was signed between Ireland and Britain in

The Beatles pictured at the Gresham Hotel, Dublin, prior to their concert in the Adelphi, 1963. From left: John Lennon, Paul McCartney, George Harrison and Ringo Starr.
Photograph: RTÉ illustrations library

Crowds line the balconies to greet the Beatles when they arrived for their 1963 concert in the Adelphi, Dublin. Similar adulation, albeit on a smaller scale, had greeted Milan Horvath during his time in the 1950s as conductor of the Radio Éireann symphony orchestra.
Photograph: G. A. Duncan

The airlift of Irish troops to the Belgian Congo, which began in 1960 and lasted for two years, was carried out using US Air Force Globemaster aircraft. One of these enormous aircraft is seen parked on the apron at Dublin airport during the airlift.
Photograph: Owen Clarke

1956, allowing BEA the right to fly on certain routes between the two countries, relationships between the two airlines had been on a steadily downward track. In 1961, BEA complained about a serious imbalance between the two airlines on the Dublin–London route, although BEA was claiming most of the increases in traffic. BEA had been responsible for handling Aer Lingus at Heathrow since soon after World War II, but in the early 1960s, the scale of charges at Heathrow prompted Aer Lingus to start its own handling, which it did from April, 1963. In 1963, BEA still had a small shareholding in Aer Lingus and that year, Patrick Lynch, the Aer Lingus chairman, proposed to Lord Douglas of Kirtleside, the chairman of BEA, that the British airline should divest itself of this shareholding. Lord Douglas agreed to the shares being sold at par and with this sale, concluded with the man who was originally responsible for choosing the Collinstown site for Dublin airport, the long and close relationship between Aer Lingus and BEA was at an effective end. That dispute with BEA over London handling charges in the early 1960s also sowed the seeds of discontent, on the part of BEA, with the way Dublin airport was being run. BEA found it incongruous that the major airline based at Dublin airport should also be responsible for the management of the same airport, a situation that affected all carriers competing with Aer Lingus.

The Government capitalised on the advantage presented by the withdrawal of BEA from Aer Lingus, even though Erskine Childers, the Minister for Transport and Power, is not remembered as having a particularly special interest in aviation matters. The Air Companies Bill (1965) was designed to reorganise the structures of the airline and of the management of the airport. A substantial change came in the status of Aer Rianta, which since its establishment in 1937, had been the holding company for Aer Lingus, and later also for Aerlínte. The State investment in these two companies was vested in the Minister for Finance. Aer Rianta was to be set up as a totally separate company, with sole responsibility for manging Ireland's main airports, Dublin, Cork and Shannon. Erskine Childers said that it was unsatisfactory for the airports to be managed by a "company so closely identified with a particular operating company". There had always been confusion in the public mind about Aer Rianta, a confusion compounded by the same capitalisation figures appearing first in the Aer Rianta accounts and then again in the Aer Lingus accounts, creating the impression that the capital structure of the two companies was double its actual amount. In 1962/63, Aer Rianta had a revenue of £530,140, excluding catering, giving it a surplus of £227,930 for the Department of Transport and Power. Aer Rianta gained fifty-three per cent of its income from landing fees and thirty per cent from airport service charges.

Meanwhile, the year that the moves started to separate Aer Lingus from its management role at Dublin airport, proved equally momentous in other ways.

The first Irish soldiers depart in 1960, destined for UN duty in the former Belgian Congo.
Photograph: G. A. Duncan

Above left: Prince Gustaf of Sweden on his arrival at Dublin airport, 1963.
Photograph: G. A. Duncan

Above right: Colonel James Fitzmaurice, co-pilot on the pioneering trans-Atlantic flight by the *Bremen*, 1928, is pictured at Dublin airport in 1964 with John Maher, (left), the first chief ground engineer in Aer Lingus.
Photograph: G. A. Duncan

While commercial aviation was moving strongly into the jet age, Aer Lingus made an aircraft acquisition that proved of temporary duration.

Two Carvairs, a very noisy and unreliable plane, were put into service in early 1963, running car ferry services between Dublin, Bristol and Liverpool; Cherbourg came later. Neither the B+I nor British Rail had introduced roll-on, roll-off ships on their Irish Sea routes, and with the growing prosperity of the British market, an increasing number of holidaymakers from there were taking their cars on holiday. The Carvair planes were slow, with a cruising speed of 207 mph, and their capacity was limited to a maximum of five cars and thirty passengers. These converted DC4s, with large front doors and an upper deck cockpit, were not popular with crews. A special terminal facility was built for the new service at Dublin airport, and it was launched with great publicity. By the end of that first season, the Carvairs had carried a total of 4,324 cars and 12,532 passengers, but in the event, the car ferry service was withdrawn in 1966, when British Rail was about to introduce a roll-on, roll-off ferry on its Holyhead–Dun Laoghaire route.

But the highlight of 1963 was the official visit of President Kennedy to Ireland. The arrival of Kennedy on the Wednesday evening of June 26 of that year, with calls to Dublin, New Ross, Wexford, Cork and Limerick before his departure from Shannon airport, made an indelible impression on all at the airport. Kennedy, forty-four years of age, cut a slim, surprisingly youthful figure at Dublin airport, when he arrived aboard the main American Government jet, Air Force One. There was a second, back-up plane, while a third Boeing brought in over 120 U S newsmen; it touched down just before Kennedy's plane. Noel Andrews gave a commentary over the specially installed public address system to the crowds assembled at the airport.

He walked down the landing steps to a full ceremonial welcome, headed by the

Erskine Childers, Minister for Transport and Power, cuts the tape for the new car ferry terminal at Dublin airport, 1962. On his left is Colonel Delamer, the airport manager.
Photograph: Independent Newspapers

In 1963, Aer Lingus started a short-lived car ferry service to Bristol and Liverpool, later adding a third route, Dublin–Cherbourg. These services were discontinued in 1966. One of the first people to use the new service was Jimmy Edwards, the English comedian famed for his handlebar moustache. This photograph shows a car being driven off a Bristol Wayfarer aircraft.

President, Eamon de Valera. The entire government, led by the Taoiseach, Seán Lemass, was also on the apron at the airport to greet Kennedy. From the moment that he set foot on Irish soil, he exuded an extraordinary personal charm and charisma that overwhelmed all who met him. The organisation of the ceremonial aspects at the airports were complex enough, but what really intrigued airport staff was the American security. Gerry Giltrap, who had joined Aer Lingus in January, 1947, had been transferred to the services manager post at the airport, his first involvement with the managerial side of the airport itself. Giltrap was deeply involved in liaising with the Kennedy entourage, what he calls the "Kennedy John the Baptists" and with the Irish security services. "I didn't have any contact with Kennedy himself, any more than anyone else did, only from twenty paces away", he recollects.

But Giltrap has the clearest memory of talking to one of the American security advisers, who remarked: "We're not worried about his visit here, but I could give you the names of five American towns where I would be very scared at what might happen". So it was to prove, five months later, in Dallas, Texas. Jack Bannon, the present head of security at Dublin airport, also has vivid recollections of the Kennedy visit. "It was the first time that we had been involved in a programme of that kind. It was unbelievable to see the helicopters flying in the way they did".

Bannon was out on runway inspection a few days before the Kennedy visit started; in the distance he saw what he thought was a flock of sparrows. As the dark dots grew closer, he saw that it was a whole fleet of American helicopters, ten in total, with, as he put it, "fellows hanging out of the windows waving. That, and the size of the machines, was unforgettable". He found the security arrangements aboard the presidential plane, Air Force One, equally dramatic. He had to take a message to the plane and when he climbed to the top of the steps, he found himself looking down the barrel of a machine gun, held by one of the American security guards, who had

Aer Lingus installed what was claimed to be the first commercial computer in Ireland at Dublin airport, 1962.
Photograph: G. A. Duncan

taken over the whole security operation at the airport for the day. Even more impressive for people working at the airport was the enormous communications system that had been airlifted from the US; no one had ever seen such a vast array of equipment, all designed to keep the American president and his entourage in constant and immediate contact with the White House in Washington.

The ceremonial at the airport lasted some ninety minutes, during which time Kennedy shook hands with every member of the Irish Government, as well as with senior officials from the Department of External Affairs and other leading dignitaries. When the official arrival functions were completed, the Kennedy motorcade swept into the city centre. The main road in from the airport was lined with cheering crowds; the outside broadcast cameras of Radio Telefís Éireann, just over two years in existence, focussed on every moment.

Among Kennedy's official duties were a visit to Leinster House, for a combined meeting of the Dáil and Seanad and a visit to City Hall, where he was conferred with the freedom of the city of Dublin. Everywhere he went, he received an ecstatic welcome. Under the grey skies that covered most of the visit, his exuberant personality, full of boyish charm and enthusiasm, his wide grin, endeared itself to everyone who met him. Beneath those glowering clouds, he injected a spirit of deep and

The Abbey Theatre company leaves Dublin airport in 1964; they were on their way to London to perform *The Plough and the Stars* at the Aldwych Theatre, before travelling on to Paris to perform *Juno and the Paycock*.
Photograph: G. A. Duncan

lasting sunshine, a zest for life, a magic charisma that is remembered to this very day. Great crowds followed his every footstep, and in one incident, outside Iveagh House, headquarters of the Department of External Affairs, the crowds rushed behind a line of dignitaries who were seeing off Kennedy. Despite the rush and the crush, the crowds remained good-humoured. Kennedy himself insisted on leaning out of the official limousine to shake the hands of bystanders in the crowds, to the chagrin of the secret service men riding "shotgun" on the car. The pattern of great welcoming crowds was followed at every stage of Kennedy's Irish visit; in New Ross, County Wexford, he told the vast throng of people that if one of his ancestors had not emigrated from Dunganstown, where there is now a poignant Kennedy memorial cottage, he (Kennedy) would have been working in the Albatross fertiliser factory in

Opposite: President Kennedy steps out of Air Force One at Dublin airport.
Photograph: The Irish Times

Two presidents greet each other, Eamon de Valera and John F. Kennedy.
Photograph: G. A. Duncan

President Kennedy makes his speech on the airport apron.
Photograph: G. A. Duncan

President Kennedy walks down the line of Irish dignitaries.
Photograph: G. A. Duncan

President Kennedy lays a wreath at the graves of the 1916 leaders at Arbour Hill cemetery.
Photograph: The Irish Times

President Kennedy at the family homestead at Dunganstown, near New Ross, County Wexford.
Photograph: The Irish Times

Frank Aiken, Minister for External Affairs, greets Maurice Couve de Murville, the French Foreign Minister, at Dublin airport in 1964.
Photograph: G. A. Duncan

the town. For the five days of the visit, Ireland was overwhelmed with delight; the Camelot years that symbolised the new soaring spirit of the 1960s, were here, in the person of John F. Kennedy.

No one who was involved in the visit even peripherally, nor indeed the general public, could ever forget the impact it made. As Jack Bannon believes, only one other arrival at Dublin airport over the years has created such an indelible impression, that of Pope John Paul II in September, 1979. When the Kennedy entourage left Shannon airport at the end of June, 1963, the American president promised to return; he was the most enthusiastic advocate of Ireland, so he said it with total sincerity. But five months later, soon after his arrival at Dallas on an official visit, the bullets of an assassin rang out, shattering the fragrant myth of the young American president as his life's blood poured away.

That evening, on Radio Telefís Éireann, the film featured Peter Lawford, ironically a brother-in-law of Kennedy. It was interrupted by Charles Mitchel, reading the news flash. Even though the television transmission was in black and white, viewers remember Mitchel appearing on screen with an ashen white face. The Dublin evening newspapers rushed out special late night extra editions; it was the last time they ever did this, for television demonstrated so conclusively that it was the medium for late, instant news. For everyone in the country, the assassination of Kennedy came like the passing of the most loved member of one's own family circle, helping to implant the memories of that Kennedy visit deep in the Irish psyche.

Everyone who was around in 1963 remembers exactly the time and the circumstances in which they heard the news of Kennedy's assassination on November 22,

Airport menu, 1962.

grills

Sirloin Steak	....	10/=
Point Steak	....	10/=
Rump Steak	....	10/=
Porterhouse Steak (2 persons)		23/6
Chateaubriand Steak (2 persons)		26/=
Minute Steak	....	10/=
Lamb Cutlets (in season)		9/6
Mutton Cutlets		8/6
Mixed Grill		9/=
Loin Chop		8/6
Pork Chop		8/=
Ham Steak		9/=
Grilled Liver and Bacon		7/6

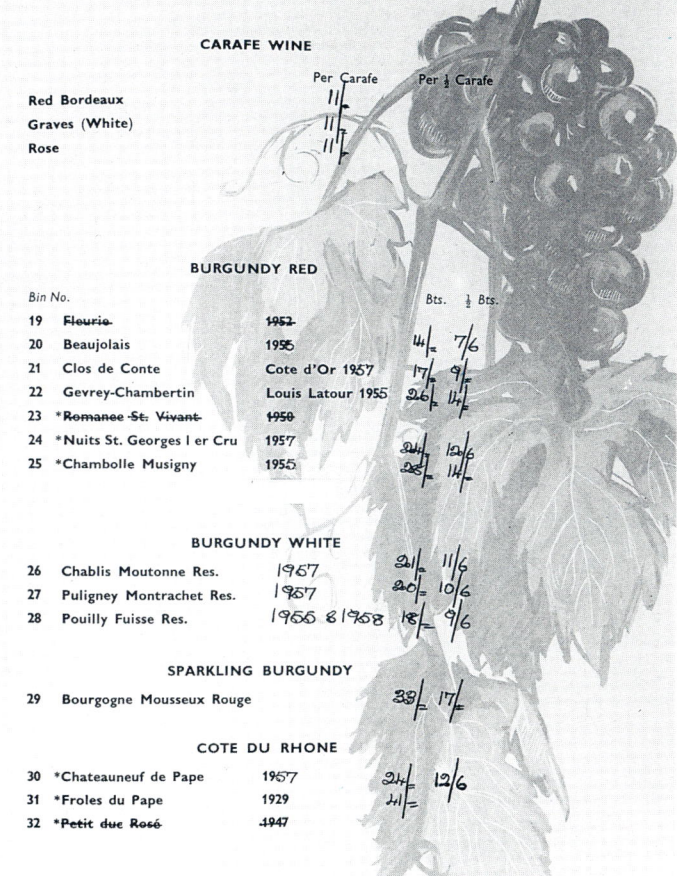

CARAFE WINE

	Per Carafe	Per ½ Carafe
Red Bordeaux	11/=	6/=
Graves (White)	11/=	
Rose	11/=	

BURGUNDY RED

Bin No.			Bts.	½ Bts.
19	~~Fleurie~~	~~1952~~		
20	Beaujolais	1955	14/=	7/6
21	Clos de Conte	Cote d'Or 1957	17/=	9/=
22	Gevrey-Chambertin	Louis Latour 1955	26/=	14/=
23	*~~Romanee St. Vivant~~	~~1950~~		
24	*Nuits St. Georges I er Cru	1957	24/=	12/6
25	*Chambolle Musigny	1955	26/=	14/=

BURGUNDY WHITE

26	Chablis Moutonne Res.	1957	21/=	11/6
27	Puligney Montrachet Res.	1957	20/=	10/6
28	Pouilly Fuisse Res.	1955 & 1958	18/=	9/6

SPARKLING BURGUNDY

29	Bourgogne Mousseux Rouge		33/=	17/=

COTE DU RHONE

30	*Chateauneuf de Pape	1957	24/=	12/6
31	*Froles du Pape	1929	21/=	
32	*~~Petit due Rosé~~	~~1947~~		

DUBLIN AIRPORT

Piet Sluís designed the cover of this Dublin airport restaurant menu, for the New Year's Eve gourmet dinner and dance, 1964.

Frank Aiken, minister for External Affairs, with Princess Grace at Dublin airport, 1961.
Photograph: The Irish Times

1963. Two days later, for his funeral to Arlington cemetery in Washington, a high level Irish delegation, led by the elderly president Eamon de Valera, left Dublin airport in an entirely different mood to that of the previous summer. A detachment of Irish troops went to the funeral, at the request of Jacqueline Kennedy. On November 26, a special Mass was held at the airport.

After the high of the Kennedy visit and the deep low of his death, it took a long while for feelings to return to some sort of equilibrium, so devastating were the news and images from Texas. Only the month before the Kennedy assassination, Lemass had left the airport, seen off by de Valera, on his official visit to the US. He started in Philadelphia and completed the tour in Boston. Aboard the Aer Lingus Shamrock Special Flight One, that left Dublin airport on October 11, 1963, at 10.20 am, were the American ambassador, Matthew McCloskey, and his wife, Hugh McCann, secretary of the Department of External Affairs and his wife, and Mrs Maud Aiken, wife of the Minister for External Affairs, Frank Aiken. The party was given a fine ceremonial send-off in the customary Dublin airport style. Only six weeks later, the news from America would be very different.

Traffic was generally buoyant at the airport, with the trans-Atlantic services performing strongly. Aer Rianta reported, for the first six months of 1963, that a total of 760,000 passengers passed through Dublin airport, an eleven per cent increase on the same period of the previous year.

The company also reported a thirty-eight per cent increase in cargo traffic, up to 11,590 tons, for this same six-month period. Revenue increased by £34,000, mainly because of increased revenue from landing fees. The result was a surplus of £130,000, a £36,000 improvement on the first six months of 1962. The growth in passenger traffic also manifested itself in the increase in catering revenue, which was £336,000 for the half year. Turnover increased in all catering sections, except outdoor. In the general administration account there was a deficit of £6,000, mainly due to increased charges for the Aer Rianta educational service. After allowing for this deficit, the Aer Rianta net surplus for the half year was £167,000, compared to £116,000 for the same period of 1962. Chief executive Gerry Dempsey pointed out, with his usual caution, that "the fortunes of a company managing an airport are inextricably bound up with the fortunes of the airlines using it and in particular with those of the

The Nevanna Swingtette played in the Collar of Gold restaurant at Dublin airport at the weekends in the early 1960s. The line-up was Bernard Hanratty (piano; now owner of the Howth Lodge hotel), master of ceremonies and vocals, Paddy Flanagan, clarinet, Billy Knight, electric piano accordeon, Paddy O'Connor, double bass, Arthur Agnew, and drums, the late Jack Hanratty, brother of Bernard. Apart from the airport gigs, the band also broadcast on *Late Dance Date* on Radio Éireann on Friday nights. This photograph was taken in 1963. Among the other bands that performed in the restaurant was Jack Flahive's; he is brother of Jimmy Flahive.

Above left: Butch Moore arrives home from the Eurovision song contest in Luxembourg, 1965. He was placed sixth with the song *Walking the streets in the rain.*
Photograph: G. A. Duncan

Right: American actors, Mel Ferrer and Audrey Hepburn, at the airport in 1964.
Photograph: G. A. Duncan

national airline".

The next year saw memorable national events. The remains of Sir Roger Casement were disinterred from Pentonville Prison in London; he had been hanged as a traitor in 1916, but thanks to the British prime minister, Harold Wilson, Casement's remains were sent back to Ireland. It was February, 1964, and the weather conditions were truly appalling. The plane carrying Casement's coffin arrived at Baldonnel for onward conveyance to Glasnevin, where the remains were finally interred. The president, Eamon de Valera, made a graveside oration in very cold and wet conditions. Baldonnel was subsequently renamed Casement aerodrome in commemoration of the event.

May 26, 1964, saw Eamon de Valera leave once again for the US. This time it was a State visit and he was given a full ceremonial departure from the airport. This year, 1964, saw some notable national events. In Dublin, the new circular-shaped American embassy, like a Martello tower, was opened at the corner of Elgin Road and Pembroke Road in Ballsbridge, Dublin. Its inauguration created considerable public interest, and a certain amount of disquiet, because of the modernity of its architecture. Nearly thirty years later, it has merged into the landscape, and no one finds it remarkably intrusive, any more than Michael Scott's Busáras, which created even more public uproar a decade earlier.

When the new airport church, Our Lady Queen of Heaven, opened in 1964, it was welcomed as an impressive new facility. For years, the question of Mass celebration on Sundays had been unsatisfactorily resolved at the airport; many airport workers were, and continue to be, faithful adherents of the Catholic Church, yet the practice of that faith proved difficult. Dublin airport lies within the boundaries of Swords parish and is under the jurisdiction of the parish priest of Swords. The airport chaplain is a curate attached to Swords parish. Before the church, facilities provided were less than satisfactory, usually a corner of one of the hangars, with a makeshift altar. Much of the impetus for building a new church came from workers at the airport. By February, 1962, the staffs of the three companies, Aer Rianta, Aer Lingus and Aer Linte, had contributed the very considerable sum of £21,000 towards the

Dublin airport restaurant, August, 1967.
Photograph: Aer Lingus

cost of the building. The three companies contributed a further £5,000 between them; the total estimated cost of the project was £36,000.

Just as the original central terminal building had set architectural precedents for the modernity of its design, by Desmond FitzGerald, so too did the new church set an example. When it was opened, it was the first church of the modern age in the Dublin diocese, yet the Archbishop of Dublin who opened the building on July 26, 1964, Dr John Charles McQuaid, had a most conservative reputation. The church was not the work of one architect, but of an architectural practice, Robinson, Keefe and Devane, still going strong today. They designed the building to suit the needs of the growing airport congregation; the entrance is through a shaded atrium, which bears some resemblance to a medieval cloister. The church itself is a rectangular shape; grey-coloured bricks and natural wood are used on the external finish. The interior of the church is much quieter in style than most modern ecclesiastical designs, with interesting stained-glass windows. It contains decorations and statuary by Helen Moloney, Sheila Corcoran and Oisín Kelly. The church has always been well used by airport staff and local people as well; just as the old Collar of Gold restaurant was very popular with local residents, so too is the church. Weddings at the church take place frequently and so many local people attend Mass there that the ensuing car parking problems brought calls for the removal of the church to another site, where less congestion would be caused. The Dublin diocese has always resisted these suggestions of a new location for the church.

The year it was opened, the new church provided spiritual sustenance for the relatives of the hundreds of Irish troops who left from Dublin airport for United Nations duty in Cyprus and for those who were killed in action there. That

Mediterranean country was embroiled in a struggle for independence, with conflicting Greek Cypriot and Turkish factions involved, and it was the first taste of UN duty for the Irish soldiers since the terrible days of the Congo, in the early 1960s.

Three other events caught the public interest in 1964; two Dublin playwrights died, Sean O'Casey and Brendan Behan. O'Casey, although a quintessential Dubliner, had long since moved to the quieter climes of Devon, but Behan had followed his rumbustious trail through Dublin and its pubs right to the end. The stories of Behan's wit, his affable persona when sober and his violently abusive outbursts when drunk, were the stuff of which Dublin legends were made. Behan worked very hard to make sure that legend and reality were in close harmony. Another building was well under way in Dublin, not entirely accepted, as was the new Dublin airport church. The enormous height of the new Liberty Hall skyscraper, a veritable monument to trade unionism in the city, was being built. It was officially opened on May 1, 1965. The architectural purists were vociferous in their criticism.

Nineteen sixty-five saw new aircraft in the Aer Lingus livery come to the airport; the airline took delivery of its first four BAC One-Eleven jets, still in the fleet today. The BAC aircraft proved their worth on UK and Continental European routes and assuaged the disappointment of Aer Lingus management earlier in the decade, when the Government refused the airline permission to go ahead with the purchase of French-built Caravelle jets. Nineteen sixty-five also saw runway 17/35 extended to 6,800 feet. Planning began for clearing the site for the new passenger terminal. On the political stage, 1965 was distinguished by the visit to Captain Terence O'Neill, Prime Minister of Northern Ireland, by Seán Lemass, the Taoiseach. The very idea of Lemass going to visit Stormont shook many fundamentalists on both sides of the border, so the year was at least memorable on the political front.

Cardinal William Conway, Archbishop of Armagh since 1963, was made Cardinal in 1965. He is seen here on his return from Rome; at the airport, he was welcomed by the Taoiseach, Sean Lemass. Cardinal Conway died in 1977 and was succeeded as archbishop of Armagh and subsequently as cardinal in 1979 by Tomás Ó Fiaich, who died in 1990.
Photograph: G. A. Duncan

Leo Carroll, senior airports' architect at the Department of Industry and Commerce in the 1960s. He was the man responsible for designing the new Dublin airport terminal, opened in 1972.

Unusual visitors continued to come to Dublin airport, as noted by aviation historian Paul Duffy. By the 1960s, aircraft from a total of forty-nine countries had touched down at Collinstown. Some of the most exotic visitors were a Cessna from Kenya, a Vagabond from Morocco and other small aircraft from as far away as Nigeria, Mexico and South Africa. DC4s and DC6s, from Lebanon, then an entirely peaceful country, with a capital, Beirut, described as the "Paris of the Middle East", were frequent visitors at Dublin airport. So too were many freighter aircraft used for shipping out meat.

The Globemasters were well-known to aircraft spotters at Dublin airport during the UN airlifts to the Congo, which started in 1962. One version of the Globemaster, the C–124, was used by a Panamanian company, Aeronaves de Panama, for freight-carrying purposes. One of these Globemaster aircraft came to Dublin in the mid-1960s, for freight operations. After five days it took off without paying the airport fees and without getting Air Traffic Control clearance to leave for Marseilles in southern France. Later on that trip, it crashed when taking off from Marseilles, killing all four people on board and bringing down the company itself. Another unusual visitor to Dublin was the Ilyushin IL–14, bringing a Bulgarian football team to Dublin. This was the first aircraft from eastern Europe to land, but by the time the decade was out, planes from Poland and Romania, as well as from Cuba, had appeared at the airport.

Two links with the past were broken in 1966, when Seán T. O'Kelly, the president from 1945 until 1959, died, and Seán Lemass retired as Taoiseach, to be succeeded by Jack Lynch. Lemass had won the previous year's election for Fianna Fáil. The most striking news story of 1966 was the blowing up of Nelson's Pillar, a Dublin landmark for generations. No one knows to this day who set off the explosion, which did little damage, apart from the pillar. When the army removed the stump of the pillar, hundreds of windows were broken in O'Connell Street.

That year was memorable at the airport, too, for not alone did Colonel Delamer retire from the position of airport manager, after twenty years' service, but detailed planning work began on the separation of Aer Rianta from Aer Lingus and Aerlínte, as proposed in the 1965 bill. Delamer retired in September, 1966, at the age of sixty-seven. His deputy, Colonel Tuohy, also retired in 1966. After he retired from his airport job, Delamer went to work for a company called Technico, in the communications business, run by his son Peter. In Technico, the colonel worked part-time and was fairly active almost until the end. He died in 1983. Delamer's retirement left something of a gap at the airport, which was temporarily filled by Gerry Giltrap, who, for a short period, became acting airport manager. Niall Weldon held the same position that year.

The job of running the airport was quite restricted in those days, remembers Gerry Giltrap. The management of the airport was the work of a department of Aer Lingus, in practice, and was limited in scope to such items as the fire service, maintenance and the letting of advertising concessions, as well as other comparatively minor matters at the time, like car parking. But this situation was to change and Giltrap recalls being a member of the working group that was set up around 1966 to advise the Department of Transport and Power on the most suitable administrative structures for the airports.

He says that the unanimous verdict of the working group was that all three airports, Dublin, Cork and Shannon, should be integrated into one national authority, under the Aer Rianta banner, and that any direct connection between Aer Rianta and Aer Lingus should be severed. The aim was that the airport managers would concentrate on providing a service to all the airport customers, so that there should be no degree of attachment between the user and the supplier of the service, nowadays considered normal practice in airport management worldwide. Apart from Giltrap, the other people on the working group were Seán O'Connor, who was the manager of Shannon airport and an employee of the Department of Transport and Power, and another civil servant, Tim O'Malley.

Not long ago, Derek Keogh, chief executive of Aer Rianta, gave a lecture in which he stated that all aspects of airport planning had been reviewed very thoroughly. As part of the exercise, the old files dating back to 1966 were dusted down and it was found that the conclusions of the working group then on how an airport should be run were not greatly different from the more recently arrived-at conclusions.

The following year saw two aircraft crashes, one at the airport, the other in nearby County Meath. On January 19, 1967, Dublin airport celebrated its twenty-seventh birthday without ever having had a single fatal air crash, but this enviable record was soon to be changed. On June 12 that year, *Papa Mike*, a Bristol 170 freighter owned by Aer Turas, was coming in to runway 17/35 after flying from Prestwick in Scotland. The plane had a crew of two, the pilot, Captain Gordon Willis, a Canadian living in Drumcondra, Dublin, and his co-pilot, Percy Maynard of Templeogue, Dublin. The aircraft was not carrying any freight. It was a quiet Monday evening at Collinstown; the port engine of the doomed plane failed. Attempting to overshoot, the aircraft slewed off the runway, hit the penthouse on the roof of pier B, and careered into a hut at the south-east corner of the airfield. The plane burst into flames, making it impossible for rescuers to save the crew. Damage to the airport could have been much worse; the plane narrowly missed hitting the oil farm on the airport perimeter.

A mere ten days later came another crash. An Aer Lingus Viscount, on a training exercise, took off from Dublin airport without incident. Just after eight o'clock in the morning of June 22, the aircraft was heard to be performing erratically, with the

Extension of runway 17/35, 1965.

Vincent Fanning, director airports, who died in November, 1973. Educated in Christian Brothers schools in Dublin and Cork, he entered the civil service. He served in the Department of Industry and Commerce and then in the Department of Transport and Power. Fanning was appointed first airport manager at Cork, when it opened in 1961, and was transferred to Dublin airport as manager in 1967. In 1972, he was made director airports. He was survived by his wife, Vera, and four sons, Gerard, John, Paul and Robert. He always preferred to stay in the background; he was very popular with his colleagues.

engines alternating between high and low power. The aircraft spun into a field near Ashbourne, Co Meath, and exploded on impact, killing the three people on board, Captain Hugh O'Keeffe and cadet pilots John Kavanagh and Rory de Paor, aged nineteen and twenty respectively. Neither of the cadets had any Viscount flying experience.

Much worse was to come in March the following year, when Aer Lingus' superb safety record was tarnished by its worst ever crash. On March 24, 1968, an Aer Lingus Viscount was en route from Cork to London, when a brief message from the crew was picked up: "12,000 feet, descending, spinning rapidly". The cause of the crash has never been conclusively determined. None of the sixty-one passengers and crew survived. Arthur Wall, then with Aer Lingus, now chairman of Ryanair, remembers going to Dublin airport and seeing the passenger list start to come through; his brother's name was third on the list. The news that emerged in sketchy form on the Radio Éireann news bulletin that lunchtime was soon confirmed and, even though the plane had taken off from Cork airport, the sense of loss was as palpable at Dublin airport, indeed nationally.

There were rumblings about the proposed new set up at Dublin airport in 1967, a certain coolness from Aer Lingus. The airline was not overly enthusiastic about the proposal to set up Aer Rianta. In 1967, Professor Patrick Lynch, the chairman of Aer Lingus, said: "I hope the Minister for Tranport and Power may be able to find satisfactory solutions to the organisational problems of Aer Rianta as a separate entity. I would look forward to seeing Aer Rianta evolve into an independent authority and with the autonomy and flexibility that would enable it to become responsible for the effective administration of Cork, Dublin and Shannon airports". Nineteen sixty-seven was also the year that the legendary J. F. Dempsey retired, the strongest personality at Dublin airport, responsible until then for the activities of both Aer Lingus and Aer Rianta. He was succeeded by the equally legendary Michael Dargan. As Dempsey retired from active service at the airport, a very famous Dublin institution closed its doors, Jammets restaurant in Nassau Street. In its demise, it joined other landmark institutions in the city, like the Russell Hotel, at the corner of St Stephen's Green and Harcourt Street, the Red Bank in D'Olier Street and the Royal Hibernian Hotel in Dawson Street, which closed down later, in 1982. As Jammets were pulling down the shutters for the last time, so too were the halcyon days of the restaurant in the original terminal building coming to an end, never to be quite recaptured. Nineteen sixty-seven also saw the demise of that great but truly eccentric poet of rough manners, Patrick Kavanagh.

The American singing star of the 1960s, Pat Boone, arrives at the airport for an Irish tour.
Photograph: G. A. Duncan

One of the "characters" of Dublin airport for some twenty years (he is now retired), was Christy Darcy, who returned home from the US and started working at the airport, as a cleaner. From there, he transferred to the car parks, and then to the vending services. He says that he enjoyed every minute of his work at the airport: "it was great, meeting different people. The majority of people are nice, decent people and I loved every minute of it". He remembers that when he came back from America, it was very hard to settle down, but when he started working at the airport, he did just that. "We worked as one big happy family, more or less", he says. Christy was one of the last of the bicycle brigade; in the early years of the airport, nearly everyone who worked at Collinstown came by bicycle. Car owners were very few and far between, right up to the end of the 1950s. But Christy maintained the bicycle tradition right to the end of his time at the airport, cycling in and out from Drumcondra every day, a four mile journey each way, even though he had a modern car parked in his driveway at home! Another great "character" on the airport payroll was Sonny Cullen, the window cleaner. John King, who was personnel manager and then company secretary at Aer Rianta for many years, remembers that although Sonny looked delicate, he must have been as "tough as nails, because he was out in all weathers, cleaning the windows at the airport". He went out in a blaze of laughter, producing his retirement speech on a toilet roll, remembers John King. Yet there was a serious side to Sonny that was not so widely known.

Sonny Cullen was always ready to help invalids on and off Lourdes pilgrimage flights. He is still widely remembered around the airport for his infectiously funny sense of humour, just as some of the older "characters" are equally well remembered, years after their retirement or death. One of the early firemen, Joe Lynch, who was very dedicated to his job, is often recalled, and so is the last survivor of the Watch Office, that venerable institution that formed the core of airport activities years ago. Frank McCartan is the last of the great bunch of fellows who were associated with the Watch Office. The Watch Office was the forerunner of the present-day Airport Duty Office.

Dr Christian Barnard, the South African heart transplant pioneer, arrived at Dublin airport for a visit to Ireland in the late 1960s.
Photograph: G. A. Duncan

The time was fast approaching for all the plans of the previous few years for Aer Rianta to be put into practice. The new company came into operation on July 1, 1968, with a board separate to Aer Lingus. A general manager, R. C. O'Connor, was appointed; he was a former assistant secretary of the Department of Transport and Power, and some staff were given the option of transferring from Aer Lingus. John Connor was appointed chairman. The embryonic operation in 1968 embraced the running of Dublin airport; it was not until April 1, 1969, that Cork and Shannon airports came under the aegis of Aer Rianta. Two of the people who transferred were John King and Jimmy O'Sullivan. King had joined Aer Lingus in 1946 and when Aer Rianta was set up in 1968, he headed its personnel function. O'Sullivan had joined Aer Lingus in 1947; after he was called to the Bar in 1951, he spent two years as assistant secretary to the three companies, Aer Lingus, Aer Rianta and Aerlínte. When Aer Rianta was established in 1968, he was offered the position of company

Inside the airport church, opened in 1964 after a twelve year fund-raising effort by Aer Rianta and Aer Lingus staff.
Photograph: Neil MacDougald

Outside the airport church. The statue (left), depicting Our Lady Queen of Heaven, was the work of Imogen Stuart.

The interior of Our Lady Queen of Heaven church, Dublin airport, officially opened July 26, 1964. When the Archbishop of Dublin, John Charles McQuaid, was blessing the church, he gave strict instructions that no photographs were to be taken. An enterprising photographer hid in a niche, but the Archbishop, duly annoyed, doused the unfortunate pressman with holy water.
Photograph: Pieter Stroethoff

secretary and took the offer.

R. C. O'Connor was subsequently made chief executive and O'Sullivan was promoted to deputy chief executive. When R. C. O'Connor retired in July, 1974, Jimmy O'Sullivan succeeded him. He remembers O'Connor well, as a strong, but likeable man, very tall, always impeccably dressed. O'Connor had been head of the aviation division of the Department of Transport and Power, but says O'Sullivan, he was a civil servant with a difference. "He was a great fighter, an aggressive man, but would treat everyone fairly. In many ways, he was the catalyst at the time of the change-over from Aer Lingus to Aer Rianta and he had the full backing of the Department, which was particularly important in that situation". O'Sullivan remembers that one would always be conscious of O'Connor's rather flamboyant presence. Another facet of his thoughtful personality is revealed by Jimmy O'Sullivan: O'Connor was a fluent Irish speaker and delighted in its use, speaking it at every opportunity, often doing interviews for Radió na Gaeltachta. He always wore a gold fáinne.

Another person who came into the ambit of Dublin airport shortly after the setting up of Aer Rianta was Vincent Fanning. He had been the first manager of Cork airport when it opened in 1961 and later became the first manager of Dublin airport under the new Aer Rianta regime. Not everyone who was offered the chance of going with Aer Rianta did so. Johnny Oppermann, whose flamboyant skills had turned the Collar of Gold restaurant into one of the culinary and social high spots of the Dublin

Dr Thekla Beere, secretary of the Department of Transport and Power and the first woman to be made secretary of a Government department. During the 1950s and 1960s, she played an influential role in the development of civil aviation, including the progress of Dublin airport.
Photograph: The Irish Times

area, especially during the 1960s, decided to opt for Aer Lingus.

He was catering manager for the airport and catering manager for Aer Lingus and did not believe that after the separation of the two companies, there would be scope for the big dinner dances and private functions that he had built up at the airport. At Aer Lingus, he organised the opening of the new airline catering division.

But although the division of the companies was in a certain sense traumatic, and posed a challenge to those Aer Lingus staff who decided to transfer to Aer Rianta, even though all pension rights and other entitlements accompanied their move, very soon, there was major work to be done. Running Dublin airport under the direct control of Aer Rianta was not simply a question of operating all facilities at the airport in a manner and style independent of Aer Lingus, something totally unthinkable even ten years previously. Serious planning was under way for a new terminal building, for it became clear in the early 1960s that the original FitzGerald terminal building was fast becoming totally inadequate for the volume of traffic. The first major task facing Aer Rianta management when the new company was set up was the start of detailed planning for the new terminal building, for which building work started in 1970. In November, 1969, work started on the Dublin airport hotel, which was opened in early 1971. Aer Rianta leased the site to Trusthouse Forte (Ireland).

Clouds were coming up on the horizon, the swinging sixties were coming to an end. In 1968, serious student riots took place in Paris, so serious that General de Gaulle was nearly toppled from power. Nineteen sixty-nine saw the Paris-domiciled Irish playwright and poet, Samuel Beckett, win the Nobel prize for literature. October that year saw the passing of Lord Douglas of Kirtleside, the man who had chosen Collinstown as an aerodrome site in World War I.

In Dublin at this same period, there was also student unrest. A typical example of their agitation came in 1969, when moves were under way to demolish two Georgian houses at the corner of Hume Street and St Stephen's Green. Large crowds, mainly of students, gathered at the site to unsuccessfully prevent the demolition of the houses. A total of 4,000 people attended a People's Democracy rally outside the GPO. The first skirmish in the Northern troubles had taken place in Dungannon in 1968, over a housing allocation, but in the summer of 1969, this unrest flared into violence. There was widespread violence in west Belfast, and in other locations, principally Derry, with the first fatalities of the troubles. So serious did the situation become that British Prime Minister Harold Wilson made the fateful decision to send

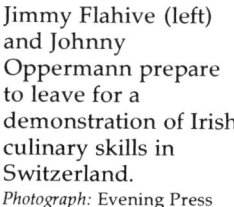

Jimmy Flahive (left) and Johnny Oppermann prepare to leave for a demonstration of Irish culinary skills in Switzerland.
Photograph: Evening Press

The King and Queen of the Belgians during their visit to Dublin, 1968.
Photograph: G. A. Duncan

Bob Hope, the American comedian, is piped into the airport, 1968. He was amused by a mural showing the first balloon flight in Ireland: "Mr Crosbie ascending from Ranelagh Gardens, January 19, 1785". "Bing's first flight", he said. "1785? Yeah, that would be about right".
Photograph: G. A. Duncan

in the British army. The first contingent arrived in Derry in the middle of August, 1969. The troubles are still going on, twenty-one years and 2,500 fatalities later. The more immediate effect of them as far as the aviation business was concerned, was to create a serious downturn in tourism. There were some lean years ahead for Aer Lingus, sparse too for Dublin airport, because of the lack of growth in passenger numbers in the early years of the 1970s. But a decision made long before the troubles started, to extend the main 06/24 runway to 7,500 feet, was put into practice at Dublin airport in 1969. It was business as usual for the new Aer Rianta company, despite the internal organisational problems of establishing the new company and the wider difficulties looming on the national tourism front. August, 1969 also saw work begin on the new airport sports' centre.

Front page, *The Irish Times*, January 19, 1970 — thirty years after Dublin airport was opened.

CHAPTER VI

Preparing for the Pope

THE 1970s began with much apprehension, a concern created by the events in the North, where the situation had been deteriorating steadily since the August of the previous year. The widescale riots in west Belfast and the Bogside district of Derry had been the signal for the start of continuing disturbances and unrest; the effects were already being felt in tourism, with substantial fallings-off in tourist traffic from Britain and America. Aer Lingus bore the brunt of this decline, but naturally the decrease in traffic affected Dublin and the other two airports under the control of the fledgling Aer Rianta company, just two years old. Yet the statistics for Dublin airport for 1969/70 were reasonable in the circumstances, a total of 1,737,151 passengers and 37,122 metric tonnes of cargo were carried, with 66,863 aircraft movements recorded for the year. In 1970/71, 1,897,917 passengers used the airport.

While the Bogside district, that depressed and deprived area of housing that lies beneath the walls of Derry, had been so much in the news for violent events during the late summer of 1969, in 1970 it shot to prominence for an entirely different reason. A young girl from the district, stage name Dana, won the Eurovision song

Dr Patrick Hillery (left), then Minister for Foreign Affairs, and Jack Lynch, then Taoiseach, sign Ireland's treaty of accession to the European Economic Community, on January 22, 1972.
Photograph: European Commission

contest with her rendition of *All Kinds of Everything,* a song written by two Dublin printers, Derry Lindsay and Jackie Smith. When Dana returned in triumph from the contest in Amsterdam, she was greeted with fervour at the airport and by a crowd of journalists, radio and TV crews, all anxious to capture the moment of arrival by this young girl.

After her arrival at Dublin airport, she transferred to a second plane, which made a celebratory flight to Eglinton airfield just outside Derry. Many media people were on that flight, along with Dana: it was a lively and somewhat rumbustious occasion. One of the people on the flight who remembers it clearly was veteran RTE commentator, now retired, P. P. O'Reilly, who was covering it for the organisation. Dana's homecoming to Derry was an exciting time for that beleaguered city, a welcome pause for a while from the troubles that gripped it and its inhabitants. Twenty years later, Dana, now married with a family, continues her singing career and remains a well-known stage and screen performer, inside and outside Ireland.

Another noted personality, this time political, who visited Ireland in 1970, made a much more low-key impact: U.S. president Richard Nixon. His rather dour character drew unfavourable comparisons with John F. Kennedy, and Nixon's Irish visit was far less exciting than the Kennedy visit seven years previously. When Nixon and his wife, Pat, arrived at Dublin airport, the contrast between them and John F. Kennedy could not have been greater. Kennedy came trailing clouds of adulation; Nixon glowered and engendered a sense of unease. His official visit to Dublin, followed by a visit to Timahoe in County Laois, burial place of his ancestors, drew widespread coverage in the media, but the uplifting enthusiasm of the Kennedy visit was totally absent. The 1960s had been a decade of youthful hope and inspiration, full of confidence and zest.

Just as the 1920s had been the time of the flapper, ceaselessly dancing away the magic hours of the night, so too had the 1960s been the time of the Beatles and the mini skirt. Yet with the events of Paris in 1968, when the students took to the streets in open warfare, and Prague the same year, when the armies of the Warsaw Pact invaded Czechoslovakia to put down the infant, liberalising "Prague Spring", and the bloody conflict of Belfast and Derry in 1969, the euphoria of the decade vanished almost like a balloon being pricked. The 1970s were dull, tedious and beset with economic and political crises; the Nixon visit to Ireland in 1970 was an entirely

Left: The Irish boxing team leaves for a contest in Glasgow, 1970. Front left is Benny Caribini, the team's trainer.
Photograph: G. A. Duncan

Right: Flying horses: Department of Agriculture officials supervise the unloading of a horse at the airport, 1970.
Photograph: G. A. Duncan

Above: The first Aer Lingus 747, the *St Colmcille,* arrives at Dublin airport on March 6, 1971. It totally overshadows the replica of the first Aer Lingus plane, the de Havilland Dragon DH84, the *Iolar,* which opened the airline's services in 1936.
Photograph: Aer Lingus

Left: A Boeing 737-300; the series came into service with Lufthansa, the German airline, in 1986. Lufthansa started scheduled services from Dublin airport in 1972.
Photograph: Lufthansa

Pier A under construction: such was the pressure of growth in passenger numbers that work started on the new terminal building (opposite page) less than ten years later.
Photograph: Frank Fennell Photography

appropriate harbinger of the decade. Restrictions started to hem in the life of the country, not only in the form of parking meters, which were introduced to Dublin amid considerable controversy, but in the increasing limitations imposed by the Northern troubles.

Jack Doyle remembers 1970, but for different reasons. He had spent over twenty years working for Aer Lingus. In 1966, he had gone over to technical control and, in 1970, he was appointed to the position of assistant airport manager at Dublin airport. He spent two years in that job, before promoted to airport manager, a post he held between 1972 and 1976. A man with a wry sense of humour, one of his stories concerns the visit by Sybil Connolly, the haute couture designer, to Dublin airport with five mannequins. The girls were photographed in endlessly different positions draped around the staircases in the old terminal building.

This was just before the old terminal building went out of public use and Doyle remembers that one airport employee, who was prone to inventing malapropisms, was asked the cause of the commotion. He replied: "Ah nothing too much, it is only Silver Connolly and her managers". Another wryly amusing episode remembered

Week forty-five of construction work on the new terminal; the photograph was taken on July 10, 1970.
Photograph: Frank Fennell Photography

Interior of the new terminal building, in the closing stages of construction, 1972.
Photograph: Frank Fennell Photography

Four Aer Rianta information girls seen in an early example of company uniform. From left: Eithne O'Sullivan, Carmel Hogan, Una Fenning and Rita Bergin.
Photograph: Robert Allen Photography

by Jack Doyle from this time was the day Mícheál MacLiammóir and Hilton Edwards came to the airport for a flight to Paris. They were late and missed the flight; to add insult to injury, they were also charged a "no show" fee by Aer Lingus and Doyle remembers MacLiammóir standing in the centre of the concourse in the old terminal building, putting on a theatrical show worthy of the old master at his height, tears streaking his mascara. MacLiammóir habitually wore stage make-up, even when wandering around town, outside the strange hours of the theatre.

Hilton Edwards is also remembered by David Lord, who worked in the airport restaurant for many years until his retirement in 1989. Edwards endeared himself by saying to Lord: "Since you left the Russell, it has gone downhill". The Russell Hotel at the corner of Harcourt Street and St Stephen's Green, and now replaced by a bland office block lacking in any kind of character, was one of the old gastronomic high points in the city. Its restaurant attracted many names on the social circuit, who dined splendidly, gazing out over St. Stephen's Green from its elegant Georgian windows.

David Lord left this haven of culinary excellence, then run by the late Ken Besson, who also ran the Royal Hibernian Hotel in Dawson Street, for the totally different confines of the airport restaurant, at the time that Johnny Oppermann was transferring over to Aer Lingus catering. Neil Fitzpatrick was put in charge of the airport catering under the new Aer Rianta regime. Lord has a vivid recollection of one incident in the airport restaurant in 1970, involving Seán Lemass and his son-in-law Charles Haughey. They were enjoying their meal, with their families, when news came through of a bomb scare. Nearly all the diners evacuated the restaurant, as requested by Lord and the other catering staff, but when they came to Seán Lemass, he replied: "No one is disturbing me from my lunch". The party sat there, in solitary splendour, while security people checked out the restaurant.

Charles Haughey, re-elected Taoiseach in 1989, has always been a very good client of the airport restaurant, says David Lord. "He is very much a family man and was always a very regular diner, with his wife, Maureen, and friends, either at night, or sometimes for Sunday lunch". On one occasion, when Pat O'Connor was in the Haughey group dining in the restaurant, O'Connor found a large pearl in his oyster, which he promptly gave to Maureen Haughey.

Matters of airport administration at this period are well remembered by James O'Sullivan, who became secretary of Aer Rianta when the company was established in 1968.

The first major task that faced Aer Rianta management was the planning and construction of the new airport terminal. The old terminal, which remained in public use until 1972, had long since outgrown its capacity, even though its architect, Desmond FitzGerald, had designed it so that the building could be expanded. Aer Lingus had already started a major building programme at the airport, first with the opening of the airline's head office in 1966, then with the new Aer Rianta cargo terminal, rented to Aer Lingus. But the Aer Lingus building, completed in 1971, was at the time the largest volume building in Ireland. The new hangar, on the north side of the airport, was built to house the Boeing 747 aircraft in the airline's fleet. The vast new building, supplemented by other new buildings for technical stores, flight simulators and an engine test cell, became a striking new feature on the skyline at the airport, one of the most telling additions to the visual appearance of the airport. But while work was being completed on this great new hangar, even more complicated design and building work was going on to complete the new passenger terminal.

P. P. O'Reilly, the veteran broadcaster, who has vivid memories of Dana's homecoming to Derry, after the 1970 Eurovision song contest.
Photograph: R. W. Hammond, Cork

The Seán Lemass memorial at Dublin airport. Lemass, Taoiseach between 1959 and 1966, died in 1971.

Left: A Bulgarian trade delegation arrives at Dublin airport, 1970. The cold war was still at its height, especially since the Warsaw Pact countries' invasion of Czechoslovakia two years previously.
Photograph: G. A. Duncan

Right: a group of handicapped people prepare to fly to Lourdes, 1971. Many Aer Rianta workers at the airport belong to the Brancardiers, a voluntary religious organisation that has helped people going on pilgrimage, especially to Lourdes, for many years.
Photograph: G. A. Duncan

Already Aer Rianta had had much experience of terminal construction, for the new terminal at Shannon was opened, on time, in 1971, despite lengthy industrial relations disputes there. For Dublin airport, the company drew up a long-term development plan which included the new terminal, a new road network, and apron and runway extensions.

Construction work on the new terminal began in 1969; the five-storey building with basement was designed to handle six million passengers a year. Leo Carroll, the chief airports architect, said at the time of its construction, that passenger traffic was expected to grow four-fold on a worldwide basis during the 1970s, a forecast that proved hopelessly over-optimistic because of the global economic crises of that decade. The Dublin passenger projections, made around 1970, for twenty years hence, 1990, were for over ten million passengers a year. The first stage in the design and construction of the new airport terminal was the appointment of AEC, an American firm of consultants, who developed the projections for the use of the new terminal. The scheme had been approved in principle, detailed planning work began in June, 1968, and the £10 million contract was placed with John Sisk & Son (Dublin). The first phase, operational in May, 1971, was the decagon concrete, steel and glass structure used as the arrival and departure facility for trans-Atlantic 747s and 707s. The second phase was the main terminal building with the top two of its five storeys designed as a car park. At ground level, the terminal building is 320 feet long and 300 feet deep, reducing to 220 feet deep at first floor level. The main concourse of the terminal is at departure level, with a series of island check-in desks. Shopping facilities were provided at this level, with bar and restaurants above it, on the mezzanine level. The buildings are fully air conditioned, for the heat generated by 10,000 people in the terminal and 3,000 in the pavilion, although the chilling units, included in the original design and meant for use in hot summer weather, were never used. They were subsequently discarded as an unnecessary luxury. Just as the first airport construction in the late 1930s was held up by strikes, so was the building of the new terminal held up by a cement strike.

The old terminal had been designed to handle 100,000 passengers a year, but by the end of its life span was handling two million. The new terminal was opened on May 31, 1972, by the then Taoiseach, Jack Lynch. The opening day was chaotic, remember airport staff who were there; the conveyor systems for taking luggage from the check-in desks to the aircraft loading areas did not work as planned, and frantic hours of work went into fine tuning those systems. But the terminal was duly opened, and if it did not have the design style of its predecessor, it was far more functional.

The mandarins of the Central Bank launch decimal currency upon an unsuspecting Irish public, February 15, 1971.
Photograph: Lensmen

Below left: Liam Cosgrave, Taoiseach of the new Coalition government in 1973.
Photograph: Lensmen

Right: the late President Cearbhall Ó Dálaigh, who resigned in 1976 to "protect the dignity of the Office" after the "thundering disgrace" remarks made by Minister for Defence Patrick Donegan.
Photograph: Lensmen

Below left: Seán Ó Riada (at piano) with singer Sean O Sé. Ó Riada (1931-1971) scaled great heights as an arranger, broadcaster and composer before dying at a tragically young age. Airport staff remember him passing through Dublin airport many times in the years immediately before his death, en route to London for medical treatment.
Photograph: RTE illustrations library

Right: in 1970, Dana, the singer from Derry, won the Eurovision song contest in Amsterdam; the following year, the contest was held at the Gaiety Theatre, Dublin. Dana (left) is seen here with the 1971 winner, "Severine", who sang for Monaco.
Photograph: RTE illustrations library

But just as the new terminal was being opened, the signs for air traffic in and out of Ireland were ominous. The first Boeing 747 in Irish colours, the *St Colmcille,* arrived at Dublin airport on March 6, 1971; a large crowd of distinguished guests saw the plane taxi-ing in. It was met on the ramp by the reconstruction of the de Havilland Dragon, named *Iolar,* with which Aer Lingus opened its flying career in 1936. Yet 1972 saw trans-Atlantic travel start sinking, largely due to the Northern troubles. That year, traffic was down six per cent. On the cross-channel and European routes, too, traffic fell, down by eleven per cent between Ireland and Britain in 1972/73 and down by six per cent on continental European routes during the same period.

Nationally, there was depressing news. Seán Lemass, the supremely skilled politician, who became a great enthusiast for aviation in Ireland after an early lack of conviction on the subject, died in May 1971.

Two years after his death, a memorial to Seán Lemass was unveiled at the airport in a ceremony attended by politicians of all parties, led by the then Taoiseach, Liam Cosgrave. Mrs Kathleen Lemass, widow of Seán, was there, along with the Haughey family. R. C. O'Connor, chief executive of Aer Rianta, and John Connor, the company's chairman, greeted the guests, who also included the former president, Eamon de Valera, John Leydon, former secretary of the Department of Industry and Commerce, and Colonel W. P. Delamer. Airport manager, Jack Doyle, kept the event moving smoothly. At the ceremony, it was noted that the stones surrounding the plaque had been brought from the Dublin mountains, where Captain Noel Lemass, brother of Seán, had been killed during the War of Independence.

The year of the passing of Seán Lemass, 1971 saw a notable happening at the airport; Aer Rianta launched *Runway* staff magazine under its first editor, John Power; it is still going strong today under editor Brian McCabe. Until the creation of Aer Rianta as a separate company in 1968, the affairs of Aer Rianta were covered, somewhat intermittently, in *Aer Scéala,* published by Aer Lingus, but it took three years to turn the aspirations for Aer Rianta's own staff magazine into a reality. 1971 saw the introduction of decimal currency, which confused many people initially, and which was also a cover for some heavy, disguised inflationary price rises. That year also saw the start of direct dialling for Dublin telephone subscribers calling Belfast and London.

Iona Airways site on the west side of Dublin airport. This photograph was taken about twenty years ago and the company has developed its base considerably since then.

Owen Clarke received a promotion in 1971. He had been senior airport duty officer, having worked in a number of management positions in both Aer Lingus and Aer Rianta. His new job involved controlling the administration process at Dublin airport. A recent arrival at Dublin airport was Dubliner Brendan Clancy, an engineer by profession, who had spent the previous ten years at Cork airport. He is now assistant chief executive–technical services.

If 1971 was full of gloomy news, 1972 was worse. January 30 saw one of the most infamous episodes in 20th century Irish history, during a march in Derry. British paratroopers fired on and killed thirteen civilians taking part in an anti-internment protest. There was widespread anger at the killings, which quickly became known as "Bloody Sunday". On February 2, during a huge march in the centre of Dublin, protesting against the killings, the British Embassy in Merrion Square was set alight. In the twenty-one years of the Northern troubles to date, these events marked one of the lowest points. Later that year, the old Unionist system of government in the North was replaced by direct rule from Britain. 1972 also saw the old Capitol cinema in Princes Street, behind the Metropole and beside the GPO, close down. The entire site, including the Metropole itself, a favourite venue for generations of Dubliners, was redeveloped and is now occupied by the British Home Stores.

Yet despite the gloomy national happenings of that year, two positive events happened at the airport: firstly the opening of the new terminal building and secondly, the start of services into Dublin by Lufthansa, the German carrier. Lufthansa started its all-year-round Dublin–Frankfurt service, with a stopover in Manchester, since discontinued. Joe Moore, the airline's general manager in Ireland, said that there was a growing demand by German holidaymakers for inclusive tours in Ireland. Other airlines operating into Dublin airport by 1972 included Alitalia, British European Airways, Iberia and SAS, the Scandinavian carrier.

Yet all was not sweetness and light between Aer Rianta and Aer Lingus, with increased rental costs projected for the new terminal at Dublin airport. Two years later, in 1974, Aer Rianta increased landing fees by thirty per cent; these increased

John Connor, first chairman, Aer Rianta. Born in Dublin and educated by the Christian Brothers, he entered the civil service in 1917, retiring in 1967. From 1955, he had been assistant secretary, Department of Industry and Commerce; in 1959, he transferred to the same position in the Department of Transport and Power.

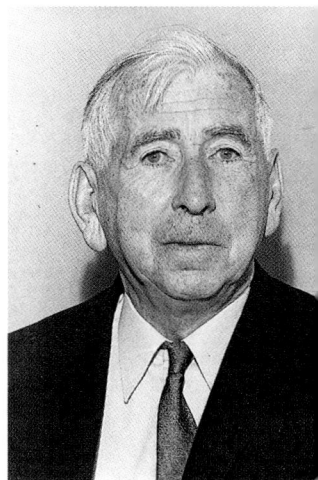

fees, as well as increased passenger load fees, brought in over £1 million extra revenue to the company. At the 1971/72 annual general meeting of Aer Rianta, chairman John Connor stated that the intention of the company was to develop revenue from non-aviation sources. In 1971/72, this revenue amounted to over £1.2 million. Despite niggling criticisms from Aer Lingus over proposals to increase fees for the use of the airport facilities, the first years of the company went well, so much so that at the 1970 annual general meeting, John Connor remarked: "There has been no significant criticism of Dublin airport; the absence of criticism is in itself a commendation".

Twenty-five-year presentations were made in 1972; recipients included Pearl Kirwan, then secretary to the chief architect. In the maintenance section, four men, Kit Johnson, Jim Gilligan, Jim Ellis and Kitt Finn, had over one hundred years' service between them. Sonny Cullen, from the cleaning section, received his twenty-five-years' membership medal from the ITGWU. Interestingly, the company ran an employee suggestions campaign to find a new name for itself. The new name, staff were told, had to be in Irish or have Irish connotations, must consist of one, two or three words and be consistent with the functions of an airports authority. The campaign drew unsuccessful conclusions; Aer Rianta continued in use.

Dublin airport saw a major improvement to its facilities with the introduction of new fire vehicles, each of which could carry 1,500 gallons of water and 200 gallons of foam liquid. Under the eagle eye of Jim McDonald, chief airport security officer, the

Left: Jack Doyle, Dublin airport manager, 1972-76.
Photograph: Robert Allen Photography

Right: Christopher Martin, now retired, once chief accountant.
Photograph: Robert Allen Photography

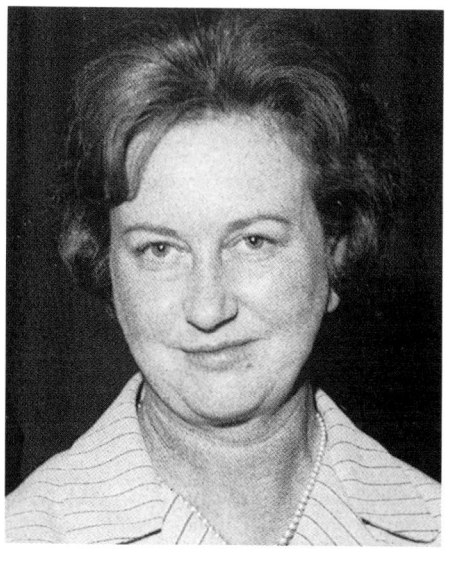

Left: Kitty Byrne, secretary to three chief executives, Jimmy O'Sullivan, Martin Dully and Derek Keogh.

Right: Johnny King, who headed the personnel function at Dublin airport and later became Aer Rianta company secretary.
Photograph: Robert Allen Photography

Left: Bill Beck, the legendary airport engineer, who worked at the airport from 1947 until his retirement in 1976.

Right: Tony McClafferty, Aer Rianta chairman, 1974-1980.

Left: R. C. O'Connor, chief executive, Aer Rianta, 1968-1974.

Right: Gerard Harvey, the first marketing director at Aer Rianta.
Photograph: An Post

new machines were put through their paces at the airport, before being permanently stationed there. Bill Beck, for so long a mainstay of the airport, was appointed to a new position, airports development engineer. He was succeeded as airport engineer by Brendan Clancy, who had been assistant engineer at Dublin, and engineer at Cork airport. Christopher Martin, the company accountant, made a presentation of a gold watch to John Langford, who retired. Langford joined the company in 1947 and in 1972 retired from the accountancy section, going home to his native Kerry to farm. The airport had a new chaplain, Fr Martin Tierney, a thirty-two-year-old Dubliner interested in athletics and golf.

The new terminal handled its first passenger, Ms Enda D. Kucher from New York, who was welcomed with a Waterford Crystal vase and a bouquet of flowers. The welcoming party consisted of Vincent Fanning, by now promoted to director–airports, and Ross Grant from the shopping centre at Dublin airport. One of the new features of the terminal was the Green/Red customs clearance system, seen for the first time in Ireland. It was already in use in a number of other European countries.

The staff suggestion scheme was hard at work. Eugene Baldwin of the maintenance section received £5 from Derek Keogh, head of administration, for his idea of an automatic battery-charging system for the fire and rescue equipment, while Jim Collier of airport maintenance also won £5 for a stick-on sign and label suggestion. The Dublin Airport Orphan Fund adopted a new name, Air Concern. During the summer season, discos were run every other Friday at the Boot Inn, to raise money for holidays for needy children.

Right: Hugh O'Hagan, an airport carpenter, whose boxing prowess was renowned. He represented Ireland in the 1948 Olympics and had 364 competitive matches.

Centre: Sonny Cullen, an airport window cleaner, well-known for his cheery sense of humour.

Far right: Joe Lynch, airport fire prevention officer, pictured on his retirement day.

Right: Two of Dublin airport's best-known secretaries, Pearl Kirwan (left) and Brenda Carley.

While 1972 saw the new terminal opening at Dublin airport, and a continuing programme of improvements being carried out within the company, a decision of major national significance was about to take place. Since the early 1930s, Irish industry had developed behind a tariff barrier, but in 1966, Seán Lemass took the first step away from this policy of protection when the Anglo–Irish free trade agreement was signed. At the stroke of midnight, on December 31, 1972, Ireland joined the EEC, along with Britain and Denmark, an accession that was to have the most far-reaching consequences for the country. Yet in the years immediately before Ireland joined what was then called the European Economic Community, one of the few political figures to realise the scale of economic and political change being proposed was Dr Garret FitzGerald, in the 1950s a familiar sight in the corridors of Aer Lingus.

The new year was another bad time: the world economic slump, caused by the oil crisis, when the Middle Eastern oil producing states started increasing their prices, had its impact in Ireland. Not only was there a general election in Ireland, which brought a Coalition government to power under Taoiseach Liam Cosgrave, but there was a presidential election, too, when Erskine Childers, once the Minister for Transport and Power, with responsibility for airports and aviation, became the

In 1974, Aer Rianta installed a new 600 line capacity telephone exchange at Dublin airport. The photograph shows Ann Smith (left) and Phil Morris working its predecessor. Ann Malone, née Smith, is now the telephone exchange supervisor.

short-lived President. Nineteen seventy-three was also a notable year for newspaper publishing; the *Sunday World* was launched and the critics were out in force, saying that the colour tabloid, full of pin-ups, would never survive. It did and now sells about 350,000 copies a week, making it the largest selling newspaper in Ireland. There was also a sombre side to life at the airport, as Jack Doyle, then the airport manager, recalls. The Northern security situation was still very volatile and a number of non-Irish airlines, notably the newly formed British Airways, were pressing Aer Rianta for security checks at the airport. British Airways even offered to run its security checks at Dublin airport, but this was unacceptable to Aer Rianta, which began its own checking system, introducing the "frisking" of departing passengers in 1973. One of the early casualties of the security situation in the early 1970s was the multi-storey car park, built on top of the main terminal building. The structure was used only briefly as a car park, before it was decided that it was too near the terminal building and apron for continued use.

At the beginning of 1973, Aer Rianta was able to display the architectural details of the new terminal building to the public, when an exhibition on the new building was opened at the Building Centre of Ireland in Lower Baggot Street. In his opening address, R. C. O'Connor, chief executive, said that the terminal was a symbol of Irish enterprise, professional expertise and a monument to the designers and builders. During the ten-day exhibition, Leo Carroll, chief airports architect, and some of the experts involved in the four-year task of designing and building the new terminal,

Left: Nicky Byrne takes a break in the airport boilerhouse.

Centre: Carol O'Donohue, the first female member of the airport security service.

Right: Jack Bannon, chief airport security officer.
Photographs: Neil MacDougald

The old Russell Hotel at the corner of St Stephen's Green and Harcourt Street; it had been acquired in 1947 by the late Ken Besson of the Royal Hibernian Hotel in Dawson Street. The Russell was closed down in 1975 and subsequently was demolished.
Photograph: Gillman Collection

The Metropole, cinema, restaurant and ballroom, was built in O'Connell Street, next to Eason's, in 1922, replacing the earlier Metropole Hotel destroyed during the 1916 Easter Rising. The "new" Metropole was demolished in 1973, making way for the British Home Stores.
Illustration: National Trust Archive

Two well-known characters about town in the 1970s: Hector Grey (left), the Scottish-born trader who changed shopping habits for generations of Dubliners and Noel Purcell (right), the quintessential Dublin actor.
Photographs: The Irish Times

gave lectures to architectural students. This public display less than a year after the terminal was officially opened was in contrast to the FitzGerald terminal, which was hidden under a blanket of secrecy during the years of the Emergency. Public attention was not focussed on FitzGerald's work until 1945; architectural sources believe the Emergency-long secrecy about the building explains why it never received its due public acclaim.

Figures released in early 1973 showed that in the financial year ended March, 1973, a total of 1,983,627 passengers used Dublin airport, while 43,694 metric tonnes of cargo was handled at the airport. Meanwhile, four barmen from the airport, Garry Benson, Paul McNally, Paddy Kelly and Martin Judge, came first, second, third and fourth respectively in the national cocktail competition. The late Garry Benson's creation was called "Garryowen".

Cupid struck in the accounts department. Mick Cashin, payroll supervisor, got married to Mary Carney, from the Dublin airport shops' section. At the celebratory party in the airport, Brian Hampson, newly appointed financial controller — he had just joined the company from Player & Wills (Ireland) — made the presentations. Another presentation made in the early summer of 1973 was to Captain Jim McGeown, assistant superintendent, technical (radar and navigational systems), Department of Transport and Power, one of the best-known people from the Department at the airport. He was especially well-known and popular with the maintenance department of Aer Rianta; he retired after thirty-five years' service with the air traffic technical service.

A number of organisational changes took place in Aer Rianta during the early summer of 1973, following the decision of R. C. O'Connor to retire from his position as chief executive in July, 1974. James O'Sullivan, the deputy chief executive and secretary, was named chief executive designate. Among the other appointments was Derek Keogh, as secretary of the company. His new responsibilities included public relations (run by Carl O'Sugrue) and personnel (headed by Johnny King). A new airport operations control centre was opened at the airport, following the decision by the international civil aviation organisation to place responsibility for aircraft

Left: U.S. president Richard Nixon, on arrival at Dublin airport for his official visit to Ireland in 1970. His visit lacked the interest, lustre and sparkle of the Kennedy tour, yet his international achievements were substantial. He withdrew American troops from Vietnam, started the process of détente with the USSR and began the American rapprochement with China.
Photograph: The Irish Times

Right: Neil Armstrong, the first man on the moon aboard the US space craft Apollo II, in 1969, came through Dublin airport in 1976, on a visit to Ireland.
Photograph: RTE illustrations library

safety on the apron with the relevant airport authorities. As part of the security system, a total of thirty-two closed circuit TV cameras were located around the airport, linked to the centre's eleven TV monitors. The engineer in charge of the project was Joe McGuinne.

A noted personality at the airport retired: Ted Sparling, who had worked with the company since 1947, when he transferred from the Air Corps at Baldonnel to work in the airport Watch Office. On his retirement, he was presented with a prototype of the new company tie by Derek Keogh, the out-going head of administration. Jim McDonald, chief airport security officer, and Jack Bannon, assistant security officer, together with a number of security officers, completed their firemanship and junior officer training courses at Stansted airfield in Essex. Meanwhile the first public baptism took place in the airport church, of Joseph Ellis, son of Brian Ellis, a former Aer Rianta staff member, and grandson of Jimmy Ellis, another Aer Rianta staff member.

The decline in passenger traffic through Dublin airport was reflected in the Aer Rianta accounts. In the financial year 1972/73, revenue was down from £4.46 million to £4.23 million, resulting in an increased loss, from £42,984 in 1971/72 to £1.03 million in 1972/73. The main factor was the continuance of the Northern troubles; passenger traffic at Dublin airport was down four per cent. A small sign of times to come happened in the summer of 1973, when a delegation from the local industries and public services union visited members of the aviation branch of the Workers' Union of Ireland, at Dublin airport. Brian Byrne, who joined Aer Rianta in 1969 from the Guinness brewery, was appointed industrial relations officer.

One of the major airlines using the airport changed its name and livery; British European Airways, which had started running scheduled flights from the UK to Dublin back in 1957, became part of British Airways, as did BOAC. The new company's first year of operation was 1972/73.

Back at Dublin airport, there were more operational changes. Brendan Murray, who was airport manager at Shannon, was promoted to head office in Dublin airport, as director–operations. Another promotion from Shannon was that of Tom

Jack Lynch, who returned as Taoiseach after the 1977 general election.
Photograph: Lensmen

Cullen, who had been working there for seven years, most recently as commercial division manager in the Shannon sales and catering service. On promotion, Tom Cullen became commercial manager in charge of the newly formed commercial division at head office, responsible for maximising revenue from all direct and indirect commercial activities throughout the organisation.

Gerry Heffernan, the shops manager at Dublin airport since 1967, was made sales manager in the new commercial division, reporting to Tom Cullen. Heffernan conducted a lot of his business at the foot of the escalator in the terminal building; it may have seemed a strange formula, but it worked. He worked morning, noon and night in the shops at Dublin airport, and Jack Doyle, then airport manager, remembers that he carried on almost like an Arab trader. Heffernan had a lot of political connections, especially with Donough O'Malley, the Minister for Education, and to the end of his days, he treasured a gold fountain pen given to him by O'Malley's widow. When Heffernan started in 1967, shopping facilities at the airport consisted of a small souvenir shop selling magazines, paperbacks, confectionery and souvenirs. Sales were £185,000 a year. By 1974, Heffernan had increased shop turnover to £1 million.

By a strange coincidence, both O'Malley and Heffernan died young, at the peak of their respective careers. With his new appointment, Heffernan continued to have direct responsibility for the shops at Dublin airport.

By the following year, Aer Rianta was putting substantial energy-saving measures into practice. Ireland was one of many countries hit by the oil crisis, which started the previous year. Britain went onto a three-day week; this was the lowest economic point of the 1970s. Financial stringency was so tight that even airport projects costing as little as £2,000 had to have departmental approval. Aer Rianta, to try and make up for the shortfall in revenue, proposed increases in landing charges, but when they came into effect on July 1, they were modified, partly due to pressure from Aer Lingus.

The airport control tower in the 1970s.

Top: Joe O'Rourke, retired chief fire officer at the airport. He still heads the Swords, County Dublin, fire service.
Photograph: Robert Allen Photography

Below: Jim Comer, crime prevention officer, Dublin airport.

A major international event that took place in Dublin in June, 1974 was the twenty-eighth conference of the Western European Airports Association. It met in Dublin over five days; the newly installed president was Jacques Block of Aéroports de Paris, which had just opened the new Charles de Gaulle airport at Roissy, north of Paris, replacing Le Bourget. When completed, the new airport, covering 7,500 acres, was scheduled to be the biggest in Europe. Here at home, there was an important communications development at Dublin airport: the new 600 line capacity telephone exchange, commissioned in co-operation with Ericsson's, the Swedish-owned telephone system manufacturers, was brought into service.

The summer of 1974 also saw the longest serving member of staff at Dublin airport retire. Joe Lynch, fire prevention officer, was the first man ever employed on firefighting duties at the airport, joining the company in 1940. He was well-known at the airport for his fire prevention lectures and fire fighting training. Another retirement was that of Danny Kelly, from airport maintenance, who had thirty years' service with the company. During 1974, substantial work took place on an overlay for runway 17/35. The runway had been built thirty years previously, and the heavy weight of aircraft like Boeing 747s was starting to break up the pavement. At a cost of £250,000, a three-tier layer of asphalt was placed on the runway surface. This new layer, explained Brendan Clancy, chief engineer, was up to 150 mm thick and a total of 17,000 tonnes of Marshall asphalt was used.

While 1974 saw progress made on the technical front at Dublin airport, there was carnage in the country. On May 17, a series of car bombs exploded in Dublin, at South Leinster Street, Talbot Street and Parnell Street, killing a total of twenty-five people. The explosions happened around 5.30 pm, during the height of the evening rush hour. Some ninety minutes later, a huge car bomb exploded outside a pub in Monaghan, killing six people. Later, two more people died from their injuries, bringing the total death toll to thirty-three. The explosions came at a time of intense instability in the North, when the loyalist workers' strike was in full swing and the Wilson government in London capitulated to their demands.

Another tragic event that year was the death of the President, Erskine Childers. Dr

Thekla Beere, for long connected with airport matters as secretary of the Department of Transport and Power, remembers vividly that she had been talking to him an hour previously on the Saturday night he died. She had left to go to another function, when the news came through that Childers had died suddenly. He was succeeded by that gentle Irish speaking scholar, Cearbhall Ó Dálaigh. However, 1974 did have its compensations; Dublin won the Gaelic football All-Ireland championships, the first of a series of four wins (the subsequent years it won were 1976, 1977 and 1983). Airport duty officer, Jack Scully, won the trophy for Aer Rianta in the pitch and putt interdepartmental match; it was the first time an Aer Rianta team had won this event.

Another prize, this time on the world stage, went to Seán MacBride, who won the Nobel peace prize. Tommy Cranitch, the airport's first resident press officer, remembers the time another Nobel prize winner, for literature, arrived at the airport. Samuel Beckett, the poet and playwright, long-time resident in Paris, was a very self-effacing man; the first time that Cranitch asked his name, Beckett walked right past. He asked him again, on the apron bus, and the great writer finally admitted his identity and shyly posed for the photographers. But he said that he never spoke to reporters. Spike Milligan was totally different, difficult to interview, because he could not be serious for one minute. When he arrived, Cranitch said: "Mr Milligan?" The reply came: "Mister Milligan! Things are looking up!"

From the start of 1975, there was a heavy emphasis on security training at the airport, tragically prophetic, as it turned out. Advanced security and firefighting training courses took place at Dublin airport, under the control of Jim McDonald, chief airport security officer, and Jack Bannon, then his assistant. One of the aims of the training was to increase still further the efficiency of security at the airport, especially in relation to what management described as "the current problem of international terrorism". For the first time ever, police dog trials were held in Ireland in June that year, at Dublin airport. They were organised by airport security and the Garda Síochána dog units; the winner was an airport dog named King, handled by Paddy Hughes of the airport security service, while third place went to Lordy, handled by Barney Reynolds, also of the airport security service. Former President Eamon de Valera died; 70,000 people filed past his coffin in City Hall. He was buried beside other national leaders, in Glasnevin cemetery.

During 1975, one particularly violent incident in the North shook the country: the Miami showband, driving North for a gig, were stopped at a bogus checkpoint, then three of its members were killed. Loyalist paramilitaries were involved, as was the case when the airport itself was attacked on November 29 that year. It was a Saturday afternoon, when the relative peace and quiet of the terminal was shattered by two bombs going off. David Lord from the restaurant was on the mezzanine balcony when it happened and remembers clearly the first bomb exploding in the arrivals area bar. The whole terminal building shook with the sound of the detonation.

It was quickly followed by a second bomb, which went off in a cubicle in an arrivals area lavatory. This explosion had tragic consequences: John Hayes, an Aer Lingus loader, was killed in the blast. Several people were injured, including two Australian tourists. The shock of the two blasts inside the terminal building caused security to be tightened even further; today, Dublin airport remains the only airport in western Europe where passengers and visitors have to go through a series of checks before they enter the building. First of all, there is an airport security checkpoint as cars approach the terminal, then going into the terminal building, passengers' luggage is scanned with a mobile scanner. The bombs at the airport in November, 1975 were profoundly shocking for everyone there at the time, as well as airport management and personnel and, as a result, the ever-tighter security vigilance has never been relaxed. One of the results, as Jack Doyle, airport manager at the time of the bombing, which was claimed by the UDA, is that delays to flights are

Left: American evangelist Billy Graham in Dublin, 1972; he was a "larger than life" arrival at the airport.
Photograph: G. A. Duncan

Right: Sybil Connolly, the fashion designer. During a photographic shoot at the airport of some of her designs, an airport worker referred to "Silver Connolly and her managers".
Photograph: Lensmen

inevitable. Passengers suffer from these delays and there is no sign that this vigilance can be relaxed in the foreseeable future, a far cry from the easy-going times up until the end of the 1960s, when passengers could stroll in and out of the terminal as they pleased. But in those far-off days, street crime in Dublin was virtually unknown, at any hour.

Energy conservation was very much on the mind of Aer Rianta management, all part of the economy drive at the airport. Board member, Frank McDonnell, was especially keen on the conservation issue, remembers Brendan Clancy. In its 1975 annual report, the company said that it was coping admirably with the twin evils of traffic stagnation and inflation. At its annual general meeting in July, 1975, the Aer Rianta chairman, Tony McClafferty, reported an operating surplus for the previous nine months of £1.67 million. By way of contrast, Aer Lingus turned in a £5.3 million loss for its year to March 31 that year. As part of the battle against rising costs, Dublin airport engineer Joe McGuinne spearheaded a campaign to cut energy costs, pointing out that if conservation steps were not taken, the company's energy bill for 1975 could top the £1 million mark. Between January and March, 1975, Dublin airport achieved a 9.19 per cent reduction in its electricity usage, and a 5.4 per cent cut in its consumption of oil and turf. After the campaign had finished, Peter Barry, the Minister for Transport and Power, wrote to Tony McClafferty congratulating the company on its energy saving, saying that he noted with satisfaction that substantial savings had been achieved at Dublin airport. The same Tony McClafferty had a narrow escape in a car crash, along with other directors and Aer Rianta's chief executive, James O'Sullivan. Going to Cork for a board meeting in O'Sullivan's car, it was involved in a crash in County Tipperary. Although the Jaguar was badly damaged, none of the party was injured.

As James O'Sullivan himself relates, the wags at the airport had a merry time for some months afterwards, asking what he was trying to do with the chairman. O'Sullivan, a tall, good-humoured man with a legal training, saw the company through the great national and international difficulties of the mid-1970s. Yet despite those problems, there was always progress to be reported at the airport. Aer Rianta head office at Dublin airport was given a new look; what had been cargo general offices was turned into new offices. The interior was completely renovated by the maintenance department; among those involved in the task were Robert Blake, Harry Clarke, George Courage, Bart Curtin, Johnny Doody, Jimmy Gilligan, Phil Meehan, John Murray and Tony Quinn. Within a matter of days, they had given the offices a brand new look, working to designs and colour schemes prepared by the technical services department.

Another innovation at the airport, introduced on October 13, 1975, was the new self-service duty free section for continental travellers. The duty free shop was relocated in the pavilion building and carried five times as much stock as the old shop in the Pier building. Cash registers were installed that eliminated the tedious task of writing duty free dockets.

Unknown to the travelling public, another major innovation was started, the building of a new two million gallon capacity reservoir, which was completed the following year.

In 1960, the average daily usage of water at the airport was 49,000 gallons, but by 1975, despite the serious recession in air travel, that figure was up to 400,000 gallons a day. Airport engineer, Brendan Clancy, described how, prior to 1970, the supply came from a six-inch pipe from Santry, which fed into a 100,000 gallon capacity tank beneath the public car park. As an interim measure, a new ten-inch pipe line was linked in to the North Dublin trunk mains in 1970, pending the completion of the reservoir. By 1975, the existing storage tanks held only about six hours' supply of water, so a site for the new two million gallon capacity tank was selected, to the east of the church. About 11,000 cubic yards of very hard limestone rock was excavated; blasting the rock presented technical problems. The radar in use at the airport precluded the use of electrical detonation for the blasting operations, so other methods had to be used. The blasting also caused problems with the computers in the nearby Aer Lingus head office. As part of the construction project, the old quarry hole which featured so prominently on the landscape of old Collinstown before the airport was built, and indeed for the first thirty-five years of the airport's existence, was drained and filled in. Workmen engaged on the draining reported some enormous eels, thicker than a man's arm, lurking in the depths. Another major infrastructural project was laying a twelve-inch sewer main from the airport to the north Dublin drainage scheme at Clonshaugh, which eliminated the need for sewage treatment at the airport.

Progress was being made in another direction, as Derek Keogh, director–administration, very much an ascendant star in the company, discussed the govern-

James O'Sullivan, chief executive, Aer Rianta, 1974-1981.
Photograph: Neil MacDougald

One of the huge US Lockheed C5A Galaxy planes used for the UN airlift to the Lebanon, 1978.
Photograph: Military Archives, Cathal Brugha Barracks, Dublin

ment's plans for worker representatives on the Aer Rianta board.

He discussed the logistics of such participation in an interview with *Runway* magazine and said, that while it should have an overall beneficial effect, it should not in any way replace the existing collective bargaining procedures. He pointed out that he had already asked the personnel department to initiate research into all aspects of worker participation. As with the issue of equal employment opportunities for both sexes, an issue that came very much to the fore in the 1980s, Aer Rianta showed itself to be at the forefront of progressive management, ahead of most other semi-state companies and many firms in the private sector.

Despite the recession, the company was looking forward to the future; there were also glimpses back into the past, with a major exhibition at Dublin airport. The air and rail transport exhibition had been based at Shannon for two years, before being transferred to Dublin airport, where it was located in the departures areas of the terminal. Many of the items came from the Irish Aviation Museum, of which Captain J. C. Kelly-Rogers was curator. Items included a Clerget 72 rotary engine, used by RAF planes in Ireland during World War I, a Rolls-Royce Dart Mark 510 engine of the type used to power a Viscount 800, a cockpit from a Viscount and an exact replica of the Ferguson monoplane, reconstructed by Captain Kelly-Rogers. The original of this plane made the first powered flight in Ireland, at Hillsborough in 1909. It was piloted by Harry Ferguson, of later tractor fame.

A series of displays portrayed the development of civil and military aviation in Ireland up to the early 1940s. The exhibition was staged at the airport on a semi-permanent basis; later, the aviation museum moved to temporary premises outside the airport perimeter. Although Aer Rianta donated a site at the airport near the hotel for the construction of a permanent building for the museum, and plans have been drawn up for its construction, progress remains slow and this dream of Captain

Kelly-Rogers, one of the most outstanding personalities in Irish aviation over the years, remains unfulfilled. In time, Dublin may yet have its own aviation museum within the airport perimeter, like the Aviodome museum at Schiphol airport in Amsterdam.

While the models and parts of old planes created much interest in the terminal building, equal interest was created by the arrival at the airport of a home-made plane. It was designed and built by Peter Garrison, an aviation journalist and private pilot, who had no prior knowledge of aircraft construction. The plane, with a bonded fibreglass body, seated two, had a cruising speed of 200 mph and a range of 3,000 miles. When it touched down at Dublin airport in the summer of 1975, it created something of a stir! As always, sport featured heavily among the airport activities. Prominence was given to Hugh O'Hagan, a carpenter at the airport, who had 364 competitive boxing matches during his career and represented Ireland at the Olympic Games in London in 1948.

During the summer of 1975, the first Aer Rianta Dublin sports day for staff and their families was held in the ALSAA grounds. Over 200 people turned out to cheer on their sons and daughters, despite the inclement weather. Later that year, in the approach to Christmas, there were three memorable functions involving serving and retired staff. The engineering section at the airport held its first dinner dance, in the Royal Hotel, Howth (the hotel is now owned by Joe Cuddy, the entertainer), and its organisation was carried out by Frank Deegan from the paint shop. He was assisted by Patsy Keegan from projects and Jim Collier and Fran Barker from administration. It was a rousing, cheerful evening of eating, drinking and sing-songs, the latter accompanied by Jim Collier on the mouth organ. At the airport, the annual Christmas party for children from the Goldenbridge Home for Children was held. Funds for the party were raised by Mary Holton, Noel Boland, Mary Doyle (all cleaning) and Jimmy Jenkinson (security). The children were entertained by members of staff, and also had a disco; the identity of Santa Claus, who gave each child a present, was not revealed! The retired staff enjoyed themselves just as much; the Christmas get together took place in Wynn's Hotel, Dublin. At the association's annual general meeting, Dr J. F. Dempsey was elected patron, with Captain Bill Scott, chairman, and Oliver Hone, vice-chairman.

James Mason, the British born film actor, resident in the US, (bearded) arrives at Dublin airport, 1976, complete with entourage. He came to Dublin on several occasions, including one for a UNICEF charity presentation in 1970.
Photograph: G. A. Duncan

But after the Christmas festivities were over, the New Year began gloomily; the economy was still in the doldrums.

People were short of money after Christmas and none of the economic forecasters held out much hope for improvements during the course of 1976. There was a continuing necessary awareness of security matters; Jack Bannon, the assistant chief airport security officer, demonstrated a new device brought into service at the airport. Known as an "explosives sniffer", it was used to detect the presence of explosives, and in addition to its use in the three Aer Rianta airports, it was also used by the security forces on both sides of the border. A security awareness scheme was put into practice at Dublin airport. A sub-committee of the airport security committee was established to draw up a programme for staff security training at the airport and all staff members attended talks on security awareness. A major construction task carried out during 1976 was the building of a security fence around the entire airport perimeter, which involved some twelve miles of fencing. How times had changed from the earlier, easy-going days; Joe McGuinne, airport engineer, pointed out the prohibition on using land for cultivation within a mile radius of the runways, because of the problem of possible bird strikes against aircraft. During the Emergency years, land on the airport perimeter had formed one of the largest wheat farms in Leinster.

Sadly, the intensity of security precautions at the airport merely mirrored the national preoccupation with the subject, heightened with the assassination of the British ambassador, Christopher Ewart-Biggs, and a UK civil servant, Judith Cooke. They were killed, and a number of other people were seriously injured, when a landmine exploded at Murphystown Road, which leads from the British ambassador's official residence, Glencairn. A sense of outrage permeated the country and was reflected in wide media coverage, both in Ireland and abroad. Nineteen seventy-six also saw equally startling political events on the domestic front. At an army dinner in Mullingar, the Minister for Defence, Patrick Donegan, made a reference to the President, Cearbhall Ó Dálaigh as a "thundering disgrace". The President was subjecting legislation relating to security matters to an intense legal scrutiny. A reporter, Don Lavery, then with the *Westmeath Examiner,* happened to be at the function and made a note of Donegan's remarks, which promptly echoed round the nation. Ó Dálaigh resigned in protest; the next president was Dr Patrick Hillery. The banks went on strike that year, from June 28 to September 6, not as long as the record-breaking bank strike of 1970, but long enough to cause much inconvenience. This was also the year that a new magazine was launched, *In Dublin,* on little more than a shoestring and a prayer. It quickly became the events "bible" of the younger set, mandatory reading; one of its early street sellers, Pete Short, is still to be seen selling copies of the magazine outside Bewley's cafe in Grafton Street. A distinguished visitor to Dublin airport that year was pioneer American astronaut Neil Armstrong, one of the two men to land on the moon in 1969.

There were comings and goings on the airport staff, too. Jack Doyle, who had been airport manager, was promoted to airport services manager. He was succeeded as airport manager by George O'Connor, the personnel manager. Doyle's new post was the last before his retirement. A very well-known personality around the airport retired: Bill Beck, the airport engineer between 1947 and 1972. For the last four years of his career at the airport, he was airport development engineer. Beck, a jovial man with a great capacity and enjoyment for telling yarns, was one of the best-known personalities at the airport for so long that, when he retired, Dublin airport lost a valuable link with its early days. Beck was a fount of information on the development of the airport. The retirement presentation to Bill Beck was made in the cocktail bar at the airport; among the attendance were Nicky Byrne, Charlie Craddock, John

Eamon de Valera, who died in 1975 at the age of ninety-two; he had been both a Taoiseach and a President.
Photograph: Lensmen

Eamon de Valera's lying-in-state, Dublin Castle, 1975.
Photograph: The Irish Times

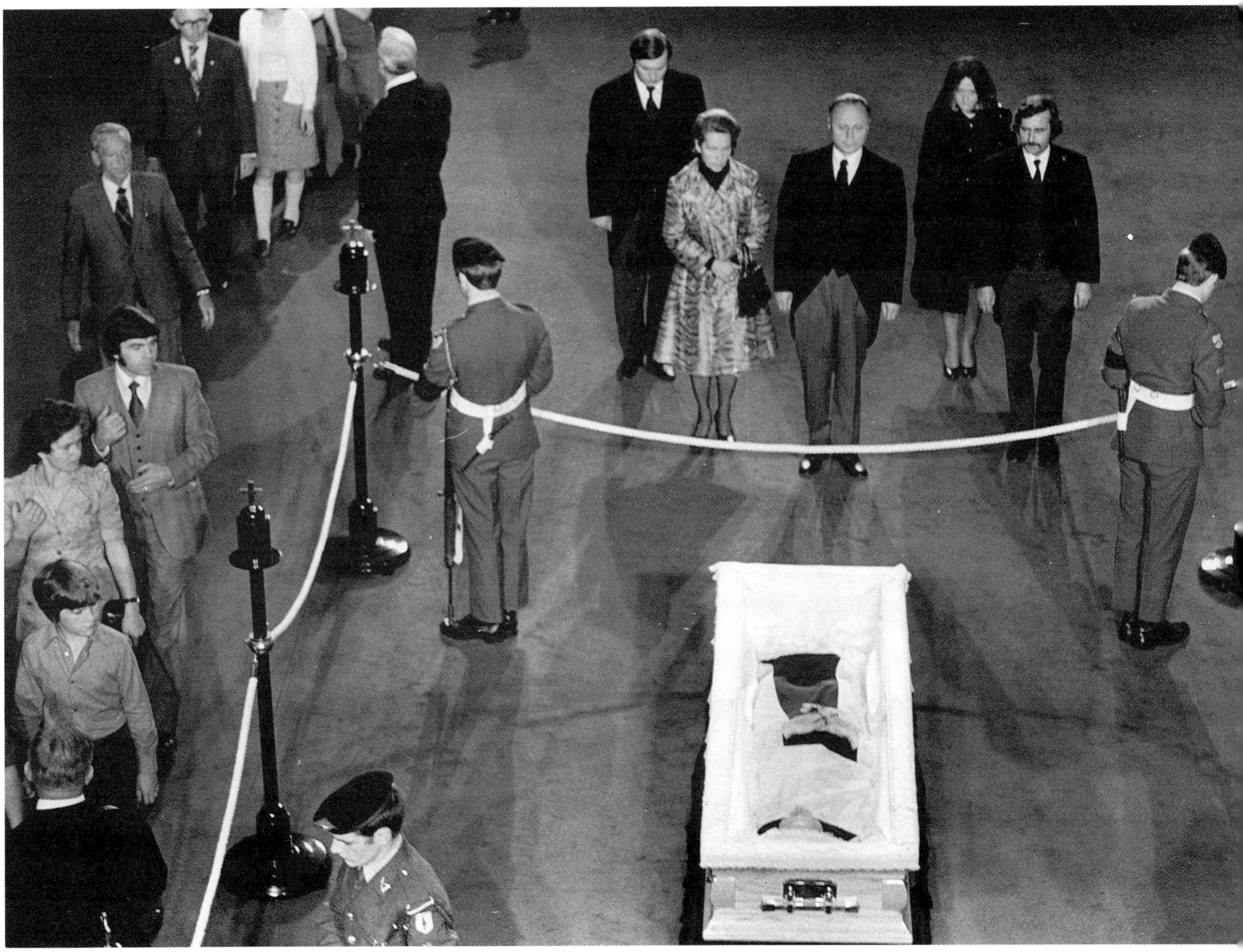

Gerry Heffernan, left, who ran the Dublin airport shops, with Senator Ted Kennedy.

Gunning, Joe Lynch and Paddy O'Daly. Beck paid an especially warm tribute to Mona Farrell, his secretary for many years. Bill Beck, a native of Dublin's northside, now lives in retirement at Kendal in Cumbria.

Other retirements included Phil Christie, Vincent Clegg and Paddy Darcy. They were all long-serving members of the airport security force. Also retiring were Brenda Carley and Peadar Breslin of airport management, while it was said that the technical services unit would never be the same again following the retirement of Pearl Kirwan. She joined the airport in 1946, in the management division and later transferred to the architect's section. Until she retired, she was secretary to Joe Clarke, chief architect, and Brendan Clancy, chief engineer. There was a promotion, too, following John Power's decision to leave the company, where he was accounting superintendent–Dublin. He was succeeded by Michael Cashin, who joined Aer Rianta accounts department in 1967 and became payroll supervisor in 1972. Before his 1976 promotion, he was training officer at Dublin airport and was keen on foreign language instruction for staff. He was instrumental in setting up a panel of airport staff, with language abilities, to translate foreign language correspondence received by the company. There were new offices for the accounts department; it moved to the ground floor of the old terminal building, where the offices were built on the site of the old shopping centre and check-in desks. James O'Sullivan, chief executive, handed over a monster-sized ceremonial key to Brian Hampson, director–finance. Another innovation at the airport were the new electronic transmissometers installed on the runways; they gave immediate visibility readings, which were then transmitted from the control tower to pilots of planes making a landing approach. The two main runways then, 16/34 and 05/23, were overlaid; they had been thirty years in use.

These readings replaced the runway visual range readings. Another technical innovation was seen in action: Lightwater brand aqueous film forming foam, which was twice as fast as conventional firefighting methods. Originally developed by the

American Navy, the new product was demonstrated at Dublin airport in 1976. Some 500 gallons of fuel was set on fire in the demonstration; the fire was brought under control in twelve seconds and was extinguished in twenty-five seconds.

On a lighter note, three arrivals caused a minor sensation at the airport. Three Welsh models, Christine Murphy, Felicity Stainthorpe and Suzanne Baker, arrived with their hair elaborately styled and dyed red and blue. They set an aviation first by having their hair trimmed in flight on a British Airways flight from Cardiff to Dublin. The effort gained the girls a place in the *Guinness Book of Records,* although Kathleen Maples and Sonny Cullen of the cleaning section were not too keen on the colour scheme. Dublin airport has its own resident barber, Benny Traynor, who has been running the hairdressing salon for men and women since 1968, and who is one of the best-known present day personalities around the airport. He has met many famous people who have passed through the airport and has often seen sides to their characters that are not public knowledge. Joe Dolan, the singer, is a quiet person, a little shy even, just like actor Peter O'Toole, in Benny Traynor's estimation, when sitting in the barber's chair. Dana, the singer, is a little pet, very gentle. One of his favourite customers is Arthur Walls, chairman of Ryanair.

The airport barmen continued to distinguish themselves in cocktail competitions. Phil Reid of the arrivals bar and Danny Toland of the mezzanine bar took two of the top awards in the 1976 Campari cocktail competition sponsored by Gilbeys of Ireland. Phil Reid's winning cocktail won him a four-day trip to Milan for two people, while Paul McNally, also of the arrivals bar, was placed fourth. Great fun was had on the variety circuit with a staff variety show presentation in the Country Club, Portmarnock, on October 14. Paddy and Rita Tierney and Barney Reynolds gave rousing renditions as members of Tierney's Country Folk group, while Bridie Hoare and Sonny Cullen did excellent impersonations of visiting Americans. The staff talent for variety had already been displayed that year when an Aer Rianta team took part, for the first time, in the Tops of the Town competition at the Player-Wills theatre on the South Circular Road. Jean Madden, Elaine Bateson, Jean Taylor, Don Treacy

Brian McCabe, editor of *Runway* magazine.
Photograph: Robert Allen Photography

In the late 1970s, the Wood Quay controversy was a very live national issue; this photograph shows the famous protest march held in 1977. All the protests were in vain, since Dublin Corporation went ahead and built two Sam Stephenson-designed tower blocks for its own use, on the Wood Quay site. Holding the banner, left, is Thomas Kinsella, the poet.
Photograph: The Irish Times

and the ever-humorous Sonny Cullen performed an Al Jolson lookalike routine.

On a more serious note, figures for the first six months of 1976 showed a very marginal increase in terminal traffic at Dublin airport (one per cent). A total of 927,000 passengers used the airport, of whom 47,000 were on domestic flights and 52,000 were on trans-Atlantic services. As from September 1, 1976, Aer Rianta introduced a ten per cent rise in landing fees, parking charges and passenger load fees.

The result of this fee rise was a twelve per cent increase in operations revenue for the first three months of 1977. Already, by the time the financial figures for 1976 were prepared, it was clear that Aer Rianta was heading for a record-breaking year; the company's insistence on strict housekeeping measures, at a time when aviation services in and out of Dublin airport were static, succeeded in producing excellent results. For Aer Rianta as a whole, 1976 turnover was £26 million and the surplus, returned to the Department of Transport and Power, was over £3 million. The Minister, Tom Fitzpatrick, paid an official visit to the airport, accompanied by the secretary of his department, Noel McMahon. The party was escorted on its tour of the airport by Tony McClafferty, chairman, and James O'Sullivan, chief executive. Among the areas inspected were the information centre, the telephone exchange, the shopping centre and the ground facilities control centre. Airport security man, Andy Simpson, demonstrated how any part of the airport could be scanned with closed circuit television, while the Minister also saw the new baggage X-ray machine, installed in Pier B to scan passengers' luggage, part of the continuing, but vital, preoccupation with the prevention of terrorism.

Twenty-five-year service medals were presented in early 1977 by Derek Keogh: they went to Bob Best, airport management, Ted Seeley and Joe Bermingham, airport engineering, Tony Nevin, technical services superintendent, Seán Denning, airport duty officer, and John Murray, a cleaner, who retired shortly afterwards.

Attending the jovial presentation of the long- service medals were Johnny King, assistant director–administration, George O'Connor, Dublin airport general manager, Brian Byrne, industrial relations manager, Joe McGuinne, airport engineer, and Frank Shortall, ground facilities superintendent.

Early that year, a number of key management personnel retired. Brendan Murray, director–airport services, retired after forty-three years in the civil service and Aer Rianta. He had begun his career as a customs and excise officer in 1934, becoming manager of Shannon airport in 1960. When he was promoted to director–operations, he was transferred to head office at Dublin airport and appointed director–airport services in 1976. Another noted name to retire was Paddy O'Daly, after thirty-six years' service at the airport. He started his career with the Office of Public Works, when the first terminal building was under construction at the airport. In 1943, he was made maintenance superintendent, a position he held for many years. In 1960, he was made airport planning superintendent and was closely involved in the planning of the new terminal that opened in 1972. Up to the time of his retirement, he was attached to the technical services department. For many years, Paddy O'Daly lived near the airfield, but on retirement, he moved to a country location, near Trim in County Meath.

There were two more retirements of note that year. First of all, Jim Comer, crime prevention officer at the airport, retired after thirty-one years; he had started as a policeman at the airport back in 1946. Also retiring was Kit Finn, a well-known personality in the maintenance section. He joined Aer Rianta in 1945 and was noted for his good humour and also for his singing abilities, which he demonstrated to melodious effect at his retirement presentation. A rather unusual retirement later that year was that of Billy Ryan, who worked in the cleaning section at the airport, as pest controller. On behalf of the staff in this section, Frank Shortall, ground facilities superintendent, Dublin, made the presentation. Billy Ryan gave an interview on RTÉ radio not long before his retirement on his unusual occupation at the airport; the job remained in the family, since his nephew, Timmy Ryan, took over. Dublin airport church also had a new chaplain; Fr Ben Mulligan succeeded Fr Martin Tierney, who was appointed to a full-time post in the Charismatic Renewal Movement. Fr Mulligan, a native of Kilmacanogue, County Wicklow, had been curate in Ballygall parish, Finglas, before his airport posting.

Amid the 737s, the 747s and the BAC One-Elevens, the regular aircraft using Dublin airport, there were some unusual visitors during 1977. Perhaps the most interesting were the two Douglas A–ID Skyraider aircraft, en route from France to Detroit. The aircraft type was developed as an attack aircraft and took part in the Korean and Vietnam wars.

The aircraft that touched down at Dublin were destined for an American aviation museum. A threatened arrival at the airport caused a great stir of interest; fortunately for the airport management, Idi Amin's intention of landing in Dublin never came to pass. On Tuesday, June 7, over fifty journalists and photographers gathered at the airport press centre, having heard that "Big Daddy" Amin, president of Uganda, intended to come to Dublin as a prelude to entering Britain. From 1.00 pm onwards that day, so many national and international media personnel started arriving that one seasoned journalist remarked that the arrival of President Nixon seven years

The airport fire service lined up: the new fire station on the west side of the field is due to open at the end of 1990.
Photograph: Neil MacDougald

previously had not generated nearly as much interest. The "scare" began when the Department of Foreign Affairs told Aer Rianta that Amin was on his way, but by late afternoon, it was clear that it was a false alarm. Amin never appeared.

Another sign of the times was noted when Joe McGuinne, airport engineer, remarked on the young plants being damaged at the airport. Since 1975, Joe McElroy, the gardener, and his team had put much work into landscaping the airport grounds and planting trees and shrubs, with up to two hundred trees planted. But around Easter, 1977, over twenty flowering cherry and maple trees were destroyed, as were their replacements; newly planted roses started disappearing from in front of the terminal building. As the old airport hands remarked, it would never have happened in the old days.

Sport, too, was disrupted not by vandalism, but by bad weather. The February and March outings of the Dublin Airport Golfing Society were disrupted due to the bad weather. Players braved the elements for the February outing to the Island golf course, but the March outing to Donabate had to be cancelled. The Aer Rianta soccer teams fared well on their travels to London, to meet teams from British Airways. While the men's team had problems with the weather, some of the players were not disappointed, since the previous night had seen lively revelries at the British Airways Trident Club. However, the Aer Rianta girls' soccer team did better, when the combined talents of Ger Dalton, Kathleen McNamara and Jean Taylor ensured a four–one win for the Aer Rianta team. Progress was also reported in the car treasure hunt, round the parishes of the Baskin, Baldoyle, Sutton, Howth and Kinsealy; again the weather proved something of a dampener. The highest score went to the car driven by Derek Keogh, with his wife, Rhona, and passengers Michael and Sheila Geoghegan; second prize went to Arthur and Ann Coughlan, with their navigators Owen and Anne Clarke.

After the retirement of Brendan Murray, substantial organisational changes were put in place. Tom Cullen, the director–commercial activities, was appointed director for Dublin and Cork airports. George O'Connor was made general manager, Dublin airport, and Gerry Heffernan was made commercial manager, Dublin airport, reporting to Tom Cullen. Other appointments included Joseph Madigan, the airports development manager, who also took over the purchasing department.

He reported to Derek Keogh, director–administration and company secretary. Work was reported as progressing satisfactorily on the new post office in the arrivals hall, while overlays were completed on four taxiways. Approval was awaited for the proposed extension to the fire station. A group of fourteen left Dublin airport in mid-October on a familiarisation tour of European catering installations; the group included Brian Byrne, industrial relations manager, Owen Clarke, staff development superintendent, and Victor Murphy, assistant commercial manager. The purpose of the visit was to see other catering locations and gather ideas that could be of use in extending the catering facilities at Dublin airport. Locations visited included St Lazare railway station and the new Charles de Gaulle airport, as well as the Renault plant, all in Paris, Zurich airport and the Penta Hotel in London.

Amid all the talk about future development of the airport, there was a sad little note about Sonny Cullen, the cheerful window cleaner at the airport. A fire at the Cullen house killed Sonny's grand-daughter Paula and almost destroyed the building. Airport staff and management rallied round in a most humanitarian manner, providing furniture, clothes and other household items, so that the Cullen house could be fitted out. The response of everyone at the airport was described by Sonny as "kind and generous".

A section of the tax-free shopping area at Dublin airport. Duty-free began, for cross-channel passengers, in 1978.
Photograph: Michael Blake

In retrospect, 1978 was a quiet year of little happening, a prelude to the great event of 1979, when the Pope visited Ireland. During 1978, a prolonged Aer Lingus cabin staff strike had a marked effect on Dublin airport traffic; members of the Federated Workers' Union of Ireland went on strike in a dispute over productivity payments, and pickets were placed. The union was unsuccessful in getting an all-out picket and many other members of staff, including management from head office, took on temporary roles as cabin staff in place of the hostesses who were on strike. Mediation proposals under the chairmanship of the late Dr Charles McCarthy were successful and the strikers returned to work on May 8, nearly two months after the dispute had begun. In the first five months of 1978, Aer Rianta figures showed a total of 699,000 passengers using Dublin airport, a reduction of 6,000 on the same period of the previous year.

Aer Rianta created a new management position, which showed a change of emphasis within the company: for the first time, there was a marketing manager, Gerard Harvey. He had had a varied management career before joining Aer Rianta, having worked for the B&I Line, where he was responsible for marketing, between 1965 and 1972. For a further four years, he was managing director of the Rank group of companies in Ireland, before being appointed group managing director of Lees, the department store. Harvey's most recent job has been as chief executive of An Post, from which he departed in the summer of 1990 to head up an international postal organisation in Brussels.

He explains why the appointment was made: like many other people, he was confused about the identity of Aer Rianta and its relationship to Aer Lingus. "I suggested at the time of my appointment that the lack of a proper identity for Aer Rianta was a disability with the opinion makers". So he started trying to build a strong corporate identity onto what he then regarded as a "very civil service type of organisation". He also felt that Dublin airport was not taking sufficient advantage of the captive audience for its shopping facilities and here he came into conflict with Gerry Heffernan, who was running the airport shops. Yet by the time Heffernan died in 1983, he and Harvey had become good friends within the organisation. Harvey's appointment came just before the introduction of duty-free facilities for

Charles de Gaulle airport at Roissy, twenty kilometres north of Paris, was opened in 1974; it is scheduled to become the biggest airport in Europe.
Photograph: Hugh Oram

passengers on cross-channel routes in the summer of 1978. A new duty free shop, with a floor space of 3,922 sq ft, was opened at the airport, with eight cash registers to speed up the flow of customers. The new facilities were inspected by Tom Cullen, director Dublin and Cork airports; chief executive, James O'Sullivan, remarked that the shop had been completed in record time, so as to be ready for the first day of cross-channel duty free trading. At its introduction, this duty free shopping facility was estimated to be worth a net £1 million a year.

The revenue from this new source was important for Aer Rianta right from the start, for as James O'Sullivan pointed out at the end of 1978, the company's trading results for that year were far worse than for the previous year, thanks to industrial disputes within the company and that in Aer Lingus. The financial shortfall was sufficiently serious, he said, to jeopardise the prospects of Aer Rianta becoming an independent airports authority. Meanwhile, Gerry Heffernan, the man at the hub of Dublin airport shopping facilities, was appointed to the Irish Goods Council by Desmond O'Malley, the Minister for Industry and Commerce. The council's aim was, and is, to persuade retailers to stock Irish-made goods, and Heffernan pointed out that ninety per cent of the goods sold in the public shop at the airport were Irish made, while in the duty free area, that figure was sixty per cent.

Bob Champion, the jockey who won his race against cancer, being welcomed at Dublin airport by John Gallagher, a former Aer Rianta press officer.

In a way, events in 1978 were a little like a repeat of old times. The year ended with the wettest December since records began in 1829. The Central Bank building in Dame Street, designed by Sam Stephenson, drew an enormous volume of public criticism; many spectators did not consider that it fitted in with the other buildings of Dame Street. The ultimately unsuccessful saga at Wood Quay continued: Dublin Corporation went ahead and built its two new Sam Stephenson-designed tower office blocks on the site of Viking Dublin.

The new bridge across the River Liffey, by the Custom House, was opened and named after Matt Talbot, the saintly Dublin worker who died in 1925 and who was declared "venerable" by the Pope in 1975. The more things change, the more they remain the same; scenes at Dublin airport in the summer of 1978 inevitably drew comparisons with the Congo airlifts of 1960–62. In June, 1978, parts of the field at Dublin airport took on the appearance of a military aerodrome, with the departure of 600 Irish Army personnel, with their military equipment, for UN peace-keeping duties in the Lebanon. A total of twenty-one flights left Dublin airport; mostly, the US air force used giant Lockheed C5A Galaxy planes, large enough to take two tanks, sixteen ¾ ton trucks and two Bell Iroquois helicopters on one flight. An even more unusual sight at the airport that year was an Ilyushin-18 aircraft in the livery of LOT, the Polish national airline. The Soviet-built plane seen at Dublin was operating a Dublin-Warsaw charter.

Meanwhile, the DC3 returned to Dublin airport in a new guise. Clyden Airways, a new local carrier, won the Department of Posts and Telegraphs contract to carry mail between Ireland and the UK. The inaugural flight left Dublin at 8.40 pm on September 17, 1978, bound for Manchester. The airline made six round trips a week, one every night except Saturdays, using two DC3s.

The two DC3 aircraft had been built in the 1940s and had been used for a while as military aircraft, C–47s, before being returned to the civilian register. The use of these DC3s by Clyden Airways was among the last of this aircraft type at Dublin airport: in the late 1940s and through the 1950s, DC3s were the mainstay of the Aer Lingus fleet. Just as the DC3s were being retired from service, so too did some prominent airport personalities retire from their duties. Kay Nagle, secretary to Tom Cullen, retired; she had joined Aer Lingus in 1947 and when Aer Rianta was set up in 1968, she transferred, becoming secretary to James O'Sullivan, then assistant general manager. In 1974, she moved to the commercial section, working first for Gerry

Heffernan and then for Tom Cullen. Very involved in charitable work, at her retirement, she was planning her next charity trip abroad, for the Legion of Mary, to Singapore. Matt Leddy retired as welfare officer, after thirty-one years at the airport. Charlie Craddock, one of the first carpenters at the airport, retired. He graduated into building maintenance and became building superintendent at the airport. A well-known figure in the airport maintenance section, Bart Curtin, died; he had worked with Aer Rianta for twenty-two years. Nicky Cash retired; he was the secretary of ALSAA and was particularly helpful to members of the newly founded Aer Rianta social and sporting clubs association when it was founded at the start of the decade.

The last year of the decade, 1979, provided a tremendous fillip not only to the airport, but for the country as a whole. The Pope, John Paul II, arrived in September; his first gesture when he arrived on Irish soil at Dublin airport was to kiss the tarmac. As Gerard Harvey remarked, when he arrived in Aer Rianta in 1978, the company was still lacking in self-confidence, still overshadowed by its subsidiary role in the shadow of Aer Lingus. In a way, the Pope's visit marked the start of new hope, new optimism within the organisation, so that within the space of a decade, it could become, in Harvey's words, one of the biggest and most successful semi-State companies, as well as one of the most forward-looking and progressive.

Some new appointments demonstrated the new thrust of the company, which was becoming keenly marketing oriented. Oliver McCann was appointed to the newly created post of marketing superintendent; he had joined Aer Rianta in 1963 and had been accounts receivable supervisor. In his new position, McCann assisted Gerard Harvey, himself promoted during the course of the year from marketing manager to director–marketing, in the development of marketing plans for existing and new commercial activities. Another new position in the marketing department, that of advertising and promotions officer, went to Frank O'Connell, who joined from the then Aer Rianta advertising agency, Domas, where he was art director and accounts executive.

Yet another appointment in the marketing department was that of Brian O'Connor, made market research officer, another new position. He joined from Aer Lingus and, in his new job, had responsibility for all market research activities in the company. In line with all this new-found marketing activity, two new external contracts were signed. The first, with Multimedia, was made in early 1979 and gave that company sole rights to the sale of advertising sites at the three Aer Rianta airports. Gerard Harvey signed the contract for Aer Rianta, while signing for Multimedia were Tom Power, managing director, and Brian Davitt, chairman. Also present at the signing ceremony was Carl O'Sugrue, Aer Rianta press and public relations manager. At the time of the contract, Aer Rianta was earning £50,000 a year from this type of advertising and Multimedia was given the brief to raise this figure to £250,000 a year over a three-year period. Later that year, Aer Rianta changed its advertising agency from Domas to Young Advertising, one of the larger Dublin agencies, which also had an airline account at that time, British Airways.

Besides all the activity in the marketing department, some more conventional appointments were made. Brian Byrne, who had worked since 1971 on the personnel side in Aer Rianta, was promoted to personnel manager. He oversaw a major reorganisation of the personnel function within the company, which included the setting up of a unit at Dublin airport to deal with day-to-day personnel matters.

In the longer term, Byrne became very involved in the development and promotion of progressive employment policies within the company, including jobsharing and equal opportunities for male and female employees. Another airport appointment was that of Clareman Gerard Dallaghan as catering manager for the airport restaurant. He had been in the first group of students to train at the Shannon

Two examples of Aer Rianta advertising, produced in 1977 and 1978, a far cry from the sophisticated commercials for radio and advertisements for other media being produced in 1990 by the company's advertising agency, CDP Associates.
Illustrations: Runway *magazine*

College of Hotel Management when it opened in 1951; he went on to work in many parts of the world, including London, South Africa, West Africa and South America, before returning home. In his new job at the airport, he reported directly to Gerry Heffernan, commercial manager. Paul McNally, who worked in the arrivals bar, was elected president of the Bartenders' Association of Ireland; thirty-one-year-old McNally was the youngest ever president. Other airport bar staff actively involved with the association were Danny Toland, a regular prizewinner for his cocktails, placed third in a world competition in late 1978 in a Paris contest, Arthur Hook and Brian O'Mara. Garry Benson, a popular figure in the airport bars in his younger days, died. He had joined the airport in 1959 as a barman and in 1975 was transferred to the training section. There were the customary retirements, too; eight cleaning ladies with a total of 138 years' service retired.

Developments continued on the technical side. The runway development committee, set up the previous year, was active in 1979, reassessing the original long-term plans to build two new east/west runways, one north, the other south of the terminal.

Decisions made by the committee during 1979 eventually resulted in the completion of the new runway opened at the airport in the summer of 1989. Yet while there was a certain optimism in the air at Dublin airport in 1979, it was not to last. That year saw a total of 2,756,581 passengers using the airport, 92,150 aircraft movements and 46,520 tonnes of cargo. As it turned out, these were peak levels, not to be achieved again until the mid-1980s. Dublin airport also made a major step forward on the computer front, with the installation of new Honeywell computer equipment, including a central processor with 384 K byte capacity and integrated diskette reader. David Hope, the computer services manager, said that a significant amount of work had to be done to ensure that the new systems reached their full information processing as soon as possible. While Aer Rianta was expanding its use of this most modern form of communications, on a national scale, one of the most traditional forms of communications was on strike. The national postal strike seemed to last for ever; it started on February 19, 1979 and lasted until June 25, dealing a severe blow to user confidence. Clyden Airways was badly hit since there was no mail to be transported to Britain, and it advertised for alternative freight business for its aircraft.

The Pope addresses the multitudes soon after landing at Dublin airport.
Photograph: Robert Allen Photography

Opposite page: Pope John Paul II emerges from the Aer Lingus 747, the *St Patrick*, moments after the plane landed at Dublin airport on Saturday, September 29, 1979.
Photograph: Robert Allen Photography

Some new aircraft arrived at Dublin. Aer Lingus acquired a third 747, from Lufthansa, while Aer Turas, the freight airline based at Dublin airport, acquired a Canadair CL–44J aircraft. This plane was developed from the Britannia type.

The aircraft had a much increased cargo-carrying capacity, up from 17,500 kg in the original version to 27,500 kg in the plane purchased by Aer Turas, which already had a Britannia in its fleet. Some unusual and historic planes came to Dublin, including a Pitts Special G–LOOP, which was used for an all-Ireland advertising promotion. B25 bombers came to the airport; several of these World War II planes, originally US Air Force B25 Mitchell bombers, spent some time on the tarmac at Dublin while returning to their private owner in the US; they had been used in the filming in England of *Hanover Street*. Two airlines started services to Dublin, Swissair and Sabena. The Swissair inaugural into Dublin took place on April 1, 1979; it operated three round trips a week between Dublin and Zurich. The service was terminated in 1988. Sabena, which had operated scheduled flights out of Dublin in the late 1940s and 1950s, restarted its Dublin–Brussels service. Airport charges went up by eighteen per cent. The cost for a Boeing 737, inward bound from Europe and landing at Dublin airport, was now £123.84. Ireland had just joined the European Monetary System and this was expected to bring a price stability to fees in future. As Brian Hampson, director–finance, explained, fluctuations between the punt and the main European currencies would be minimal, so future increases could not be higher than the European norm. Energy conservation was still a key issue at the airport, ever since the oil crisis of 1973. In 1979, further substantial increases in world oil prices meant that energy conservation continued to be just as essential.

Pope John Paul II chats to President Hillery soon after his arrival. In the background can be seen the helicopter which took the Pope from the airport to the Papal Nunciature on the Cabra Road.
Photograph: Robert Allen Photography

Lisa Drumgoole and Russell Gleeson present flowers to the Pope. On the right, in jovial mood, is the late Cardinal Tomás Ó Fiaich.
Photograph: Robert Allen Photography

Tony McClafferty, Aer Rianta chairman, pointed out that between 1973 and 1978, electricity consumption at Dublin airport had been reduced from 12.2 million units a year to 10.4 million units. At the airport, extra space was provided for the apron area, with an additional 28,859 square metres for aircraft to ease the problem of congestion around the pavilion area. While extra parking for aircraft was provided, the provision of car parking space for passengers continued to present problems; a multi-storey car park had been built on the top levels of the new terminal building, but was never used, because of the international terrorist threat. Behind the scenes, there was a flurry of activity with a simulated plane crash at the airport, part of the regular training exercises that are carried out. The sound of the siren heralded the start of a "without warning" exercise; within eighty seconds, the first of the airport fire vehicles was at the scene of the "crash", with the major foam tenders only seconds behind. Eastern Health Board ambulances were on the scene in twenty-five minutes, good timing considering the heavy traffic conditions on a wet day. That year, the Dublin emergency plan was put into practice for real, when a train crash at Dalkey, County Dublin injured thirty-three people. At the airport, staff were much saddened by the sudden passing of Frank Weldrick; he died only a short while after being promoted to welfare superintendent.

On the wider scene, there was much disruption from strikes. Dublin barmen, binmen and bus drivers all went on strike. PAYE taxpayers, some 200,000 of them, went on the march through Dublin, demanding tax reforms. The Wood Quay site was peacefully occupied by protestors objecting to the building of the new civic offices. 1979 also saw the first women bus conductors in Dublin and there was a summit of EC premiers at Dublin Castle. Also on the political front, Jack Lynch retired as Taoiseach, to be succeeded by Charles Haughey. Fianna Fáil had won a spectacular success in the 1977 general election; now there was an equally fascinating change at the top, when Charles Haughey became Taoiseach for the first time.

For the Pope's visit to Ireland in September, Dublin airport was scheduled to play a substantial part in the proceedings. The preparations began well in advance. Gerard Harvey, director–marketing, managed the airport arrangements for the

Pope's arrival at Dublin and departure from Shannon. Harvey remembers that they had two months to plan the details; the task force behind the scenes involved everyone from the gardai to the fire service and CIE. Dublin airport management staff liaised very closely with this task force. Harvey remembers: "It was a delicate mission to have the airport staff openly and willingly liaise with this task force, but because of the sanctity of the event, no one seemed to fight, argue or disagree". He remembers in particular Frank Shortall, the operations manager at Dublin airport: "absolutely fantastic".

Four new communications supervisors were appointed to handle the VIPs connected with the Papal visit: Rita Bergin, Una Fenning, Carmel Hogan and Eithne O'Sullivan. A reception area on the apron was designed by Tony Kelly of Technical Services; the podium was designed so that the Pope could be seen by all present. This podium and reception area were to be filled with flowers, the most outstanding of which were to be the yellow and white display on the front of the podium, depicting the Papal colours. Around the pier buildings, link buildings and airbridges, banners in four languages, English, Irish, Italian and Polish, were to be draped. The team of airport gardeners made sure well in advance that the grounds of the airport looked at their best, while Dublin County Council planned to erect a flag display platform at the entrance road to the airport. Staff at the airport were preparing in other ways, too; a special retreat took place in the airport church for nearly a week before the Pope's arrival. This retreat was led by Fr Lomán Mac Aodha, superior of St Isodore's College, Rome; the airport chaplain, Fr Ben Mulligan, said that the aim of the retreat was to renew the heritage of faith, in preparation for the Pope's historic visit to Ireland.

There was a behind the scenes row over the travel arrangements. It had been decided that the Pope would fly to Ireland on an Aer Lingus plane; Alitalia lobbied furiously to have the Pope travel on one of its planes. When Archbishop Marcinkus travelled to Dublin a fortnight before the visit, he was told in no uncertain terms that his request for a change in the travel arrangements would not be acceded to. Pope John Paul II left Rome early in the morning of Saturday, September 29, 1979; the *St Patrick* 747 arrived over the city of Dublin just before 10.00 am, preparing for its descent to Dublin airport. Already, the excitement among the populace was palpable. The plane touched down at 10.00 am and when the door of the plane opened and the Pope appeared, there was a huge cheer from the 11,000 crowd, including many Aer Rianta staff, who were waiting to greet him. His first action on descending the steps from the aircraft was to kiss the ground. He was greeted by the President, Dr Hillery and by Cardinal Ó Fiaich. After the playing of the national anthems, four Air Corps Fouga jets flew over the airport in a cross-shaped formation. Then the Pope made his first address to the Irish people after the ceremonial welcome. Next came the presentation of flowers by two children of airport workers, Lisa Drumgoole, whose father Noel was catering supervisor in Aer Rianta, and Russell Gleeson, whose father worked in Aer Lingus. After the presentation, Lisa admitted that they had both been nervous and excited, but not frightened. "He was a very kind man", said Lisa. Both children received a present of a rosary from the Pope.

After the children came the VIPs. Among those to meet the Pope were Tony McClafferty, chairman, and the board of directors of Aer Rianta, and all wives.

Others from Aer Rianta to meet the Pope included James O'Sullivan, chief executive, and George O'Connor, Dublin airport manager. After the VIP introductions, the Pope moved along a line of 100 children of airport and airline employees, where he stopped and spoke with them for several minutes. Once all the arrival ceremonies were completed, the Pope took off in an Irish Helicopters' flight from the airport to the Papal Nunciature in Cabra. The two climaxes of the Pope's visit to Dublin were the motorcade through the city and the Papal Mass in the

Phoenix Park; over a million people went to the park. The city was deserted and countless families made their way to the Mass, the site of which is commemorated by the Papal cross, which still stands today.

The Pope did a good job for the corporate identity of Aer Rianta, recollects Gerard Harvey. The company logo was posted in prominent positions all over the terminal buildings at the airport and the air bridges were painted in the Aer Rianta colours. The intense television coverage of the Pope's arrival gave excellent shots of the Aer Rianta insignia. That night, the board had a dinner to celebrate and says Harvey, "we had all met the Pope. It was a lovely occasion and we brought the wives along and we met the Pope again that night. We weren't supposed to, but we did; it was a little bit irregular". It was a good experience for the children, too, and the sense of the fun and excitement of the whole occasion is captured in photographs of Derek Keogh and his family on the plane to Shannon.

When the Pope left from Shannon on October 1, the weather was wet, in contrast to the bright, windy day that greeted the Pope at Dublin airport. The Pope remarked at Shannon: "It is nice that it rains on my last day in Ireland". His whirlwind tour of the country, taking in such historic localities as Drogheda, was short, lasting from the Saturday to the Monday, but it left an indelible impression in Ireland and is remembered to this day by the entire airport staff at Dublin airport. In the whole fifty year history of Dublin airport, only one other ceremonial arrival created such a frisson of excitement — that of US president John F. Kennedy in June, 1963. The Pope's arrival at Dublin airport in September, 1979 brought an otherwise rather dull decade at the airport, marred by the effects of the national economic crises and the impingement of terrorism, to a glorious and stirring conclusion.

Taking off into the sunset at Dublin airport.
Photograph: Neil MacDougald

Front page of *The Irish Times*, January 19, 1980 — forty years after the airport opened.

CHAPTER VII

Up to the present

Johnny Logan, pictured during the *Johnny Logan Special* on RTE television, 1980. He won the Eurovision song contest twice, first in 1980 with *What's Another Year?* and then in 1987 with *Hold Me Now.* For the 1984 contest, he wrote *Terminal Three,* an appropriate title for the aviation world, for singer Linda Martin.
Photograph: RTÉ illustrations library

WHAT'S ANOTHER YEAR, written by Shay Healy of RTE television's Nighthawks fame and sung by Johnny Logan, won the Eurovision song contest in 1980. For the second time, Ireland had won this prestigious international contest, a decade after her first win. What's another year, what's another decade could well have been the feeling among airport staff, as the new year bells of Christchurch rang in 1980. The economy was in recession, matching the state of the world economy, and the aviation industry was entering one of its periodic downturns. There had been reasonable forecasts of air traffic growth at the beginning of the year, but these proved hopelessly optimistic as the year wore on. By the end of the year, James O'Sullivan, chief executive, was warning that the financial performance of the airport authority had fallen far short of expectations. Much of the blame was placed on American aviation deregulation and also on the global recession; trans-Atlantic passenger traffic to Ireland slumped substantially, although this decline had a far more serious effect on Shannon than on Dublin. 1980 saw the Aer Rianta surplus halved, cut to £2.5 million because of the aviation industry recession. Yet as from April 1, charges had to be increased by eleven per cent. At Dublin airport, landing charges for all aircraft went up to £2.86 per metric tonne.

The landing charge for a Boeing 737 arriving from Europe went up from £123.84 in 1979 to £137.28 in 1980. Yet amid this economic gloom, Aer Rianta took very significant steps to improve its corporate image, a move that stood the organisation well for the future. A survey carried out on a selective basis throughout the Republic revealed that only sixteen per cent of people interviewed were aware of Aer Rianta's existence and the precise nature of its business. Much work went into designing the new logo for the company, which was unveiled on the 1980 annual report, published in May, 1980. Gerard Harvey, who as director–marketing oversaw the progress of the new corporate identity campaign, estimated that it would take about two years to complete the new design style for all the company's activities. At the same time, new identification signs were erected at Dublin airport.

A number of key appointments were made at Dublin airport in 1980. Brendan Wall was made terminal facilities manager, a new position. He had joined the planning department as a draughtsman in 1965. In 1968, he transferred to airport management. Jim Collier was appointed to another new position at Dublin airport, as ground services manager. He transferred from the personnel department, where he had been industrial relations superintendent. He was succeeded in this post by Ray La Comber, who transferred from Aer Lingus to Aer Rianta in 1969. There were appointments, too, on the marketing side.

207

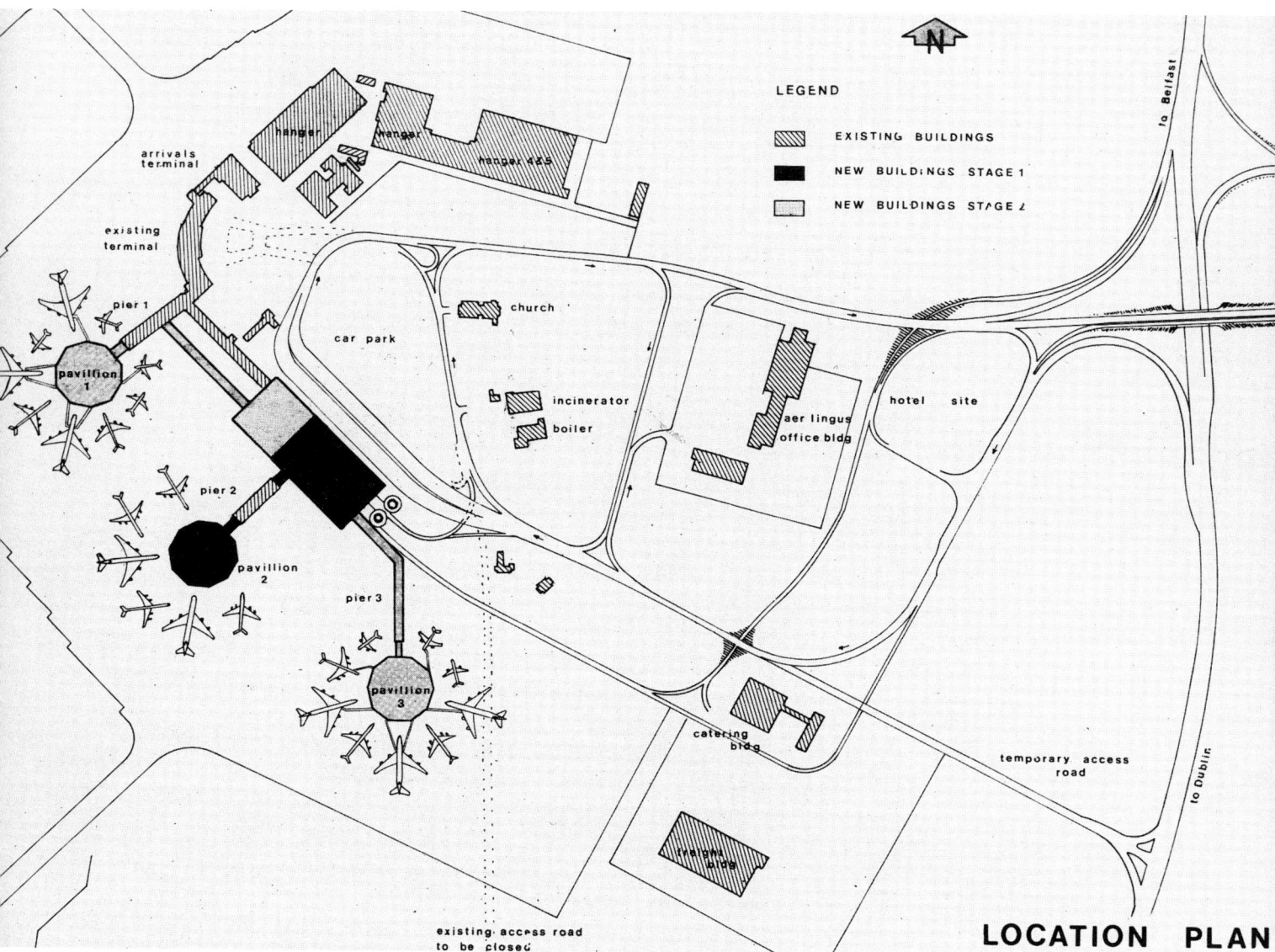

Above and right: Plans for the present terminal building at Dublin airport.

Frank O'Connell was appointed advertising and promotions superintendent, while Brian O'Connor was made market research superintendent. In an interesting development, Brian Lennon was made the first male information assistant at Dublin airport, a job previously the preserve of female staff. Alan Lowndes, a third-year apprentice painter in the maintenance section of Aer Rianta at Dublin airport, came second in the national Apprentice of the Year competition.

Brian McCabe took over temporarily at *Runway* magazine, when the then editor, Phil Treacy, went on maternity leave. Phil's temporary leave became permanent when she decided to devote all her time to motherhood, so Brian McCabe took over as *Runway* editor. Although he has always had a keen interest in writing poetry and plays, he joined the magazine from a completely different background, the airport maintenance section. Phil Treacy, who had edited the magazine for six years, joined Aer Rianta in 1970 as secretary to Carl O'Sugrue, press and public relations manager.

Management moves in 1980 included Derek Keogh, who was made acting assistant chief executive, with the task of running the day-to-day aspects of the company for chief executive James O'Sullivan, who retired in 1981. The company had a new board and a new chairman in 1970. Peter Hanley was appointed chairman; a native of Rooskey, County Roscommon, he was described at the time of his appointment as a businessman of international repute.

At the time of Peter Hanley's appointment, his positions included chairman and

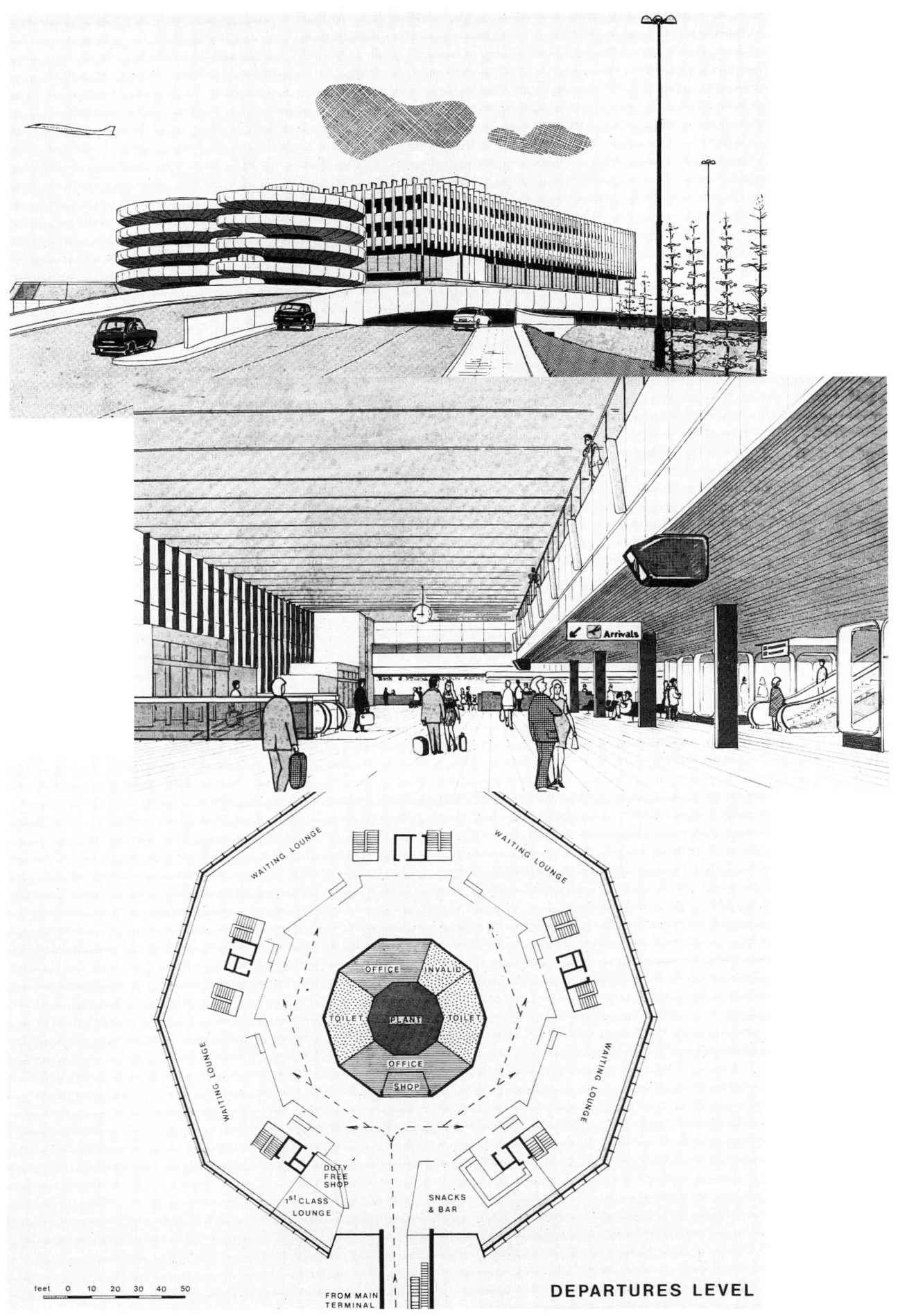

DEPARTURES LEVEL

Dr. Garret FitzGerald, T.D., then Taoiseach, welcomes George Bush, then U.S. vice-president, and his wife, Barbara, to Dublin airport in 1983. Bush became U.S. president in 1989.

Dan-Air, the U.K.airline, inaugurated its Dublin–Gatwick service on June 28, 1982. Pictured at Dublin airport are from left: Martin Dully, then Aer Rianta chief executive, Martin Clough, product planning manager, Dan-Air, John Varrier, head of the airline's scheduled services, Charlie Cullinane, head of GSA airport handling, and Gerard Harvey, then marketing director, Aer Rianta. The service was discontinued in 1990.
Photographs: Robert Allen Photography

210

managing director of the Hanley Meat Group, County Roscommon. He said that he saw the new job as a very interesting challenge and that he was already aware of the wealth of talent working in Irish airports. One of the company's new directors was Michael Mullen, general secretary of the Irish Transport and General Workers' Union, who remarked that the staff at Irish airports were first class. "I am constantly meeting people who have come from abroad and they all speak so highly of the courtesy and helpfulness of all airport employees". Johnny King was made company secretary and George O'Connor was appointed deputy director Dublin airport, reporting to Tom Cullen, director–Dublin and Cork airports.

On the airline side, Dan-Air started a new Dublin–Cardiff service; during the 1980s, the mainstay of its operation at Dublin was its daily service to Gatwick, which was terminated in 1990. In early 1980, British Airways introduced a new aircraft on its Dublin–Heathrow services, a Super 737. The airline also became embroiled in controversy, with its decision to drop the word "Airways" from its title. A glimpse of the past reappeared at the airport, when a 1961 vintage double decker bus in cream and blue livery came to the airport to publicise the transport museum at Castleruddery, County Wicklow. On the streets of Dublin, there was widespread disruption when PAYE workers again took to the streets in an attempt to secure tax reform. In January, 700,000 PAYE workers demonstrated.

George O'Connor, Dublin airport general manager, 1981–1984.
Photograph: Frank Fennell Photography

The death occurred in June, 1980 of R. C. O'Connor, the retired chief executive of Aer Rianta. Born in Cork in 1908, he went to Foynes in 1945 as assistant airport manager and then on to Shannon in the same capacity, before returning in 1948 to the civil service. In 1968, he was seconded from the Department of Transport and Power, where he headed the aviation section, to become the first chief executive of the newly constituted Aer Rianta. He retired from that position in 1974, but remained on the board. R. C., as he was known at the airport, was a warm personality, with a soft spot for the underdog; in many ways, he was the father figure of the company in the early days of its existence, seeing it through its establishment as an independent airports authority. Another death in 1980 was that of Jim Gallagher, in the airport police/fire service, which he had joined in 1961.

Among the people retiring that year were Christina Murphy, well-known on the airport cleaning staff; on her retirement, a presentation was made to her by Eamon Clancy, foreman cleaner, and Christy Sheridan, cleaning supervisor. Joyce Farrelly,

Avair, a short-lived Irish aviation aspiration of the early 1980s.
Photograph: Lensmen

Above: Former U.S. president Ronald Reagan makes his speech of farewell at Dublin airport, 1984.
Photograph: Robert Allen Photography

Dr Garret FitzGerald, then Taoiseach, welcomes the Spanish prime minister, Felipe Gonzales, to Dublin airport, 1984.
Photograph: Robert Allen Photography

President Hillery and Taoiseach Charles Haughey, T.D., greet the then president of India, Sanjiva Reddy, 1982.
Photograph: Robert Allen Photography

Javier Perez de Cuellar, United Nations' secretary-general, is escorted across the tarmac on his arrival in 1983 by Peter Barry, T.D., then Minister for Foreign Affairs.
Photograph: Robert Allen Photography

known as the "uncrowned queen of airport maintenance", also retired. She joined the company in 1949 and spent most of her career at the airport in the maintenance section, before becoming secretary to Joe McGuinne, manager–facilities and planning. Joe Madigan retired; he had transferred from the Department of Transport and Power to Aer Rianta in 1969, as contracts manager, before being appointed airport development manager.

Jim Power, a senior police fireman at the airport, retired after thirty-three years service. He was keenly interested in sports and was a founder member of the security service Gaelic team. Also retiring was Jimmy Gilligan, who had spent the war years painting in the Belfast shipyards before joining Aer Rianta in 1946 as a painter. A craftsman of the old school, he was responsible for many of the hand-painted signs around the airport.

There was more strike trouble at Aer Lingus; on May 30, 1980, a major strike started, of tradesmen, over a relativity claim. The strike was not settled until early July; the strikers returned to work on July 4. This was the second major strike at Aer Lingus in three years; on this latter occasion, it caused some disruption at the airport, because tradesmen in the Aer Rianta maintenance section refused to pass the pickets. Still, there was some humour amid the economic gloom of another poor tourist season. Benny Traynor, the airport hairdresser, had made a prediction on RTÉ television, while cutting Frank Hall's hair, that long hair would never catch on: "Irish people are much too conservative". Before long, everyone, from teenagers to bank managers, was wearing long hair! Long before he came to the airport barber's shop, he had his experiences in the Dublin hairdressing trade, having served in O'Rahilly's of O'Connell Street. He specialised in theatrical hairdressing, for such

Robert Mugabe, prime minister of the newly independent African state of Zimbabwe, steps out of an Air Zimbabwe plane at Dublin airport to a wet Collinstown welcome, 1983.
Photograph: Robert Allen Photography

Martin Dully, appointed chief executive of Aer Rianta in 1981. In early 1988, he was made executive chairman of Bord Fáilte and was succeeded at Aer Rianta by Derek Keogh.
Photograph: Bord Fáilte

personalities as Anew McMaster, Brendan Behan and Eddie Golden. Benny's comments on one of the great long-haired events of 1980 were not recorded: a new rock group called the Boomtown Rats staged a very lively concert at Leixlip, which attracted 14,000 fans, an unprecedented number for a concert of that kind.

Towards the end of that year, 1980, there was an interesting management appointment. Jack Doyle, once a manager of Dublin airport and now airport services manager, was made secretary general of the Western European Airports Association. The current president was James O'Sullivan, chief executive, so two Irish appointees held the top two positions in the organisation, which was founded in 1950 to represent all the major European airports. On November 13, many dignitaries attended the plaque-unveiling ceremony at the airport marking the papal visit the previous year. Albert Reynolds, Minister for Transport and Power, unveiled the plaque set into the airport apron. The late Cardinal Ó Fiaich, speaking in Irish and English, recalled the deep significance of the visit and commended Aer Rianta's initiative with the plaque, before imparting his blessing.

Traffic statistics for the twelve months to the end of December, 1980 confirmed the depressing downward trend. In Dublin, the main decline was in trans-Atlantic traffic; total passenger numbers for this period were 2,582,000, a six per cent decrease. Freight was down by twelve per cent.

Belt-tightening was the order of the day. Assistant chief executive Derek Keogh said that while Aer Rianta did not intend to follow the Aer Lingus example of increased voluntary redundancies and accelerated retirements, stringency was necessary. With the serious decline in passenger traffic, the company's surplus had been substantially reduced, cut from £5 million in 1979 to half that figure in 1980. The recession in Britain affected Dublin traffic and the Aer Lingus tradesmens' dispute cost Dublin airport 50,000 passengers. The only traffic increase in Dublin came from the operations of the European charter companies, Aviaco and Spantax, which brought about a two per cent increase in European traffic. With those figures not only down, but considerably lower than the company's worst expectations, revenue from new sources had to be developed. As it turned out, Dublin airport produced a quite healthy surplus for 1981, of £3.98 million, balancing out the serious revenue declines at Shannon airport. But much of the surplus at Dublin came from the operations of its duty free shops. The presentation to Dublin airport of a statue of the Madonna of Loreto, patron saint of aeronauts, could not have come at a more appropriate time. Pope Benedict XV had proclaimed the Madonna patron

Joe McGuinne, general manager, technical services, Dublin airport.
Photograph: Robert Allen Photography

in 1920; the saint is commemorated at most airports throughout the world. Fr Giovanni Leonardi, head of the congregation of the Holy House of Loreto, presented the statue to James O'Sullivan at Dublin airport.

The most newsworthy event of 1981 in Aer Rianta was the retirement of James O'Sullivan as chief executive and his succession by Martin Dully. O'Sullivan had worked in the aviation business for thirty-four years, since joining Aer Lingus in 1947. His early work there also involved Aer Rianta; in 1968, he transferred to the new company as secretary, becoming deputy chief executive in 1969 and chief executive in 1974. He remembers about his days with Aer Rianta that there were also the characters at Dublin airport, but never the flamboyance of some of the personalities associated with the earlier days of Irish aviation development, like the late Captain J. C. Kelly-Rogers. In O'Sullivan's recollection, R. C. O'Connor, the first chief executive of Aer Rianta, had a touch of the Kelly-Rogers extroversion, but in a more restrained way. "He was not bombastic and did not expect everyone to genuflect". O'Sullivan's own style was quiet and dignified and he played a substantial part in seeing the company safely through the great recession in the aviation industry that lasted for most of his tenure of office as chief executive. He was greatly influenced in his management style by his training as a barrister; he was cool and analytical in his management approach.

Martin Dully was born and brought up in Athlone, County Westmeath, interestingly not too far from where Colonel Delamer, the first manager of Dublin airport, had been raised. Dully started work with Bord na Móna, then graduated to the Sea Fisheries Board, the predecessor of Bord Iascaigh Mhara. He joined Aer Lingus in 1952, in a junior clerical capacity and worked his way up, tackling such tasks as

The snows of January, 1982 brought chaos to the country and temporarily closed down Dublin airport.
Photograph: Beryl Stone Photography

Above: Henry Kissinger, former U.S. Secretary of State, signs the distinguished visitors' book, 1983. He was arriving for a Heinz Corporation meeting at Tony O'Reilly's estate in Kilcullen, County Kildare. Kissinger is an adviser to Heinz.
Photograph: Robert Allen Photography

In March, 1985, top American politician Tip O'Neill, the former Speaker of the U.S. House of Representatives, arrived for a visit to Ireland; Aer Rianta hostess Breda Mulligan is seen presenting him with some shamrock.
Photograph: Robert Allen Photography

Michael Mullen, general secretary of the ITGWU, now part of the SIPTU union. He was appointed to the Aer Rianta board in 1980, but his directorship was short-lived; he died in a Frankfurt hospital in 1982.
Photograph: SIPTU

managing the airline's operations in Europe and in North America. While he found a lot of career opportunities in Aer Lingus, he was aware that his skills in managing people and in marketing could be of crucial importance to Aer Rianta, a company which he says was still trying to find its identity in the shadows of Aer Lingus. "It was beginning to realise that it had the making of a good business, but no one was quite sure what to develop and how to make Aer Rianta a household name in Ireland". He says that the strange aspect of his transfer was that even though he was working in Aer Lingus at Dublin airport, some 250 yards from Aer Rianta's head office, he hardly knew any of the top management in Aer Rianta. The whole question of deregulation in the U.S. had thrown the world aviation business into turmoil, so it was a time of great change. Up to 1981, says Dully, the state was very reluctant to commit money to airport development, so Aer Rianta had to generate that money itself. "We started by attacking a number of traditional ways of doing business", he recollects.

He cites the famous restaurant at Dublin airport as a classic case of a section of the airport business waiting to be turned round. Catering at the airport had been synonymous with romance and marriages, and people went there at weekends for dress dances, but gradually the demand for the product fell off, yet the company continued to provide the service, even though the airport restaurant became increasingly unprofitable. Says Martin Dully of that time: "We had to start thinking in terms of what the customers really wanted. It was a traumatic time for everyone, but it was evidence of a new corporate philosophy". Changes had to come with the airlines, as well. Year by year, Dublin airport had been losing out to the shipping companies on the cross-channel routes, so much so that by 1981 the airlines had less than half of that passenger traffic. As soon as he arrived at the Aer Rianta head office, where he enjoyed the same view of the old terminal building as he had done when he joined Aer Lingus as a grade four clerk in cargo operations in 1952, he set about seeing all facets of the Aer Rianta operation for himself. At Dublin airport, the extro-

Dublin-born Chaim Hertzog, president of Israel, arrived for an official visit to Ireland in 1985. He was elected president for the first time in 1983 and re-elected for a second term in 1988.
Photograph: Robert Allen Photography

Above: Crown Prince Akihito of Japan, subsequently Emperor, greets compatriots at Dublin airport, 1985. Also included in the photograph are President Hillery and Dr. Garret FitzGerald, T.D., then Taoiseach.
Photograph: Robert Allen Photography

The King and Queen of Spain are greeted by President and Mrs Hillery on their arrival at Dublin airport for a State visit in 1986.
Photograph: Robert Allen Photography

Left: Aer Rianta was a pioneer of equal employment opportunities for women; it was the first Irish company to implement an equality programme. Judy Donaghy was appointed affirmative action co-ordinator in 1982.
Photograph: Robert Allen Photography

Right: Marion Keating, who joined Aer Rianta in 1973. Ten years later, she was made employment officer.
Photograph: Robert Allen Photography

vertive Dully quickly impressed himself upon the staff as a totally committed chief executive, bringing a very hands-on approach to even the smallest aspect of the airport operations.

That year proved traumatic in national terms. The H-Block hunger strike in the North was at its height and a demonstration in support of the political prisoners ended with a riot outside the British Embassy on the Merrion Road, Dublin. Damage estimated at over £1 million was caused to surrounding property. H Block demonstrators occupied the offices of British Airways, then in Lower Grafton Street, but for Aer Rianta there was great concern when a group of demonstrators managed to get onto the airside of the terminal at Dublin airport and occupy a British Airways plane for eight minutes. What was a very anxious situation was resolved quickly, with the minimum of force, and thanks to the intense security that surrounds the airport, the incident was never repeated. During the year, a security team from the UK arrived at Dublin airport at the behest of major UK airline users of the airport and declared that Dublin airport security was excellent in every respect. While the H-Block events caused considerable political strains and much concern nationally, even having an influence on the general election, which was won by a Coalition headed by Dr Garret FitzGerald, political violence was by no means confined to Ireland. That summer, Anwar Sadat, the president of Egypt, who had done so much to try to normalise relations with Israel and bring some sanity into the deeply troubled politics of the region, was assassinated during a military parade in Cairo. Throughout the world, there was anguish that such a palpable man of peace in the Middle East had met a violent end. President Hillery was the chief Irish mourner at the official funeral ceremonies in Egypt and he was given a full ceremonial send-off from Dublin airport.

Death was in the air that year. A well-known Dublin character, Thomas Studley, otherwise known as "Bang Bang" because of his habit of 'shooting' people with an imaginary gun, died. But the real tragedy was on the night of St Valentine's Day, February 14, when the Stardust disco on Dublin's northside caught fire. In the ensuing blaze, which trapped many dancers, a total of forty-eight young people died; it was the worst tragedy in the city since 1596 and was the subject of intense media coverage. Jimmy Kiernan, senior plumbing supervisor, lost his daughter, Margaret. But there was some pleasant news that year; the National Concert Hall,

Above: Bob Geldof plays his last concert with the Boomtown Rats, at the RDS, Dublin, on May 17, 1986.
Photograph: Terry Thorp

The Boomtown Rats at their last gig.
Photograph: Terry Thorp

Self-Aid at the RDS, Dublin, in May, 1986: Bono and Adam Clayton are on stage.
Photograph: Terry Thorp

The late John Feeney, the *Evening Herald* columnist who was killed in the Eastbourne plane crash, on the south coast of England, in November, 1984. His irrepressible sense of fun is sadly missed.
Photograph: Independent Newspapers

converted from the Aula Maxima of University College, Dublin, in Earlsfort Terrace, was opened and so too was the Powerscourt Townhouse shopping centre, converted from a 1771 mansion. In San Diego, California, Dubliner Eamonn Coghlan set a new world record for the indoor mile and came home to a hero's welcome at Dublin airport; it was reminiscent of the old days, when Ronnie Delaney arrived home from Melbourne in 1956.

There were some celebrations at the airport, too. *Runway* magazine, which had started out as a rather tentative staff magazine, celebrated its tenth birthday. Brian McCabe, still its editor, paid tribute to John Power, who had the especially hard task of getting the early issues airborne and Phil Treacy, its first full-time editor, who covered such momentous occasions as the Pope's arrival at Dublin airport in September, 1979. New airline services added sparkle to the apron at the airport. A brave new venture, Avair, was launched.

Early in the year, Avair started its operations with a daily service to Eglinton airport, which serves Derry and the North-West. That summer, Avair, in conjunction with Aer Lingus, launched a daily service to Belfast, using a Shorts 330, an upgrade from the fifteen-seat Beechcraft turboprop used on the Derry run. In early 1982, it began flights to Cork. Despite the brave words of Avair's managing director, Gerry Connolly, neither the new Dublin–Belfast service, nor the new airline itself, were to prove durable. Of all the domestic routes in Ireland, Dublin–Belfast has proved among the most difficult to develop over the years; the most recent incumbent was the UK-based Capital Airlines, whose parent company went into receivership in July, 1990. Three other inaugurations out of Dublin that summer failed to achieve permanent lift-off. Olympic Airlines started a charter service between Dublin and Athens, using a Boeing 707. As part of the reception given at Dublin airport, both Irish and Greek music was played, a stirring combination, as the plaintive sounds of the bouzouki wove their way around the Aer Rianta offices. There has long been considerable and fierce national rivalry between Greece and Turkey. Interestingly,

The late Eamonn Andrews, the Dublin-born broadcaster, whose Irish home was at Portmarnock. He commuted every week to and from London, a familiar figure at Dublin airport. This photograph was taken on the stairs at the Gaiety Theatre, Dublin.
Photograph: The Irish Times

Meteorological office at Dublin airport.
Photograph: Neil MacDougald

Turkish Airlines also had an inaugural into Dublin that summer, with the start of a new summer only charter service from Dublin to Istanbul and Ismir. Balkan Tours, which ran inclusive tours based on this service, praised Aer Rianta for its cooperation in opening up the new route. Air Ecosse started a scheduled service from Dublin to Aberdeen, using Bandeirante aircraft.

The timings of the Aberdeen service connected with Aer Lingus services to and from Cork and Shannon, with the hope of attracting oil-related business; in 1981, the oil industry in Aberdeen was still enjoying a tremendous boom. Air Ecosse had been flying into Dublin airport since 1979, running a five nights a week charter between Luton and Dublin. In 1981, it took over the Dublin–Liverpool mail service, following the collapse of the local carrier, Clyden Airways. Other cross-channel mail services were taken over by Humberside-based Eastern Airways. They operated, on an *ad hoc* basis, into Dublin for a period of four months during 1981, and when their service was terminated, it was also an historic moment for Dublin airport: regular DC3 operations at the airport came to an end. In another throwback to the late 1940s and 1950s, when many military aircraft visited Dublin, giant Hercules aircraft belonging to the Canadian Air Force made regular stopovers at Dublin, en route from Germany to Canada.

Many international guests were welcomed at Dublin airport for the 1981 Eurovision song contest. Following Ireland's win the previous year, RTÉ staged the contest in the Simmonscourt Extension of the RDS (which incidentally celebrated its 250th anniversary that year). The UK group, Bucks Fizz, won, and on their departure from Dublin airport, received an especially friendly farewell.

On one unusual occasion, many passengers intending to use Dublin airport found themselves at Shannon. Bad weather causes diversions from Shannon from time to time, but diversions in the other direction, from Dublin to Shannon, especially because of fog, are very rare. One such event happened on April 9 that year when a heavy fog at Dublin airport meant the diversion of many aircraft to Shannon, where the apron became packed with extra aircraft. Another cause of delays and worse was tackled, with the setting up of a national committee, aided by local airport committees, to deal with the problem of bird strikes. A series of recommendations was put into effect. At Dublin airport, an ornithologist was employed; he advised that cutting the

Don Treacy, Dublin airport operations manager.
Photograph: Robert Allen Photography

Above: Sean Kelly from Carrick-on-Suir, County Tipperary, (right, in white jersey) receives a hero's garland at the airport. Included in the photograph are Stephen Roche's wife Lydia (left, with flowers) and Kelly's wife Linda (right, with flowers).
Photograph: Robert Allen Photography

After Stephen Roche, the world-class cyclist from Dundrum, Dublin, won the Tour de France in 1987, he returned home to a hero's welcome. From left: Roisín Shannon, Aer Rianta, Frank Fahy, T.D., Minister for Sport, Stephen Roche and Martin Dully, then chief executive, Aer Rianta.
Photograph: Robert Allen Photography.

In 1982, the film *Educating Rita* was shot entirely on location in Dublin, including Dublin airport. In this photograph, the two stars of the film, Michael Caine and Julie Walters, are seen in the customs' hall.
Photograph: Robert Allen Photography

Benny Traynor, the airport barber. On one occasion, he gave Jack Benny, the American comedian, a trim, but was given strict instructions not to touch the top of his head. Jack Benny had covered his large bald spot with grease paint. In the summer of 1990, his most popular client was Mick McCarthy, captain of the Irish team in the World Cup soccer finals held in Italy.
Photograph: Neil MacDougald

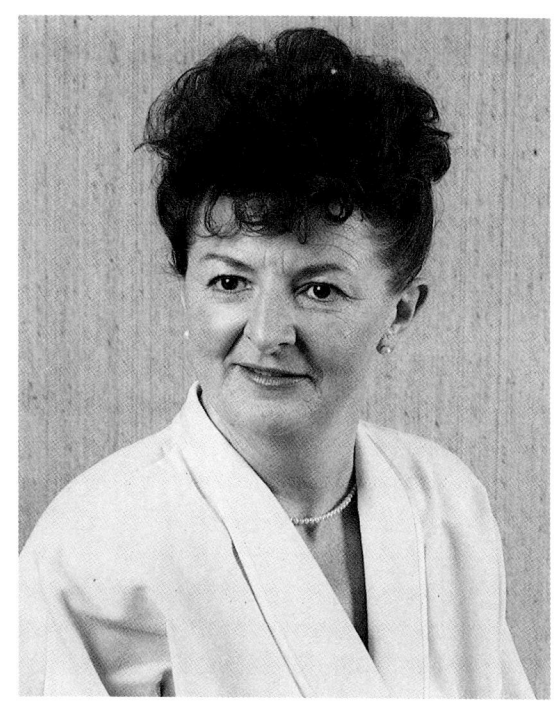

Left: Peter Hanley, a former chairman of Aer Rianta.
Photograph: Robert Allen Photography

Right: Breege O'Donoghue, a director of Penney's, was the first woman to be appointed a director of Aer Rianta, in 1985.
Photograph: Robert Allen Photography

grass around the runways to a certain height would discourage birds from nesting there. A ban was placed on rubbish dumps nearer than eight kilometres to the airport. At a technical level, the airport got another aid to safety, a friction tester that produced continuous printouts of pavement friction, rolling resistance, speed and distance on the runways.

In the boilerhouse, there was more positive news. Nicky Byrne who runs the establishment and uses it to grow cacti, begonias and an orange tree, won £600 in the staff suggestion scheme. It was the largest amount awarded so far under the scheme; his idea reduced the dependence on oil and was expected to save up to £35,000 a year in fuel costs. A native of the Milltown/Dundrum area in south Dublin, Nicky Byrne has long cycled to work at the airport, where he is one of the best-known personalities, a great storyteller and retailer of humorous tales. Over the years, the boilerhouse has used several different types of fuel, including turf, which was essential during the Emergency and for long afterwards, oil and coal. Two years ago, the present boilerhouse changed to natural gas, which has meant big savings on fuel costs. While gas is very efficient, it has also meant a halving of the boilerhouse staff; Nicky Byrne believes that, in the longer term, there will be no staff at all because boilers will be decentralised into those areas of the airport that need hot water, like the catering section.

Brian Byrne (no relation) heralded another substantial change of direction in 1981, when he played a major part in an airport seminar on encouraging equal opportunity. Derek Keogh, assistant chief executive, said that the percentage of females employed in the company was not reflected in the higher grades. He said that he preferred to work with women because they were not as egotistical as men; neither did they seem to need to assert themselves at the expense of others. He also said that he liked the meticulousness with which most women approached their job. Company attitudes and practices would be changed, he concluded. Brian Byrne, the present deputy general manager at Dublin airport, says that women's rights became an issue for Aer Rianta long before it was generally fashionable. Just as the company struck historic precedents with its commitment to give its thirty per cent female workforce at Dublin airport equal opportunity, so too was the company the first in Ireland to introduce a job-sharing scheme, in 1983. It was also one of the first organisations to introduce flexi-time working, with the aim of making the work experience more positive and satisfying for employees and more productive for the company. Management were clearly in cracking form; the annual Dublin airport question time was again held in Maguire's pub in Dorset Street; the airport management team, comprising Owen Clarke, Arthur Coughlan, Alan Levey, Joe Kelly and Joe O'Connell, won the day. Oliver McCann emerged as the "Brain of Dublin".

Eileen Dale became the first female executive in the company to take an Irish Management Institute course. In 1981, she attended the Aer Rianta/IMI course on industrial relations for line managers. Another "first" happened that year when Oonagh Doyle became the first woman technician to work on the Department of Posts and Telegraphs' staff at Dublin airport.

There were some interesting managerial appointments at the airport during the course of the year. Frank Shortall, the manager of airport facilities and services, had his area of responsibility extended. He now looked after airport maintenance as well, and also deputised in the absence of George O'Connor, deputy director–Dublin airport. Shortall was often held up as an example of how the path to the top at the airport is open to all; ability and talent are the main requirements. He began as a carpenter with Aer Lingus in 1947 and was let go with hundreds of others during the big aviation recession of 1948. The following year, he joined Aer Rianta as maintenance carpenter and worked his way up, becoming ground facilities superintendent in 1973. Frank Shortall was a Dubliner, while Joe O'Connell, who was appointed maintenance manager in 1981, is a native of Kildysart, County Clare. He joined the company in 1963, working in commercial and administrative areas. Denis Murray, who joined Aer Rianta in Shannon in 1969 and transferred to Dublin in 1976 to work in airport administration, was appointed maintenance control supervisor, reporting to Tony Nevin, maintenance facilities superintendent. Frank Cruise was made airport engineer. Cruise, a native of Dublin, joined the company in 1969. Chuni Phukan, appointed division head–civil engineering, is a native of Assam, India. He came to Ireland in 1968 and worked with the ESB on the new generating station at the Pigeon House in Dublin, before joining the Department of Transport and Power in 1970, transferring to Aer Rianta in 1973. In his new job, he played a crucial role in engineering services at the airport.

Eamonn O'Leary, who is a police/fireman at Dublin airport, is also a member of the crew of Dun Laoghaire lifeboat. In August, 1990, he carried out a daring single-handed rescue of five men and a boy, all from Crumlin, Dublin; their boat had gone down off Dalkey Island, County Dublin. A Garda spokesperson said that O'Leary should be cited for gallantry for saving so many people. He had been out fishing when he saw the six people floundering in the water.
Photograph: Neil MacDougald

Jean Taylor, advertising and promotions officer, Aer Rianta.
Photograph: Neil MacDougald

Left: Larry Hagman, alias J. R. Ewing, the oil baron of *Dallas*, the TV series, does some duty free haggling at Dublin airport, 1986.
Photograph: Robert Allen Photography

Right: Gay Byrne, the radio and TV broadcaster: in praise of Dublin airport.
Photograph: The Irish Times

Longer serving members of staff were honoured. Ten members of staff at the airport each received twenty-five-year-service medals: they were Harry Clarke, Owen Clarke, Hugh Connolly, Brendan Dolan, Johnny Doody, Paddy Kelly, Martin Judge, Danny McLoughlin, Jimmy McNulty and Danny Toland. Five of the long-serving members of staff all came from one section; they were all bar staff. RALSA, the association for retired members of the company, set a "first"; it was the first such organisation to have its own official headquarters. These were opened in the North terminal on January 8, 1981. Two noted personalities at the airport retired. Billy Bizzell worked from 1946 to 1977 as Dublin airport's foreman painter; then he became building maintenance contracts supervisor. One of his tasks in his last years at the airport was assessing the satisfactory completion of contracts, so that payment could be authorised. Just before he died, in December, 1989, he confessed that many contractors' employees had reason to dislike him intensely. Yet he always retained a stylish patrician air that caused many people meeting him for the first time to mistake him for an airport director. His farewell presentation was attended by a huge number of airport colleagues, including Tom Cullen, the director of Dublin and Cork airports. Another retirement was that of Christopher "Kit" Johnson, the airport's longest-serving carpenter, who had been closely involved with the fund-raising for the airport church. He had also been very active on the sporting side of the company. Kit died shortly after his retirement.

Two other outstanding airport personalities died, Captain J. C. Kelly-Rogers early in the year, Ted Sparling in the autumn. Kelly-Rogers had been appointed assistant general manager (technical) of Aer Lingus, Aer Rianta and Aerlínte in 1947, and in 1952, was appointed deputy general manager, a post he held until his retirement in 1967. During World War II, he had been a pilot for Churchill. After his retirement, he became honorary curator of the Irish Aviation Museum and collected many items of interest. Ted Sparling came to Dublin airport from the Air Corps at Baldonnel; he had been involved in the formation of the Air Corps in the early 1920s. At Dublin airport, he became a supervisor attached to the Watch Office, an early institution at Collinstown. Later, he worked with the engineers' department.

At the airport itself, little development took place in 1981, although Seaborne opened a new Georgian-style delicatessen shop on the departures level and new payphones were installed, which allowed people to direct dial trunk calls. On the sporting front, Dublin airport got a new staff pitch and putt course. Eighteen members of the Aer Rianta Dublin hurling team went to Boston to play.

The annual triangular golf match between Dublin, Cork and Shannon airports took place at the Island golf course on May 15. Dublin won the title, with Brendan Murray winning the best card of the day. Chief executive James O'Sullivan, president of the Dublin Golfing Society, made a light-hearted speech and Martin Dully, then chief executive designate, although not expecting to be called on to speak, winged it in great style, drawing peals of laughter from the diners. Shortly afterwards, when the Dublin Airport Golfing Society held its captain's outing to Baltray, Derek Keogh won the top prize. Christopher Martin, head office accountant, for fourteen years secretary of the Irish Aviation Club, until 1980, made further progress with his yachting activities. One of the trips he undertook at this time in his own yacht was a voyage from Howth Yacht Club down to Castletownbere and Glengarriff. Robert Allen, the airport photographer, captured the Lord Mayor of Dublin, Councillor Fergus O'Brien, with an enormous photographic reproduction, presented to him at the Mansion House.

The new year, 1982, began with a snowstorm that paralysed the Dublin area for a week. The airport was closed for the duration and many staff were unable to leave the building. The storm began on Friday, January 8, and by the following day, the airfield was covered in ten inches of snow. On access roads, winds had blown the snow into eight feet high drifts. Hundreds of motorists had to abandon their cars on the Swords Road and on the roads leading to the airport.

At the height of the blizzard on the Friday evening, there were 1,500 people marooned in the airport. There was an ESB power failure and airport staff performed heroic deeds to keep light and heat going in the main areas of the airport. Three fitters, Mark Gilmartin, Robert McAlpine and Martin Nolan, battled through six feet high snowdrifts to get emergency heaters to the medical centre, the hangars and the main terminal building. Many catering staff worked throughout the Friday night to provide food for stranded passengers and airport workers. The first runway was cleared by Sunday evening but it was not until Tuesday that the second was opened and Wednesday when the access roads to the airport were cleared. For five days, Dublin airport had been caught in a snowstorm unprecedented in its history.

Some major management changes took place at the airport. Tom Cullen, director Dublin and Cork airports, was appointed assistant chief executive with responsibility for sales. His specific task was to boost Aer Rianta's income from shop sales. By this time, Gerry Heffernan, for so long associated with the Dublin airport shops, had been promoted to deputy general manager, Dublin airport, and in that capacity, in early 1982, he welcomed Björn Borg, the Swedish tennis star, to the airport. In another appointment, Joe O'Rourke, an aerodrome fire officer, was appointed to the

Samuel Beckett, the Irish dramatist, novelist and poet, who lived in Paris for many years; he died there in December, 1989. On the very rare occasions that he visited Ireland, he always wished to pass through Dublin airport with total anonymity.
Photograph: The Irish Times

Left: The grave of Beckett and his wife in the Cimetière Montparnasse, Paris.
Photographs: Hugh Oram

British Midland inaugurated its Dublin–Heathrow service at the end of April, 1989, offering an all business class service. Previous routes operated out of Dublin by the company included Liverpool and East Midlands airport.
Photograph: British Midland

new position of fire chief–Dublin. He had joined the airport fire service in 1946.

Owen Clarke was appointed airport facilities manager. John Brennan became sales manager in charge of all the retail outlets at the airport; already, there was strong pressure from the EC for the abolition of duty free facilities. Aer Rianta began a strong lobbying campaign against the concept, pointing out that if duty free shopping was abolished, landing charges at Dublin and its other airports would have to be increased by forty per cent. Also on the political front, Dublin airport laid on full-scale ceremonial for the departure of the Taoiseach, Charles Haughey, to the U.S. on March 15. He had become Taoiseach of a minority Fianna Fáil government, supported by independent T.D., Tony Gregory, the previous month. In December 1982, a Coalition government, headed by Dr Garret FitzGerald, came to power.

During the year, interesting developments took place at the airport. Runway markings changed, because of the oscillation of magnetic north. The main runway changed from 06/24 to 05/23 and runway 12/30 changed to 11/29. Dan-Air inaugurated its Dublin–Gatwick service and Avair, having started three domestic services the year before, began its first international service, to the Isle of Man. The training scheme for Libyan students got into full swing, with sixty trainees arriving at the specially built school premises at the airport. Headmaster of the school was Ray Bolger, previously a maintenance facilities assistant, electrical, at the airport.

The Libyans studied mechanical and electrical engineering subjects, as well as electronics and communications. A noted airport personality retired: Frank Shortall, who in the words of George O'Connor, the airport manager, left a benchmark for everyone else to follow. He died less than a year later. There was sadness when Michael Mullen of the ITGWU and a board member of Aer Rianta died in a Frankfurt hospital on November 1. As branch secretary of Number Four branch of the union, he looked after the interests of airport workers most assiduously. His tenure of office as an Aer Rianta director lasted just over two years. Paul Kimmage, the cycling star, hit the headlines, as he has continued to do in 1990. At the time of the 1982 publicity, he was an apprentice plumber at the airport, but already held the all-Ireland cycling championship.

That summer saw the plans revealed for the new ALSAA club at the airport. A ten

Ryanair brought the first Airbus A320 into Ireland in April 1988, as part of its sponsorship of the Eurovision song contest.
Photograph: Ryanair

Ryanair commenced services from Dublin on May 23, 1986, with a flight to London. Pictured at Dublin airport prior to the first flight is Martin Dully, then chief executive, Aer Rianta, making a presentation to Arthur Walls, chairman of Ryanair. On the right of the photograph is Derek Keogh, Aer Rianta.
Photograph: Ryanair

year development plan called for the building of an elaborate sports complex at Toberbunny, on the east side of the main Dublin–Belfast road. Facilities were to include a ten pin bowling alley, three squash courts, a large multi-purpose sports hall and a clubhouse. By 1990, the development of the ALSAA complex has been virtually completed. A blast from the past came in the shape of Fokker Friendships. British Midland used the aircraft type on its new Dublin–East Midlands service, while the Dutch Air Force band arrived on one of these aircraft to take part in Dublin's St Patrick's Day parade.

Two well-known journalists gave outsiders' views of the airport scene for *Runway* magazine. Jim Dunne, then editor of *Business and Finance*, now senior finance editor with *The Irish Times*, described Aer Rianta as an organisation still in search of an image. With tongue firmly in cheek, he said it was disappointing that the company could not mobilise itself for a really disruptive strike. Michael Foley, writing as tourism correspondent of *The Irish Times*, said that the 1982 tourism season had not turned out as badly as feared. The effects of the H-Block hunger strikes were still

Left: The late Carl O'Sugrue, who used to head the press and public relations function at Dublin airport.
Photograph: Robert Allen Photography

Right: Flan Clune, press and public relations manager, Aer Rianta from 1986.
Photograph: Robert Allen Photography

Gillian Bowler, managing director, Budget Travel, Dublin. Her company operated thirteen charter flights a week out of Dublin airport in the summer of 1990, to such destinations as Corfu, Cyprus and Nice. Ten of those flights were on charter from Aer Lingus.

being felt, but for Aer Rianta, the year turned out well, with a surplus of £6 million. Dublin airport showed a minor drop in traffic of just 0.8 per cent, but chairman Peter Hanley said that this concealed a worrying fall in international travellers. During the year, North American passengers fell by 1.5 per cent to 193,000 and cross-channel by three per cent to 1,422,100. European passenger figures were up one per cent to 959,500, while domestic passengers were up 13.6 per cent to 128,900. One interesting new service was started in April, 1985, by Dublin City Helicopters, whose managing director was John Riordan. Using a Sikorsky S61, it ran flights from the airport to Holyhead in north Wales. The service had its own check-in and ticket desk on the departures level of the terminal at Dublin airport. The operation lasted a year.

During 1983, major technical improvements took place at Dublin airport. The main runway was resurfaced, a temporary job until such time as the new runway could be completed. Work on placing a thin asphalt overlay on runway 05/23 began on April 18 and was finished, on schedule, in early July. The main contractors were Roadstone, who employed about forty men on site. Daily asphalt laying averaged a total of 400 tonnes, with a peak of 900 tonnes. During the work, the shorter runway 17/35 was used and when it came to resurfacing the pavement at the intersection of the two runways, both had to be closed, so the work for this section was carried out on four nights a week. The work was designed by head office technical services staff, under Pat Hackett, while the construction work was supervised by Hugh Tremble with the co-operation of airport engineer, Frank Cruise. Jack Scully, airside maintenance and safety manager, kept a close eye on the proceedings. When the work was completed, the new surface had to be totally cleaned; the smallest piece of debris left behind could have caused havoc to an aircraft engine. The other substantial development at the airport in 1983 was the new look for the main terminal building. Chief architect, Joe Clarke, explained that when the terminal was built in the early 1970s, materials such as aluminium and glass were used, since they have an almost indefinite lifespan. However, management decided that the arrivals and departures areas should be given a new appearance.

The arrivals concourse was redesigned, with a new seating area placed near the Customs' exit doors. The information desk was relocated and redesigned to reflect the company's corporate image. Careful consideration was given to colour schemes, and a bright red was chosen for the carpet and furnishings, to contrast with the dark brown rubber tiles on the floor. Lighting, too, was improved; the overall effect of the new look arrivals area was a much more "user friendly" section of the airport. The security service at the airport got new accommodation; its offices had been scattered around the terminal site and link buildings. In 1982, the Aer Rianta board decided to use the space intended for car parking on the roof levels of the terminal for office facilities, and the airport police were the first to benefit. The office suite, with its own entrance hall, has accommodation that includes a mess hall, a briefing and lecture room and a recreation area. The area was designed by Tony Kelly of technical services under chief architect Joe Clarke. For the security staff, headed by Jim McDonald and his deputy, Jack Bannon, the new centralised accommodation meant much easier office working conditions. The other substantial change at the airport that year was the concession arrangement between Aer Rianta and SAS Catering, part of Scandinavian Airways System, for running the airport catering.

Since the new terminal opened to the public in 1972, the workings of the catering arrangements had never been entirely satisfactory, principally because it never proved possible to generate the turnover and profit levels that existed in the restaurant in the original terminal building. Under the terms of the ten-year contract, SAS Catering committed itself to spending £620,000 on development work for the airport catering area. Jimmy Doyle had been head chef for many years, but with the new regime, a new head chef, Michael O'Carroll, was appointed, to work under new general manager, Per Arnborg. Of the 120 catering staff who had been working in the airport, seventy-three were transferred to the new operation. Dick Lennon, the ITGWU branch secretary, who was involved in the transfer negotiations, said that SAS Catering's industrial relations style was excellent, equal to that of Aer Rianta. "Prior consultation is their hallmark and staff have been very adequately protected

Irish competitors at the Paraplegic Olympics in Seoul, 1988, return to a rapturous welcome from supporters.
Photograph: Robert Allen Photography

A British Airways Boeing 757, which the airline used on its Dublin–Heathrow services. British Airways is the world's leading international airline; it carried 18 million scheduled passengers in 1989.
Photograph: British Airways

in terms of pay and conditions". A self-service fast food fair, the first such operation in the airport, was opened on the mezzanine floor and a self-service café was opened on the arrivals concourse. The main restaurant, which had been closed, despite many protests from customers, including Charles Haughey, according to David Lord's recollections, reopened. Dick Lennon made the telling point that since the glamour traffic had disappeared from the airport, in favour of volume traffic, catering at the airport had been going downhill. From 1975 until 1982, airport catering lost a total of £1.3 million.

One of the staff who transferred under the new arrangements was David Lord, who remained restaurant manager until he retired in 1989. Another veteran of the catering services who transferred was Seán Clancy, who became head waiter and assistant manager in the restaurant. Naturally, there was regret among the staff that the catering arrangements could not have been handled locally, but in the seven years since the contract was signed with SAS Catering, the catering side of the airport has been greatly stabilised and developed. One other area of the airport's operation celebrated a milestone: in October, 1983, the VAT free shop sales at the airport exceeded £1 million. In 1981, the shop had turned over £580,000, but with the move to the new location during the summer of 1983, sales soared. Passing the £1 million mark in October, by the end of that year they had soared to £1.2 million. The airport staff were intrigued with all the innovations: with Martin Dully installed as new chief executive, the old adage about the new broom took shape, fast.

The usual crop of staff appointments and promotions were made at the airport. Gerry McEvoy, manpower planning officer, was promoted to organisation services manager, reporting to deputy personnel manager, John Burke. Gerry Weir, who was training officer, was promoted to training manager, at a time when the expansion of training facilities within Aer Rianta was about to lead to the setting up of a custom-built training centre for inhouse and overseas courses at the historic Castlemoate House, a landmark at Cloghran since the early 19th century. In a welcome move as part of the company's employment equality drive, Marion Keating, secretary to Gerard Harvey, was promoted to employment officer, assisting the personnel administration manager with staff recruitment programmes. Another female management appointment came when Kathleen Keatley was made construction contracts superintendent. She had begun her Aer Rianta career in 1973 as a grade four clerk. A career switch came with the appointment of Michael Houlihan as ground facilities officer; he had spent the last ten years in the accounts department. Barney Boylan, field electrical supervisor, won £400 for improving the lighting in the public car park, in a way that would save energy costs. Retirements included that of Gerry Monks, for long the property services manager at the airport.

Tragedy struck, too. Gerry Heffernan, for long one of the most flamboyant and popular personalities around the airport, who made such an impact on retailing at the airport, went home from work on Thursday, May 5, 1983. He collapsed and died that night. He had joined the airport staff in 1967 and, at the start, he was seen as having an unconventional management style that did not fit in readily with the largely non-commercial approach that characterised Aer Rianta's earlier years. But Gerry Heffernan, through his presence in the shopping centre, became one of the best-known people at the airport, as well as in the business life of the greater Dublin area. Strongly nationalistic in outlook, he saw the airport shops as a means of selling quality Irish goods to foreign visitors; the airport was a commercial shop window on the world. A great friend of Michael Mullen, the trade unionist, one of his most treasured possessions was a photograph of himself with Senator Ted Kennedy during Heffernan's visit to the U.S. in 1981 as part of the then Taoiseach's official party. His good friend, Fr Joe Drumgoole, said at the funeral Mass that Gerry Heffernan's greatest characteristics were his integrity and loyalty. At the funeral, to his parish church in Howth, the attendance included the Aer Rianta board of directors, many business friends, the President's personal representative, Charles Haughey, leader of Fianna Fáil, and Dublin's then Lord Mayor, Councillor Dan Browne.

Just a week before Gerry Heffernan died, he had been made a Governor of Jervis Street hospital. Another tragedy was remembered just two days before Gerry Heffernan died. A Mass was held in the airport church for the soul of Declan Flynn, who worked in the ground services department at Dublin airport and who was remembered by his colleagues as a very quiet and gentle person, popular with all who knew him. He had been murdered in most brutal fashion in Fairview Park the previous September. When sentence was eventually passed in what became known as the Fairview Park trial, there was widespread concern at the alleged leniency and Dublin airport staff sent a petition in protest to the Minister of Justice.

Many new aircraft were seen at Dublin airport during 1983. Dan-Air flew a new British Aerospace 146 jet into the airport; it was claimed to be the quietest short-

David Lord, who retired as manager of the Silver Lining restaurant in 1989.
Photograph: Robert Allen Photography

Left: Edward F. MacSweeney, producer of the RTÉ Radio 1 programme, *Sunday Miscellany*. He has broadcast and written extensively on aviation matters, for RTÉ, *The Irish Times* and aviation magazines.
Photograph: RTÉ illustrations library

Right: Jack Fagan, for long aviation correspondent of *The Irish Times*, whose reports included many events at Dublin airport. He is now property editor of *The Irish Times*.
Photograph: The Irish Times

Joe Walsh of JWT Holidays. The firm has been operating from Dublin airport for the past thirty years and in 1990 will have a total of about three hundred charter flights from Dublin, excluding flights to Lourdes and special flights to the World Cup soccer finals in Italy.

range commercial jet in the world. Aer Arran was using Bandeirante aircraft into Dublin for its new commuter service to Shannon, while Aer Lingus introduced its new Shorts 330 aircraft on cross-channel routes to Liverpool and East Midlands airport, starting on May 1. This new thirty-seater aircraft became a useful low-cost plane on cross-channel and domestic routes, but was superseded by the thirty-five seater Shorts 360. For the first time, Air France started a scheduled service between Dublin and Charles de Gaulle airport in Paris. The airline had long been a regular user of Shannon, so the new Dublin service, using Boeing 737s, was a departure.

Since 1983, the Air France service has had its daily frequency increased considerably and in 1989, a new direct route was opened between Dublin and Nice. This service runs from the spring to the autumn each year; the next Air France service out of Dublin is likely to be a direct route to Lyons. For the first time, a Concorde supersonic aircraft visited Dublin; on October 1, an Air France Concorde landed at the airport. The roofs of the airport were especially opened to cater for the thousands of aviation enthusiasts, keen to catch a glimpse of this plane of the future that holds one hundred passengers and cruises at a height of about 55,000 feet, at a speed of 1,350 mph. Concorde, with its white fuselage and red and blue Air France markings, created a tremendous stir, reminiscent of the great aviation days of the late 1940s and 1950s, when unusual aircraft, like the "Connies" brought huge crowds out to the airport. The second Concorde visit to Dublin was on September 30, 1988; it returned to Paris that night after having once more proved its crowd-pulling capacity.

More spectacular aircraft were seen around the airport that summer. Aer Rianta had been closely involved in sponsoring the Air Spectacular since 1982. The event that took place in the summer of 1983 was described as the most spectacular ever to have taken place. An American Jolly Green giant helicopter, three US Air Force Thunderbolt anti-tank aircraft and a World War II Spitfire Mk XIV gave the great crowds at Fairyhouse treat after treat. Some aircraft arrived and departed via Dublin airport.

Sabena, more than forty years after its introduction to Dublin, still runs regular scheduled flights between Dublin airport and Brussels.
Photograph: Airprint, Brussels

Ryanair BAC-One-Elevens at Dublin airport. In the summer of 1990, a total of fourteen scheduled airlines were using the airport: Aer Lingus, Aeroflot, Air France, British Airways, British Midland, Brymon Airways, Delta Airlines, Iberia Airlines, Lufthansa–German Airlines, Manx Airlines, Ryanair, Sabena–Belgian World Airlines, SAS and TAP-Air Portugal.
Photograph: Ryanair

A new land-based transport system also created a frisson that year, for 1984 was the year that the DART electrified railway system came into operation. Running from Howth on the northside to Bray in County Wicklow, it soon became a popular commuter service, efficient and on time. Another event that year was the new style *Sunday Tribune,* edited by Vincent Browne. The paper had been launched in 1980 as a rebirth of the old *Hibernia* magazine, but this first version collapsed. Browne's version has proved considerably more durable. 1983 also saw some very distinguished visitors to Dublin airport, including Javier Perez de Cuellar, the UN secretary-general, who was greeted on arrival by Peter Barry, then Minister for Foreign Affairs, Sean Donlon, then secretary of that department and now with Guinness Peat Aviation, and Martin Dully, Aer Rianta chief executive. American vice-president, now president, George Bush, also got the full airport welcome, as did Henry Kissinger, a former U.S. Secretary of State. He was visiting Dublin in his capacity as an advisor to Heinz Erin Foods; he spent two days as a guest of Dr A. J. F. O'Reilly, of Heinz and Independent Newspapers. The year also saw the last "Connie" at the airport. This Constellation began life in 1947 under the KLM colours; much later, after a bizarre series of adventures, the plane ended up on the tarmac at Dublin

Louisa Hopkins, great granddaughter of the late Hugh Cahill, senior, founder of Iona National Airways, made her first solo flight in 1990 at Iona's commercial flying school in Cork. She is pictured here with her uncle Peter (right) and grandfather Pearse Cahill at Iona's Dublin headquarters.
Photograph: Dara MacDonaill/ Sunday Independent

Eamonn Moran, Dublin airport services manager.
Photograph: Robert Allen Photography

An Air France Concorde at Dublin airport, September 30, 1988. The airline has seven Concordes in its fleet.

airport. Finally, its lack of airworthiness meant that the plane had to be dismantled on the spot. Jack Fagan, then aviation correspondent, now property editor of *The Irish Times,* wrote a feature for *Runway* on the recession in world aviation. He described the considerable Aer Lingus cost-cutting programme that was going on within the Irish airline, with the aim of making that organisation leaner and slimmer for better times ahead. But Jack Fagan pointed out that the interests of national airlines and national airports are not always identical. Revenue figures for Dublin airport for 1983 showed total passenger numbers of 2,562,000, a five per cent decrease on the previous year. 1,363,000 of those passengers were travelling on routes to and from Britain. The biggest decline, twenty-two per cent, was on trans-Atlantic routes, while the one area to show an increase was domestic flights, where the number of passengers was up fourteen per cent to 151,000. Terminal freight increased by 5,023 metric tonnes, while terminal mail increased by 356 metric tonnes. Considering the state of the aviation industry, Dublin airport performed well during 1983. Martin Dully said in his Christmas message that Aer Rianta had been trading well during a difficult period for aviation and tourism. No major setbacks were expected during 1984. He became president of the Chartered Institute of Transport in Ireland. Appropriately, in line with a tradition that is now firmly established, the airport terminal was most colourfully lit up for the Christmas season, with lights and decorations galore.

When 1983 finally drew to a close, Martin Dully echoed the sentiments of many when he said that most businesses would rather forget the year completed. Numerous companies closed down or contracted, direct and indirect taxation soared and spending power diminished. A dismal year on the national economic front turned

A Belfast-built Shorts SD360 in the livery of Manx Airlines; both the plane type and the airline are daily "visitors" at the airport.

out to be reasonably satisfactory for Aer Rianta. At the airport, two new restaurants were opened, the first signs of the new catering arrangements with SAS Catering. The Silver Lining was opened as the new upmarket venue; in his speech, Aer Rianta chairman Peter Hanley said that many people remarked nostalgically to him about the old days in the Collar of Gold: the new restaurant restored Dublin airport to its old place among gourmets. Manager of the new restaurant was David Lord. The other catering innovation opened was the Food Fair, a fast food restaurant, where the eating area was designed like a garden. On the electronics front, there were developments, too. The company opened a new computer software library to loan books and cassettes for the computers issued under the company's staff purchase scheme. It was based in Castlemoate House. The airport had a good effect on Gay Byrne, because on his radio show at the beginning of 1984, he said: "I went out from Dublin airport on New Year's Day. It was a rotten stinking morning, the morning after the night before. I wasn't feeling too well myself and by the looks of some people, they weren't feeling too well either. But I got a lovely atmosphere in Dublin airport. It was quite quiet and low keyed, but everybody was being very kind. I was most taken with it. If you were on the staff of Dublin airport on New Year's Day, take a bow . . . well done. I was kind of taken with it".

Positive action was taken on a number of fronts. The company's affirmative action programme came in for close scrutiny on RTÉ radio. Derek Keogh remarked how in the old days one would never see a private office for women. They were all bashing away at typewriters while the top management jobs were held by men. The affirmative action co-ordinator, Judy Donaghy, outlined some of the advances that had been made within the company. Job-sharing arrangements were also detailed. To complete the interest, a competition called "Jobs for Women in the Future" was staged in Castlemoate House. Nuala Fennell, Minister of State for Women's Affairs, opened the event. One poster showed a female chief executive, while another depicted a female Pontiff named Pope Mary. Ruairi Quinn, the Minister for Labour,

Oliver Costello, financial manager, Dublin airport.
Photograph: Robert Allen Photography

When the Irish soccer team returned home from the European Cup matches in Germany in the summer of 1988, they were met by a rapturous reception at Dublin airport. Watched by Charles Haughey, T.D., Taoiseach, team manager Jack Charlton addressed the multitudes.
Photograph: Robert Allen Photography

extended the Worker Participation Act to include Aer Rianta. Subsequently, three workers were elected to the board. Welcoming the legislature news, chairman Peter Hanley said that Aer Rianta had always been in favour of industrial democracy. As part of the management changes initiated at Aer Rianta in 1983, Tom Cullen moved back to his original discipline of accountancy by being appointed assistant chief executive–finance, with responsibility for the finance department.

The move was cited by Martin Dully as an excellent example of how people can move around within the organisation, bringing their talents and skills to bear in different areas. Tom Cullen had previously been director, Dublin and Cork airports, and subsequent to his finance posting was made general manager of Dublin airport. Derek Keogh was appointed assistant chief executive–operations and general manager, Dublin airport. He was also given responsibility for the customer standards programme, which Dully described as becoming the main plank of the company's policy. Following intense lobbying, including regular trips to Brussels by Martin Dully and Gerard Harvey, good news came through from the EC Commission. The EC recognised that duty free sales were a legal entity. Had the ruling gone the other way, the company would have been faced with the contraction of a major source of income, said Gerard Harvey. In those management changes in early 1984, no sooner had it been announced that Harvey was to become assistant chief executive–trading than he surprised everyone by resigning from the company to take up the position of chief executive, An Post. Other appointments that year reflected the fast-growing emphasis on customer-related marketing operations within the company. Frank O'Connell was made marketing manager, a further stepping stone in his swift ascent of the company ladder. His new appointment also showed the extent to which marketing had become a major element in Aer Rianta's corporate thinking.

Five years previously, as Martin Dully pointed out, the setting up of the marketing department had been greeted with some considerable scepticism. Aer Rianta appointed Frank Hanlon as general manager–trading; he came to the airport from Dunnes Stores. His appointment reflected the policy of the company in making each section of the enterprise totally viable in its own right, giving it the best of personnel and expertise. Other appointments at the airport included Patrick Harrington as aerodrome fire officer; he had joined the airport police and fire service in 1961. Theresa Wearen was made senior cleaning supervisor; she had joined the airport cleaning section in 1966. Her husband, Austin, who works with the outside cleaners at the airport, is a church organ builder by trade. A new social club at the airport was that for the cleaners; it was the brainchild of Eddie Cromwell, its first treasurer.

The retirement of Jim McDonald as head of the airport police and fire service came after thirty-seven years' service. He had seen the airport improve beyond all recognition, recalling that in the early days, paraffin landing lights burned on the runways and, in conditions of bad visibility, firemen would fire Verey cartridges at the runway thresholds to give the runway position to pilots. Jim McDonald was succeeded by Jack Bannon, from Clonshaugh, which was a very rural part of north County Dublin when he was a boy, but which is now just beyond the airport perimeter fence and the site of a large industrial estate.

Derek Keogh, the new general manager of the airport, referred to the complexity of the operation. Between Aer Rianta, Aer Lingus and all the other airlines and services at the airport, some eight thousand people were employed on the site. 2.6 million passengers used the terminal every year and a further four million people came to see them off, or welcome them on their return. The 1984 budget for the airport was £17 million. In 1984, the biggest problem at the airport was the question of funding the much-needed new main runway. Discussions had been continuing

Oliver McCann, public relations officer, Aer Rianta.
Photograph: Robert Allen Photography

Kealys is a popular hostelry on the old Swords road; dating back well over a century, it is the nearest pub to the main airport buildings. For many years this century, it was run by Pat Murtagh and his daughter May; in the early 1960s, it was sold to Michael Woods, who had returned from the U.S. In 1966, it was sold to Joe Kealy, father of the present owner, Derry Kealy. Although the pub has the airport at its back, the immediate location is very rural. There used to be a turkey farm behind the pub and also a national school, just across the road.
Photograph: Neil MacDougald

with the various bodies concerned, the Departments of Communications and Finance and Dublin County Council, but no specific government approval had been given for the project. It was stated that the safety in use of the old runway 05/23 for larger aircraft could no longer be guaranteed by 1989, which was in fact the year the new east-west runway was opened. Good financial housekeeping showed up in the boilerhouse. In 1973, the year of the first global oil crisis, the airport was using 2,546,363 litres of oil; by 1984, that figure had been reduced to 80,000 litres. Brickeens dropped from 2,281 tonnes in 1973 to eighty-five tonnes in 1984, but in the same period, the use of macerated turf rose from 11,231 tonnes to 16,000 tonnes. Three years later, the last of the turf fired the boilers; they were converted to natural gas.

Work was progressing well on the motorway status road linking the airport to Whitehall. It opened to traffic the following year, 1985. The eventual plan is for these new roads in the vicinity of the airport to be an integral part of a Dublin–Belfast motorway. 1985 also saw the new East Link toll bridge opened across the Liffey, the first such toll section in Ireland since 1816.

The highlight of the year at the airport was the departure of President Reagan. The American president had arrived at Shannon on June 1; the tour to the south and west of the country included the much publicised visit to the small south Tipperary town of Ballyporeen, home of his ancestors. Today, the visit, which generated intense media coverage, is remembered by the name of the Ronald Reagan pub on the Main Street in Ballyporeen and by the heritage centre at the village crossroads, named in his honour. On Monday, June 4, the presidential party left from Dublin airport. After their three days in Ireland, both Ronald Reagan and his wife, Nancy, looked extremely relaxed. The media facilities, including those for live television and radio coverage, were compared to those needed for a moonshot. As usual, for these big ceremonial occasions at the airport, everything worked flawlessly, despite the odd behind the scenes panic. The national and international media, including Pat Kenny on RTÉ radio, praised the smoothness of the operation.

An example of Aer Rianta computerisation: Gerard Lawlor operates the IBM AT computer-aided drawing system at Dublin airport. The system designs such projects as circuits, ducting, runways and airfield lights and has a 20 mb capacity.
Photograph: Neil MacDougald

Above: The evening approach to the Dublin International hotel at Dublin airport.
Photograph: Neil MacDougald

The perfumes section of Dublin airport tax free shop.
Photograph: Michael Blake

The old and new Dublin: reflected in the River Liffey are the two new tower blocks housing Dublin Corporation's main offices and Christchurch cathedral.
Photograph: Neil MacDougald

Despite the air of forward progress and development at the airport, there were tragedies and disasters. There was a fire disaster at Trinity College, when the historic dining hall caught fire. Fortunately, there were no injuries and the building was eventually restored to its former architectural glory. But there was tragedy in the Lebanon, in the grip of a civil war that has continued for almost as long as the conflict in the North; the Lebanese war has reduced Beirut, once described, with good reason, as the Paris of the Middle East, to virtual ruin. Irish troops have been leading players in the UN peacekeeping mission in that troubled country; the price was high. During 1984, there were fatalities among the Irish contingent and bodies were returned home to Baldonnel, just as they had been in earlier years from the Congo and Cyprus. In November that year, 1984, a small charter aircraft took off from Dublin bound for the Beaujolais wine race in France. Its complement of nine included leading Dublin journalists, like John Feeney of the *Evening Herald* and Kevin Marron, a former editor of the *Sunday World*. The plane came down near Eastbourne on the south coast of England; all on board were killed. Tragedy struck, too, in the world of entertainment, when Luke Kelly of the Dubliners died suddenly. Among his notable renditions was that of Patrick Kavanagh's plaintive, elegiac poem, *Raglan Road*. The next year, 1985, saw the passing of veteran Dublin character actor, Noel Purcell, while Hector Grey, a native of Scotland, but long-time resident of Dublin, also died. His inimitable style of trading, a little reminiscent perhaps of Gerry Heffernan's, was long a feature of central Dublin shopping.

Pop music filled the airwaves; the Dublin rock group, U2, one of the most successful the world has known, who helped turn the city into a world rock capital, filled Croke Park with no bother at all. Another city son, Bob Geldof, organised the international television "Live Aid" appeal for famine relief in Africa. The customary Irish generosity was much in evidence. President Hillery was reappointed for another seven-year term in the Park. Also on the political front, the controversial Hillsborough Agreement was signed between the Irish and British governments; for the first time, it gave the Irish government a formal role in the governing of the North and drew protests from the loyalist section of the community there.

At Aer Rianta, Frank Boland was appointed chairman in 1985 by the Coalition government; he succeeded Peter Hanley for a five year term of office. A prominent Cork businessman, he started Ireland's first car and van rental company in Cork in 1967. His other extensive interests include property development; he is chairman of a leading estate agents in Cork. He has had many interests in transport over the years; a former chairman of Cork Harbour Commissioners, he is still a board member of that body. He is a former director of Aer Lingus and is a former chairman of the B & I Line. His five year mandate as Aer Rianta chairman ran until the end of July, 1990, and during that period, the greatest change he has seen at Dublin airport has been the virtual doubling of passenger numbers. The Aer Rianta arts festivals have been another milestone, in his view, part of management's determination to humanise the airport. Passengers are not treated as captive customers, he says, and an especial effort is made to make the airport as sympathetic an environment as possible for those passengers who are still nervous of flying. Air travel is now accessible to all segments and Dublin airport has a very high level of "meeters and greeters", part of the Irish culture, a customer need that has to be reflected in airport facilities. Boland reflects that in all his time in business, he has never seen such a committed management as that in Dublin airport: "they treat every day as a pioneering day and there is a fantastic kindred spirit between all the staff".

Frank Boland, chairman of Aer Rianta, 1985–1990.
Photograph: Robert Allen Photography

Sculptures at Dublin airport, summer 1990

Above: "Amobea". Bronze on granite by Noel Hoare.

Right: "Robed demon". Sculpture in welded copper by Vincent Browne.

Below left: This strikingly red ferro cement creation by Dick Joynt is entitled "Earth Mother".

Below centre: "Ammonite", made in ferro cement by Niall O'Neill.

Below right: Another "Earth Mother" sculpture by Dick Joynt.

Above left: The sculpture that greets people arriving at Dublin airport on the main approach road: "Afar", a ferro cement and stainless steel creation by Niall O'Neill.

Above: On the approach road to the departures level, this untitled arch-like sculpture in wood and steel is the work of Michael Verdon.

Left: "Miss Swanlinbar" bids farewell to people leaving the airport; this pitch pine and red deal statue was created by James McKenna.

Below: On display in the departure level of the airport, the whimsical bicycle sculpture entitled "Quest" was made from leather, limestone and steel by Remco de Fouw.
Photographs: Neil MacDougald

247

A trio of politicians at the airport: from left, Brian Lenihan, Ben Briscoe and Ted Kennedy.
Photograph: Robert Allen Photography

He says that the airport owes much to the work of successive governments in expanding the facilities; out of his time as chairman of the company, he says that his real memories are of courtesy and co-operation from every single individual working in the airport. "Controversial points were discussed but there was no rancour, it was all for the betterment of Dublin airport". Frank Boland succeeded Peter Hanley and in turn, Boland was succeeded as chairman by Dermot F. Desmond.

John Cahalan made the type of big career change that is quite common and indeed encouraged within Aer Rianta. He joined the airport in 1978 and spent all his career there working as a technician before moving to become a ground facilities officer. Chuni Phukan, division head, civil engineering, went off for a three month UN secondment to Maseru, capital of the African kingdom of Lesotho. There, he carried out consultancy work at the newly built airport. Before he left, he expressed his pleasure at the task ahead, saying that it was good for Aer Rianta and the country that someone from Irish Airports should have been chosen. Two members of staff at Dublin airport, property superintendent Brian Vaughan, and airport police/fireman Jim Treanor, were called to the Bar, following the precedent set over thirty years previously by James O'Sullivan, a former chief executive.

Dublin airport saw the start of substantial physical changes, with the beginning of a five-year landscaping programme for the grounds. Besides planting trees and flowers to make the site look more attractive, the construction of roadways was planned so as to make a logical traffic flow system for passengers arriving and leaving and parking their cars. There were plans to plant trees in the car park to give people visual reference points, so they could find their cars more easily.

One of the last elements in the new landscape design for the airport was the completion of a new lake by the entrance road to the terminal. This lake was finished and filled in 1990, bringing back memories to older people at the airport of the quarry lake that stood at the airport until the early 1970s. Dublin airport joined the

Above: West German president Dr Richard von Weizsacker came to Ireland on holiday in 1987; an official party, led by President Hillery and the Taoiseach, Charles Haughey, T.D., met him at the airport. In 1980, there had been an official visit by the then German president, Carl Carstens and his wife.

Left: In June, 1988, Crown Prince Abdullah bin Abdulaziz Al Saud, first deputy prime minister and commander of the national guard of the Kingdom of Saudi Arabia, arrived on a State visit. He was welcomed to Dublin airport by Tom Cullen, general manager.
Photographs: Robert Allen Photography

Cardinal Tomás Ó Fiaich, Primate of All Ireland, seen at the airport in happier times in 1984 with Fr Niall O'Brien, the Irish priest imprisoned in the Philippines.

Below: His remains arriving at the airport, May, 1990; the Cardinal had collapsed and died during a diocesan pilgrimage to Lourdes.
Photographs: Robert Allen Photography

"Wrong Way" Corrigan pictured in 1988, fifty years after his famous flight to Ireland, when he says he took a wrong turning on take-off in the U.S. and ended up in Ireland instead of the American west coast.
Photograph: The Irish Times

Left: John Hume, the Northern Ireland MEP, with Derek Keogh, chief executive, Aer Rianta.
Photograph: Robert Allen Photography

Right: Three Dublin "institutions": Pete Short sells *In Dublin* magazine outside Bewley's café in Grafton Street.
Photograph: In Dublin

new Swords Business Association, a means of linking the 8,000 people working in the airport with the nearest town. At a function in the airport hotel at which the airport was formally introduced to the association, ex-Minister for the Environment Ray Burke, then out of office, and in 1990 Minister for Communications and Justice, stressed the need for the new runway at the airport. A new service was inaugurated, when Shannon Executive Aviation launched its Shannon–Dublin route, using a Metroliner 2 Turboprop aircraft. Sadly, like the new helicopter service to Holyhead, this new service proved of rather short duration. The fuselage of the old Aer Lingus Viscount, the *Naomh Fiachra*, was taken from the aeronautical museum in Dublin airport for display in the Young Scientists Exhibition and Competition in the RDS, Dublin.

At the forefront of technology, the company appointed its first-ever information technology manager, John O'Connor. Part of his job was advising users in the airport on their computer needs. In another step forward, January 1985 saw the cover of *Runway* magazine go full colour; it was also the first magazine in Ireland to be produced on a desktop publishing system, which not only handled the typesetting, but also the graphics and layout.

Dublin airport welcomed its two millionth passenger of 1985 on October 24; for the year as a whole, there were 2,618,627 passengers, an increase of 0.8 per cent over the previous year. The two millionth passenger was a Manchester travel agent, Harry Nixon, who came to Dublin with his wife, Margaret, as part of a group from the Association of British Travel Agents who were guests of Bord Fáilte at the ABTA Irish Golf Open at the Royal Dublin course. Although this was the first time the Nixons had been in Ireland since their honeymoon in Bray in 1953, Harry Nixon had been instrumental during the intervening years in sending many travellers from the North of England through Dublin airport. Derek Keogh, airport general manager,

President François Mitterrand of France is greeted by Charles Haughey, T.D., Taoiseach, at the start of his Irish visit, 1988. Looking on are President Hillery and four members of the cabinet, Brian Lenihan, Dr. Michael Woods, Ray Burke and Bertie Ahern.
Photograph: Robert Allen Photography

presented the Nixons with a plaque and a case of champagne. But Jack Fagan of *The Irish Times* noted in *Runway* magazine that although there were signs of the world aviation industry coming out of the recession, for the previous six years Irish airport traffic had been virtually static. He said: "In a nutshell, the airlines have failed to deliver. Some would suggest that they have been more concerned with feather-bedding than with increasing the number of tourists to Ireland". Martin Dully was accorded a singular honour: he became the first Irishman to be elected to the world-wide Airport Operators' Council International, as director for a three-year term. This body represents some 230 airports in five continents; over three-quarters of the world's airline traffic passes through these airports.

For Dublin airport, the long-awaited decision came at the tail end of 1985, when government approval was given for the new 8,650 feet east-west runway. It was designed to be 1,150 feet longer than the existing main runway; for some years, Aer Lingus and other carriers had had to accept payload penalties on long distance flights to the Canary Islands and Greece. One of the aims of the new runway design was to remove all payload penalties from all flights using the airport. Completion date for the new project was set as the first quarter of 1989; it was to be the biggest single construction job in the State during the 1980s. At the time the project was announced, it was stated that aircraft noise would be much reduced in areas like Ballymun and Swords, as well as in northside suburbs like Beaumont, Clontarf, Glasnevin and Killester.

Work began on the new runway the following year, 1986. That year is remembered for tragedies and a vast storm. Hurricane Charlie struck on August 25 that year; within the space of twenty-four hours, 3.1 inches of rain fell in the Dublin area, the heaviest rainfall since 1905. Normally placid rivers, like the Dodder, which flows through Ballsbridge, burst their banks. Traffic movements at the airport were severely disrupted for the duration of the storm. When the Loreto convent at St

Australian prime minister Bob Hawke inspects the guard of honour at the start of his official visit to Ireland, 1988.
Photograph: Robert Allen Photography

The terminal at Dublin airport illuminated for Dublin's Millennium, 1988.
Photograph: Robert Allen Photography

Stephen's Green caught fire that summer, six nuns died. Mrs Jennifer Guinness was kidnapped from her home in Howth, but was released unharmed, after eight days in captivity. Later, she suffered another tragedy, when her husband was killed in a mountain walking accident in North Wales.

A new political party was formed, the Progressive Democrats. Four years later, they found themselves in a coalition government as minority partners of Fianna Fáil. Samuel Beckett, one of the greatest Irish-born writers of the 20th century, celebrated his eightieth birthday in Paris. He had lived in France since before World War II; he died in Paris in December, 1989. In the divisive divorce referendum, Dublin was the only part of the country where the supporters of change had a majority over those who preferred the status quo, but only by the slimmest of margins. 49.9 per cent of those who voted were in favour of allowing divorce, 49.7 per cent were against, a dramatic contrast to the rest of the Republic, where the "no change" lobby gained up to 71 per cent of the vote.

At the airport, there was celebration of a golden jubilee and also the start-up of a new service that was to play a significant part in ending the traffic stagnation that had characterised Dublin airport for nearly a decade. On May 26, 1986, Aer Lingus celebrated its fiftieth anniversary. *Runway* magazine pointed out that not only was the airline the jumbo customer for Aer Rianta, but that "like most Irish people, we take great pride in the success and worldwide reputation of the national flag carrier". As part of the celebrations, it had been planned to fly the *Iolar*, a replica of the first plane used by the airline, back in 1936, on a repeat of its first journey for the airline, from Dublin to Bristol, but gale force winds forced the cancellation of the flight.

The main celebrations were transferred at short notice to Hangar 1, where the master of ceremonies was Pat Kenny, the broadcaster. Guests included Dr Garret FitzGerald, then Taoiseach, who had worked for Aer Lingus. Dr J. F. Dempsey and Dr Michael Dargan also came to the rostrum. Leading the Santry marching band, who serenaded the diners, was Niall Fitzgerald of Aer Rianta's trading department. In the terminal building, Gay Byrne presented an edition of his morning radio show, while on the Friday of that week, his *Late Late Show* on RTE television also presented a blockbuster on the anniversary. Appropriately, the giant banner at Dublin airport read: "Jumbo congratulations to our No 1 customer", signed by Aer Rianta. In a subsequent ceremony at the airport on October 23, Frank Boland, chairman of Aer Rianta, and Brian Slowey, chairman of Aer Lingus, unveiled a plaque mounted on a 1½ ton block of Wicklow granite. The plaque shows an impression of the *Iolar*.

But while Aer Lingus was celebrating its golden jubilee anniversary, Ryanair was starting its new Dublin–Luton service. The subsequent development of Ryanair was to have an even greater impact on Dublin airport than the ending of the Aer Lingus cross-channel monopoly in 1957. The airline had started its scheduled services with a Waterford–Gatwick route in June, 1985, using a fifteen-seater Bandeirante aircraft. On May 23, 1986, it opened its Dublin–Luton route, using forty-four seat Bae 748 aircraft. The unrestricted return fare was £94.99. At this stage, the airline was capitalised at £2 million. It had just one hundred employees then. The chairman of the company was, and is, Arthur Walls, for long a senior member of staff at Aer

Frank Sinatra, one of the biggest names in international show business to have arrived at Dublin airport in recent years. In 1988, he gave memorable concerts at Lansdowne Road rugby stadium.
Photograph: The Irish Times

In the Silver Lining restaurant at the airport, Seán Clancy (left) head waiter and assistant manager, and Noel Drumgoole, manager.
Photograph: Neil MacDougald

Left: Brian Byrne, deputy general manager, Dublin airport, with years of experience in personnel management.
Photograph: Frank Fennell Photography

Right: Frank O'Connell, general manager–trading, Dublin airport.
Photograph: Robert Allen Photography

Lingus, a man with a long background in aviation engineering. He said, at the time of the launch in Dublin, that never before had an Irish airline started up with such a sound financial base and wealth of experience. He also remarked that Ryanair was here to stay. In December that year, Ryanair took delivery of its first BAC One-Eleven aircraft, on lease from a Romanian charter airline. Over the past four years, Ryanair has continued to expand, despite the inevitable hitches, like the Dublin–Glasgow route, which proved uneconomic. The airline is now a substantial customer of Dublin airport, with up to two dozen departures and an equal number of arrivals each day. Another new service opened at Dublin in 1986 was the Jersey European Airways' route to Exeter. At the launching ceremony, the hope was expressed that the scheduled service would prove successful: it did not.

More management changes took place at the airport in 1986, reflecting the trend over the previous 2½ years, as Dublin airport took over more functions from Aer Rianta head office. The trading department, under Frank Hanlon, its general manager, was reintegrated with the airport, so that Dublin airport now became responsible for its own commercial, financial, marketing, personnel and technical functions. A personnel and administration division was set up, headed by Owen Clarke.

Brian Byrne, the personnel manager, was made general manager–services, while airport engineer, Joe McGuinne, became general manager–technical and Joe O'Connell, the maintenance manager, became general manager–marketing and finance. The airport was preparing itself well for the huge increases in traffic volume caused by the lower air fares. The revolution in deregulated Irish aviation, pioneered by Ryanair, was well and truly under way.

Following the tragic death of County Kerry born Carl O'Sugrue, the Aer Rianta press and public relations manager since 1970, who had been ill for some time, Flan Clune took up this position in February, 1986. He had worked for Aer Lingus for many years, from 1963, before being seconded for a short time to the Department and Transport and Power. From 1981 until his Aer Rianta appointment, he was press manager for the PMPA, the motor insurance firm founded in controversial circumstances by the late Joe Moore. John Gallagher held the position of Aer Rianta press officer from 1981 until 1990, when he was seconded to the Department of Justice. Meanwhile, there were some long-service celebrations to be enjoyed. Fire chief Joe O'Rourke chalked up forty years' service as the longest serving employee of Aer Rianta in 1986. He had joined the airport fire station in 1946 and was promoted to fire chief in 1982. Celebrations were also the order of the day in the early summer of 1986, when chief executive, Martin Dully, congratulated Joe Walsh of JWT, Ireland's leading private holiday company, on the firm's twenty-fifth anniversary.

Left: Brian Hampson, assistant chief executive–finance and corporate services, Aer Rianta.
Photograph: Robert Allen Photography

Right: Arthur Coughlan, marketing manager, Dublin airport.
Photograph: Robert Allen Photography

August, 1986 was the busiest month ever for the airport. A record number of passengers, almost 395,000, passed through Dublin airport, a seventeen per cent increase on the previous August. General manager Derek Keogh attributed the increase in traffic to the reduction in air fares: the government policy of air service liberalisation was beginning to work. The increases were particularly strong on the cross-channel routes, which had an extra 25,000 passengers over August, 1985. Irish-originating trans-Atlantic traffic remained strong and on the European routes there was good demand for charter holidays in the sun. Yet, as Martin Dully, Aer Rianta chief executive, warned in his address to the Irish Travel Agents' annual general meeting in Wexford, significant challenges were being posed. "American deregulation has spread similar expectations among consumers throughout Europe and indeed, in other parts of the world. All the EC governments and carriers are under great pressure to reduce fares and open up the industry". He remarked that, under the banner of liberalisation, a new deal was being fashioned: "this will make 1986 a special year when the history of aviation is being updated". But with the Europe of 1992 being planned, a European Community without border and frontier checks, Dully said that the logical outcome was the abolition of duty free sales. Shannon would not be affected, because most of its duty free trade is with the U.S., but for Dublin airport, Aer Rianta would have to find means of replacing a significant part of the company's income. "The best prospect lies in the extra volume of travel resulting from liberalisation". Another threat came from the continuance of international terrorism. Martin Dully said that Aer Rianta, like all airport authorities, is in the front line of the security battle. "We have had to develop good control systems which are regularly checked by the FAA, the British CAA, the pilots' associations, by the airlines and by the Gardai. Our arrangements have passed those tests". Stanley Clinton Davis, the EC transport commissioner, said that Dublin airport's security arrangements set a standard that should be followed by the other major airports in the European Community.

The status of Aer Rianta was set for change. Previously, the company acted as agent for the Minister for Communications, with the Minister owning the physical facilities and providing the finance for construction and land acquisition. The new plan was for Aer Rianta to own the three airports in its control, with the Minister being the principal shareholder in the company. This had been in discussion since 1969, Martin Dully pointed out, with the question of the valuation of the assets being the key issue. A more immediate and tangible sign of progress at the airport came on June 25, when Derek Keogh, together with David Kennedy, Aer Lingus chief executive, opened the new ALSAA complex. The clubhouse, containing the biggest

Derek Keogh, chief executive, Aer Rianta.
Photograph: Neil MacDougald

sports hall in Ireland, was opened with a gala ball. Aer Rianta's planning superintendent, Declan O'Dwyer, designed the complex through his company, Declan O'Dwyer Associates. His wife, Sheila, through her company Sheila Jones Interior Decor, was responsible for the internal decor of the complex. That summer was also notable for the retirement of Johnny King, Aer Rianta's company secretary, after forty years' service. He had been working as a booking clerk in Westland Row railway station and was lured to Aer Lingus as a reservation clerk in the Cathal Brugha Street terminal for £4 16s a week, a princely sum in 1946. His interest in aviation went right back to his childhood days; he remembers vividly seeing the ill-fated RIOI airship over Dublin on November 18, 1929. The airship crashed in northern France the following autumn on its maiden voyage to India, with the loss of forty-eight crew and passengers. Before becoming company secretary, he had brought his long years of personnel experience to the job of industrial relations superintendent. John Burke, who joined Aer Rianta in 1969, took over as company secretary. Besides Johnny King, another well-known airport personality retired, Kevin Flood of the boilerhouse. He joined the airport staff in 1963, moving from the cleaning section to the boilerhouse the following year. In his previous existence, he had been known to numerous Aer Rianta people: for many years, he ushered them in and out of the old Whitehall cinema.

A series of tragedies struck the airport security service during 1986. Brendan Dempsey collapsed and died on duty at the security checkpoint in the arrivals hall at nine o'clock on the morning of April 3. Jack Bannon, in a tribute, said that the security force had suffered an immense loss with the passing of Bren, as he was affectionately known. He carried out his police duties with a discretion which called for wisdom, patience and understanding, said Bannon. During that summer, during a routine training session in the airport fire station, Paddy Doyle met with a tragic and fatal accident. Aged thirty-four, he died in the neurological unit of the Richmond hospital on September 3 without regaining consciousness. At the funeral, the coffin was carried by six men from C crew, under Joe O'Rourke, while Jack Bannon commanded the fifty strong guard of honour. In addition to all the local tributes, there were also messages of sympathy and wreaths from as far away as the Belfast fire brigade, the British Airports Authority and the UK Civil Aviation Authority. Aer Rianta set up an immediate internal inquiry to find out exactly how airport police/fireman Paddy Doyle was hit on the head by a branchpipe or hose coupling. Another well-liked and respected member of the airport security service, Jim Murray, died the following month. The litany of loss was added to with the passing of Limerick man Joseph Madigan, who retired as airports development manager in 1979. He was best remembered as chairman of the committee that prepared the report on the development of Dublin airport's runway systems. Yet amid the gloom of all this tragic news, Nicky Byrne, the boilerhouse supervisor, had a humorous word or two that as usual brought smiles. He celebrated forty years' service with the airport; he made the 1963 boilerhouse a showpiece. At the celebrations, he remarked on how short a time forty years really is; while the boilerhouse tradition was carried into the third generation of the Byrne family, with Nicky's son, Thomas. Nicky remarked on why he had refrained from calling his son after him, in case people got into the habit of calling him "Auld Nick".

Celebrations at management level were the order of the day, too. During the twelve months of 1986, a total of 2.93 million passengers used Dublin airport, a twelve per cent increase on the previous year. Later in 1987, Dublin airport welcomed its three millionth passenger of the year; the honour fell to Mrs Shirley Samuels from Pinner, near London, who had travelled from London on a British Airways flight with her husband, Oliver, to attend the Wexford opera festival. Derek Keogh, airport general manager, made a suitable presentation, before the couple were

Tom Cullen, general manager, Dublin airport.
Photograph: Neil MacDougald

whisked off to Wexford in a vintage Rolls-Royce. Behind the scenes at the airport, considerable progress was taking place. A new maintenance building was constructed in the "red brick area" to house workshops for the airport carpenters and painters. The site of the new building was the original avenue leading to Corballis House; the complex was equipped with the latest facilities, including dust extraction equipment for the carpentry workshop, a far cry indeed from the first such airport workshop, forty years previously. A £1 million expansion scheme was carried out in the terminal.

A new check-in island for Aer Lingus was built, giving that airline fourteen extra desks. New check-in facilities were created for Ryanair, as well as for two newcomers to the airport. Club Air was started by Liam Lonergan, the man behind Club Travel, to run charter flights to Mediterranean sun spots. The new airline aimed to carry 50,000 passengers a year, but was ultimately unsuccessful, closing down two years later. The other new airline at the airport, Virgin, was also given facilities. Run by the flamboyant Richard Branson, whose business empire also includes the Virgin Megastore in the former McBirney's department store premises on Aston Quay, the airline started off with Viscounts on the Dublin–Luton run. The one-way fare of just £29 added a further notch to the already intense price war on the Dublin–London routes. Besides all the new check-in facilities, the biggest change to the terminal was moving all the shops to the airside of the building, where the aviation museum once

Plans exist for extending the DART line to the airport terminal.
Photograph: Iarnród Éireann

stood. The brand new shopping mall was designed by Dublin airport architect, Paul Keatley, and his team; they also designed the new VAT-free shopping area.

Work also began on the new runway. On October 24, 1987, John Wilson, Minister for Tourism and Transport, poured the first load of concrete into the foundations, watched by Frank Boland, Martin Dully and Derek Keogh. The contract was placed with Walls Tarmac, a joint venture, and was scheduled to employ 200 people during the three-year construction period. The new runway was opened in June, 1989.

A time capsule was buried in the foundations; it contained microfilmed records of the history of Aer Rianta and the development of Dublin airport, along with historic photographs and a copy of the 1987 annual report, as well as contemporary airline tickets giving data on travel conditions. The aim of the capsule was to give historians an insight into Dublin airport in a century's time. At the airport that year, Aer Rianta hosted a jubilee dinner at which John Wilson, the Minister responsible for the airports, was guest of honour, along with seven of his predecessors, Peter Barry, Paddy Cooney, Padraig Faulkner, Tom Fitzpatrick, Brian Lenihan, Jim Mitchell and Albert Reynolds. Plans were put in hand to mark the fiftieth anniversary celebrations of the airport itself. Owen Clarke was assigned to head the small committee supervising the project; among the ideas put forward in 1987 was this history of the airport. While the company was looking to its past events with an appropriate feeling of its history, it was looking forward with its customary determination. A £1.6 million contract was signed with Digital, the computer manufacturers, for the last stage in the Aer Rianta computerisation programme. A VAX cluster system was installed at the airport to drive the new system of visual display units, printers and micros and a new data network cable was laid through the airport to link the stations. Another sign of the times was to be seen on the apron on October 30, when the first of the new generation Boeing 737–300 aircraft, purchased by Aer Lingus, arrived.

This aircraft, and the second identical type, which arrived a month later, represented the first phase of the Aer Lingus European fleet replacement programme. The second phase included Fokker 100 aircraft; devotees of the Fokker Friendship planes of the 1950s and 1960s were delighted to see planes from the Fokker factory back on the apron. Three major appointments were made during the course of the year by Aer Rianta. John Murphy, a native of Cork, who joined Aer Rianta at Shannon in 1970 for the construction of the jet runway there, was made airport engineer for Dublin. Tony Nevin, who joined Dublin airport as an electrician in 1950, working under foreman electrician Kevin McKeon, was made maintenance manager. Another electrician was promoted in 1987, Ray Bolger, who joined the

Brendan Clancy, assistant chief executive — technical, came to Dublin airport from Cork airport in 1970. He oversaw the planning and construction of the new main runway, opened in June, 1989.
Photograph: Robert Allen Photography

Owen Clarke, head of administration, Dublin airport. From its inception, he has been closely involved with this book on the history of Dublin airport and has contributed significantly to its research and production.
Photograph: Neil MacDougald

Above: Inside the new air traffic control tower, showing the tower with view of the field.

Right: The electronic heart of the tower, where aircraft movements in and out of Dublin airport are plotted on screen.
Photographs: Neil MacDougald

The new air traffic control tower on the west side of Dublin airport.
Photograph: Neil MacDougald

Air traffic control at Dublin airport is run by the Air Traffic Services division of the Department of Tourism and Transport; it moved in the summer of 1990 from the cramped and uncomfortable conditions in the old central terminal building to the new State Services building on the west side of the airfield, next to the new fire station, due to be completed in November 1990.

The first two control officers in the State were Captain Ned Stapleton and Captain Michael Cumiskey; the latter died recently. They began work when Aer Lingus started services in 1936. Immediately after the Emergency, the Department of Industry and Commerce took over the functions of civil aviation, with the late Captain J. P. Saul the first chief control officer. Over the years, air traffic control has progressed from Aldis signalling lamps to UHF and VHF communications, primary and secondary radar and computer applications. Since the early 1960s, recruitment to the Irish air traffic control service has been from school-leavers; it takes up to ten years for a controller to be fully trained and hold all ratings for this high stress occupation.

At Dublin airport in 1955, a visual control cab was added to the top floor of the old terminal building and new radar equipment was added. Working conditions were very uncomfortable.

Life did not become easier for the air traffic controllers after the new centre was opened in 1965. It was known as the "blue room" because of the type of fluorescent tubes used in conjunction with the then new Philips radar. This new centre was never environmentally or operationally satisfactory and provided difficult and uncomfortable working conditions for the staff. Yet during its quarter century in existence, it handled a vast increase in aircraft movements, which advanced from slow piston and turbo-prop aircraft to modern jet types. The centre also handled complex civil-military interfaces and overflights from Belfast and other regional airports.

The new building became operational in June, 1990; moving from the old centre to the new was technically complex. Aer Rianta designed and built the new centre for the Department; the total cost is up to £12 million. It has primary and secondary radar; the latter activated by transponders, or radio transmitters, on all commercial and military aircraft, which relay to the control centre such details as altitude. They also enable messages to be sent to the centre in an emergency. The Dublin control zone is a parallelogram covering the east coast; the Dublin centre is responsible for controlling flights from 5,000 feet to 24,000 feet. Higher altitude flights are controlled from Shannon. The Dublin radar can "see" aircraft movements as far as 200 miles from the airport, extending as far as north-west France.

When the second phase of the civil aviation integrated radar display equipment project for Dublin is completed by early 1991, the airport will lead the field with the latest in radar and flight data processing, ready to meet the new age of integrated air traffic control systems planned for Europe.

About eighty air traffic control staff work at the new Dublin centre, a third of the total in Ireland. All training of Irish ATCs is carried out in the new training centre in the building. The new centre and tower is well situated for the new main runway and also for the second new runway, planned to run east-west across the northern side of the airfield. The new building provides a striking contrast to the old control centre and provides a vast improvement in working conditions; like engineers and pilots, Air Traffic Controllers are responsible for many lives.

company in 1972, was made airfield and lands manager. From 1982 until 1984, when the Libyan training contract ended, he was headmaster of the international training school at the airport. At the end of 1987, Albert Baker, the marketing and promotions manager at the airport, was made manager of the tax free shop. Tax free shopping turned over £2.7 million in 1986, and the concept was considerably expanded following Baker's appointment.

There were the inevitable retirements. Bobby Best retired from airport management after thirty-five years' service, while Harry Clarke, who worked for many years in the paintshop and later became senior supervisor, also retired. John Gunning, the airfield supervisor, retired after thirty-four years' service. He lives in Garristown, north County Dublin, where his carefully preserved mementoes of his airport days include what are probably the last existing paraffin runway flares, as used during the Emergency years. Paddy Corrigan, a well-known figure in the maintenance department for almost thirty years, also retired, as did Jack Doyle, a former airport manager, whose other involvements during a forty-year career at Dublin airport included heading the Libyan training project. Tommy Cranitch retired; he was the first press

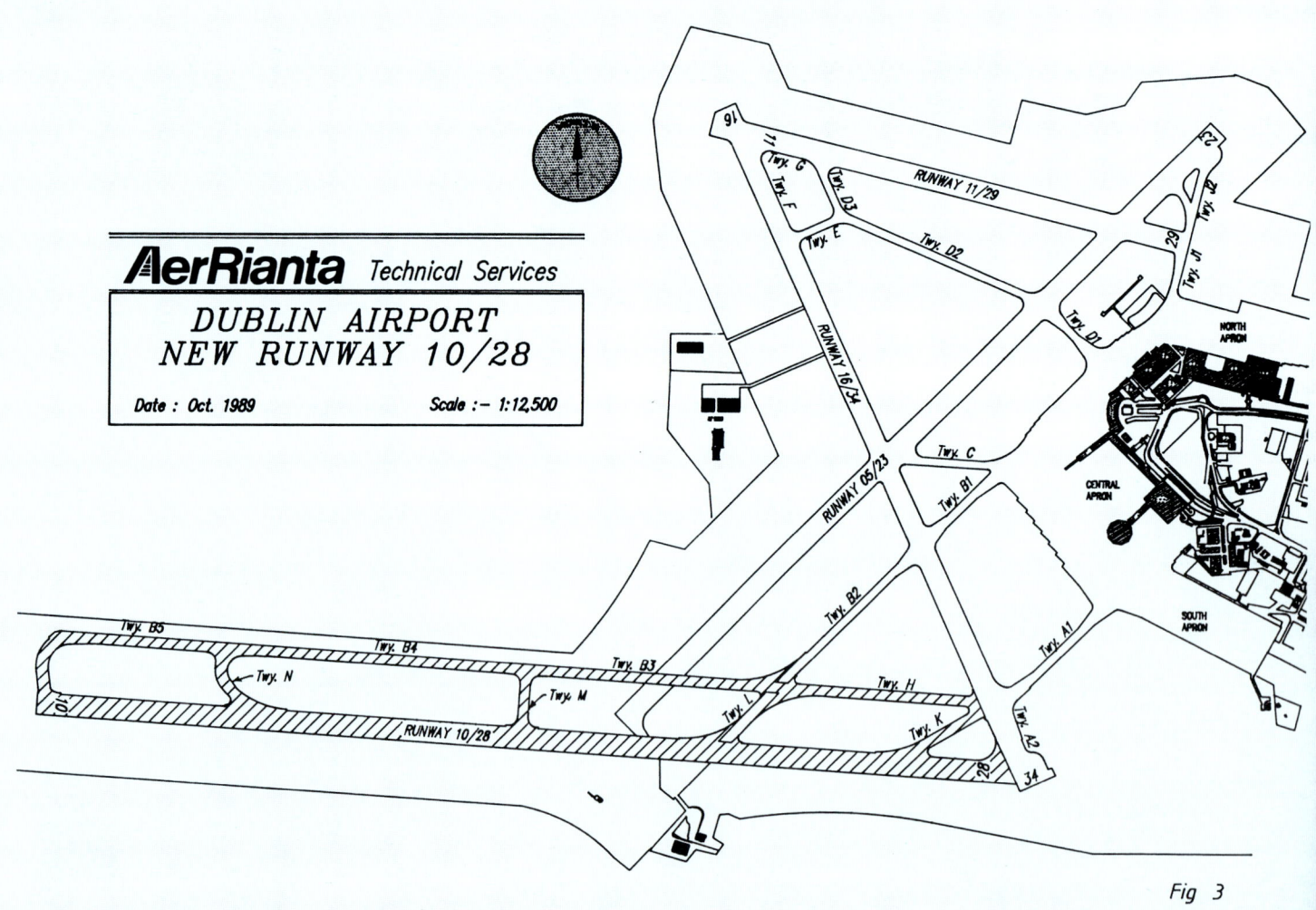

Below: Plan of the new main runway at Dublin airport, opened in June, 1989, with the old runways. The old main runway, 05/23, is likely to be closed shortly.
Illustration: Aer Rianta technical services

Fig 3

At the official opening of the new main runway 10/28, on June 21, 1989, Taoiseach Charles Haughey, T.D., cuts the ribbon. Included in the line-up are Ben Briscoe, then Lord Mayor of Dublin (second from left), Frank Boland, Aer Rianta chairman (fifth from left), John Wilson, T.D., Minister for Tourism and Transport (sixth from left), Ray Burke, T.D., Minister for Industry and Commerce (fourth from right) and Derek Keogh, chief executive, Aer Rianta (third from right).
Photograph: Robert Allen Photography

Left: John Wilson, when Minister for Tourism and Transport, buries a time capsule with items of historical interest on the new main runway, 1988.
Photograph: Robert Allen Photography

Right: Taoiseach Charles Haughey, T.D., signs the distinguished visitors' book for Derek Keogh, Aer Rianta chief executive, on June 21, 1989, the day the new main runway was opened.
Photograph: Robert Allen Photography

Map of the present Dublin airport area, showing the new main runway and the proposed new north parallel runway.
Illustration: Ordnance Survey/ Aer Rianta technical services

The vast new addition to the Dublin airport skyline, the new engineering hangar being built by Aer Lingus; it is intended to use this new facility for engineering servicing for the world aviation industry.
Photograph: Robert Allen Photography

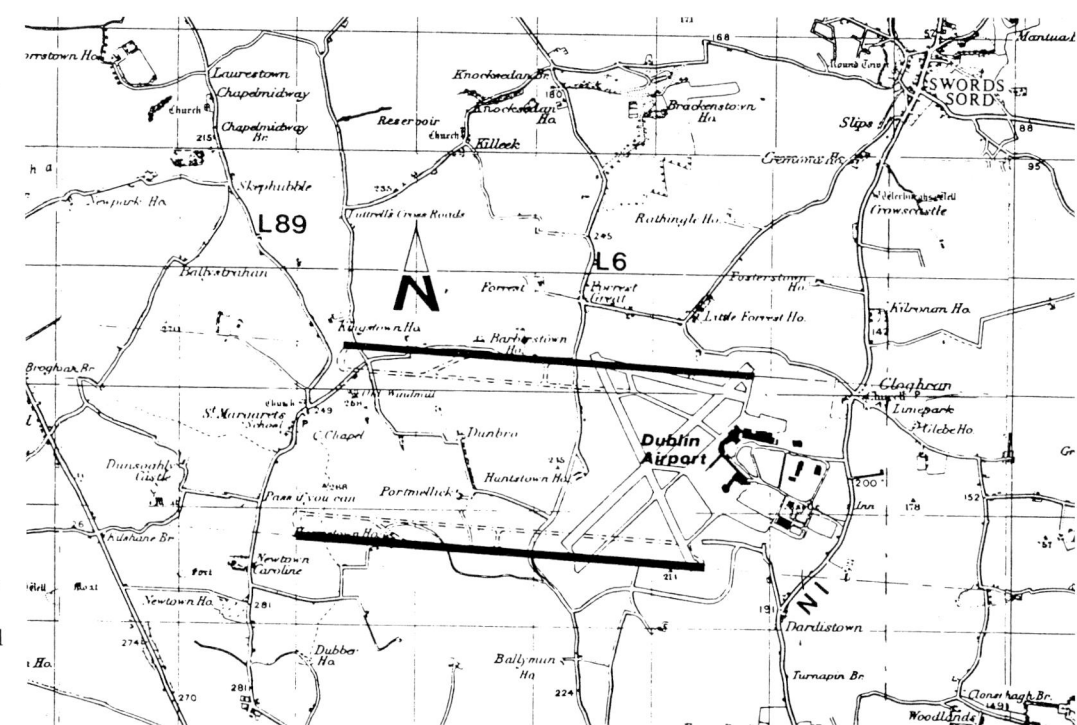

officer to be based at Dublin airport, where the Watch Office was pressed into service, conveniently handy to the makeshift VIP room. Another anniversary marked at the airport was that of Harold Murray; his car hire firm was fifty years old in 1986 and, in early 1987, Martin Dully presented Murray with a gift of Irish crystal. Murray's was the first car hire company to have desks at the three Aer Rianta airports. A team from the airport won Aer Rianta the first place in the commercial section of the St Patrick's Day parade in Dublin; among the "exhibits" was an eight foot "bottle" of Bailey's Irish cream.

International delegates from airports in every corner of the world were able to see Dublin's facilities for themselves, when the conference of the Airport Operators Council International met in Dublin in early June. It was the biggest aviation gathering in Ireland for twenty years. Derek Keogh delivered the main passenger service paper, on the topic of humanising airports and spoke about the "Putting the Customers First" programme at Dublin. Several hundred delegates went home highly impressed by the efficiency of Dublin airport and the friendliness of the Irish welcome.

That efficiency was well tested during 1987. Just after an Iberia A300 Airbus landed on runway 16 at 1.09 pm on Saturday, February 14, the port engine caught fire. All 238 passengers were evacuated down the emergency chutes; a total of thirty-four were treated for minor injuries in the medical centre, while duty manager, Noel Donohue, sustained a broken finger while helping passengers to evacuate the aircraft. Frank Khan, the tourism correspondent of the *Irish Independent,* was returning to Dublin on a Cyprus Airways flight from Larnaca, when it was thought he was suffering a form of heart attack. Two doctors on the flight had the pilot radio ahead for an ambulance to meet the plane; as it turned out, fortunately Khan's condition was a false alarm. He wrote to *Runway* magazine praising the efficiency of the emergency services at the airport.

Nineteen eighty-seven saw Dublin airport exceed 3½ million passengers for the first time, so the extensive new catering and shopping facilities were well needed. There were many dramatic events happening outside the airport that year; Charles Haughey was Taoiseach once again, heading another minority Fianna Fáil government. The State bought Rathfarnham Castle.

Left: Seamus Brennan, T.D., Minister for Tourism and Transport since 1989, the minister responsible for Aer Rianta.
Photograph: Lensmen

Right: Denis Lyons, T.D., Minister of State at the Department of Tourism and Transport since 1989, with responsibility for the meteorological service.
Photograph: Lensmen

Donal O'Mahony, secretary, Department of Tourism and Transport.

Section of the departures level at Dublin airport with the new ceiling in place, photographed in June, 1990.
Photograph: Neil MacDougald

The present telephone exchange at Dublin airport, soon to be updated. Operators from left are: Maureen Byrne, Susan Metcalfe, Irene McNally, Ann Malone (exchange supervisor), Siobhan Forde and Majella Rutter.
Photograph: Neil MacDougald

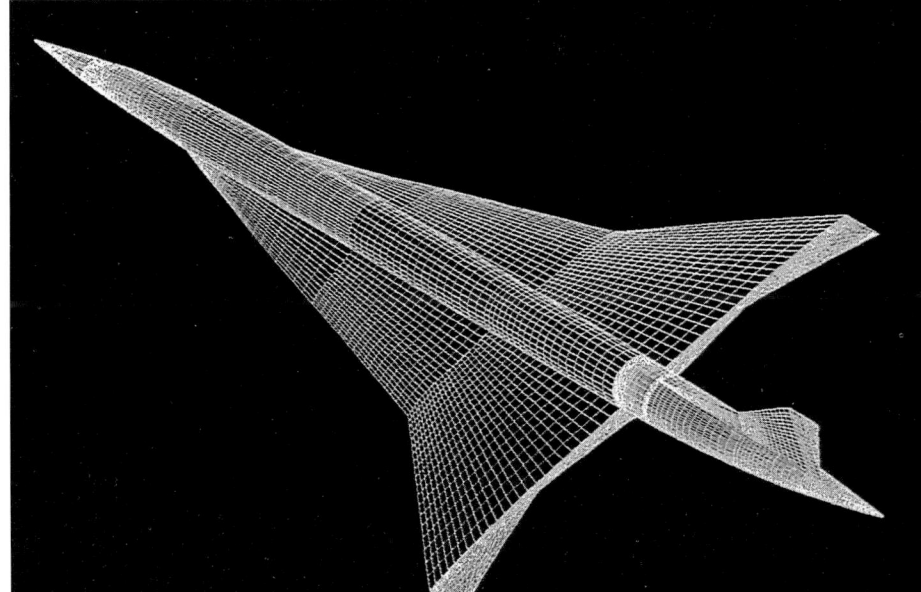

The next generation of Concorde, scheduled to come into service in 2005, travelling at 1,500 mph. Fifteen years further down the line, a hyper Concorde is projected, with a cruising speed of 3,000 mph, capable of reaching Tokyo from Paris in two-and-a-half hours. Concorde has made two appearances at Dublin airport; the next generation could be a regular visitor.
Illustration: Aerospatiale

A Lockheed L–1011 of Delta Airlines, which originates six flights a week out of Dublin airport to the US. In winter, its flight frequency is lower from Dublin, three a week.

A gas explosion in a block of flats in Serpentine Avenue, Ballsbridge, killed three people. The national lottery was launched and soon became a huge money spinner. For the second time, Johnny Logan won the Eurovision Song Contest, this time with his song *Hold Me Now*. The Dubliners hit the UK charts, having had their first big chart successes back in 1962. But the biggest headlines that year belonged to the cyclist from Dundrum, Dublin, Stephen Roche, who won the world championships in Austria, the Giro d'Italia and capped his triumphs by winning the Tour de France. He returned to a hero's welcome at Dublin airport, where a crowd of thousands included many airport staff. For the occasion, Roche signed the distinguished visitors' book. The Aer Rianta banner especially painted read "Stephen you're magic". When another big name, Bono of U2 passed through the airport, he met an old school friend, Noel Carroll, of the financial division, Dublin airport; they shared the same

THE IRISH TIMES

PRICE 65p (incl. VAT) 55p sterling area DUBLIN, FRIDAY, JANUARY 19, 1990 NO. 41,579 CITY

Azerbaijan 'at war' with Armenia

INSIDE TODAY

BUDGET '90
Limited scope for income tax relief — daily series □ page 14

A PR obsession
Sean Flynn on Ireland's EC presidency □ page 7

Mad cow disease
Britain's 600 cases a month □ page 13

13% exports rise likely
Exports are expected to rise to £16.4 billion this year, an increase of 13 per cent over 1988, according to Alan McCarthy, chief executive of Coras Trachtala □ page 14

INDEX
Home News............ 5, 8, 9, 10
Sport........................ 2, 3, 4
World News............. 6, 7
Business & Finance.. 14, 15
Arts, Reviews........... 12
News Features........ 13
Letters to the Editor. 11
Weather................... 10
Countdown to College. 8
Entertainments........ 28
TV and Radio........... 29

WEEKEND Tomorrow
Homosexuality and Irish Society
Salman Rushdie's latest dilemma

From Conor O'Clery, in Moscow

AZERBAIJANI officials declared yesterday that their republic was at war with neighbouring Armenia, as the Soviet Union began mobilising reservists and moving troops by helicopter into areas of fighting between Azerbaijanis and Armenians.

As the death toll in the ethnic civil war which flared at the weekend reached 66, Azerbaijani crowds tried to blockade railway stations and the airport in Baku, the capital of Azerbaijan, to prevent the deployment of Soviet troops sent to end the conflict.

The deputy chief of the Azerbaijani office in Moscow, Mr Zaur Rustam-Zade, accused Armenia of "armed aggression" by using helicopters to shoot at Azerbaijani villages.

"Military actions with the use of helicopters and other means of destruction cannot be described as anything other than war," he told a press conference, accusing Armenia of trying to annex the Azerbaijani-administered region of Nagorno-Karabakh, the population of which is 75 per cent Armenian, and which is at the centre of the outbreak of fighting.

Announcing the call-up of reservists, the Soviet Defence Minister, General Dmitri Yazov, described the conflict in the USSR's southern republics as a "major disaster". Troops have been authorised to drop their restraint of recent weeks and fire their weapons to protect lives and military equipment.

The USSR Interior Ministry yesterday issued statistics of six days of turmoil which have left 220 people injured, including 26 militiamen and 31 soldiers. Sixty-six raids on armouries have taken place as militants armed themselves for battle.

More than 200 houses or apartments were destroyed or set on fire and 136 freight trains have been paralysed as Azerbaijanis resumed a deadly economic blockade of Armenia, which receives almost all of its essential supplies through Azerbaijan.

Despite the allegations of aggression by the Azerbaijanis, it is the Armenians who continue to bear the brunt of the suffering. A total of 4,658 Armenians, mostly women, children and old people, have been evacuated by sea from Baku, where more than 40 people, mainly Armenians, have been killed in a series of pogroms which began last Saturday night.

No deaths were reported in the city in the last 24 hours, according to the Soviet news agency, Tass, but "pogroms are continuing in other areas." A curfew which the Supreme Soviet in Moscow said should be imposed on Baku has not been enforced. A spokesman for the Azerbaijani Popular Front said it would fan fresh passions.

Soviet army officers began evacuating their families from Baku yesterday in the face of threats by Azeri militants to use them as hostages if Soviet troops continued to help Armenians escape from the city in Caspian Sea ferries, according to the government newspaper, Izvestia.

Militants went to Baku airport to block Soviet troops flown to the region to try to halt the mounting bloodshed in the mountains around Nagorno-Karabakh.

There were also attempts to disrupt the deployment of Interior Ministry troops at railway stations in Udzhary and Khachmas in Azerbaijan, the Interior Ministry reported, and water pipelines leading to the town of Shusha in Nagorno-Karabakh were blown up.

Helicopters taking troops to the areas of fighting came under fire near Nagorno-Karabakh from militants armed with air defence weapons and machineguns, according to a report on Soviet television, which said thousands of armed men from both sides in bulletproof vests were present in the area.

Despite a total armed forces strength of nearly four million, General Yazov has taken the unprecedented step of calling up unmarried conscripts who were recently discharged from the army.

The 5,000 Interior Ministry troops in the region for the past few months were insufficient to control the situation because of the size of the terrain and the inflamed passions of its inhabitants.

"In this connection a decision has been adopted to carry out a full mobilisation of formations from certain regions of the Soviet Union to enable them to take part in maintaining order, discipline and good organisation in the state of emergency," he said.

It was vital, General Yazov said, "to control centres of population, roads and state enterprises and institutions to prevent chaos from arising." On Monday the Supreme Soviet authorised martial law in Nagorno-Karabakh and some other areas as the ethnic clashes got out of control.

The Azerbaijani border with Iran, where militants tore down fencing earlier in the month, has also been placed under martial law, and yesterday the Armenian news agency, Armenpress, claimed the border had been totally closed.

● Some 20,000 demonstrators gathered outside the Central Committee headquarters in Baku late yesterday amid further protests against the Soviet military presence to quell unrest, nationalist sources said. The Azeris have thrown up barricades against Soviet troops who are attempting to take control of the city. Paratroopers who landed by helicopter yesterday in one of the town's main squares were immediately surrounded by a large crowd and forced to take off again, the sources reported. (AFP)

Armenian volunteers on patrol alongside armed personnel carriers yesterday in Yerevan, the capital of Armenia. — (EPA wirepicture)

Rabble obstructing reforms—Gorbachev

From Conor O'Clery, in Moscow

THE Soviet President, Mr Mikhail Gorbachev, under increasing pressure from opponents to the left and the right, hit out at those obstructing his reforms as a "rabble".

Addressing a Kremlin conference of workers and specialists on the problems of the Soviet economy, Mr Gorbachev defended perestroika and attacked those who blamed it for the failures of the economy.

"Work is in progress," he said in a speech broadcast live by Moscow Radio. "This too must be seen, so as not to get into a flap, saying everything is going to pieces. What is falling apart are the old ways."

In an uncharacteristic outburst clearly aimed at conservative officials and mushrooming patriotic groups resisting reform, Mr Gorbachev said: "The main tendency consists of the spiritual renaissance of our society, of the formation of a new moral atmosphere on the basis of socialist and universal human values.

"It is this tendency which must be strengthened, and we must fight resolutely against all the rabble, all those who are putting in their oar to muddy this process of moral renaissance."

The power struggle within the Soviet leadership was reiterated in the press yesterday, with two newspapers printing articles critical of speedy reform.

Sovetskaya Rossiya published an attack on perestroika and leading reformers by Mr Valentin Romanov, a People's Congress deputy, who said: "We could have avoided many of today's ills and misdeeds if we had, in a timely way, listened to the wise conservatives in the bureaucracy, who cautioned against hasty and poorly-thought-out decisions."

The new workers' daily, Rabochaya Tribuna, signalled an end to the sympathetic treatment of striking miners, saying work stoppages were aimed at extorting as much as possible for the workers at the expense of the state.

Mr Gorbachev is coming under increasing pressure from radicals for not pressing ahead with political reform quickly enough, in particular from the radical Moscow deputy, Mr Boris Yeltsin, who said in Japan this week that the Soviet leader had perhaps only three months to show results.

Mr Gorbachev claimed in his speech — which indicated that he was moving on to the offensive to stem the wave of criticism — that "we are already gathering fresh momentum in favour of the industries producing consumer goods and services, primarily in favour of light and food industries. For the first time in many years, production of consumer goods has started to overtake the growth of heavy industry."

He faces an assault from his enemies at a plenum of the Communist Party central committee on January 29th which will discuss his recent trip to Lithuania where he failed to persuade Lithuanian communists to moderate their pro-independence policy.

In the face of a so far unco-ordinated chorus of dissent from old-style party members, Mr Gorbachev repeated that there was no other way ahead for Moscow. "I stress that life itself, and not someone's inventions, subjective desires, aspirations or ambitions, have brought us to the idea of radical perestroika," he said.

TURN OVER A NEW LEAF

If you want to do your bit for the environment, Jumbos are the natural choice. Now Jumbos are made with 100% recycled paper.

And Jumbos — the softer, stronger toilet tissue — are now even better value than ever. There are 300 sheets in every roll.

Sure you'd be out of your tree to use anything else!

Stalker renews NI allegations as friend is cleared of fraud

From Ella Shanahan, London Editor

MR JOHN STALKER says that if it had not been imperative to get him off the inquiry into the alleged RUC shoot-to-kill policy, Mr Kevin Taylor, yesterday cleared on all counts of fraud, would never have been investigated or charged.

The former Deputy Chief Constable of Greater Manchester said yesterday that he has the minutes of a meeting, probably of senior British cabinet office civil servants, at which the decision to take him off the investigation in 1986 was taken.

He is prepared to produce that document in court, if asked to do so. "What difference it will make to me or Mr Taylor, I don't know. Mr Taylor's life is in tatters. I have made a new life for myself," he said.

Mr Stalker said people were identified only by initials at that meeting, but he could guess who some of them were. He had been given the document legitimately in relation to another case.

Mr Stalker said the decision to throw out the case, and the discovery that documents were missing from files relating to the case, left some very important questions hanging over very senior police officers in Greater Manchester.

"The prosecution of Mr Taylor, as I said in my book, was a contrivance to take the spotlight away from Northern Ireland, and I am still totally convinced of that, and everything now tends to show that was true."

The stage his investigations had reached in Northern Ireland by 1986 demanded some quick measures to have him taken off the investigation, he says. This the authorities, "at senior political level, the cabinet or certainly the cabinet office," had attempted to do by trying to discredit him through his association with Mr Taylor, a Manchester businessman.

He said senior policemen were also involved, but would not elaborate further.

On Wednesday, Detective-Inspector Anthony Stephenson had told the court that documents were missing and he could not answer the questions being put to him about them.

After the case had been adjourned to yesterday to allow three more senior police officers to give evidence, they also said they could give no explanation about the missing papers. They said the Taylor investigation had been shrouded in secrecy and directed by even more senior police officers.

Mr Stalker, who was removed from the Northern Ireland investigation and suspended from duty for a time, resigned from the police force in 1987.

Mr Taylor, then a multi-millionaire property developer, was charged in 1986, with three associates, with fraudulently obtaining loans to finance property developments, based on the inflated value of their properties. Mr Taylor has since lost his luxurious house and his businesses.

The case collapsed at Manchester Crown Court yesterday after the prosecution accepted defence counsel claims that detectives had misled Manchester's Recorder, Judge Arthur Prestt, QC, when in March, 1986, they obtained orders giving them access to Mr Taylor's bank accounts.

Throughout the 16-week trial, which is estimated to have cost £1 million, Mr Taylor (58) and his co-defendants denied defrauding the Co-Operative Bank. Detectives had admitted during the trial that the investigation of Mr Taylor would not have proceeded if they had not obtained the orders for access.

The defence argued that Mr Taylor's solicitor had invited the police to interview him, but the detectives neglected to tell the Recorder this, saying instead that there was no likelihood of Mr Taylor allowing access to his bank accounts. Inspector Stephenson said yesterday that the information give to the Recorder "was not accurate".

Mr Michael Corkery, QC, prosecuting, told Judge Michael Sachs: "I have taken the view that, in all the circumstances of this case, it would not be proper that the prosecution should seek an adverse verdict at the hands of the jury against these four defendants."

Judge Sachs then directed the jury to return verdicts of "not guilty".

Afterwards, Mr Taylor said the collapse of the case proved the authorities had been out to get Mr Stalker and had used him as the tool to do it.

TCD students pass abortion vote

By Patricia Hegarty

STUDENTS in Trinity College, Dublin, voted almost three to one in favour of providing information on all pregnancy options, including abortion, in a campus-wide referendum held in the college. The referendum poll at 65 per cent was the highest poll among students in the college and shows decisively that majority student opinion supports the distribution of information on abortion, according to TCD students' union president, Ms Ivana Bacik.

The Trinity decision is one of a series of decisions taken by students over the last year and a half, and brings the total number of colleges in favour of abortion information to 22 in the Republic. Five colleges in the South voted against in that period. The Union of Students in Ireland says that roughly 11,000 students have indicated opposition to such information; about 33,000 voted for, by way of either referendum or general meeting, in the South, while students in Northern Ireland overwhelmingly supported the provision of such information.

The women's rights officer with USI, Ms Karen Quinlivan, said: "The most important aspect of the decision is the fact that today Irish students have reasserted their position that they will never turn away a woman looking for abortion information."

Ms Bacik said that the high turnout discredits claims that the union has been undemocratic and added: "We're going to continue union policy on abortion information and will have discussions amongst ourselves on how best to do this with due regard to the interlocutory injunction."

Ms Bacik was referring to the injunction SPUC successfully sought to deter Trinity Students distributing information until the European Court decides on the matter, following a referral to it by the Supreme Court.

A spokesman for Students for Life, who opposes the distribution of information on abortion, said they accepted majority student opinion as represented by last night's vote but they feel that they would have had more support if they had had more time to campaign.

The president of USI, Mr Stephen Grogan, said that the high turnout demonstrated that Trinity students were well informed on this issue. "It's a decisive result — it shows that students will get involved and have a legitimate right to get involved in this issue," he said.

At 2 a.m. this morning, the unofficial result was approximately 3,900 for and 683 against, with 61 spoilt votes.

The vote was taken by students from all faculties in Trinity and in the affiliated colleges of St. Catherine's College of Domestic Science and the Froebel College of Education. A total of about 7,300 students were eligible to vote.

FOR A LIMITED PERIOD

THINKING ABOUT A PENSION?

If you are self-employed there's never been a better time to secure your future with a pension plan from Irish Life.

• TAX RELIEF ON CONTRIBUTIONS
• TAX FREE GROWTH ON YOUR INVESTMENT
• TAX FREE LUMP SUM ON RETIREMENT

PLUS "A TASTE OF THE FUTURE"
OPEN A RETIREMENT ACCOUNT NOW FOR £100 PER MONTH OR MORE AND TAKE A FREE WEEKEND FOR TWO AT ANY OF JURYS' THREE LUXURY HOTELS COURTESY OF IRISH LIFE.

Contact your Insurance Broker or Irish Life Representative today, or phone Rose Johnson at 720288

Offer applies to all Retirement Accounts with 5 years or more to maturity.

Irish Life
The largest and most successful investment company in the land.

Front page, *The Irish Times,* January 19, 1990 — fifty years after Dublin airport was opened.

Above: On January 19, 1990, exactly fifty years after Dublin airport was officially opened, the Minister for Tourism and Transport, Seamus Brennan (third from right), unveiled a plaque depicting the original terminal building. Also in the photograph are Derek Keogh, chief executive, Aer Rianta (second left), Frank Boland, chairman, Aer Rianta (second from right) and Tom Cullen, airport manager (far right).
Photograph: Robert Allen Photography

Coverage of the fiftieth anniversary celebrations at the airport in the *Irish Independent*.

Board of directors, Aer Rianta, as at July, 1990. Back row, from left: Derek Keogh (chief executive), Des Mullally, Frank Boland (chairman), Dermot Desmond and John Burke (company secretary).
Front row, from left: John Carroll, John Anglim, Peter Hanley, Tom Keaveney, Seán Murray and Alan Morris.

Photograph: Robert Allen Photography

classroom at Mount Temple Comprehensive.

Early 1988 saw Derek Keogh take over as chief executive. After seven years at the helm, Martin Dully left on March 30 to become executive chairman of Bord Fáilte. Many parties were held to mark his departure from Aer Rianta, a time that saw some of the most spectacular growth in the company's history. Chairman Frank Boland remarked: "We are very sorry to lose Martin Dully, but we regard his appointment as a recognition that he is the right man for a challenging task". Derek Keogh worked from 1959 to 1968 in the civil service. At the time that Aer Rianta was being set up as a separate company, he was involved with the new company from the Department of Transport and Power side. In 1969, he joined Aer Rianta as executive assistant to the secretary of the company, progressing upwards through the ranks. He says that only within the last six years has Dublin airport been organised with its own orientation, separate from the mother company. The running of Dublin airport is now very separate from the running of the national airports authority, which happens to be located at Dublin airport. From Keogh's time as general manager of the airport, it started to develop its own management structures. The aim is to run the airport as a separate, major business unit on an entrepreneurial basis. Says Derek Keogh: "Tom Cullen, the general manager, is the chief executive of Dublin airport and is answerable for everything that happens there. He is also expected to feel a sense of ownership of that entity and deliver customer service and plans for the future, as well as deliver a good economic return". The long-term landscaping programme and the Christmas lights are just two examples quoted by Keogh of the efforts to humanise the airport. He recalls that when the Christmas lights were first put up, with a sign reading "Welcome Home, Happy Christmas from Aer Rianta", the airport police were puzzled to see cars stopping. Was there something wrong with the signpost? "After a while, we discovered that people were stopping to have a little cuddle; they were moved by the message".

That sort of happening feeds back into people's commitment, reflects Derek Keogh. Soon after his appointment as chief executive, structural changes and also changes at senior management level were put into practice. Liam Skelly was made deputy to the chief executive and commercial supremo, while Aer Rianta International was set up under Michael Guerin to handle all overseas work, such as the duty free shops in the Soviet Union. Tom Cullen was made assistant chief executive–marketing. In a change of policy, marketing decisions for Dublin airport were brought much closer to base, away from corporate marketing decisions made for the overall company. A new corporate identity was unveiled, including new staff uniforms.

Other quite radical changes took place. The maintenance department had its first plumber in a pony tail. Nineteen-year-old Elaine McLoughlin from Baldoyle was working on a work experience programme with FÁS. She may have been the first female plumber in the country. The following year, more equal employment history was made when Carol O'Donohue was appointed the first female member of the airport security service. She was brought up on the family farm at Cloghran, near the airport; always interested in security work, she applied to the airport police and was taken on the staff in 1989, one girl among over two hundred male security staff. While she was training with the fire section, the main problem was that there were no female facilities and a Portacabin had to be built on the airfield just for her. She has had no problems with the rest of the staff, and has got used to the roster times. Shifts run from 7.00 am until 3.00 pm, from then to 11.00 pm and the hardest one of all, from 11.00 pm until 7.00 am. "The nights were a 'downer' at the start, but you get used to them", she comments. Other innovations at the airport that year, 1988, included the first Aer Rianta arts festival at Dublin airport. Classical ballet, heavy rock, these were just some of the sights and sounds that filled the terminal. Ireland's oldest company, Rathborne's on East Wall Road, founded in 1488, gave a display of its candle-making craft.

New facilities at the airport included the new Aer Rianta cargo terminal, which was opened on March 7, 1988. The fastest-growing sector in the freight business is overnight express and the new building was designed to satisfy the demands of this market. Customers of the new terminal included Elan and Express Mail; Aer Lingus itself set up a new joint venture company with Securicor and called it AerSecuricor.

John Burke, appointed Aer Rianta company secretary in July, 1986.
Photograph: Robert Allen Photography

Dermot Desmond, appointed Aer Rianta chairman in August, 1990.

Aer Rianta Arts Festival, Dublin airport, 1990

A stilt walker from Circus Belfast takes a bow.

Below left: Face painting at the airport only happens during arts events.

Below right: Viewing works of art at the airport during the 1990 "Gateway to Art" exhibition.

274

Above: The Dublin Junior Ballet performs during the 1990 Arts Festival at Dublin airport.

Paul Fanning (violin) and Marian Doherty (piano) play for the 1990 Arts Festival.
Photographs: Frank Fennell Photography

Jack Charlton moves through the crowds at the airport on the return of the Irish football team from the World Cup, 1990.
Photograph: Frank Fennell Photography

The new Fáilte bar café was opened on the arrivals floor of the terminal; it was designed to look like a stylised version of a Continental street and represented the last phase of the five-year catering investment programme at the airport. Frank O'Connell was made general manager–trading; he took over from Frank Hanlon, who left to pursue other business interests. O'Connell was now responsible for running Aer Rianta's retailing operations at Dublin airport. At the world tax-free trade show held in Cannes that October, Aer Rianta won the airport retailer of the year award.

Ryanair threw a "millionaire's" champagne reception at the boarding gate at Dublin airport on October 20, for the departure to London of the airline's one millionth passenger since the airline was launched 2½ years previously. Twenty-one-year-old Jane O'Keeffe from Cabinteely, County Dublin, was given free travel for life on Ryanair. Dublin airport was really buzzing; during August, it had half a million passengers, a record for one month. SAS Scandinavian Airlines inaugurated a new service, from Dublin to Glasgow, onwards to Copenhagen. The new service, running six days a week, broke the monopoly held on the route until then by Aer Lingus. The new flights were part of the opportunities being given to "fifth freedom" foreign carriers, enabling them to operate between Ireland and Britain en route to mainland European destinations. Under these same rights, Aer Lingus opened new routes out of Dublin, via Manchester to such destinations as Copenhagen, Hamburg and Zurich, as well as via Birmingham to Brussels. To cater for the extra traffic, Aer Lingus leased two extra Boeing 737s and a Shorts 360, adding to the considerable number of planes now using the airport on a daily basis. The first Lufthansa aircraft in that airline's new livery arrived at Dublin airport; the new design style included the famous crane logo in use since the 1920s. The plane was checked in by Lufthansa's station manager in Dublin, Juergen Behrens. Air France station manager, Marcel Henri Lamarque, welcomed the Air France Concorde that arrived at Dublin airport on September 30.

On the inward journey, it brought one hundred French passengers to Ireland, while an equal number of passengers from Ireland, including this writer and his wife, travelled to Paris via the mid-Atlantic at the plane's cruising speed of 1,350 mph, 55,000 feet above the ocean. There was great excitement at the airport that summer with a very well-behaved but large and lively group of soccer supporters. Ireland performed well in the European cup matches in Germany, with the Irish team managed by the inimitable Jack Charlton. When the victorious team arrived back at the airport, they were given a tumultuous welcome. An equally enthusiastic, but more restrained welcome was given to Bob Hawke, the Australian prime minister, and his wife, when they arrived at the airport for an official visit. President Mitterrand of France also arrived, conveniently just before the presidential elections in France; airport wags declared that he was playing the green card. Another distinguished visitor was Douglas "Wrong Way" Corrigan, so called because when he took off from New York in 1938, the authorities would not give him permission to fly the Atlantic. Several airmen had already been lost on the route and Corrigan was rebuffed when he applied for permission. When he took off, due to fly to Los Angeles, he made a navigational error, as he has claimed ever since, and eventually made landfall in Ireland, to a hero's welcome. In 1988, Corrigan returned the

Jack Charlton speaks to the crowds at the airport on his return, with the Irish team, from the World Cup football competition in Italy, during the summer of 1990. Among those watching, from left, are: Tom Cullen, Dr Michael Woods, T.D., Minister for Social Welfare and the Taoiseach, Charles Haughey, T.D.
Photograph: Frank Fennell Photography

The "family photograph" of the EC heads of Government taken during the June summit at Dublin Castle. Ireland held the EC presidency for the first six months of 1990 and many heads of state and numerous dignitaries and officials from every other country in the EC came through Dublin airport. Included in this photograph are the Taoiseach, Charles Haughey, T.D., (front row, fifth from right), the Minister for Foreign Affairs, Gerard Collins, T.D., (back row, sixth from left), Spanish prime minister, Felipe Gonzales (front row, first left), Chancellor Kohl of West Germany (front row, fourth from left), French president François Mitterrand (front row, sixth from right) and British prime minister, Mrs Margaret Thatcher (front row, fourth from right).
Photograph: Lensmen

conventional way, on a scheduled flight into Dublin airport. There was plenty of gas of a different kind at the airport; the boilerhouse was converted to natural gas.

The gas was piped up from the Kinsale gas field in the national gas grid that serves Dublin and other towns and cities. The new fuel is cost efficient and effective, but the certain romance that surrounded the turf used for so many years vanished into history. Another piece of airport history vanished in 1988: the Cloghran pill box that was built near Corballis House in 1939, just before the outbreak of World War II, was finally demolished. Dublin's Millennium year, 1988, was another excellent one for the airport, with passengers totalling over 4.4 million. Carmencita Hederman, then Lord Mayor, came out to the airport to inspect the special Millennium illuminations on the terminal building.

During 1989, the big event was the official opening of the new east-west runway by Charles Haughey, the Taoiseach. The new runway cost £35 million to build. The first aircraft to land officially on the new runway, designated 10/28, was a European Airbus, an A320 chartered by Aer Rianta for the occasion. It took off from the old main runway and after a circuit of the city, landed on the new pavement. Disembarking with Charles Haughey were Frank Boland, Aer Rianta chairman, and assistant chief executive–technical, Brendan Clancy. On their arrival, the Taoiseach was greeted by Aer Rianta chief executive, Derek Keogh, and Dublin airport general manager, Tom Cullen. The speeches were made by Tom Cullen and the Taoiseach before the latter cut the huge red ribbon. The Garda band played a selection of melodies. Hundreds of airport workers took part in a 1.7 mile race that covered most of the new runway. Lunch took place for guests in Pier A, while that evening, Aer Rianta staff jived to jazz in temperatures that rivalled those in New Orleans.

A second cargo-handling facility was opened at the airport, when the new Servisair depot was constructed. Said Tom Cullen, airport general manager: "It is the practice in western Europe and America to allow the customer some choice in cargo handling

Éamon de Buitléar recently made a short TV film about the airport's wildlife, called *Dublin Airport — Life in Harmony*. This photograph shows him filming house martins in a hangar roof. Every spring, these birds travel from Africa to nest in the hangars and are undisturbed by all the workshop activity going on far below their lofty perches. House martins are too few and too small to interfere with aircraft.

Wildlife living within the airport boundaries includes hares, pheasants, pigmy shrews and woodmice, unruffled by the constant noise of aircraft. Hares are often seen in the staff car park. The miles of hedgerows have their own kinds of wildlife, including an endless variety of insects, attracted by the profusion of wildflowers.
Photograph: Cian de Buitléar

A fox seen at Dublin airport.

An airport woodmouse.
Photographs: Éamon de Buitléar

Above: Nelson Mandela's message to the people of Ireland, written in the airport VIP book when he arrived in Dublin to receive the freedom of the city in July, 1990. Mandela had been imprisoned in South Africa for twenty-seven years. He praises the support given by the government and people of Ireland.

Right: Nelson and Winnie Mandela with Gerard Collins, T.D., Minister for Foreign Affairs.
Photographs: Robert Allen Photography

at airports. We are very encouraged by Servisair's plans for cargo development at Dublin airport". The same Tom Cullen was among the eighteen recipients of twenty-five-year service awards, along with other airport luminaries, such as Ray La Comber, Oliver McCann and Hugh Mulligan. Two well-known airport characters retired: Christopher Darcy, trolleys and vending supervisor, and Christy Sheridan, cleaning supervisor. After twenty-one years running the print room, mailroom and stationery stores, Felix Carpenter succeeded Christopher Darcy. The year was memorable for a new development on the broadcasting front. Capital Radio went on the air in Dublin in July, the first of the new independent radio stations. A year later, there were nineteen local stations in operation and a national one, Century Radio. On the broader international front, the political ice in eastern Europe began to break up and countries like Czechoslovakia, Hungary and Poland were soon to gain non-communist governments. The biggest change is in Germany; monetary union of the two Germanies during the summer of 1990 was followed in the autumn by unification. Germany is set to become the economic and political centre of Europe, a far cry from the events of 1940, the year the airport opened.

The annual air spectaculars started in 1978; the first seven were held at Fairyhouse racecourse, north of Dublin. Since 1982, they have been sponsored by Aer Rianta. Many of the incoming aircraft for the displays, like the Dunlop Pitts special and the B17 Flying Fortress, touched down at Dublin airport, providing a striking contrast with the commercial aircraft that use the airport.
Photograph: Billy Strickland

Cross-channel traffic at the airport developed strongly in 1988, as a result of airline liberalisation. The arrival of yet another carrier on the Dublin–London route, British Midland, in April, 1989, stimulated traffic growth. A regional airline, Manx Airlines, began to step up its services from Dublin, with plans to develop Dublin airport into a hub on its network. During the month of June, over half a million passsengers used the airport, a record. As the airport frequently passed its maximum designed capacity of 5.5 million passengers a year, management style changed with the appointment of Tom Cullen as general manager and Brian Byrne as deputy general manager. Tom Cullen's style is to delegate. He remarked, soon after his appointment, that his aim is to push the decision-making process down to the coal face, in line with Aer Rianta's declared objectives of being a customer oriented, participative company. Brian Byrne foresaw each division at the airport evolving into a self-managing business centre. New appointments to this end included Eamonn Moran as airport services manager, Don Treacy as operations manager and Arthur Coughlan as marketing manager. The aim of Tom Cullen and Brian Byrne is to make Dublin airport the best airport of its size in the world. As part of that process, Aer Rianta took a dramatic step forward, with the election of three worker directors for the first time. 1989 saw Dublin airport handle 5.1 million passengers and make a profit of £21.1 million. The Dublin–London route, on which British Midland started as an extra competitor at the end of April, 1989, is now the second busiest air route in Europe.

On January 19, 1990, Aer Rianta held a gala lunch in the Silver Lining restaurant at Dublin airport, to mark the fiftieth anniversary of the first official flight from the airport. People who had contributed so much to the airport over the years were there, like Dr J. F. Dempsey; Frank Delaney, the flight engineer on the first plane to leave the new airport at Collinstown, was also there. On April 30, Derek Keogh laid the foundation stone for the new airport fire station, on the west side of the field. It is due to be ready at the end of 1990. Now into its fifty-first year, Dublin airport takes off into a brand new future, the new Europe, where ninety per cent of all flights will be domestic, within the twelve states that at present form the European Community. Only ten per cent of flights will be international, a far cry from that first flight to Liverpool in 1940. The airport of the present looks to the next century, when air travel will change beyond anyone's wildest dreams.

Dermot F. Desmond, who was appointed chairman of Aer Rianta in August, 1990, is a prominent figure in the Irish financial services industry. Before setting up his own firm, NCB Stockbrokers, in 1981, he worked for such organisations as the World Bank. His own firm was set up to act as a foreign exchange and currency

Brian Keenan, the Belfast lecturer who spent over four years in captivity in Beirut, returned to Dublin airport in August, 1990. Disembarking from the government jet, he is greeted by the Taoiseach, Charles Haughey, T.D. Centre is Gerard Collins, T.D., Minister for Foreign Agfairs.
Photograph: Robert Allen Photography

deposit agency broker to Ireland's banks; in 1984, it diversified into stockbroking. Today, the NCB group of which Dermot Desmond is executive chairman, is one of Ireland's leading financial services groups. It was the primary sponsor of *NCB Ireland*, the Irish entry in the 1989/90 round the world yacht race.

Although his appointment to Aer Rianta, first as a director and now as chairman, is his first board appointment in the semi-State and public sector, his group has advised many semi-State companies on such matters as acquisitions and general development plans. He says that the main value of Aer Rianta is its people and its management team; the priority is to enhance the value of that strong blend of talents. Programmes have to be drawn up and implemented for the 1990s and Dermot Desmond intends to be very closely involved in the direction and detail of the company's commercial development. He says that while the likely abolition of duty-free sales within the EC after 1992 is perceived as a major problem, it is not, although he acknowledges that they are a substantial contribution to Aer Rianta profits.

Through its unique marketing programmes, Aer Rianta can replace any loss of duty free sales with other products for other markets. But he stresses that any change in the duty free status is not a foregone conclusion. Aer Rianta thrives on new opportunities: "having a captive market can make for complacency, which we do not want in the company. We want Aer Rianta to be measured as an open market operator". He does not see any possible change in financial status for Aer Rianta as a key issue in operating the business: "the key issue is developing and growing the company and if there are any restrictions on the capital needed, we will tackle that problem". He wants to see Dublin airport developed as a model airport for the 1990s, with an identity and a life of its own, rather than just a service facility. He is impressed with the central philosophy of Dublin airport: care for the passengers, which is reflected in the current level of capital expenditure to improve and extend facilities. He has also been very impressed by what he calls the "fantastic commitment" at all levels of staff in the airport. Dermot Desmond promises to be a very active and very involved chairman of the company, injecting his own great financial expertise into the running of the company's affairs, as it heads into the uncharted airways of the 1990s.

Aer Rianta is a public limited liability company incorporated under the Companies

Shortly after his arrival, Brian Keenan addresses a news conference at Dublin airport, flanked by his sisters, Elaine Spence (left) and Brenda Gillham.
Photograph: Robert Allen Photography

Opposite page:
Aeronautical chart showing the Dublin air traffic control zone. To the west and south, aircraft movements are controlled by Shannon, while those to the north are the responsibility of Prestwick.
Map: Based on the Ordnance Survey by permission of the Government. Permit No. 5312.

Acts. Its authorised share capital is £60,000 divided into 60,000 £1 shares. The Minister for Finance is the sole shareholder, apart from eleven holders of qualifying shares, who are the nine board members and the Secretaries of the Department of Finance and the Department of Tourism and Transport. The Minister for the latter Department appoints the board of Aer Rianta with the agreement of the Minister for Finance. Seamus Brennan, T.D., has been Minister for Tourism and Transport since 1989, with Denis Lyons, T.D., as Minister of State. Donal O'Mahony, who is now Secretary of the Department, has had a long and close working relationship with Aer Rianta during his distinguished career with the civil aviation division of the Department. He succeeded Noel McMahon.

During the past fifty years, the airport itself has changed beyond recognition; a humble dream has developed into a colossus and the modest airport at Collinstown has become the vast construction known as Dublin airport, preparing itself for the twenty-first century, a vast journey in time and spirit from the fields, trees and cottages that within living memory once occupied this part of north County Dublin.

POSTSCRIPT

A glimpse into the future

WITH Dublin's airport's main terminal building literally bulging at the seams, having nearly reached its passenger capacity of 5½ million people a year, construction work is beginning on extensions that will carry the terminal through to the mid-1990s, when major new terminal buildings are due to be completed. While passenger numbers are likely to be about 5½ million in 1990, Derek Keogh believes that there could be as many as ten million passengers by the end of the century. Increasing air traffic congestion in Europe could open up new transit possibilities for Dublin.

At present, six wide-bodied aircraft use Dublin airport; as part of the huge likely expansion of traffic, much more room will have to be found at the airport for handling many more wide-bodied jets on a daily basis. In the immediate future, the extension at arrivals and departure levels will cost up to £10 million. The first phase of a long-term multi-storey car parking facility will be started shortly; by 1992, it should be ready to hold 4,500 cars. A major update on the airport telephone exchange is planned for 1991. Catering and shopping facilities in the terminal are also being expanded in the near future, as are executive lounges in the pavilion area. Business travel is expanding just as much as the cheaper end of the market. By the end of 1990, Dublin airport will be providing a range of executive facilities to match the best of European airports. Major extensions to the existing terminal could handle up to ten million passengers a year, which would take the airport to the year 2000.

By the time the airport is handling eight million passengers a year, there will be a need for a second and completely separate terminal building. This is likely to be built on the opposite side of the airport, in keeping with already well-established practice at some other major European airports. But by the time the passenger level reaches seven million, there will be a strong need for a better public transport connection in the shape of a DART line into the airport. The favourite place for branching off is Howth Junction. The plan for this rail link to the airport is well-advanced and the two miles of track are costed at about £5 million, a very small proportion of Aer Rianta's capital expenditure programme of £135 million over the next five years for its three airports. There are also plans by a UK developer for a £50 million hotel and leisure complex near the airport. With the takeover of Great Southern Hotels by Aer Rianta in the summer of 1990, a second airport hotel is likely. In the more immediate future, there is still a serious threat to abolish duty free shopping for travellers within the EC, after 1992, and the major loss of revenue this would pose for Dublin airport will have to be addressed. But with a company that is so innovative as to be developing duty free locations in Hungary, China and in the Soviet Union, Aer Rianta can be guaranteed to tackle the duty free problem, as well as the wider opportunities of airport development, with its customary aplomb. Under the guidance of Joe McGuinne, who heads the technical department at the airport, the details of the future are being worked out with fine precision.

The technical department takes with an everyday matter-of-factness the possibility of Super Concorde, which is scheduled to take to the air in 2005. Flying at a speed of 1,500 mph, with a range of over 6,000 miles, it will carry 200 passengers, bringing supersonic travel into the mass market. Perhaps it will be as common a sight every day on the apron at the Dublin airport of the future as the 747 and the European Airbus are today, and as the Viscounts, the Fokker Friendships and the DC3s were in previous generations. The future holds no fears for Aer Rianta and the planning has already started for the next century.

A chronology of events

1169 Earliest reference to Cloghran.
1573 Dunsoghly Castle built.
1641 Townland of Corballis documented.
1719 Thomas Wilkinson, owner of Corballis House, is made Lord Mayor of Dublin.
1820 Castlemoate House is built (approximate date).
1900 Queen Victoria's state visit to Dublin.
1909 Harry Ferguson makes first successful flight in Ireland, at Hillsborough, County Down.
1912 Royal Flying Corps brings first military aircraft to Ireland.
1914 World War I begins.
1916 Easter Rising.
1917 Sholto Douglas selects Collinstown as site for aerodrome. Construction work starts almost immediately.
1918 Collinstown military aerodrome partially completed. End of World War I.
1919 Raid on Collinstown base.
1921 War of Independence ends. Treaty signed.
1922 British forces withdraw from Irish Free State. Collinstown abandoned as military airfield.
1923 Civil war ends.
1929 The R101 airship flies over Dublin.
1930 Iona Airways starts up at Kildonan airfield in Finglas.
1935 Planning and development starts on new Dublin airport.
1936 Aer Lingus begins operations, using Baldonnel.
1937 Work begins on new grass runways at Collinstown. Aer Rianta established.
1938 Building begins on new terminal, designed by Desmond FitzGerald, Office of Public Works. It was completed in the spring of 1941.
1939 World War II begins; Ireland declares neutrality.
1940 Dublin airport officially opened on January 19, with first Aer Lingus flight from the new airfield, to Liverpool.
1942 BOAC begins short-lived Dublin–Bristol service, while Aer Lingus starts an equally short term service to Shannon.
1943 Planning begins on new runway construction, to start after the Emergency.
1945 End of World War II in Europe; it ends in the Far East the following year.
1946 Colonel W. P. Delamer appointed first airport manager. Air transport agreement between Ireland and Britain; Aer Lingus given sole rights on all cross-channel routes. Work begins on concreting the runways.
1947 KLM begins first service from Dublin airport by a continental carrier. The first Constellations arrive at the airport for the new Aer Lingus Aerlínte trans-Atlantic service, which is scrapped before it begins.
1948 New runways completed. First jet aircraft, an RAF Meteor, lands at Dublin airport.
1949 Declaration of the Republic.
1950 Dublin airport third busiest in these islands, after Heathrow and Northolt in London.

1954 First Vickers Viscount lands at Dublin airport.
1955 First helicopter comes to the airport.
1956 Ronnie Delaney's win at the Melbourne Olympics; given tremendous reception at the airport on his homecoming. Aer Lingus loses its monopoly on cross-channel routes.
1957 BEA starts services into Dublin from Heathrow and Birmingham.
1958 Aer Lingus introduces Fokker Friendships as it phases out its DC3 fleet. Aer Lingus also starts its trans-Atlantic service. Lourdes terminal opened.
1958 North terminal opened.
1960 First Aer Lingus jet arrives at Dublin airport.
1961 Visit by Prince Rainier and Princess Grace of Monaco, who arrive at Dublin airport; it is the first state visit to Ireland for sixty-one years.
1962 Car ferry terminal built at airport.
1963 President John F. Kennedy arrives at Dublin airport to begin his Irish tour. He is assassinated in Dallas five months later. BEA divests itself of remaining shares in Aer Lingus. Beatles arrive at the airport for their Adelphi concert.
1964 Airport church opened.
1965 Air Companies' Bill lays foundation for separation of Aer Rianta from Aer Lingus.
1966 Colonel Delamer retires as airport manager.
1968 Aer Rianta set up as separate company; at first it manages Dublin airport, but soon afterwards also assumes responsibility for Cork and Shannon airports.
1969 Construction work begins on new terminal. Vincent Fanning is appointed airport manager.
1970 US president Nixon arrives at Dublin airport at start of official visit to Ireland.
1972 New terminal is opened, replacing old building. Jack Doyle is new airport manager.
1973 Ireland joins the EEC.
1974 R. C. O'Connor retires as chief executive of Aer Rianta and is succeeded by James O'Sullivan.
1975 Aer Lingus worker killed by bomb in terminal.
1976 Bill Beck, first airport engineer, retires. George O'Connor made airport manager.
1979 Pope John Paul II starts Irish visit with rapturous welcome at Dublin airport.
1981 Martin Dully appointed chief executive.
1986 Ryanair starts flights from Dublin airport; the air fares "war" creates huge growth in passenger air traffic from the airport.
1988 Derek Keogh succeeds Martin Dully as chief executive.
1989 Tom Cullen made general manager, Dublin airport. New main runway opened.
1990 January 19 is fiftieth anniversary of airport opening. Plans are advanced for terminal and other facilities to take Dublin airport into the twenty-first century.

Sources

Much of the research material in this book came from the personal recollections of many people associated with Aer Rianta since its inception, as well as historical documents collected by the company, minutes of board meetings and annual general meetings, annual reports and *Runway*, the Aer Rianta staff magazine. The following printed sources were consulted:

Aer Lingus 1936–1986, a business monograph, Dublin, 1986.
Aer Scéala, 1946–
A History of the Royal Air Force and United States Naval Air Service in Ireland, 1913–1923. Irish Air Letter/Karl E. Hayes, Dublin, 1988.
Air disasters. Stanley Stewart, London, 1986.
Air spectaculars — air displays in Ireland. Madeleine O'Rourke, Dublin, 1988.
An Irishman's Aviation Sketchbook. R. W. O'Sullivan, Dublin, 1988.
Aviation Ireland, Journal of the Aviation Society of Ireland, Dublin, 1971–
Cara magazine, May/June, 1986. 50th anniversary of Aer Lingus.
Development magazine, no. 132, 1972. Aer Rianta: Dublin airport's new terminal.
Dublin churches. Peter Costello, Dublin, 1989.
Dublin's fighting story, 1913–21. Collinstown aerodrome raid, Patrick Houlihan. The Kerryman, Tralee, nd.
Evening Press, various dates. Dubliner's Diary by Michael O'Toole.
Green in my Sky. A. A. Quigley, Co Dublin, 1983.
History and description of Santry and Cloghran Parishes, County Dublin. Rev Benjamin William Adams, D.D., London, 1883.
History of Aviation in Ireland. Liam Byrne, Dublin, 1980.
International aviation quiz book. Michael Barry, Fermoy, Co Cork, 1989.
Ireland and world aviation. Liam M. Skinner and Tommy Cranitch, Dublin, nd.
Irish Aviator magazine.
Irish Builder magazine, July 28, 1945. Feature on original airport terminal building.
Irish Independent, various dates, 1936. Passenger lists, Aer Lingus, Baldonnel.
Irish Independent, January 19, 1990. Supplement on Dublin airport fiftieth anniversary.
Runway magazine, Aer Rianta, Dublin 1971–
Studies magazine, xxiv, 1935. Desmond McAteer, "Suggested airport for Dublin".
The Annals of Dublin — Fair City. E. E. O'Donnell, Dublin, 1987.
The Emergency. Bernard Share, Dublin, 1978.
The Flight of the Iolar — the Aer Lingus experience, 1936–1986. Bernard Share, Dublin, 1986.
The Irish Times, March 23, 1989. Feature on Air France services to Ireland.
Those magnificent men in their flying machines at Leopardstown, Liam Clare, Dublin, 1981.
UCD News, November 1987. Feature on Joseph P. MacHale, a former Aer Rianta accountant.
Vom flughafen Zürich — Start in alle Welt/Zurich airport — Gateway to the world. Erich Meier, Zurich, 1980.
Years of Combat. Volume I of the autobiography of Lord Douglas of Kirtleside, London, 1963.

Aer Rianta directors
Dublin airport statistics

AER RIANTA CHAIRMEN AND DIRECTORS, 1967-1990

Chairmen

John Connor, 1967/68-1974
A. P. McClafferty, 1974-1980
Peter Hanley, 1980-1985

Frank J. Boland, 1985-1990
Dermot F. Desmond, 1990-

Directors

John Anglim, 1989-
D. G. Beddy, 1967/68-1974
Tony Brazil, 1985-1989
D. A. Browne, 1975-1980
John Carroll, 1982-1990
J. A. Daly, 1980-1985
Dermot Desmond, 1989-
Gerald Doyle, 1967/1974
P. O. Ferguson, 1974-1977
Peter Hanley, 1980-1985, 1989-
Tom Keaveney, 1989-

F. J. Kinahan, 1974-1977
A. P. McClafferty, 1967-1980
F. V. McDonnell, 1977-1985
Alan Morris, 1989-
Des Mullally, 1989-
Michael Mullen, 1980-1982
Sean Murray, 1985-1990
R. C. O'Connor, 1968-1980
Breege O'Donoghue, 1985-1989
Barra Ó Tuama, 1977-1984

Dublin airport operating surpluses, 1967-1989

Year	Amount	Year	Amount
1967/68	£198,866	1979	£5,566,000
1968/69	£243,819	1980	£4,536,000
1969/70	£895,000	1981	£5,925,000
1970/71	£967,000	1982	£4,598,000
1971/72	£996,000	1983	£6,298,000
1972/73	£727,000	1984	£7,394,000
1973/74	£583,000	1985	£7,821,000
1974	£988,000	1986	£10,060,000
1975	£1,206,000	1987	£13,713,000
1976	£1,614,000	1988	£18,536,000
1977	£2,125,324	1989	£21,129,000
1978	£3,631,000		

Dublin airport aircraft movements, 1967-1989

Year	Movements	Year	Movements
1967/68	65,154	1979	92,150
1968/69	64,404	1980	94,381
1969/70	66,863	1981	92,645
1970/71	64,063	1982	90,444
1971/72	65,395	1983	93,494
1972/73	69,982	1984	89,049
1973/74	65,434	1985	87,074
1974 (9 months to December 31)	57,473	1986	96,071
1975	79,416	1987	99,368
1976	80,622	1988	111,169
1977	85,053	1989	113,729
1978	89,799		

Dublin airport, freight traffic, 1967–1989
Metric tons. From 1974, statistics include mails

Year	Tons	Year	Tons
1967/68	33,757	1979	46,520
1968/69	40,048	1980	42,347
1969/70	35,004	1981	40,295
1970/71	37,738	1982	40,790
1971/72	38,315	1983	42,748
1972/73	43,694	1984	47,271
1973/74	52,280	1985	41,956
1974 (9 months to December 31)	40,275	1986	40,314
1975	44,731	1987	39,488
1976	46,637	1988	46,823
1977	48,965	1989	46,932
1978	41,955		

Dublin airport passenger movements, 1967–1989

Year	Passengers	Year	Passengers
1967/68	1,510,677	1979	2,756,581
1968/69	1,602,405	1980	2,582,417
1969/70	1,737,151	1981	2,732,928
1970/71	1,902,984	1982	2,700,368
1971/72	2,068,749	1983	2,562,308
1972/73	1,983,627	1984	2,599,064
1973/74	2,155,206	1985	2,618,627
1974 (9 months to December 31)	1,702,323	1986	2,925,573
1975	2,195,688	1987	3,551,032
1976	2,208,882	1988	4,418,356
1977	2,267,089	1989	5,099,253
1978	2,514,169		

Index – Text

A
Abbey Theatre, 99
Aberdeen service, 223
ABTA Irish Golf Open, 253
Adcock direction finding, 34
advertising, 198
AEC, 170
Aer Arran, 236
Aer Lingus, 1, 24, 58, 163, 169, 218, 231
  and Aer Rianta, 34, 54, 70, 72, 74, 82, 84, 91-2, 94-5, 109, 173-4, 196
    separation, 127, 129, 134, 154-5, 156-7, 159-60
  car ferry, 140
  catering, 65, 160
  celebrations, 119
  crashes, 99
  cross-channel monopoly, 72, 117
  established, 25
  expansion, 43, 69-70
  finances, 58, 109, 115-16, 122, 215, 238
    fares, 115
    share capital, 72
  first flight from Collinstown, 39
  first service, 27
  fleet, 70, 84, 88-9, 91, 114, 119-21, 153, 172, 197, 202, 236, 261, 264, 277
    jet aircraft, 79, 86, 97, 127
  Golden Jubilee, 254, 255
  inaugural flight, 39, 45
  mail service, 69
  name, 24
  and other airlines, 138-9, 276
  personnel, 93, 97, 152, 157, 159-60, 227-8, 245
    ex-military, 59, 61
    lay-offs, 87
  routes, 222-3, 276
  statistics
    passengers, 74, 89, 115, 122, 133-4
  strikes, 91, 196, 214, 215
  training facilities, 7
Aer Lingus golfing society, 124
Aer Lingus Young Scientists' Event, 252
Aer Rianta, 5, 7, 8, 39, 101, 150, 255
  and Aer Lingus. *see under* Aer Lingus
  air displays, 24, 113, 236
  arts festival, 273
  cargo terminal, 273, 279
  change in status, 258
  charter operation, 84-5
  commercial division, 181
  computers, 239, 252, 261
  corporate image, 207, 232, 273
  educational service, 119, 124, 150
  during the Emergency, 54-5, 58
  energy conservation, 181, 184
  established, 34
  finances, 87, 93-4, 104, 113, 115-16, 117, 122-3, 139, 150-1, 174, 180, 184, 192, 197, 207, 232, 238-9, 241, 284
    cutbacks, 215
    share capital, 72
  financial structure, 283-4
  fleet, 110
  marketing, 196, 241
  offices, 94, 190
  personnel, *see under* personnel
  plans, 43, 285
  re-organisation, 157, 159, 161
  security checks, 177
  shops, 229
    airport retailer of the year, 277
  shareholders, 284
  social and sporting association, 198
  staff, *see under* personnel
  status, 257, 283-4
  technology manager, 252
  training, 8, 230, 264, 267
Aer Rianta International, 273
Aer Scéala, 104, 109, 172
AerSecuricor, 273
Aer Turas, 113, 155, 202
Aerlínte, 74, 86-7, 106, 109, 152, 157, 228
Aeronaves de Panama, 154
Agaginian, Cardinal, 136
Aiken, Frank, 1-2, 136, 150
Aiken, Maud, 150
Air Companies Bill, 1965, 139
Air Concern, 175
Air Corps, 16, 19, 21, 24, 86, 180, 204, 228
  during Emergency, 51
  helicopter, 113
  testing Dublin airport, 35, 38
air displays, 24, 114, 119, 236
Air Ecosse, 223
Air France, 236, 277
Air Navigation and Transport Bill, 1936, 25
Air Navigation School, Bishopscourt, 52
air service liberalisation, 257, 281
Air Services Exhibition, 12
air traffic control, 27, 30, 263
Air Transport Bill, 1966, 129
Airline Pilots and Navigators, Guild of, 99
Airport Duty Office, 157
Airport Operators Council International, 253, 263
Airspeed Consul aircraft, 85
Akef, Group Captain Hassan, 89-90
Albatross DI aircraft, 12
Aldergrove airport, 11, 15, 16, 18, 113
Alitalia, 173
Aly Khan, 74, 101-2
Allen, Robert, 229
ALSAA, 230-1, 257-8
American Embassy, Ballsbridge, 151
American Overseas Airlines, 69
Amhurst, Lord, 91
Amin, Idi, 193-4
Amsterdam service, 43, 89, 91, 113
Andrews, Noel, 140
Andrews, Dr Tod, 125
Anglo-Irish free trade agreement, 177
Anson aircraft, 50-51, 52
Apprentice of the Year, 208
Armée de l'Air, France, 113
Armstrong, Neil, 188
Armstrong Whitworth Whitley bomber aircraft, 51
Arnborg, Per, 233
Artane, 6
Artane Boys Band, 102
arts festival, 276
Ashbourne crash (1967), 155
Association of British Travel Agents, 253
Athens service, 222
Avair, 222, 230
Aviaco, 215
aviation museum, 186-7
Avro 504K aircraft, 21
Avro Tudor aircraft, 99

B
B & I Line, 245
B17 Flying Fortress aircraft, 279
B25 bomber aircraft, 202
B25 Mitchell bomber aircraft, 202
BAC One-Eleven aircraft, 153, 196, 256
BAE 748 aircraft, 256
Baker, Albert, 264
Baker, Suzanne, 191
Baldonnel aerodrome, 1, 11, 14, 15-16, 39, 51, 68, 228
  Aer Lingus terminal, 27
  Air Corps HQ, 19
  civilian aviation, 25, 27, 30
  designated as civil airport, 24
  famous passengers, 31-2
  mail flights, 21, 24
  renamed, 151
  training depot, 13
Baldwin, Eugene, 175
Balkan Tours, 223
Bandeirante aircraft, 223, 236, 255
Bannon, Jack, 92, 107, 142-3, 148, 180, 183, 188, 233, 241, 259
Bannon, Jim, 92
barber's shop, 214
Barker, Fran, 187
Barnard, Dr Christian, 17

Barry, Peter, 184, 237, 261
Bartenders' Association of Ireland, 199
Baskin, The, 6, 35
Bateson, Elaine, 191
BEA, 74, 91, 102, 104, 113, 119, 136
    and Aer Lingus, 138-9
BE2A aircraft, 11
BE2C aircraft, 11
Beatles, The, 127, 164
Beck, Bill, 79-80, 82, 92-3, 106, 175
    retirement, 188, 190
Beckett, Samuel, 160, 183, 254
Beech 18 aircraft, 90
Beechcraft Expeditor aircraft, 90
Beechcraft turboprop aircraft, 222
Beere, Dr Thekla, 61, 110, 129, 183
Behan, Brendan, 153, 215
Behrens, Juergen, 277
Beirut, 244
Belfast service, 87, 222
Bell Iroquois helicopters, 197
Belvelly project, 24
Benedict XV, Pope, 215
Benny, Jack, 225
Benson, Garry, 179, 199
Bergin, Rita, 204
Bermingham, Joe, 193
Bernhard, Prince, 89, 136
Besson, Ken, 168
Best, Bobby, 193, 264, 267
Bewley family, 10
Beyers, Lieutenant General, 90
Biarritz service, 115
bird strikes, 223, 226
Birmingham, Patrick, 6
Birmingham service, 119, 277
Bizzell, Billy, 117, 228
BKS Air Transport, 119
Blackburn Bluebird aircraft, 21
Blake, Robert, 185
Block, Jacques, 182
Bloody Sunday, Derry, 173
Board of Works, 19
Boeing 737-300 aircraft, 261
Boeing 707 aircraft, 222
Boeing 720 aircraft, 127
Boeing 737 aircraft, 193, 202, 207, 236, 277
Boeing 747 aircraft, 169, 172, 182, 193, 202, 285
Boeing B-50D aircraft, 102
Boeing B-17F flying fortress aircraft, 49, 50
Boeing company, 127
boiler plant, 104, 106
Bokassa, Emperor, 113
Boland, Frank, 245, 248, 255, 261, 272, 279
Boland, Frederick, 129
Boland, Noel, 187
Bolger, Ray, 230, 261, 264
bombs, 182, 183, 188
Bono, 269
Boomtown Rats, 215
Boot Inn, 1, 9, 20, 32, 56, 175
Bord Fáilte, 107, 253, 272
Bord Iascaigh Mhara, 218
Bord na Mona, 218
Borg, Björn, 229
Boston service, 120

Bouchier-Hayes, Dr, 82, 93
Bourke, Patrick "Pakie", 1
Boylan, Barney, 235
Bradley, Walter, 111
Brancardiers, 170
Branson, Richard, 260
Brennan, John, 230
Brennan, Robert, 59
Brennan, Seamus, 5, 284
Breslin, Peadar, 190
Bristol 170 freighter aircraft, 155
Bristol fighter aircraft, 15, 16
Bristol freighter aircraft, 91
Bristol service, 47, 69, 140
Bristol Sycamore helicopter, 113
Britannia aircraft, 202
British Aerospace 146 jet aircraft, 235-6
British Airports Authority (BAA), 259
British Airways, 117, 177, 180, 191, 194, 198
    demonstration against, 220
    fleet, 211
British European Airways (BEA), 97, 117, 138-9, 173, 180
British European Airways, 72
British Midland, 231, 281
British Overseas Airways Corporation (BOAC), 47, 72, 87, 180
British Rail, 140
Broad, Hubert, 17
Browne, Dan, 235
Browne, Dr Noel, 99
Browne, Vincent, 237
Browne, Vincent (sculptor), 246
Brussels service, 87, 89, 117, 197, 202, 277
Bruton, C., 1
Bucks Fizz, 223
Building Centre of Ireland, 177
Burke, John, 234, 258
Burke, Ray, 252
Busáras, 109, 151
Bush, George, 237
Business and Finance, 231
Byrne, Alfie, 22-5, 27, 29, 117
Byrne, Brian, 180, 193, 195, 198, 226, 256, 281
Byrne, Gay, 134-5, 239, 255
Byrne, Nicky, 81, 82, 84, 188, 226, 259
Byrne, Thomas, 260

C
C-47 aircraft, 70, 88, 89, 113, 197
Cahalan, John, 248
Cahill, Hugh, 21, 22, 30, 121
Cahill, Pearse, 121
Campbell, Captain D., 77
Canadair CL-44J aircraft, 202
Canadian Air Force, 223
Canary Islands service, 253
Capital Airlines, 222
Capital Radio, 281
Capitol Cinema, 173
car bombs, 182
car hire, 267
car parking, 114-15, 154, 177, 203, 233

Caravelle jet aircraft, 153
Cardiff service, 191, 211
cargo traffic, 150
Carley, Brenda, 190
Carney, Mary, 179
Carolan, 7
Carpenter, Felix, 281
Carroll, Major G. T., 1, 30
Carroll, Leo, 170, 177
Carroll, Noel, 269
Carstens, Charles, 249
Carvair aircraft, 140
Casement, Sir Roger, 35, 151
Casement aerodrome, 151
Cash, Nicky, 198
Cashin, Michael, 179, 190
Castlemoate House, 8, 234, 239
Castleruddery, County Wicklow, 211
Catholic Herald, 97
Caul, Matthew, 34
CDP Associates, 199
Century Radio, 281
Cessna 180 aircraft, 114
Cessna aircraft, 154
Chamberlain, Neville, 38
Chance Brothers, 34
charity fundraising, 187, 198
Charles de Gaulle airport, Paris, 182, 195
Charles II, King, 6
Charlton, Jack, 278-9
Chartered Institute of Transport in Ireland, 238
Chaumont air base, France, 111
Cherbourg service, 134, 140
Childers, Erskine, 128-9, 139, 176, 182-3
China, 284
Christie, Phil, 190
Christmas lights, 273
Churchill, Clementine, 129
Churchill, Winston, 228
Churchill-Guest, Rt. Hon. Ivor, Baron Wimborne, 12
cinema, 4, 116
Civil Aviation Authority, U.K., 259
civil aviation conference, Chicago, 59
Civil War, 15-18, 63
Clancy, Brendan, 173, 175, 182, 185, 185, 190, 279
Clancy, Eamon, 211
Clancy, Seán, 121, 234
Clarke, Anne, 194
Clarke, Harry, 185, 228, 267
Clarke, Joe, 190, 232, 233
Clarke, Owen, 173, 194, 195, 227, 228, 230, 245, 256, 261
Clegg, Vincent, 190
Clerget 72 rotary engine, 186
Cloghran, County Dublin, 5, 8, 10, 55, 234, 278, 281
Clonshaugh, County Dublin, 185, 241
Club Air, 260
Club Travel, 260-61
Clune, Flan, 256
Clyden Airways, 197, 201, 223
Cobham, Alan, 16-17, 24
Cobham flying circus, 16-17, 24-5

cocktail competitions, 179, 191, 199
Coghlan, Eamonn, 222
Collier, Jim, 175, 187, 207
Collins, Michael, 17
Collinstown, County Dublin, 5-6
Collinstown airport, 13, 19-20, 21, 283
   as Dublin Airport, 27, 29, 30-31
   inaugural flight, 1-3, 5
   IRA raid, 7, 14-15
   military mails, 15, 17
   radio station, 2, 18
   RAF base, 16-18
   terminal building, 2, 17
   during World War I, 10-14
Collinstown Cross, 9
Collinstown House, 10, 14
Comer, Jim, 193
Comet 1 aircraft, 127
communications,
   closed circuit TV, 125
   GCA radar, 119
   lack of, 80
   radio direction-finding equipment, 101
Communications, Department of, 242
computerisation, 201
Concorde aircraft, 236, 277
Connell, Dr Desmond, 5
Connolly, Gerry, 222
Connolly, Hugh, 228
Connolly, Sybil, 166
Connor, John, 172, 174
Constellation aircraft, 104, 237-8
control tower, 109
Convair 240 aircraft, 91
Convair 340 aircraft, 113
Conway, Cardinal, 136
Cooke, Judith, 188
Cookstown airfield, Tallaght, 11 12, 13, 14, 30
Cooney, Patrick, 261
Copenhagen service, 277
Corballis, County Dublin, 5-6
Corballis House, 6-8, 260, 281
Corcoran, Sheila, 152
Cork airport, 43, 94, 139, 157, 223
   crash, 156
   opens, 134
   personnel, 173, 211, 228, 229, 240
Cork Harbour Commissioners, 245
Corrigan, Douglas "Wrong Way", 277-8
Corrigan, Paddy, 264
Cosgrave, Liam, 72, 74, 172, 176
Costello, John A., 90, 91, 102, 113
Côte d'Azur airport, Nice, 122
Coughlan, Ann, 194
Coughlan, Arthur, 194, 227, 281
Courage, George, 185
Couve de Murville, Maurice, 136
Craddock, Charlie, 55-6, 92, 188, 198
Cranitch, Tommy, 183, 264
crashes, 68, 74, 99, 110, 119, 155-6
   Aer Lingus, 156
   crashlanding, 135
   Dublin airport, 132-3, 155
   Eastbourne, 244
   Liverpool, 88

Munich, 124
   simulated, 203
   training for, 203
Cromwell, Eddie, 241
Cronin, John, 56
Crosbie, Richard, 1
Crosby, Bing, 102
cross-channel service, 72, 117, 172, 281
Croydon flights, 69
Cruise, Frank, 227, 232, 245
Cuckoo Stream, 65, 68
Cuddy, Joe, 187
Cuddy, Mick, 19
Cullen, Sonny, 157, 174, 191-2, 195
Cullen, Tom, 181, 194, 197, 198, 211, 228, 272-3, 279, 281
   appointments, 180-1, 194, 229, 240, 281
Cumberbatch Trophy, 99
Cumiskey, Captain Michael, 25, 27, 263
Cummins, Peggy, 116
Curragh, The, 11, 86
Curtain, Bart, 185, 198
customs clearance system, 175
cycle park, 104
Cyprus Airways, 267
Czechoslovakia, 164, 281

D
Dakota aircraft, 86
Dale, Eileen, 227
Dallaghan, Gerard, 198
D'Alton, Cardinal, 97, 102
Dalton, Ger, 194
Daly, Colin, 93
Dan-Air, 211, 230, 235-6
Dana, 163-4, 191
Darcy, Christopher, 157, 281
Darcy, Paddy, 190
Dargan, Michael, 92, 157, 255
DART railway system, 237, 284
Davis, Stanley Clinton, 257
Davitt, Brian, 198
Dawnflights, 87
DC3 aircraft, 45, 68, 70, 84, 88, 89, 91, 101, 119, 120, 197, 223, 287
   crash, 99
DC4 aircraft, 68, 106, 114, 154
DC6 aircraft, 154
DC9C aircraft, 17
de Cuellar, Javier Perez, 237
de Fouw, Remco, 247
de Gaulle, General, 111, 160
De Havilland Aeroplane Hire Service, 16
De Havilland Albatross aircraft, 32, 34, 35
De Havilland Dragon aircraft, 27, 172
De La Noyde family, 6
de Paor, Rory, 156
de Valera, Eamon, 18, 20-21, 24, 91, 99, 102, 121, 150, 172
   Casement oration, 151
   death, 183
   and the Emergency, 38, 41
   inaugurates trans-Atlantic service, 120-1
   and Kennedy visit, 142

   visits U.S., 151
de Valera, Sineád, 18, 20-21
decimal currency, 172
Declan O'Dwyer Associates, 258
Defence, Department of, 24
Delamer, Colonel Bill, 22, 61, 65, 76, 79-80, 94, 101, 109, 136, 172, 216
   in charge of airport, 61, 63, 65
   retirement, 154
Delamer, Peter, 61, 154
Delaney, Frank, 45, 281
Delaney, Ronnie, 117, 222
Dempsey, Brendan, 258
Dempsey, Dr J. F., 1, 45, 54-5, 58, 65, 82, 92-3, 104, 121, 129, 187, 255, 281
   on finances, 115, 150-1
   retirement, 157
Dempsey, Mrs., 99
Denning, Sean, 193
Desmond, Dermot F., 248, 281-3
Devlin, Denis, 59
DH9 aircraft, 16
DH.86 aircraft, 45, 46, 69, 70
Digital, 261
Dillon, James, 29
divorce referendum, 254
Dodd, Christopher, 8
Dodder River, 253
Doherty, Jim, 136
Dolan, Brendan, 228
Dolan, Joe, 191
Domas, 198
Donaghy, Judy, 239
Donegan, Patrick, 171, 188
Donlon, Sean, 237
Donohoe, Alf, 94
Donohue, Noel, 267
Doody, Johnny, 185, 228
Douglas, Lord Sholto, 11-12, 18, 72, 85, 91, 138, 160
Douglas A-ID Skyraider aircraft, 193
Dowanstown, 6
Doyle, Jack, 74, 135, 166, 168, 172, 177, 183, 188, 215, 264
Doyle, Jimmy, 233
Doyle, Mary, 187
Doyle, Oonagh, 227
Doyle, Paddy, 258-9
Dragon aircraft, 119
Drogheda, Countess of, 12
Dromgoole, Lisa, 204
Dromgoole, Noel, 204
Drumgoole, Fr Joe, 235
Dublin airport
   air traffic control, 263
   airspace intrusions, 68
   arts festivals, 245
   boilerhouse, 79-80, 226, 242, 278
   bombs, 183
   buildings, 30-31, 39
   construction strike, 34-5
   extensions, 89, 111, 119, 121
   FitzGerald terminal, 35, 38, 54, 65, 84, 97, 109-10, 119, 152, 160, 170, 179
   North terminal, 125
   second terminal, 153, 160, 169-70, 175, 177

exhibition, 177, 179
cargo facilities, 179, 281
catering, 54, 101, 233-4, 239, 276. *see also under* Restaurants
   revenue, 122-3, 150
check-in facilities, 260-61
church, 107, 151-3
Collinstown proposal, 27, 29
commemoration, 5
communications, 80
control centre, 179-80
cross-channel traffic, 218
diversions from Shannon, 88
emergencies, 132-3, 135, 155, 183, 267
   training for, 203
during the Emergency, 41-59
   air raid shelter, 46
   extensions, 52, 54
   military occupation, 43, 45, 57
   unauthorised landings, 47-52
   wheat growing, 45, 58
exhibitions, 186
export charters, 91
finances, 207, 283
fire services, *see under* Fire services
first jet, 86
fuel, 278
future plans, 286-7
Golden Jubilee, 261, 281
ground transport, 74, 79, 87
hairdressing salon, 191
identification sign, 41
improvements, 114-15, 119, 153, 169, 184-5, 190, 195, 201, 203, 228, 230, 232, 284
landing rights, 91
landing systems, 69-70
landscaping, 194, 248, 252, 273
lounge bars, 54, 119, 191, 199
   cocktails, 179, 191, 199
Lourdes terminal, 98, 121
maintenance building, 260
management changes, 136, 138-9, 256
museum, 186-7, 252
new runway, 253, 261, 279
new terminal, 170
post-war expansion, 61-95
proposals for, 29
quarry lake, 248
redesign, 232-3
religious services, 80, 88, 92
reservoir, 185
restaurants. *see under* Restaurants
runway extension, 232
safety, 223, 226
security. *see under* security services
separate organisation, 272-3
service charges, 139
sheep grazing, 45, 51, 54, 58
shops, 181, 185, 196-7, 261. *see also under* Duty-free facilities
   tax-free, 264
   VAT-free, 234
sports centre, 161
statistics
   freight, 215

passengers, 1, 87, 89, 101, 102, 104, 116-17, 150, 163, 179, 180, 192, 196, 201, 238, 241, 252-3, 257, 260, 269, 277, 281, 283, 284
   revenue, 238
   traffic, 215, 232
training schemes, 230
trans-Atlantic services, 68-9
unauthorised landings, 35
VAX system, 261
visitors to, 101
VOR equipment, 119
Watch Office, 157, 180, 228, 267
Water storage, 185
weather, 229
Dublin Airport Golfing Society, 194, 229
Dublin Airport Hotel, 160
Dublin Airport Orphan Fund, 175
Dublin City Helicopters, 232
Dublin Corporation, 2-3, 29, 30, 197
Dublin County Council, 30, 34, 242
Dublin Golfing Society, 229
Dublin Millennium, 278
Dublin United Tramway Company, 27
Dubliners, The, 244, 269, 272
Duffy, Neil, 77
Duffy, Paul, 154
Dully, Martin, 97, 107, 229, 238, 240, 241, 256, 257, 258, 261, 267
   chief executive, 216, 218, 220, 234, 237
   goes to Bord Fáilte, 272
Duncan, Michael, 127
Dunlop Pitts special aircraft, 279
Dunne, Jim, 231
Dunnes Stores, 241
Dunsoghly Castle, 9-10
Dutch Air Force, 231
duty-free facilities, 215, 230, 240, 257, 284

E
East Link toll bridge, 242
East Midlands service, 231, 236
Easter Rising (1916), 10, 11
Eastbourne air crash, 244
Eastern Command, 38
Eastern Europe, 281
Eastern Airways, 223
Education, Department of, 55
Edwards, Hilton, 168
Edwards, Jimmy, 141
EC Commission, 240
EC, 1992, 283
Egan, Nurse, 82
Eglinton airfield, Derry, 164, 222
Egypt, 89
Elan, 273
Electricity Supply Board (ESB), 227, 229
Ellis, Brian, 180
Ellis, Jimmy, 174, 180
Ellis, Joseph, 180
Emergency, The, 2-3, 38, 41-59, 88
   blackout, 46
   rationing, 45, 47, 54
   transport difficulties, 54, 55-6
emigration, 101

energy conservation, 202-3
equal opportunities, 186, 198, 226, 234, 239-40, 273, 276
Ericsson's, 182
Eucharistic Congress (1932), 21
European Airbus, 285
European Airbus A320 aircraft, 281, 287
European Community (EC), 176, 230, 257, 283, 284
European Monetary System (EMS), 202
Eurovision Song Contest, 207, 223, 269
Evening Herald, 2, 244
Evening Mail, 2, 4, 25, 135
Evening Press, 113, 135
Ewart-Biggs, Christopher, 188
Exeter service, 256
exhibitions, 186
Express Mail, 273
External Affairs, Department of, 136

F
Fagan, Jack, 238, 253
Fairchild C-82 Packet aircraft, 101
Fanning, Mrs M. A., 54
Fanning, Vincent, 134, 159, 175
Farouk, King, 89
Farrell, Mona, 190
Farrelly, Joyce, 211, 214
FÁS, 276
Faulkner, Padraig, 261
Federated Workers' Union of Ireland, 196
Feeney, John, 244
female equality at airport, 239, 273
Fennell, Nuala, 239
Fenning, Una, 204
Ferguson, Harry, 186
Ferguson monoplane, 186
Fermoy, County Cork, 11, 16
Ferris, Mr, 58
Fianna Fail, 254, 269
fifth freedom rights, 277
Finance, Department of, 242
Finglas airfield, 21
Finglas family, 10
Finn, Kit, 193
fire services, 81, 154, 182, 190-1, 204
   emergencies, 267
   fire station, 195, 283
   personnel, 157, 211, 230, 241, 257, 259
   training, 180, 276
   vehicles, 174-5
FitzGerald, Desmond, 2, 17, 35, 39, 65, 84, 97, 109, 152, 160, 179
FitzGerald, Dr Garret, 16-17, 35, 87, 176, 220, 230, 255
Fitzgerald, Niall, 255
Fitzpatrick, Tom, 192-3, 261
Flahive, Jimmy, 121
flexi-time, 226-7
Flood, Kevin, 258
Flynn, Declan, 235
Flynn, J., 34
fog, 223
Fokker 100 aircraft, 264
Fokker Friendship 27 aircraft,

119-20
Fokker Friendship aircraft, 89, 231, 261, 264, 287
Fokker F.XII aircraft, 21
Foley, Michael, 231-2
Fonteyn, Margot, 129
Foreign Affairs, Department of, 237
Forrest Little, 9, 20
Fouga jet aircraft, 204
Fox Moth aircraft, 21, 24
Foynes, County Limerick, 32, 35, 47, 211
Franco, General, 2
Frankfurt service, 173

G
Gallagher, Jim, 211
Gallagher, John, 256
Galvin, Jim, 57
Garda Siochana, 183
Gardiner, Captain W. H., 113
Garrison, Peter, 187
gas explosion, Ballsbridge, 269
Gatwick airport, London, 211, 230, 256
Geldof, Bob, 245
Geoghegan, Michael, 194
Geoghegan, Sheila, 194
German unification, 281
Germany, 281
Gilligan, Jimmy, 174, 185, 214, 281
Gilmartin, Mark, 229
Giltrap, Gerry, 99, 142, 154
Glasgow service, 256, 277
Gleeson, Russell, 204
Globemaster C-124 aircraft, 154
Gloster Meteor aircraft, 86
Goebbels, Heinrich, 2
Gogarty, Oliver St. John, 24
Golden, Eddie, 215
Goldenbridge Home for Children, 187
Golien, Captain, W. G., 69
Gormanston aerodrome, 11, 13, 14, 86
Grace, Princess, 129, 135, 136
Grant, Ross, 175
Great Southern Railway, 56
Greece, service to, 253
Greene, Denis, 35
Gregory, Tony, 230
Gresham Hotel, 128
Grey, Hector, 245
Guerin, Michael, 273
Guinea Airways, 45
Guinness, Jennifer, 254
Guinness Book of Records, 191
Guinness Peat Aviation, 237
Gunning, John, 70, 190, 264

H
H-Block hunger strikes, 220, 232
Hackett, Pat, 232
Halifax bomber aircraft, 106
Hall, Frank, 214
Hamburg service, 277
Hampson, Brian, 179, 190, 202
Hanley, Jack, 19
Hanley, John, 81, 98-9
Hanley Meat Group, 211
Hanley, Paddy (Butsey), 81

Hanley, Paddy (Gaffer), 81
Hanley, Peter, 81, 208, 211, 232, 239, 240, 245, 248
Hanlon, Frank, 241, 256, 277
Harcourt Street railway line, 125
Harrington, Patrick, 241
Harvey, Charles, 195
Harvey, Gerard, 196, 198, 204, 205, 207, 234, 240
Haughey, Charles, 168-9, 172, 203, 230, 234, 235, 267, 279
Hawke, Bob, 277
Hawker Hurricane aircraft, 47
Hayes, John, 183
Hayworth, Rita, 101
HD.32 aircraft, 114
Healy, Shay, 207
Heathrow airport, London, 76, 102, 113, 138, 211
Hederman, Carmencita, 278-9
Heffernan, Gerry, 181, 195, 196, 197, 198, 199, 229, 235, 245
Heinkel aircraft, 2
Heinz Erin Foods, 237
helicopters, 113, 232, 252
Henry VIII, King, 5
Hercules aircraft, 223
Hillery, Dr Patrick, 188, 204, 220, 245
Hillsborough Agreement, 245
Hoare, Bridie, 191
Hoare, Noel, 246
Hoey, Laurence, 81
Hogan, Carmel, 204
Hogan, T. L., 77
Hollywood family, 7
Holton, Mary, 187
Holy Year, 1950, 97-8
Holyhead service, 232, 252
Hone, Oliver, 187
Honeywell computer, 201
Hook, Arthur, 199
Hope, Bob, 102
Hope, David, 201
Houlihan, Michael, 234-5
Howth Yacht Club, 229
Hughes, Paddy, 57, 183
Hume Street demolitions, 160
Hungary, 281, 284
Hunting Air Travel, 97-8
Hurricane Charlie, 253

I
Iberia A300 Airbus, 267
Iberia airlines, 173
Iceland, 90
Idlewild airport, 122
Ilyushin-18 aircraft, 197
Ilyushin IL-14 aircraft, 154
Imperial Airways, 32, 35
Imperial Defence, Committee of, 11
In Dublin, 188
Independent Newspapers, 237
Independent radio stations, 281
Indian Air Force, 119
Industry and Commerce, Department of, 34, 39, 58-9, 69, 77, 122, 263
and Aer Rianta, 109
and Shannon Air Services, 128-9
and Shannon Airport, 74, 94

inflight catering, 129
International air transport conference (1949), 91
international civil aviation organisation, 179-80
Iolar, the, 172, 255
Iona Airways, 21, 121
Irish Aero Club, 35
Irish Air Lines, 21
Irish Air Transport, 24
Irish Army, 57, 63, 136, 150
  occupies Dublin airport, 43, 45
  UN duties, 129, 153, 197, 244
Irish Aviation Club, 119, 229
Irish Aviation Museum, 186
Irish Builder, 65
Irish Continental Hotels, 128
Irish Goods Council, 197
Irish Helicopters, 204
Irish Independent, 2, 31-31, 267
Irish Junior Aviation Club, 1
Irish Management Institute (IMI), 227
Irish Press, 1-2, 111
Irish Republican Army (IRA), 7, 14-15, 63
Irish Shipping, 54
Irish Times, The, 2, 4, 39, 91, 119, 231-2, 238, 253
  on Armistice Day, 13-14
  on bomber aircraft, 102
  on IRA raid, 14-15
  sent by air, 27
  on trans-Atlantic flight, 68-9
Irish Transport and General Workers' Union (ITGWU), 63, 174, 211, 230, 233
Irish Travel Agents, 257
Isle of Man service, 230
Istanbul service, 223

J
James, Duke of York, 6
Jammet's restaurant, 157
Jenkinson, Jimmy, 187
Jephson-Norreys, Brigadier, 114
Jersey European Airways, 256
jet planes, 86, 97, 114, 119, 121, 125, 127
job sharing, 226
John Paul II, Pope, 148, 198, 203-5, 222
  visit to Ireland commemorated, 215
Johnson, Christopher, 174, 228
Jolly Green Giant helicopter, 236
Joyce, Michael, 77
Joynt, Dick, 246
Judge, Martin, 179, 228
Junkers aircraft, 68
Justice, Department of, 257
JWT, 256

K
Kavanagh, George, 20
Kavanagh, John, 156
Kavanagh, Mr, 81
Kavanagh, Patrick, 157, 244
Kavanagh, Sean, 35
Kaye, Danny, 102, 135
Keating, Marion, 234

Keating, Ned, 101, 102
Keatley, Kathleen, 234
Keatley, Paul, 261
Keegan, Patsy, 187
Kelly, Canon, 92
Kelly, Danny, 182
Kelly, Joe, 227
Kelly, Luke, 244
Kelly, Oisin, 152
Kelly, Paddy, 179, 228
Kelly, Tony, 204, 233
Kelly-Rogers, Captain J. C., 186-7, 216, 228
Kennedy, David, 257
Kennedy, Edward, 235
Kennedy, John F., 127, 136, 140-8, 150, 164, 205
Kenny, Pat, 242, 255
Keogh, Derek, 155, 175, 180, 185, 193, 194, 195, 205, 215, 226, 229, 239, 241, 252, 257, 261, 267, 272, 279, 281
   appointments, 179, 208, 240
   chief executive, 272-3, 281
   opens clubhouse, 258
   paper given by, 260
   and worker participation, 185-6
Keogh, Rhona, 194
Khan, Frank, 267
Kiernan, Jimmy, 220
Kildonan airfield, Finglas, 21-2, 30, 121
Kimmage, Paul, 230
King, John, 157, 179, 193, 211, 258
Kirwan, Pearl, 94, 174, 190
Kish lightship, 52
Kissinger, Henry, 237
KLM, 21, 24, 84, 89, 91, 104, 113, 237
Knock airport, 231
Knocksedan, 10
Kucher, Enda D., 175

L
La Comber, Ray, 207, 281
Labour Party, 34
Lamarque, Marcel Henri, 277
Lancashire Aircraft Corporation, 106
landing charges, 101, 123, 139, 173-4, 181, 192, 202, 207, 230
Langford, John, 175
Larkin, James, 63, 65, 79
Lavery, Don, 188
Lawford, Peter, 148
Le Bourget airport, Paris, 76, 182
Leddy, Matt, 198
Legge, Hector, 91
Legion of Mary, 198
Lemass, Kathleen, 172
Lemass, Captain Noel, 172
Lemass, Seán, 27, 30, 58, 91, 109, 121, 125, 142, 154, 168, 172, 176
   Air Transport Bill, 129
   and Dublin airport, 27, 29
   opens Cork airport, 134
   visits Northern Ireland, 153-4
   visits U.S., 150
Lenihan, Brian, 261
Lennon, Dick, 233, 234
Leonardi, Fr Giovanni, 216
Levey, Alan, 227

Leydon, John, 45, 54, 59, 61, 110, 172
Liberty Hall, 153
Libya, 230, 264, 267
Lightwater foam, 190
Lindsay, Derry, 164
Liverpool service, 39, 45-6, 47, 69, 79, 223, 236, 283
   car ferry, 140
Lloyd George, David, 2
Lockheed 14 aircraft, 1, 39
Lockheed aircraft, 45
Lockheed C54 Galaxy aircraft, 197
Lockheed Constellation aircraft, 86-7
Logan, Johnny, 207, 269
Logan, Robert, 32
Logue, John, 77
London service, 43, 87, 91, 102, 113, 119, 281
Lonergan, Liam, 260
Lord, David, 168, 169, 234, 239
Lorenz landing system, 34, 69
Loreto Convent, St. Stephen's Green, 253-4
LOT airline, 197
Lourdes service, 88, 89, 91, 98, 111, 113, 115, 157
   centenary flights, 123
   crashlanding, 132-3
   new terminal, 98, 121
Lowndes, Alan, 208
Lufthansa, 104, 173, 202, 276-7
Luftwaffe, 2
Lunde, Col. Oswald W., 102
Luton service, 223, 255-6, 261
Lynch, Jack, 154, 170, 203
Lynch, Joe, 157, 182, 190
Lynch, Patrick, 138, 156-7
Lyons, Denis, 284

M
McAlpine, Robert, 229
McAteer, Desmond, 29
MacBride, Sean, 183
McCabe, Bill, 208
McCabe, Brian, 172, 208, 222
McCafferty, Tony, 184, 192, 203, 204
McCafferty, Private, 15
McCann, Hugh, 150
McCann, Oliver, 198, 227, 281
McCartan, Frank, 157
McCarthy, Dr Charles, 196
McCarthy, J. C. B., 109-10
McCarthy, Mick, 225
McClafferty, Tony, 184, 192, 203, 204
McCloskey, Matthew, 150
McConnell, Charlie, 27
MacCurtain, Thomas, 3
McDonald, Jim, 56-7, 174, 180, 183, 233, 241
McDonald, Mary, 92
McDonnell, Frank, 184
McElroy, Joe, 194
McEvoy, Gerry, 234
McGeown, Captain Jim, 179
McGuinne, Joe, 180, 184, 188, 193, 194, 214, 256, 272
McGuinness, Christopher, 20
MacHale, J. P., 70
McKenna, James, 247

McKeon, Kevin, 261
MacLiammoir, Micheál, 168
McLoughlin, Danny, 228
McLoughlin, Elaine, 273
McMahon, Noel, 192, 284
McMaster, Anew, 215
McNally, Paul, 179, 191, 199
McNamara, Kathleen, 194
McNulty, Jimmy, 228
McQuaid, Dr J. C., Archbishop of Dublin, 99, 152
MacReady, General Sir Neville, 18
Madden, Jean, 191
Madigan, Joseph, 195, 214, 259
Madonna of Loreto (statue), 215-16
Magee, Myles, 81
mail services, 15, 17, 69, 134, 197
Manchester service, 135, 197, 277
Manchester United crash, 124
Mannin Airways, 88
Manx Airlines, 281
Maples, Kathleen, 191
March Hare, The (film), 116
Marcinkus, Archbishop, 204
Marron, Kevin, 244
Martin, Christopher, 94, 109, 175, 229
Martin, Kingsley, 31
Martin, Linda, 207
Maseru, Lesotho, 248
Maxwell family, 9
Maynard, Percy, 155
Meehan, Phil, 185
Meteor jet aircraft, 119, 127
Meteorological Office, 39
Meteorological Service, 59
Metroliner 2 Turboprop aircraft, 252
Metropole, 121, 173
Miami showband, 183
Miles Gemini aircraft, 85, 110-11
Milligan, Spike, 183
Mitchel, Charles, 148
Mitchell, Jim, 261
Mitterrand, François, 277
Model Aeronautics Council of Ireland, 119
Moloney, Helen, 152
Molyneux, Dr Thomas, 6
Monaghan, T. J., 59
Monahan, John, 81
Monks, Gerry, 235
Monks, Michael, 32
Moore, Joe, 173, 257
Moran, Eamonn, 281
Moran, James, 93-4
Moran, T. J. and Co., 77
Morgan, John, 6
Morgan, Terence, 116
Morton, W. H., 34
Mount Temple Comprehensive, 272
Mountbatten, Lord Louis, 73
Movietone News, 55
Moynet, André, 113
Mullen, Michael, 211, 230, 235
Mulligan, Fr Ben, 193
Mulligan, Hugh, 281
Multimedia, 198
Murphy, Christina, 211
Murphy, Christine, 191
Murphy, John, 261
Murphy, Victor, 195

Murray, Brendan, 180, 193, 194, 229
Murray, Captain, 51
Murray, Denis, 227
Murray, Harold, 267
Murray, Jim, 259
Murray, John, 185, 193

N
Nagle, A. H., 59
Nagle, Kay, 197-8
National Concert Hall, Dublin, 220, 222
National Lottery, 269
natural gas, 279
Naul, The, 10
NCB stockbrokers, 281-2
NCB Ireland, 282
Nehru, Pandit, 90, 119
Neill, Lieutenant - Colonel Frank, 135-6
Nelson's pillar, 154
Nevin, Tony, 193, 227, 261
New Year's celebrations, 121-2
New York service, 120
Newcastle service, 119
Nice service, 236
Nixon, Harry and Margaret, 252
Nixon, Richard, 164, 193
Nolan, Martin, 229
Noone, Michael, 77
North Atlantic route conference, 70, 72
Northern Ireland, 153-4, 173
   troubles, 160-61, 163, 164, 166, 180
   UWC strike, 182
Northolt airport, London, 102, 113
Nugent, Gerald, 5
Nutt's Corner airport, Belfast, 113

O
O'Brien, Fergus, 229
O'Carroll, Michael, 233
O'Casey, Sean, 153
O'Connell, Frank, 198, 208, 240-41, 276
O'Connell, Joe, 227, 256
O'Connell, S. M., 1
O'Connor, Brian, 198, 208
O'Connor, George, 188, 193, 194, 204, 211, 227, 230
O'Connor, John, 252
O'Connor, Pat, 169
O'Connor, R. C., 157, 159, 172, 177, 179, 211, 216
O'Connor, Richard, 22
O'Connor, Sean, 155
Ó Dalaigh, Cearbhall, 183, 188
O'Daly, Paddy, 57-8, 81, 91-2, 94, 121, 190, 193
O'Dea, Jimmy, 4
O'Donohue, Carol, 273
O'Driscoll, T. J., 1
O'Dwyer, Declan and Sheila, 258
O'Ferrall, George More, 116
Ó Fiaich, Cardinal Tomás, 153, 204, 215
O'Hagan, Hugh, 187
Ó hUadhaigh, Mrs, 27
Ó hUadhaigh, Seán, 24, 34, 54, 93
   oil crisis, 181
O'Keeffe, Captain Hugh, 156

O'Keefe, Jane, 276
O'Kelly, Sean T., 89, 113, 154
O'Leary, J. J., 34
Olympia Theatre, 4
Olympic Airlines, 222
O'Mahony, Donal, 284
O'Malley, Desmond, 197
O'Malley, Donough, 181
O'Malley, Tim, 155
O'Mara, Brian, 199
O'Neill, Niall, 246-7
O'Neill, Captain Terence, 153
Oppermann, Johnny, 55, 65, 90, 92, 95, 97, 121, 124, 129, 168
   joins Aer Lingus, 159
O'Rahilly's hairdressers, 214
O'Reilly, Dr A. J. F., 217, 237
O'Reilly, Charlie, 81, 92, 93
O'Reilly, P. P., 45, 90, 164
Orly Airport, Paris, 76
Order of Malta, 104
Ornithologist at airport, 223
O'Rourke, Joe, 81, 82, 132, 229-30, 256, 259
O'Sugrue, Carl, 179, 198, 208, 256
O'Sullivan, Eithne, 204
O'Sullivan, James, 84, 87, 91, 157, 169, 184, 190, 192, 197, 198, 204, 215, 229, 248
   on finances, 207
   retirement, 208, 216
O'Sullivan, R. W., 12, 29-30, 59
O'Sullivan, Seán, 113
Our Lady Queen of Heaven, church of, 151-3, 180, 193, 204

P
Pan American Airways, 32, 128
Panaytou, Dr Paris, 114
Papal visit, 1979, 203-5
Paris service, 43, 87
"Pat and Pete", aero twins, 25
PAYE protests, 203, 211
payload penalties, 253
People's Democracy, 160
personnel, 54, 61, 79-82, 84, 92-3, 97, 152, 157, 159-60, 166, 168, 179, 180, 187-8, 198, 199, 207-8, 211, 216, 226-7, 229-30, 234-5, 240-41, 245, 248, 256-7, 264, 277
   25 years' service, 174, 193, 228, 281
   cleaning staff, 92-3, 241
   deaths, 199, 228, 235, 256, 259
   entertainment, 95, 97, 187, 191-2, 227, 261, 281
   ex-military, 59, 93
   numbers of, 91, 241
   recruitment, 93-4
   reminiscences, 55-8, 77
   retirements, 179, 180, 182, 190, 199, 211, 214, 216, 228, 230, 235, 264, 267, 281
   retreat for, 204
   shepherd, 58
   social club, 241
   sports, 98-9, 183, 187, 194, 214, 228, 229
   staff suggestions, 175, 226
   unionisation, 63, 65
   worker directors, 283

   worker participation, 240
Phoenix Park, 18, 29-30
Phukan, Chuni, 227, 248
Pickardstown, 9
pilgrimages, 88-91, 97-8, 111, 113, 132-3, 157
Pitts Special G-LOOP aircraft, 202
Plunkett, John, 10
Plunkett family, 10
PMPA, 256-7
Poland, 281
police, *see* security services
police service, 211, 233
Post, An, 240
postal strike, 201
Posts and Telegraphs, Department of, 59, 227
Power, Jim, 214
Power, John, 172, 190, 222
Power, P. J., 119
Power, Tom, 198
Power, Tyrone, 129
Powerscourt, Lord, 101
Powerscourt Townhouse centre, 222
Progressive Democrats, 254
protocol, 135-6
Public Works, Office of, 30
Purcell, Noel, 245
Purchasers of Aviation Materials, Committee of, 102

Q
Quidnunc, *The Irish Times*, 68
Quinn, Eamon, 115
Quinn, Feargal, 115
Quinn, Ruairi, 239-40
Quinn, Tony, 185

R
Radio Éireann, 4, 117
Raglan Road poem, 245
Raidió na Gaeltachta, 159
Railway Air Services, 69, 74
Rainier, Prince, 129, 135, 136
RALSA, 228
Rapide aircraft, 88, 119
Rathborne's, 273
Rathfarnham Castle, 267
rationing, 101
Reid, Phil, 191
Reagan, Nancy, 242
Reagan, Ronald, 242
Red Island holiday camp, 115
Renault, Paris, 195
Rennes service, 134
Republic F-84 Thunderjet aircraft, 110-11
restaurants, 55, 65, 168-9, 195, 199
   Collar of Gold, 121-2, 129, 157, 160, 239
   Silver Lining, 239, 283
   unprofitable, 218
Reynolds, Albert, 215, 261
Reynolds, Barney, 183, 191
RFC Sopwith Camel aircraft, 12
Rineanna, 32, 34
RIOI airship, 258
Riordan, John, 232
Riordan, Kathleen, 10, 13, 20-21
Riordan family, 15
Robinson, Keefe and Devane, 152

Roche, Stephen, 269
Rogers, Mr, 35
Rolls-Royce Dart Mark 510 engine, 186
Rome service, 87, 97-8
Rooney, Colonel Eamonn, 61
Royal Air Force (RAF), 2, 12, 13, 14, 18, 21, 43, 86, 119, 127, 186
   Collinstown base, 16-18
   IRA raid, 14-15
   personnel to Aer Lingus, 59
   unauthorised landings, 47, 50-51, 52
Royal Canadian Air Force, 70
Royal Dublin Society (RDS), 223
Royal Flying Corps, 10-12, 43, 61
Royal Institute of the Architects of Ireland, 39
Royal Naval Air Service, 12
RTÉ Radio, 239
Runway magazine, 172, 186, 231-2, 238, 253, 255, 269
   colour, 252
   editors, 208
   tenth birthday, 222
runways, 34-5, 75-6, 77, 79, 123, 127, 153, 201, 230, 232, 241-2, 252
   24, 114
   10/28, 253-4, 261, 281
   17/35, 182
   23 ILS, 101
   time capsule, 261
Russell, Colonel Charles, 24, 27, 34
Russell Hotel, 168
Ryan, Billy, 193
Ryan, Timmy, 193
Ryanair, 93, 117, 120, 255-6, 260, 276

S
Saab Scandia aircraft, 88-9
Sabena, 84, 87, 88, 89, 117, 119, 197, 202
Sadat, Anwar, 220
Salmon, Mrs, 92-3
Samuels, Shirley, 259-60
Sandymount airport proposal, 29
Santry Demesne, 20
Saul, Captain J. P., 263
Scandinavian Airways System (SAS), 173, 233, 276
   SAS Catering, 233, 239
Scannell, Flight-Lieutenant, 86
Schiphol airport, Amsterdam, 89, 187
Scotland service, 155
Scott, Captain Bill, 187
Scott, Michael, 109, 151
Scully, Jack, 79, 80, 183, 232
Sea Fisheries Board, 218
Seaboard & Western Airlines, 106, 113, 120
Securicor, 276
security services, 142, 177, 183-4, 220, 233, 257, 259
   explosives sniffer, 188
   first female member, 276
security system, 180, 192-3
Seeley, Ted, 193
Serpentine Avenue gas explosion, 269
Servisair, 279-81

Shannon airport, 32, 58, 65, 91. *see also* trans-Atlantic services
   control of, 74, 94, 109, 134, 139, 154, 157
   diversions to, 223
   diversions to Dublin, 88
   Dublin-Shannon service, 46-7, 236
   duty-free facilities, 257
   exhibitions, 186
   new terminal, 170
   personnel, 180, 193, 211, 227, 264
   Shannon-Dublin service, 223, 252
   Pope departs, 205
   slump, 207, 215
   sports, 229
   strike, 113
   tested by TWA, 68
   trans-Atlantic service, 120-1
Shannon College of Hotel Management, 199
Shannon Executive Aviation, 252
Shannon Repair Services, 128-9
Sheila Jones Interior Decor, 258
Sheridan, Christy, 211, 281
Short, Pete, 188
Shortall, Frank, 193, 204, 227, 230
Shorts 330 aircraft, 222, 236
Shorts 360 aircraft, 236, 277
Sikorsky S61 helicopter, 232
Silver City Airways, 91
Simpson, Andy, 192
Sisk, John, & Son, 170
Skelly, Liam, 273
Skymaster aircraft (DC4), 68-9
Slater, M. L., 109
Sligo, Marquess of, 32
Slowey, Brian, 255
Sluis, Piet, 149
Smith, Jackie, 164
Sneyd, William, 6
South African air force plane, 90
Soviet Union, 273, 284
Spanish Civil War, 2
Spantax, 215
Sparling, Ted, 180, 228
Spitfire Mk XIV aircraft, 236
Stainthorpe, Felicity, 191
Stapleton, Lieutenant E. F., 25, 27, 263
Stardust fire, 220
Starflights, 87
Starways, 132
Stenson, Billy, 117
Stephenson, Sam, 197
Stokes Kennedy Crowley, 94
strikes, 34, 113, 170, 201, 20
   Aer Lingus cabin staff, 196
   pilots, 91
   tradesmen, 214, 215
Studley, Thomas (Bang Bang), 220
Sukarno, President, 136
Sunday Independent, 91
Sunday Press, 91
Sunday Tribune, 237
Sunday World, 177, 244
Super 737, 211
Super Concorde aircraft, 285
Super Constellation aircraft, 120-1
supersonic travel, 285
Supplies, Department of, 45
Sweden, 89

Swissair, 114, 197, 202
Switzerland, 76
Swords, 20
Swords Business Association, 252

T
Taillour family, 6
Talbot, Matt, 197
Taylor, Jean, 191, 194
Technico Communications, 61, 154
Telefís Éireann, 134, 143
Temple, Dr, Archbishop of York, 2
Terry (sheepdog), 58
Theatre Royal, 4, 101, 135
Thunderbolt anti-tank aircraft, 236
Tierney, Fr Martin, 175, 193
Tierney, Rita, 191
Tisdall, Bob, 117
Tobberbonney House, 6
Toberbunny, 6, 231
Toher, Fr, 92
Toland, Danny, 191, 199, 228
Tolka River, 113
Tops of the Town, 191-2
Tostal, An, 107, 109
tourism, 107, 163, 180, 253
trade unions, 230, 233
trams, 91
trans-Atlantic services, 38, 55, 65, 97, 114, 150, 172
   Aerlínte Eireann, 86-7
   conference, 1946, 70, 72
   Dublin airport, 68-9, 120-21, 123
   flying boats, 46-7
   international agreement, 32
   jet aircraft, 127
   landing rights, 91
   plans for Dublin, 58-9
   post-war, 106-7
   slump, 207
Trans World Airlines (TWA), 68, 104
Transport and Power, Department of, 61, 139, 192
   advised on administrative structure, 154-5
   control of Shannon, 134
   personnel, 179, 211, 214, 227, 256, 272
transport museum, 211
Traynor, Benny, 191, 214
Treacy, Don, 191, 281
Treacy, Phil, 208, 222
Treanor, Jim, 248
Tremble, Hugh, 232
Trinity College, Dublin, 243
Trusthouse Forte (Ireland), 160
Tuohy, Colonel Michael, 63, 79, 93, 97, 101, 106, 136
   retirement, 154
Turkish Airlines, 223

U
U2, 245, 272
Ulster Defence Association (UDA), 183
Ulster Television, 117
unemployment, 4, 54
United Nations troops, 129, 153, 154, 197, 244
United States, 102, 111, 232
   airline deregulation, 207, 218, 257

Civil Aeronautics Board, 107
United States Air Force (USAF), 101, 113, 197, 202, 236
    unauthorised landing, 49-50
    unlicensed intrusions, 68
United States Air Service, 13

V
Vagabond aircraft, 154
vandalism, 194
Vaughan, Brian, 248
Verden, Michael, 247
Vickers Viking aircraft, 84
Viking aircraft, 89, 97
Virgin airline, 260
Viscount 700 aircraft, 119
Viscount 800 aircraft, 186
Viscount aircraft, 89, 91, 113, 116, 119, 121, 261, 287
    crash, 155-6
    Naomh Fiachra, 252

W
Walcott, Sergeant Salvatore, 47
Wall, Arthur, 156
Wall, Brendan, 207
Wall, Miss, 7
Walls, Arthur, 93, 120, 191, 256-6
Walls Tarmac, 261
Walsh, Joe, 256
Warsaw service, 197
Watkins, Kathleen, 135
Wearen, Austin, 241
Wearen, Theresa, 241
weather, 5
Weekly Irish Times, 4
Weir, Gerry, 234
Weldon, Matt, 1
Weldon, Niall, 154
Weldrick, Frank, 203
West Coast Airways, 25, 46, 69, 72, 74
Western European Airports' Association, 215
    conference, 182
Weston airfield, County Kildare, 114, 119
Weston airlines, 119
Whelan, Liam, 124
Whitaker, T. K., 127
Whittle, Sir Frank, 85
Whoriskey, Joe, 74-5
Wilkinson, Sir Henry, 7
Wilkinson, Thomas, 7
Willis, Captain Gordon, 155
Wilson, Harold, 151, 161, 182
Wilson, John, 261
Wood Quay, 197, 203
Woods, Major, 15
Worker Participation Act, 240
worker representation, 185-6
Workers' Union of Ireland, 180
Works, Board of, 34
World Cup, 278-9
World War II. *see also* Emergency

Y
Years of Combat (Douglas), 11
Yeats, Elizabeth Corbet, 3
Young Advertising, 198

Z
Zeppelins, 12
Zurich airport, 195
Zurich service, 197, 202, 277

Index – Illustrations

A
Abbey Theatre company, 143
Aer Lingus
 bus, 136
 cargo terminal, 125
 Carvair terminal, 141
 computer, 142
 engineering hangar, 266
 first jet arives at airport, 165
 fleet, 42, 80, 111, 165
Aer Rianta
 accounts department, 64
 advertising, 199
 air spectacular, 281
 arts festival, 274
 board of directors, 272
 carpenters' shop, 63
 charter division, 74-5, 84
 Christmas dinner, 64
 computerisation, 242
 information staff, 168
 staff, 51, 174-7
 staff entertainments, 99, 104, 115
Agaginian, Cardinal, 132
Ahern, Bertie, 252
Aiken, Frank, 148, 150
Airbus, 231
Air France, 238
Air Traffic Services, 263
Airbus A320 aircraft, 231
aircraft, 75, 84, 230, 236, 279, 283.
 see also individual types
 first commercial aircraft, 22
 first jet, 128
 horse unloaded, 164
 types of, 39
Akihito, Prince, 219
Al Saud, Prince Abdullah bin
 Abdulaziz, 249
Andrews, Eamonn, 222
Anglim, John, 272
Armstrong, Neil, 180
Army in Emergency, 47, 49
Attlee, Clement, 87
Avair, 211

B
BAC One-Elevens, 237
Baker, Carmel, 176
Bannon, Jack, 177
Barnard, Dr Christian, 157
Barry, Peter, 213
Beatles, The, 137
Beck, Bill, 64, 175
Beckett, Samuel, 229
Beere, Dr Thekla, 160
Belgians, King and Queen of the, 161
Bergin, Rita, 168
Bernhard, Prince, 79
Bewley's Café, 251
Blandford Arms, 10
Boeing 720-048 aircraft, 128

Boeing 737-300 aircraft, 165
Boeing 747 aircraft, 165, 201
Boeing 757 aircraft, 234
Boland, Frank, 245, 265, 271, 272
Bono, 221
Boomtown Rats, 221
Boone, Pat, 157
Boot Inn, 14
 ball alley, 17
Bouchier-Hayes, Dr Thomas, 113
Bowler, Gillian, 232
Boxing team, 164
Brabazon, Noel, 82
Brennan, Seamus, 267, 271
Briscoe, Ben, 248, 265
British Airways, 234
British Midland, 230
Brown, Jack, 31
Browne, J., 56
Buitléar, Éamon de, 279
Bulgarian trade delegation, 170
Burke, John, 273
Burke, Ray, 252, 265
Bush, George, 210
Butler, Johnny, 90
Butler, Ned, 31
Byrne, Alfie, 35
Byrne, Brian, 256
Byrne, Gay, 228
Byrne, Kitty, 174
Byrne, Nicky, 177
Byrne, Paddy, 62

C
Cahill, Hugh, 23
Cahill, Pearse, 237
Caine, Michael, 225
Caribini, Benny, 164
Carley, Brenda, 176
Carroll, Gerry J., 42
Carroll, J., 56
Carroll, John, 272
Carroll, Leo, 120, 154
Carvair service, 141
Castlemoate House, 7, 12, 41
Caul, P., 56
Central Bank, 171
Champion, Bob, 197
Charles de Gaulle airport, Paris, 196
Charlton, Jack, 240, 276, 277
Chevalier, Maurice, 86
Childers, Erskine, 128, 141
Christchurch cathedral, 244
Clancy, Brendan, 261
Clancy, Seán, 255
Clarke, Owen, 261
Clayton, Adam, 221
Clifford, Stan, 92
Cloghran, 12
Cloghran bunker, 41
Clough, Martin, 210
Clune, Flan, 232

Coachman's Inn, 10
Cobham, Sir Alan, 23
Cobham's Flying Circus, 23
Cogan, Angela, 100
Collins, Gerard, 278, 282
Collins, J., 56
Collinstown
 lake, 18
 map of, 3
 Old RAF hangars, 22
Collinstown airfield, 18, 24
 aerial views, 8, 9
Comer, Jim, 182
computers, 142, 242
Concorde aircraft, 238, 269
Congo airlift, 138-9
Connolly, Sybil, 184
Connor, John, 173
Constellation aircraft, 68, 69
Consul aircraft, 75
Conway, Cardinal William, 153
Coras Iompair Éireann (CIE), 136
Corballis, 5, 8, 31
Corrigan, Douglas, "Wrong Way", 251
Cosgrave, Liam, 171
Costello, John A., 84
Costello, Oliver, 239
Coughlan, Arthur, 257
Couve de Murville, Maurice, 148
Craddock, Charlie, 62, 64, 90
Cronin, Mick, 31
Crosby, Bing and Cathy, 154
Crosby, Jack, 31
Cullen, Sonny, 176
Cullen, Tom, 249, 259, 271, 277
Cullinane, Charlie, 210
Cushing, Cardinal, 132

D
Daily Mail, 16
D'Alton, Cardinal John, 116
Dan-Air, 210
Dana, 172
Dardis, Mr, 31
DART railway system, 260
DC3 aircraft, 80
decimal currency, 171
de Buitléar, Éamon, 279
de Cuellar, Javier Perez, 213
de Valera, Eamon, 145, 189
Delamer, Colonel Bill, 64, 97, 99, 104, 141
Delamer, Helen, 99
Delaney, Frank, 115
 drawing by, 39
Delaney, Ronnie, 109
Delta Airlines, 269
Dempsey, J. F., 42, 54, 68, 99, 129
Dempsey, Mrs, 99
Dennis, Jim, 31
Department of Industry and
 Commerce, 32

Desmond, Dermot, 272, 273
Doherty, Marian, 275
Donaghy, Judy, 220
Donnelly, Mick, 31
Douglas, Sholto, 11
Doyle, Jack, 100, 174
Drumgoole, Lisa, 203
Drumgoole, Noel, 255
Dublin airport
   1972 terminal, 167-8, 208-9
   aerial views, frontispiece, 60, 71, 106
   Aer Lingus aircraft (1940), 42
   aeronautical map, 285
   air traffic control, 103, 262-3
   aircraft, 39, 124
   apron scene, 122
   arts festival, 274-5
   boilerhouse, 62, 81
   car ferry terminal, 141
   car park, 123
   carpenters' shop, 63, 90
   celebration of mass, 85
   check-in desks, 114, 131
   church, 158-9
   construction, 25-31, 66-7
   control tower, 82, 103, 182, 262-3
   departures bar, 76, 100, 107
   departures level, 268
   drawing office, 43
   during Millennium, 254
   fire engine, 103
   fire service, 194
   fiftieth anniversary, 271
   first jet, 78
   first passenger landing, 39
   first shop, 108
   FitzGerald terminal, 36-7, 38, 46, 94, 95, 105, 110, 112, 130-1
   football team, 89
   grass cutting, 70
   gun emplacements, 49
   identification sign, 38
   illuminations, 254
   kitchen, 92
   landscape surrounding, frontispiece
   Lourdes terminal, 118, 170
   main bar, 107
   maps, 266
   Mass, 85
   Meteorological Office, 223
   new runway, opening, 265
   new runway plans, 264, 266
   newsagents' shop, 114
   new terminal, 46, 167
   North terminal, 120, 134
   passenger lounge (1945), 57, 100
   Pier A, 166
   plan of, 33
   plans, 208-9, 264, 266
   refuelling, 80
   restaurant, 99, 104, 108, 150, 152, 255
      menu, 149
   runway construction, 25-9, 66-7, 155, 265
   saving the hay, 56, 70
   sculptures, 246-7
   shops, 108, 114, 195, 243
   snowbound, 216
   staff, 90, 112
   staff entertainments, 149
   tax free shopping, 195, 243
   telephone exchange, 268
   telephone switchboard, 177
   viewing balcony, 98
   wildlife, 279
Dublin city, 244
Dublin Corporation offices, 244
Dublin International Hotel, 243
Dublin Junior Ballet, 275
Duff, Carmel, 100
Dully, Martin, 210, 215, 224, 231
Dunsoghly Castle, 19

E
Educating Rita (film), 225
Edwards, Maura, 108
Ellis, Jimmy, 90
European Community heads of government, 278
European Cup (1988), 240
Eurovision, 207, 231
Everett, James, 124

F
Fagan, Jack, 235
Fahy, Frank, 224
Fanning, Paul, 275
Fanning, Vincent, 156
Feeney, John, 222
Fenning, Una, 168
Ferrer, Mel, 151
Ferris, Micky, 31
Finn, C., 56
fire service, 103, 194
first fast food equipment, 92
Fitzgerald, Colm, 115
FitzGerald, Desmond, 34
FitzGerald, Desmond drawings by, 36-7
FitzGerald, Dr Garret, 210, 219
Fitzmaurice, Colonel James, 140
Flahive, Jimmy, 104, 160
Fonteyn, Margaret, 88
Formby, George and Beryl, 83
Forrest West, 13

G
Gaiety Theatre, Dublin, 222
Galaxy aircraft, 186
Gallagher, John, 197
Galvin, Jim, 31
Gannon, Peter, 31
Garland, Judy, 83
Gavin, Tony, 100
Geldof, Bob, 221
Gillham, Brenda, 283
Gleeson, Russell, 203
Globemaster aircraft, 138, 186
Gonzales, Felipe, 212, 278
Goodwill restaurant, Dublin, 55
Gorman, James, 128
Grace, Princess, 133, 150
Grafton Street, Dublin, 251
Graham, Billy, 184
Grand Canal, 44
Grant, Cary, 116
Greene, June, 100

Grey, Hector, 179
greyhounds, 84
Guinness, Alec, 135
Gunning, John, 62
Gustaf, Prince, 140

H
Hagman, Larry, 228
Hallinan, Tom, 64
Hampson, Brian, 257
Hand, Tom, 31
Hanley, Jack, 31
Hanley, John, 81
Hanley, Peter, 56, 226, 272
Hanratty, Bernard, 150
Hanratty, Frank, 108
Harvey, Gerard, 175, 210
Haughey, Charles, 213, 240, 249, 252, 265, 277, 278, 282
Hawke, Bob, 253
Heffernan, Gerry, 190
Henry, "Stacks", 31
Hepburn, Audrey, 151
Hertzog, Chaim, 218
Hillery, Dr Patrick, 163
Hillery, Mrs, 219
Hillery, Patrick, 202, 213, 219, 252
Hogan, Carmel, 168
Hope, Bob, 161
Hopkins, Louisa, 237
Hopkins, Peter, 237
Horses at airport, 164
Hudson, Jack, 64
Hughes, Mick, 31
Hume, John, 251

I
In Dublin, 251
Industry and Commerce, Minister of
   instructions from, 32
Iona Airways, 24, 173
Ireland joins EEC, 163
Irish Army
   gun emplacements, 49
   26th battalion, 47
   UN troops, 138, 139
Irish Independent, 271
Irish Times, The, 40, 96, 126, 162, 206, 270
Irish Weekly Independent, 53

J
John Paul II, Pope, 200-3
Johnson, Kit, 63, 90

K
Kavanagh, J., 31
Kaye, Danny, 83
Kealy's pub, 241
Keating, Marion, 220
Keaveney, Tom, 272
Keenan, Brian, 282, 283
Kelly, D., 56
Kelly, Linda, 224
Kelly, Sean, 224
Kelly-Rogers, Captain J. C., 115, 140
Kennedy, Edward, 190, 248
Kennedy, John F., 144-7
Keogh, Billy, 31

Keogh, Derek, 231, 251, 258, 265, 271, 272
Khan, Aly, 77
Kilbride, Jimmy, 92
Kildonan, Finglas, 22
King, Johnny, 174
Kinsella, Thomas, 192
Kirwan, Pearl, 176
Kissinger, Henry, 217
Kohl, Helmut, 278

L
Lawlor, Gerard, 242
Lawlor, J., 56
Lebanon airlift, 186
Le Bourget airport, Paris, 34
Lemass, Seán, 68, 75, 111, 120, 128, 132, 153
   memorial, 169
Lemass, Seán and Kathleen, 129
Lenihan, Brian, 248, 252
Leydon, John, 68
Lockheed 14 aircraft, 42, 269
Lockheed L-1011 aircraft, 269
Logan, Johnny, 207
Lord, David, 235
Lufthansa, 165
Lynch, Jack, 129, 163, 181
Lynch, Joe, 176
Lynch, Liam, 104
Lynch, Patrick, 120, 128
Lyons, Denis, 267

M
MacBride, Seán, 87
McCabe, Brian, 191
McCann, Oliver, 241
McCarron, Eamon, 124
McCarthy, J. C. B., 120
McClafferty, Tony, 175
McCormick, Colonel Bertie, 79
McCormick, Paget, 115
McGuinne, Joe, 215
McGuinness, Christopher, 15
McGuirk, Tom, 31, 56
McKeon, J., 124
McKettrick, Jes, 31
McQuaid, Dr J. C., Archbishop of Dublin, 132
MacSweeney, Edward F., 235
Madigan, Joe, 51
Maguire, Josie, 31
Malone, Ann, 177
Mandela, Nelson, 280
Mandela, Winnie, 280
Manning, Jack, 31
Manx Airlines, 239
map, aeronautical, 282
Markey, Jim, 31
Markey, Mick, 31
Markey, Tommy, 31
Martin, Christopher, 174
Martin, Mother Mary, 132
Mason, James, 187
Mass parade, Emergency, 51
McCormick, Colonel Bertie, 79
McGuinness, Christopher, 15
Merryweather foam carrier, 103
Metropole Cinema, 48, 178
Miles Gemini aircraft, 74

Mitterrand, François, 252, 278
Monaghan, John, 31, 63, 90
Mooney, Leo, 64
Moore, Butch, 151
Moore Street, Dublin, 52
Moran, Eamonn, 238
Morris, Alan, 272
Morris, Phil, 177
Morton, Billy, 73
Mountbatten, Edwina Lady, 73
Mugabe, Robert, 214
Mullally, Des, 272
Mullen, Michael, 218
Mulligan, Breda, 217
Murphy, Mike, 64
Murray, Seán, 272
Murray-Jones, Tony, 135

N
Nagle, Bill, 31
Neagle, Anna, 116
Nehru, Pandit, 72
Nevanna Swingtette band, 150
New engineering hangar, 264
New Year's Eve dance (1951), 104
night mail service, 124
Nixon, Richard, 180
Noonan, Joe, 63
Noonan, Paddy, 63
Norton, Jim, 87
Norton, William, 124
Nulty, Kit, 31

O
O'Brien, Fr Niall, 250
O'Broin, Leon, 124
O'Connell, Frank, 256
O'Connell Street, Dublin, 48, 50
O'Connor, George, 211
O'Connor, John, 173
O'Connor, R. C., 175
O'Dálaigh, Cearbhall, 171
O'Daly, Paddy, 64, 93
O'Donoghue, Breege, 226
O'Donoghue, Carol, 177
Ó Fiaich, Cardinal Tomas, 203, 250
O'Gorman, James, 128
O'Hagan, Hugh, 63, 176
O'Hara, Maureen, 88
Ó hUadhaigh, Sean, 42, 111
O'Kelly, Phyllis, 111
O'Kelly, Sean T., 111
O'Leary, Eamonn, 227
O'Leary, J. J., 111
O'Mahony, Donal, 267
O'Neill, Tip, 217
Oppermann, Johnny, 88, 92, 99, 104, 108, 110, 160
O'Reilly, P. P., 169
O'Riada, Sean, 172
O'Rourke, J., 31
O'Rourke, Joe, 182
O'Rourke, Johnny, 31
O'Sé, Seán, 172
O'Sullivan, Eithne, 168
O'Sugrue, Carl, 232
O'Sullivan, James, 51, 185
Our Lady Queen of Heaven, church of, 158-9

P
Papal visit (1979), 200-3
paraffin flares, 62
Paraplegic Olympics, 233
Pearse Street, Dublin, 55
Phillips, Leo, 51
Purcell, Noel, 179

R
RAF Meteor jet aircraft, 78
Rainier, Prince, 133
Reagan, Ronald, 212
Reddy, Sanjiva, 213
Rickards, Billy, 31
Riordan family, 18
Riordan, Kathleen, 20
Roche, Lydia, 224
Roche, Stephen, 224
Rock House, 15
Rugby, Lord, 87
Runway magazine, 191
Russell Hotel, 178
Ryan, Bill, 31
Ryan, Joey, 31
Ryan, Timmy, 81
Ryanair, 231, 237

S
Sabena, 236
Safir, Sidney, 116
St Doulagh's church, 7
Sandymount strand, 21
Saudi Arabian visit, 249
Savage, Henry, 31
Savage, Mick, 31
sculptures, 246-7
Self-Aid, 221
Severine, 172
Shannon, Roisín, 224
Shields, Larry, 63
Short, Pete, 251
Shortall, Frank, 63
Shorts SD360 aircraft, 239
Sinatra, Frank, 255
Skentelbery, Leo, 134
Spain, King and Queen of, 219
Spence, Elaine, 283
sports
   boxing team, 164
   football team, 89
   World Cup football team, 240, 276-7
Stafford, T., 56

T
Taylor, Jean, 227
Thatcher, Margaret, 278
Tierney, Peter, 31
Traynor, Benny, 225
Treacy, Don, 223
turf-loading, 44

U
U2, 221

V
Valentine, Nick, 31
Varrier, John, 210
Viscount aircraft, 111
von Weizsacker, Dr Richard, 249

W
Walls, Arthur, 115, 231
Walsh, Joe, 236
Walters, Julie, 225
Weldon, Niall, 120
Wilson, John, 265
Wood Quay demonstration, 192
Woods, Dr Michael, 252, 277
World Cup (1990), 276, 277
Wyse, May, 114

Signatures from the distinguished visitors' book, Dublin airport

ARCHBISHOP MARCEL LEFEVRE,
1985

JIM MITCHELL,
Minister of Communications, 1987

RICHARD BRANSON,
Virgin Atlantic, 1987

STEPHEN ROCHE,
Tour de France Winner, 1987

CARMENCITA HEDERMAN,
Lord Mayor of Dublin, 1987–88

PAUL & MARY HOFFMAN,
Montana, U.S. Two millionth passenger arrival, Dublin airport, 1987

HRH PRINCE YAZID SAUD,
Saudi Arabia, 1987

JIM McKIERNAN,
Senator, Western Australia, 1988

EPHRAIM MIRVIS,
Chief Rabbi of Ireland, 1988

EAMONN DOHERTY,
Commissioner, Garda Síochána, 1988

MILES WALKER
Chief Minister, Isle of Man Government, 1988

CARDINAL O'CONNOR
Archbishop of New York, 1988

SINÉAD O'SULLIVAN,
Melbourne Rose, 1988

CHRISTINE BRIERS,
Southern California Rose, 1988

BOBBY ROBSON,
U.K. Football Association, 1988

DOUGLAS "WRONG WAY" CORRIGAN,
California, 1988

LIZA MINELLI,
New York, 1988

FRANK SINATRA,
Palm Springs, California, 1988

MR LEE,
Chairman, Samsung, Korea, 1988

MIKE MURPHY,
RTÉ, 1988

EMMANUEL GERADA,
Apostolic Nuncio, 1989

DESMOND CONNELL,
Archbishop of Dublin, 1989

MAEVE BINCHY,
The Irish Times, 1989

RICHARD A. MOORE,
U.S. Ambassador to Ireland, 1989

NELSON & WINNIE MANDELA,
South Africa, 1990

SEAN HAUGHEY,
Lord Mayor of Dublin, 1989–90

Date	Name	Address
Sept 4 '85	+ Marcus Welsh	Archbishop Bishop of Tuile
6.3.87	Jim McLeod	Minister of Government Catering
8 June 87	Rich Branson	Virgin Atlantics Inaugural Flight
Sept 1987	Stephen Roche 28 Meadowmount	Tour de France Winner 1987
10/8/87	Carmencita Hederman	Lord Mayor of Dublin
18/8/87	Paul E. Hoffmann + Mary L. Hoffmann	P.O. Box 113, 59931 Rollins Montana U.S.A.	2,000,000! arrivals at airport
5.10.87	H.R.H. Prince Yazid Saud	— Saudi Arabia —
9/4/88	Jim W. Kiernan	Senator for Western Australia
19.5.88	Ephraim Mirvis	Herzog House Zion Rd, Rathgar, Dublin 6	Chief Rabbi
6/6/88	Eamon Doherty	Commissioner Garda Siochana
15-7-88	Miles R. Walker	Chief Minister Isle of Man Government
27 July 1988	John Cardinal O'Connor	Archbishop of New York U.S.A.
17/8/88	Sinéad C. Sullivan	Melbourne Rose
17/8/88	Christine Briers	Southern California Rose
28/8/88	Bobby Robson	The Football Association. London W2